AF291838

A LOST LEGIONARY
IN
SOUTH AFRICA

A LOST LEGIONARY
IN
SOUTH AFRICA

Colonel George Hamilton-Browne

Introduced and Annotated
by
John Laband

Greenhill Books

A Lost Legionary in South Africa

This edition first published in 2026 by
Greenhill Books,
c/o Pen & Sword Books Ltd,
George House, Units 12 & 13
Beevor Street, Off Pontefract Road,
Barnsley, S. Yorkshire S71 1HN

www.greenhillbooks.com
contact@greenhillbooks.com

ISBN: 978–1–03615–307–6

The Publisher's authorised representative in the EU
for product safety is Authorised Rep Compliance Ltd.,
Ground Floor, 71 Lower Baggot Street, Dublin D02 P593, Ireland.
www.arccompliance.com

CIP data records for this title are available from the British Library

Designed and typeset by Donald Sommerville

Printed and bound in the UK by CPI Group (UK) Ltd,
Croydon, CRO 4YY.

Typeset in Century Old Style Standard 10/12.5,
and ITC Franklin Gothic LT Pro 9/12.5

Contents

Illustrations

The illustrations between pp. 2 and 251 are reproduced from the original edition of Hamilton-Browne's book and were by S. Velda, of whom no further details have been found. Hamilton-Browne's group of medals are in a private collection, photographs reproduced by permission.

Prologue

George Hamilton Browne's *A Lost Legionary in South Africa.*

George Browne, later self-hyphenated to become the more socially acceptable Hamilton-Browne, remains one of the most intriguing and controversial characters to emerge from the Anglo-Zulu War. He was by nature an adventurer, and a garrulous one at that, whose own stories are the principal cause of the confusion that still surrounds his life and career. Cast from the mould of harsh colonialism but rejected for formal military training, he was a true frontiersman, picking up wars and battles from Europe, America, Southern Africa and on to Australia and New Zealand. He was a prolific writer – however, what he wrote was invariably unsubstantiated and prone to great exaggeration, deliberately blending fact with fiction. Being sensational and exciting, *A Lost Legionary in South Africa* was lauded by contemporary reviewers as a worthy and fascinating account of the Anglo-Zulu War.

Professor John Laband's fresh analysis is the result of painstaking research and effectively deconstructs Hamilton-Browne's text by comparing his subject's fiction with known facts. It provides the first welcome and truly academic approach, furnishing experts and those who know little about the war with answers to many unanswered questions about this enigmatic Zulu War soldier.

Adrian Greaves
Chairman,
Anglo-Zulu War
Historical Society

Introduction

Sir Edmund Backhouse, a highly respected Sinologist, left on his death in 1944 the unpublished journal of his life in China. When Hugh Trevor-Roper, the Regius Professor of History at Oxford, examined the manuscript, to his astonishment he found that the memoirs were suffused with lascivious details of sexual encounters. Not everything Backhouse had recorded rang true to him, however. He assiduously checked for verifiable biographical facts against the external sources, and in *The Hermit of Peking*, published in 1977, he demolished many of Backhouse's palpably false claims. In Trevor-Roper's estimation, the line for Backhouse between reality and fabrication had become more than blurred, and he had convinced himself of his own falsehoods because there was always a small kernel of fact from which his tales flourished so luxuriantly.[1] On the other hand, it is not uncommon for imaginative raconteurs exuberantly to embroider the circumstances of their tales, to introduce themselves into the anecdotes they repeat, to appropriate the parts played by others, or to give themselves unwarranted leading roles. Is this not being inventive rather than delusional as Backhouse appears to have been?

This is the question the historian must ask when approaching the three books of adventure tales George Hamilton-Browne – 'Maori Browne' – published in the early years of the twentieth century. To disentangle fact from fiction in what Hamilton-Browne aptly always referred to as his 'campfire yarns', and to establish what really had or had not taken place, becomes an obsessive exercise of historical sleuthing such as Trevor-Roper undertook with Backhouse.

The difference, however, between Backhouse and Hamilton-Browne is that the latter was never deluding himself. Rather, he was a confidence trickster. His books were written in his penurious retirement as money-spinners intended to appeal to a very specific readership whose interests and prejudices he shared and consciously pandered to. He knew that what they wanted were ripping yarns of Empire. As a reviewer wrote of his first book, *With the Lost Legion in New Zealand* (1911), 'those who delight in the reading of heroic actions of British dare-devils and loyal comradeship will revel in these exciting pages.'[2]

1. Sisman, *Honourable Englishman*, pp. 463–4.
2. *Sporting Times*, 21 September 1911.

The New Zealand book was woven around an invented character called Richard Burke whom the reader was led to believe was none other than the author himself. Hamilton-Browne's second book, *A Lost Legionary in South Africa* (1912), was made all the more personal and vivid by his giving himself the leading role, even if he declared it was 'much against [his] inclination [. . .] to blow his own trumpet', apologising that 'this must occur when a man writes about events in which he has taken a hand'.[3] This apologia was disingenuously intended to give the impression that everything he was about to recount was true. It was not. Take the many pages he devoted to his description of the battle of Gingindlovu during the Anglo-Zulu War where he claimed to have been present, but where research has established that he was in fact in Cape Town at the time. But if some inventiveness was required to add zest to the tales his readers required, that did not faze him one whit. Nor did he baulk at concocting a more glamorous and adventurous back-story for himself in his books. After all, he was a practised imposter. When he landed at the Cape during the Ninth Cape Fronter War, he obtained his commission as a lieutenant in Pulleine's Rangers on 26 February 1878 and his nickname of 'Maori' on the strength of his false claim that he was a veteran of the final stages of the New Zealand Wars (1860–6) and the campaigns against Tītokowaru (1868–9) and Te Kooti (1868–72)[4] – a claim that required him to falsify the date of his birth from 1851 to 1844 in order to make him old enough to have fought. And we have evidence that over the following years, when yarning with his comrades, he was assiduously honing and rehearsing what he would later write down in his books.

The most complete expression of the legend Hamilton-Browne was weaving about himself before he put pen to paper is to be found in Major-General Robert Baden-Powell's history of the Matabele Campaign. On 9 December 1896 he entertained Hamilton-Browne in his tent outside Umtali, and wrote this of him:

> To-night we had to dinner 'Maori' B., who was with me with the Native Levy in Zululand in 1888. Celebrated over Africa for his yarns of fighting and adventure. Originally of a fine old Irish family – arrested, while a schoolboy from Cheltenham on his way to shoot at Wimbledon, on suspicion of being a Fenian; enlisted as a gunner; blew up his father with a squib cigar; shot his man in a duel in Germany; biked into the Lake of Geneva; went to New Zealand, where for twelve years he fought the Maoris; ate a child when starving; and afterwards hunted the bushrangers in Australia; took a schooner in search of a copper island, or anything else of value; next, a Papal Zouave; under Colonel Dodge, in America, he fought the Sioux. When with Pullein's corps in South Africa, his men shot at him while bathing; he beat them with an ox-yoke; they

3. Hamilton-Browne, *South Africa*, below, p. 9.
4. The war correspondent Charles Norris-Newman, who met H-B during the Anglo-Zulu War, confidently wrote of him in his *In Zululand*, p. 21: 'Commandant Hamilton-Browne, who had been through the New Zealand campaign'.

> stole an ostrich and hid it; a row among themselves followed, begun
> by a Kentish navvy, who complained he did not get his fair share of the
> 'duck.' . . . Then he became gold-digger; later, fought in the Galeka
> war, then the Zulu, Dinizulu, first Matabele campaigns, and lastly the
> present operations, in which he is a major in the Umtali forces.[5]

Lieutenant-Colonel Edwin Alderson, who fought in the same campaign as Baden-Powell and brought out his own account soon after, served alongside Hamilton-Browne and commended his 'excellent work' with the Umtali Rifles. In a footnote he added that '"Maori's" experiences of the world in general, and of irregular corps in particular, was undoubtedly great.' He went on to repeat in substance Baden-Powell's resumé of his career, adding that Hamilton-Browne had earned his nickname for fighting the Māoris for 'twelve years'.[6] A newspaper interview with Hamilton-Browne in 1908 stated misleadingly that he 'broke the monotony of fighting New Zealand natives by running over to the United States, and taking part in the Indian rebellion of 1873.'[7] Another newspaper report, only a few months later, wrote equally speciously that 'his long military career began in New Zealand in 1866, and was continued in South Africa, where he won great distinction. He was commended for gallantry at Rorke's Drift.'[8] To cap it all, doubtless on information he himself supplied, the *Cheltenham College Register 1841–1910*, compiled in 1911, stated that he had 'served in various campaigns in New Zealand and South Africa for which he was awarded medals'.

Clearly, then, by the time he came to write his books, Hamilton-Browne had his fabricated life-story down pat. And the public swallowed it. *Lost Legionary in South Africa* was widely and favourably reviewed. The *Dublin Times* was typical when its reviewer enthused: 'To those who wish to know something of the life of a soldier and the kind of fighting he has done in those early days for the aggrandisement of the Empire, we can give no better advice than to procure this book. It is full of candid criticism and genuine information.'[9]

It was easy for a 'book packed full of lively incidents, told in a quick, easy and vivid style' to 'find many readers all the Empire over.'[10] General readers – and book reviewers and school magazines too – were seldom inclined to check the veracity of Hamilton-Browne's yarns or were in a position to do so. Nevertheless, in other circles Hamilton-Browne's story had begun to unravel in 1908. The War Office in London made a small grant to this now indigent officer, and wrote to the New Zealand Ministry of Defence for confirmation of his military record there with the suggestion that it be responsible for further assistance. The bemused

5. Baden-Powell, *Matabele Campaign*, pp. 483–4.
6. Alderson, *Mashonaland Field Force*, pp. 64–5.
7. *Sheffield Evening Telegraph and Star*, 23 September 1908.
8. *Dundee Courier*, 31 December 1908.
9. *Dublin Times*, 9 August 1912.
10. *Illustrated London News*, 31 August 1912.

researchers in Wellington found that his name did not appear in the Register of the Colonial Issue of the New Zealand Medal for 1845–7 and 1860–6,[11] though a person of his name had enlisted as a trooper – and not an officer – in the Armed Constabulary in July 1872, after the cessation of hostilities. Further investigation by the authorities, and following the publication of *Lost Legionary in New Zealand* in 1911, the indignant reaction by some of those who had fought in the New Zealand Wars and knew Hamilton-Browne while he was serving with the Armed Constabulary, sealed the matter.[12]

However, this information passed the general public by, and did not percolate down to professional historians in the United Kingdom and South Africa, who continued to be hoodwinked by Hamilton-Browne's yarns. In 1959 Major Geoffrey Tylden, the doyen of South African military historians, published an extensive article on Hamilton-Browne's career. He began by declaring that Hamilton-Browne had left in his three books 'a very fair picture of what he saw and did himself'. He uncritically bought the invented aspects of Hamilton-Browne's story, including his service in the New Zealand Wars, fighting bushrangers in Australia and the Sioux in the United States, and his presence at the battle of Gingindlovu.[13]

In 1985 a New Zealand researcher, Barbara Cooper, published an article conclusively disproving Hamilton-Browne's account of his active military service in New Zealand and outlining instead his peacetime service in the Armed Constabulary.[14] Her findings were supported in 1993 by Bryan Gilling in the *Dictionary of New Zealand Biography*.[15] Yet Hamilton-Browne's fabrications continued to be perpetuated by reputable historians.

In their *Who's Who in the Zulu War*, published in 2007, Adrian Greaves and Ian Knight, two leading authorities on the Anglo-Zulu War, reaffirmed Hamilton-Browne's spurious birthdate of 1844 and declined to reject his dubious account of his New Zealand career and of his adventures in Australia and the United States. Moreover, they accepted his presence at the battle of Gingindlovu.[16] In a later work, *Zulu Rising* (2010), although retaining Hamilton-Browne's bogus birthdate of 1844, Knight showed himself more guarded about the veracity of his adventures as related in his books, and cautioned that 'Quite how much of this is true it is difficult to determine.'[17] More recently, Chris Peers in *Rorke's Drift and Isandlwana* (2021) would concede only that Hamilton-Browne 'possibly was not in the Maori

11. *See* Appendix: Hamilton-Browne's Medals.

12. Cooper, 'Hamilton-Browne', pp. 76, 78–81; Herron, *Hamilton-Browne*, pp. 116–22.

13. Tylden, 'Hamilton-Browne', pp. 153–60.

14. Cooper, 'Hamilton-Browne', pp. 76–81.

15. Gilling, 'Hamilton-Browne'.

16. Greaves and Knight, *Who's Who*, vol. II, pp. 6–8, 10. In Castle and Knight's earlier work of 1994, *Fearful Hard Times*, pp. 198–9, 208, Hamilton-Browne's sham eye-witness account of Gingindlovu is taken at face value.

17. Knight, *Zulu Rising*, pp. 161–2.

Wars in New Zealand'.[18] In my own work I was similarly circumspect, in 2023 characterising Hamilton-Browne as 'a swashbuckling adventurer and the self-proclaimed hero of many an unattested exploit in his melodramatic memoirs'.[19] But, to my embarrassment, considering that the contrary evidence was already to hand, in a subsequent book that came out in 2024, I continued to give his birth-date as 1844.[20]

The sources I should have consulted then, but have only now, are the pains-taking work of two pertinacious scholars who charted Hamilton-Browne's career in accurate detail, and winnowed the verifiable particulars of his life from his falsifications. Kristine Herron's *Georg [sic] Hamilton Brown: A Misjudged Man* (2019), a sprawling, comprehensive compendium of material about him and all his family, is readily available online. In it, Herron does her best to give Hamilton-Browne's intentions behind what she calls his 'storytelling' an indulgent gloss. The other work is not yet accessible, and I am more grateful than I can say to Cameron Simpson for permitting me to make full use of his as yet unpublished manuscript, 'Imperial and Colonial Officers of the Anglo-Zulu War of 1879', which contains succinct and thorough biographical information about Hamilton-Browne.

My footnotes to Hamilton-Browne's *Lost Legionary in South Africa* owe a great deal to these two works. Much additional information about his life will be found in those footnotes that provide a running commentary on the text. It is sufficient here to give a short but accurate resumé of his life.

His German birth certificate gives his name as Georg [sic] Hamilton Browne.[21] He was born in Bonn, in the Rhine Province of the Kingdom of Prussia, on 9 January 1851, the fifth son of Major George Browne of Comber House, Londonderry, Ireland, a member of the Protestant Ascendancy.[22] An older brother of the same name had been born at Cheltenham, Gloucestershire, on 22 December 1844 but had died the following year. To make his real age fit the tale he would spin about his military service in New Zealand, Hamilton-Browne appropriated the birthdate of his dead bother. He was educated at Malvern College along with two brothers (1863–5) and at Cheltenham College (1865–9). He was enrolled as a Gentleman Cadet at the Royal Military College, Sandhurst (1869–70), but left without taking a commission. His yarns of being thereafter a driver in the Royal Horse Artillery, serving in the Papal Zouaves and fighting a duel in Belgium are inherently unlikely for a youth not yet twenty years old, and have not been verified.

18. Peers, *Rorke's Drift and Isandlwana*, p. xxi.

19. Laband, *Shadow of Isandlwana*, p. 254.

20. Laband (ed.), *Charlie Harford*, p. 182.

21. 'Deutschland Geburten and Taufen, 1558 –1898', database, *Familysearch* https://. familysearch.org/ark:/61903/1.1 [accessed 1 November 2024].

22. This short biography is based mainly on Herron, *Hamilton-Browne*, pp. 10, 18–20, 23, 30–9, 41–3, 45–50, 53–6, 125; and on Simpson, 'Imperial and Colonial Officers'.

What has been established is that he arrived in New Zealand aboard the *Queen Bee* on 10 January 1872, just too late to have fought in the New Zealand Wars. Intriguingly, in a testimonial presented to the captain of the ship by several grateful passengers, he signed himself 'G. Hamilton Browne, Lieut 1st Reserve'[23]– surely an early instance of awarding himself a rank to which he was not entitled. He enlisted on 16 July 1872 as a trooper in the New Zealand Armed Constabulary and was posted to the Taupō District where he served as a despatch rider. Subsequently he was stationed at Opepe, Runanga and Tara Wera. A good marksman (at Cheltenham College he had been in the Shooting XI of 1867), in January 1875 Constable Hamilton Browne won the Colonial Prize for Firing.[24] He took his discharge in October 1875 and then tried various lines of employment, including working as a tour guide at Rotorua and as a valet to rich tourists. On 6 August 1877 he finally became the publican of the Cascade Hotel at Te Wairoa, Lake Tara Wera, and very soon thereafter went bankrupt. Disappointed with New Zealand, he sailed for the Cape Colony in late 1877, and not in April 1877, as he claimed in *Lost Legionary in South Africa* so as to accommodate his false assertion that he had fought in the early engagements of the Ninth Cape Frontier War during the last months of that year. There is every reason to doubt whether his claimed exploits in Australia, the United States and the South Seas during this period ever occurred.

Landing in the Cape early in 1878, he was commissioned as a lieutenant in Pulleine's Rangers on 26 February 1878, and was promoted captain on 1 May 1878. When Pulleine's Rangers were disbanded, he transferred on 4 August 1878 as a lieutenant to the Transkei Rifles. On 6 December 1878 he was appointed captain with the 1st Battalion, 3rd Regiment, Natal Native Contingent, and was promoted commandant of the 1/3rd NNC on 12 January 1879. He served with the Centre Column during the first phase of the Anglo-Zulu War and saw service throughout the Isandlwana campaign. On 8 February 1879 he was ordered from Rorke's Drift, where he was serving with the garrison, to the Cape to recruit for Lonsdale's Mounted Rifles. Although he claimed to have been present at the battle of Gingindlovu on 2 April 1879, he was in Cape Town at the time, and arrived in Durban only on 24 April with drafts for Lonsdale's Mounted Rifles. Returning to Cape Town, on 7 June 1879 he was injured when loading mules onto the *Ontario* and was incapacitated. On 25 June 1879 he married Dolphina Johanna Spolander (1856–1904) in Cape Town. However, in order to give the impression that he had secured a first-hand account of the death of the Prince Imperial of France, he pretends in his book to have remained on board the *Ontario* and to have sailed on to Natal to recuperate in Pinetown.

In September 1879 he resigned his commission as major in Londale's Horse and failed to secure a commission with the Cape Mounted Rifles. From 1880 to 1881 he served with the Cape Town Volunteer Engineers. On 15 November 1880

23. *New Zealand Mail*, 13 January 1872.
24. *Evening Post*, 10, 276 (13 January 1875).

he was appointed lieutenant. He claimed to have served in the Gun War and Transkei Rebellion (1880–1) and wore the campaign medal, but he is not listed in the medal rolls,[25] so this too must be considered a fabrication. Perhaps for that reason, he was highly reticent about his service in this campaign.

He then moved to Kimberley and on 1 January 1885 was appointed captain in the 3rd Mounted Rifles during Warren's Bechuanaland Expedition. Returning to Kimberley, where he joined his family, on 13 July 1887 he was appointed lieutenant (permanent) in the Diamond Fields Horse, and was promoted captain and adjutant on 1 January 1890. During mid-1888 he took temporary leave to serve as commandant of Carrington's Levy during the uSuthu Rebellion in the Colony of Zululand. He resigned from the Diamond Fields Horse in July 1891 to join the De Beers Mashonaland expedition. He continued to live in what in 1898 became known officially as Southern Rhodesia, serving as major in the Salisbury Horse during the First Matabele War of October–December 1893, and as major in command of the Umtali Rifles (Volunteer Corps) during the Second Matabele War of March–December 1896, as well as during operations in Mashonaland up to October 1897.[26] Having apparently lost all his livestock in Southern Rhodesia in the rinderpest epizootic of the late 1890s, he sailed for England in the *Carisbrooke Castle* and landed in September 1902.

For the next few years knowledge of his activities is scanty. There was a newspaper report in October 1902 that he had been found unconscious in the street close to Westminster Abbey 'with a paralytic seizure of his right side'.[27] He apparently soon recovered, but misfortune followed, and on 26 May 1904 his wife Dolphina, whom he evidently had left behind in South Africa, died in Cape Town aged only forty-eight. He seems to have stayed on in London, and in August 1904 a newspaper correspondent reported that he had met him in the billiard room at the Royal Palace Hotel in Kensington High Street (since demolished). Hamilton-Browne was still spinning his yarns, for he claimed that he was 'just back from Central Africa where he had been big game shooting'. The reporter had his measure, though. He wrote that Hamilton-Browne had some 'marvellous tales to tell', and that 'most of the yarns were new, although some . . . may have done the rounds'. Nonetheless, he suggested that '"Maori" Browne should write a book,' even if 'fighting [were] more probably in his line than writing'.[28] Perhaps he planted a seed in Hamilton-Browne's mind, and he would be proved quite wrong that writing was not in his line.

Hamilton-Browne is next reported to have resided between 1905 and 1907 at Cumber Claudy, Londonderry, Ireland. He was presumably living on the charity of his successful and prosperous surviving brothers: Captain William Lecky Hamilton Browne, RN (1848–1900), their father's heir (he had died in 1887); Ernest de

25. *See* Appendix: Hamilton-Browne's Medals.
26. *See* Appendix: Hamilton-Browne's Medals.
27. *London Daily News*, 6 October 1902.
28. *Sporting Times*, 27 August 1904.

Sylly Hamilton Browne (1855–1946), renowned lawn-tennis player and landowner; and Lieutenant-Colonel Cecil Hamilton Browne-Lecky, Royal Irish Fusiliers (1856–1927) who lived at Cumber House.[29]

It appears that they grew tired of supporting their black sheep of a brother for, in September 1908, a newspaper reported that he was living in penury in a London lodging house, a hard fate for 'one of the Empire's fighting heroes . . . where no native war seemed complete unless "Maori" Browne . . . was well to the front'. The newspaper continued in pathetic vein: 'Now this fine gentleman . . . has come to the end of his resources. From the publicity of having his name in print, he shrinks, but he hopes that the outcome might be the offer of work, so that he may maintain his steady independence.'[30]

Whether Hamilton-Browne really was on his uppers is not known, but the publicity he evidently courted rapidly bore fruit. Newspapers excitedly reported on 'a matrimonial event . . . quite romantic enough for a penny novelette'.[31] On 1 January 1909, at the Parish Church of St John at Hackney, he married Sarah Wallis Wilkerson (1869–1932), a union that miraculously plucked him from his desperate situation where he reportedly had only been scraping by from the sale of his medals. But as with everything to do with Hamilton-Browne, the whole business was wrapped in deliberate misinformation, transforming it into one of his yarns. The bride was described as 'a lady of wealth and position', or at the very least, 'a lady of independent means', whereas she was the eleventh and youngest child of a retired farmer, and was a lowly assistant schoolteacher living with her married eldest sister in Brighton. Are we to believe the more than unlikely tale that she contacted Hamilton-Browne when she saw him mentioned in the newspapers and recalled his name from a treasured bundle of letters from her betrothed who had died in the Sudan, but who mentioned Hamilton-Browne as having saved his life in the Anglo-Zulu War? And then, to cap it all, the bride wore as her only ornaments the miniatures of the four medals Hamilton-Browne sported, including two to which (with his typical effrontery) he had no right: the New Zealand War Medal and the Cape of Good Hope General Service Medal.[32]

The happy couple set up home in a semi-detached house at 18 Robinson Road, Colliers Wood, Merton, London, and it was there that Hamilton-Browne, describing his profession as author and journalist, wrote the three books for which he is remembered. There is a suggestion that Baden-Powell assisted him in finding a publisher.[33] The publishing house was T. Werner Laurie, founded in 1904 by Thomas Werner Laurie (1866–1944), that brought out memoirs, poetry, avant-

29. Herron, *Hamilton Browne*, pp. 18, 21, 24–8, 30, 40, 62–3.

30. *Sheffield Evening Telegraph and Star*, 23 September 1908.

31. *Evening Star*, 11 February 1909.

32. *Dundee Courier*, 31 December 1908; the *Gloucester Graphic*, 2 January 1908; *The Sketch*, 6 January 1908. *See* Appendix: Hamilton-Browne's Medals.

33. *Otago Witness*, 24 May 1916: letter to the editor, Captain Gilbert Mair, New Zealand Mounted Rifles, 15 May 1916.

garde and racy books including works by William Butler Yeats and Oscar Wilde, *The Jungle* by Upton Sinclair (1906), which exposed corruption in government and business, and *A Text-Book of Sex Education for Parents and Teachers* by Walter M. Gallichan (1919), which speaks for itself. *With the Lost Legion in New Zealand* (1911) was followed in swift succession by *A Lost Legionary in South Africa* (1912) and *Camp Fire Yarns of the Lost Legion* (1913). The last in the series was a compendium of tales about New Zealand and South Africa, gleaned from people Hamilton-Browne had met or from books he had read and given an autobiographical gloss. In all three books he fraudulently calls himself 'Colonel' Hamilton-Browne, a rank he never held.

These three books, all written in his recognisably individual and colloquial style, are extraordinary crossbreeds where fiction is disguised as autobiography and real events are given a fictionalised gloss. But they are more than mere tales of adventure tailored for a generation imbued with the grand romance of the imperial frontier. For in these books Hamilton-Browne was attempting to make sense of the tough life he had led, and he found it in the concept of the Lost Legion, encapsulated by the yarns its members told each other around the campfire.

Who were these Lost Legionaries?[34] They were the renegade gentlemen of Hamilton-Browne's own class who were the natural leaders, and the ruffians and rogues of every complexion who served under them. They were bonded by their shared hardships, dangers and lucky escapes that effaced their social and educational disparities, as well as their religious differences. Theirs was the practical, masculine camaraderie of the campfire. And although they were despised outsiders, all too often the bane of civil society, they were nevertheless a select, courageous fraternity who served the cause of Empire and expanded its sway. As Hamilton-Browne recognised, none put his finger on it better than Rudyard Kipling in his poem of 1896, 'The Lost Legion':

> There's a Legion that never was 'listed,
> That carries no colours or crest,
> But, split in a thousand detachments,
> Is breaking the road for the rest.
> Our fathers they left us their blessing –
> They taught us, and groomed us, and crammed;
> But we've shaken the Clubs and the Messes
> To go and find out and be damned
> (Dear boys!),
> To go and get shot and be damned.

For, as numerous passages in Hamilton-Browne's *Lost Legionary in South Africa* reveal, although wedded to the ideal of Empire, Hamilton-Browne had no

---

34. For the Lost Legion and the ensuing discussion, see MacDonald, *The Language of Empire*, pp. 175–91.

time for the petty absurdities of the regular army, even if by social upbringing he identified with the officer class whose company he enjoyed. He knew all too well that, unlike the Lost Legionaries, professional soldiers were largely ignorant of the nature of warfare waged on the frontier with the disastrous consequences he witnessed at Isandlwana. If his attitude to the regular army was consequently ambivalent, Hamilton-Browne's perception of politics was unnuanced. He had no interest in the rights or wrongs of any campaign he fought in, and was typical of his own conservative caste in blaming any imperial difficulties on the Liberal government when in office. Related to that, he was always ready to censure the corrupt gang of politicians, do-gooders, and Little Englanders for leaving the Lost Legion in the lurch. He especially dismissed their qualms over the violent nature of frontier warfare for, as an affirmed Social Darwinist, he firmly believed that the spoils of conquest went by right to the most powerful nation, namely the British.

Indeed, for the modern reader, many of Hamilton-Browne's attitudes and assumptions – to which he adhered without discernible qualm – are particularly questionable. They are particularly evident in the pages in *Lost Legionary in South Africa* that are given over to the lengthy, purportedly humorous yarns interpolated into the narrative, with a knowing wink, to entertain readers who were expected to share the author's conservative outlook and essential contempt for anyone or anything which was not 'English'. It was conventional at the time to treat the Irish with their brogue and drinking habits as comic, and Hamilton-Browne has a field day with Irish soldiers, sailors, priests and, time and again, with his 'man' Quin, the quintessential fall-guy. The treatment is less affectionate and more edgy when he makes fun of the Africans of the Natal Native Contingent, and the derogatory names he calls them (along with the Khoisan he encountered in the Cape), while common enough then in colonial circles, grate on modern ears. Always, the way they and the Irish are portrayed serves to proclaim Hamilton-Browne's own superior status and their dependent and subservient station.

On occasion, Hamilton-Browne is capable of some sympathy towards his Zulu enemies on account of their commendable martial culture. But his true racial sentiments are exposed when he contemptuously lambastes his own men of the Natal Native Contingent for their cowardice. His deeply engrained racial prejudice against Africans – a mindset that was all too prevalent in the British Empire at this time[35] – is most blatantly expressed in the two disturbing yarns he spins of his exploits while in garrison at Rorke's Drift: the lynching of the Zulu 'spy' and the shooting of the two 'witchdoctors' (see pp. 151–3). What makes these episodes particularly distasteful is the heavy-handedly 'humorous' style he adopts which serves effectively to belittle and dehumanise the victims. If anything sums up his attitude to Africans, it is the illustration in Baden-Powell's book about the Matabele campaign where the photograph accompanying the

_____

35. Brendon, *British Empire*, pp. 146–8.

story of his dinner with '"Maori" B.' on 9 December 1896 is of Hamilton-Browne aggressively holding a rifle to the head of an African cowering at his feet.[36]

Colonial politicians and traders, the diamond capitalists, clergymen, lawyers and children – all of these groups also come in for Hamilton-Browne's contemptuous and antagonistic handling. But his greatest bile was reserved for the Jews, more often than not contrived stock figures with negative racial and cultural characteristics, who repeatedly feature in his yarns.

Antisemitism has been present in Great Britain since the Middle Ages, and the anti-Jewish stereotype has long been part of British culture, even if unconsciously. In the late nineteenth century, the immigration of Litvak Jews fleeing persecution in the Russian Empire affronted the insular British mentality, and there was growing conservative resistance to Jews as unassimilable aliens. Eugenics-inspired notions of Jewish racial inferiority and fears of racial mixing were in the air. Moreover, racial discourse increasingly characterised Jews as feeding parasitically off other racial groups – hence the popular distrust of cosmopolitan Jewish financiers and the connections of these magnates with the British establishment.

Hamilton-Browne unswervingly subscribed to these views, as he makes only too plain on repeated occasions in *Lost Legionary in South Africa* – and it should incidentally be recorded that contemporary reviewers of his book found nothing untoward in that. Jews were not new to South Africa, and had found their way to the Cape almost from the beginning of colonial settlement. But it was the discovery of diamonds in 1867 that attracted Jews among a stream of other enterprising emigrants hoping to make their fortunes. When Hamilton-Browne encountered these Jews in South Africa, the majority had remained relatively poor. But some had become prominent traders and entrepreneurs, while others were major investors in the diamond industry. This success bred resentment, shared by Hamilton-Browne, and is expressed in his deeply unpleasant lampooning of Jews in his writings.[37]

Hamilton-Browne died at Up-Park Camp, the headquarters of the British Army in the heart of Kingston, Jamaica, on 28 January 1916. He was buried with full military honours in the garrison cemetery. His widow was left in severely reduced circumstances, last heard of in 1920 working at a munitions depot in England repairing soldiers' clothing.[38]

To the end, Hamilton-Browne's life was a mystery, for why he was in Jamaica remains unknown. And to the very last he succeeded in persuading others of his invented persona. The brigadier-general and officers of the garrison who attended his impressive burial ceremony evidently believed that they were laying to rest the mortal remains of a 'gallant Colonel',[39] whereas he had never held that rank,

---

36. Baden-Powell, *Matabele Campaign*, p. 484.

37. Hodes and Reznek, 'Antisemitism and racism in modern South Africa', pp. 30–1, 38–9, 43, 49.

38. Cooper, 'Hamilton-Browne', p. 82.

39. *The Gleaner*, 31 January 1916.

nor served in the regular British Army. Hamilton-Browne died and was buried the considered confidence trickster he had ever been, never a fantasist of the likes of Sir Edmund Backhouse. His exuberant yarns and manipulated half-truths have lived on after him through his books, to beguile and mislead.

A LOST LEGIONARY
IN
SOUTH AFRICA

BY

Colonel G. HAMILTON-BROWNE
"MAORI BROWNE"
Late Commandant in Colonial Forces

ILLUSTRATED BY S. VALDA

THE AUTHOR IN 1879.

THIS WORK IS

DEDICATED TO THE MEMORY

OF

MY OLD COMRADES
OFFICERS AND MEN

OF H.M. 24TH REGIMENT, THE 3RD NATAL NATIVE

CONTINGENT, THE PIETERMARITZBURG CARBINEERS, AND THE

NATAL MOUNTED POLICE, WHOSE BONES LIE BURIED

BENEATH THE SHADOW OF ISANDLWANA WHERE

LOSING ALL SAVE THEIR HONOUR, THEY

FELL FIGHTING BRAVELY FOR

QUEEN AND FLAG ON THE

22ND OF JANUARY

1879

" Theirs not to reason why,
Theirs but to do and die,
Though every soldier knew
Someone had blundered."

TENNYSON.

Contents

"But I've cut my cake, so I can't complain,
And I've only myself to blame,
Ah! that was always their tune at home,
And here it is just the same.
Of the seed I've sown in pleasure,
The harvest I'm reaping in pain;
Could I put my life a few years back,
Would I live that life again?

Would I? Of course I would!
What glorious days they were!
It sometimes seems the dream of a dream,
That life could have been so fair.
A sweet but if a short time back,
While now, if one can call
This life, I almost doubt at times
If it's worth the living at all.

One of these poets, which is it?
Somewhere or another, sings,
That the crown of a sorrow's sorrow
Is remembering happier things.
What the crown of a sorrow's sorrow
May be, I know not; but this I know,
It lightens the years that are now
Sometimes, to think of the years ago."

A. LINDSEY GORDON.[1]

1. Adam Lindsay Gordon was born in England in 1833 and emigrated to Australia in 1853. Long considered Australia's first national poet, he was besides a horseman, police officer and politician. He shot himself in 1870. His poetry struck a strong chord with Hamilton-Browne.

Preface

BEFORE saying anything about this present work I think it is my bounden duty to tender my hearty and sincere thanks to the innumerable critics, both British and Colonial, who so unanimously reviewed my first attempt at literature, *With the Lost Legion in New Zealand,* with a kindness that has greatly surprised me and in a manner, so obviously to myself, closing their eyes to the manifold faults in the work and most probably actuated by their sportsmanlike wishes to help a worn-out old war dog along the rough road of his declining years, have held out a helping hand, tried to lighten his swag and cheer him along the line of march by making the most of the few good things in his book and treating with leniency its many failings. I hereby again gratefully thank the members of the Press and many of my old comrades for their generous sympathy and warm support.

Much against my inclination I have written the present work in my own name,[1] for no real Lost Legionary ever wishes to blow his own trumpet or pose as a hero even should he have done deeds worthy to be so styled, and I have certainly no right to the appellation. I must therefore apologize for the frequent appearance of the big capital "I," but this must occur when a man writes about events in which he has taken a hand. Again I have tried to eliminate as much as possible accounts of petty skirmishes and cattle-raiding excursions that are so frequent in savage warfare and have contented myself by trying to make the book entertaining without thrilling my readers with bloody happenings many of which had better be forgotten.

1. In the Preface to his *With the Lost Legion in New Zealand* (1911), Hamilton-Browne (henceforth H-B) had stated that he was not writing about his own experiences, but had woven his tale of the New Zealand wars between 1866 and 1871 around a fictional character, Richard Bourke, purportedly a member of Whitmore's Corps of Guides. Nevertheless, he gave the impression that the work was in fact autobiographical – even though he had only landed in New Zealand in June 1872, after the fighting was over – and many critics and readers accepted it as such.

My frail bark is launched and must sink or swim on its own merits and if it does the former I can only hope it will go down with colours flying, after having, as Umvubie would say, a good fight first.[2]

2. Mvubu (isiZulu for hippopotamus) is a Zulu clan name. 'Umvubie' was the senior African soldier in No. 8 Company, 1st Battalion, 3rd Regiment, Natal Native Contingent commanded by H-B in the Anglo-Zulu War of 1879.

PART I

Baby Farming off Cape Horn[1]

ONE fine day towards the end of April, in the year of Our Lord 1877, two men might have been seen walking down Queen Street, Auckland, New Zealand, towards the wharf, and as one of them is the author of this book, in whose pages the name of the other frequently occurs, let me introduce myself and companion to you. I had three months previous to that date turned thirty years of age,[2] stood just over 5ft. 7in. in my bare feet, with a chest measuring over 40 inches in circumference and limbs of almost too great a magnitude for my size yet withal, when in good health, which I was not at that moment, as active as a cat and capable of undergoing any amount of exertion and hardship. As for my face, well you must judge that for yourself. Look at the portrait in the book, knock off some thirty-four years, allow for the wear and tear of over thirty strenuous years of South African frontier life, many of which have been passed in warfare, and there you are.

My companion, by name Edward Quin, called himself, and in reality was my servant but there were bonds that tied us together far stronger and more lasting than any services received or wages paid could forge.[3]

---

1. Cape Horn is the southernmost headland of the Tierra del Fuego archipelago of southern Chile.

2. In fact, he was twenty-six, having been born on 9 January 1851 in Bonn, in the Rhine Province of the Kingdom of Prussia (*see* Introduction).

3. Edward Quin remains a shadowy figure. H-B states that he was accompanied to New Zealand by his 'man' Quin, a fellow Irishman he had saved from a brawl in Brighton, and who had sworn to follow and serve him wherever he went. Of him, H-B declared: 'a truer, braver comrade, friend or soldier, never took the Queen's shilling' (H-B, *New Zealand*, p. 32). There is evidence that Quin accompanied H-B to the Cape from New Zealand and that he served alongside him in the Anglo-Zulu War in the 1st Battalion, 3rd Regiment, Natal Native Contingent (where a 'Quinn' is listed as a sergeant and a 'J. Quinn' as a corporal) and then with Lonsdale's Mounted Rifles. His prime function in H-B's book was to provide a lay figure on which to hang many of his yarns in which Quin provided stock Irish 'humour' expressed in brogue and in which he exemplified the author's belief in the comradeship – despite discrepancies in class and status – that existed between 'Lost Legionaries'. (*See* Introduction.)

Par exemple,[4] we both came from the same county, a very strong tie to an Irishman, and although Quin had not been born on my father's estate,[5] still as he put it, "he had seen dayloight, for the first toime, so moighty adjacent to it, that the short intervaneing distance made no matter." Again, just before he joined me, I had done him a trivial service, which he, with the warm-hearted gratitude of the true Irish peasant, God bless them, magnified to an enormous extent, and although he had repaid by faithful service and devoted attachment, the trifling obligation, ten thousand times over, still the simple fellow fancied he was my debtor. Stronger, however, than all these put together, was the fact, that for many a year we had fought side by side, we had looked after one another when wounded, we had shared one another's meagre rations,[6] but above and beyond all we had suffered hunger, thirst, cold and privation equally in company and neither master nor man had ever heard the other grumble or repine. This being so, no matter how wide apart we were separated by the difference of birth, education, religion and what the world calls social position, we were comrades in every sense of the word, and the love of man for man surpasses that of the love of man for woman. Such was the case with Quin and myself, though the innate good breeding and tact of my humble mate never permitted him to take any liberty with me, more than is usual for a trusty old family servant to take with an indulgent master. In person he stood over five feet eleven in height, was broad in the shoulder and narrow in the flank and was some three or four years older than myself, while both of us, in our own individual ways, were as reckless a pair of blades as ever Old Ireland has produced.

Well here we were proceeding to the wharf, for the purpose of looking at the ships, for we were Homeward Bound.[7] You good people who live at Home, know but little what the meaning of the word Homeward Bound conveys to the world wanderer; and I'll be shot if I can tell you, anyhow, such feelings we possessed as, leaning on Quin's arm, we descended Queen Street and reached the wharf. I was in no ways fit, having some time previously got in the way of a bullet, and although convalescent,

4. For example (French).

5. The estate of H-B's father, Major (retired) George Browne (1815–87), was Cumber House, Claudy, in County Londonderry, Ireland.

6. H-B had served in no military campaign prior to the final stages of the Ninth Cape Frontier War in 1878, and had never been (nor ever would be) wounded in battle, although he fancifully claimed to have been shot while hunting bushrangers in Australia at some unspecified date.

7. In fact, H-B did not embark for England in late April 1877 as he states in the opening of this chapter. He was still in New Zealand on 3 August 1877, when he gave evidence in a court case in Wairoa, Tara Wara (see Introduction), and the next day the Licensing Court of Maketu district granted his application for the transfer to him of the licence of the Cascade Hotel in the same place from W. H. Wakeham, a former steward in the Royal Navy.

was under the doctors' orders to go home and knew they were quite right in sending me. On reaching the quay, I found two vessels that, having completed their lading, were getting ready for sea and looked them over, so as to make my choice as to which should have the honour of conveying Cæsar and his fortunes; there being no direct steam communication, at that time, between New Zealand and England.

One of these vessels was a very smart-looking, full-rigged, clipper-built ship, of some six hundred tons; the other a bluff-bowed old bark, about the same tonnage, which looked as if she had been built by the mile, cut off by the foot and then the ends boxed in.[8] Of course I chose the clipper and stepping aboard was accosted by a man who, informing me he was chief mate, asked me my business and on being told I was a prospective passenger showed me into the cuddy, which I found to be a comfortable little saloon with the usual so-called state rooms, *i.e.*, square boxes of cabins, opening out of it. One of these I entered and found it furnished with two wooden bunks, placed one above the other, and these were all the necessaries, provided by the ship-owners. As the ship (the *Electric*) was advertised to sail only one day after the bark I determined to take passage in her, so without making any further inquiries, which was very foolish on my part, I went straight to the shipping office, paid our passage money and then visited an outfitter, to whom I gave instructions to rig up our state room in a comfortable manner.[9] As only two days intervened before the ship sailed and I had many things to attend to I did not again go on board until the hour advertised for the departure; reaching the wharf, just as the dock hands were beginning to cast off our moorings and the tug was alongside to pick up our hawser. As I passed along the gang plank the mate informed me the skipper was on board and that we should get under way at once, so I went into the cuddy to see that Quin had fixed up our cabin to my satisfaction. The good ship *Electric* was a poop-built vessel, with the door of the cuddy opening out on the main deck and on my entering the saloon, I was struck dumb and nearly fainted, to find it overrun with children of a tender age. Troth they were everywhere, on the deck, on the settees, crawling out of the state-room doors, and among them were many women, and a sky-pilot or two, all in tears, taking leave of one another. The howling of some of the kids was ex-cruciating, and on my getting hold of the far from clean-looking steward he informed me, to my horror, that three of the females

8. A clipper was a sleek, fully rigged sailing vessel designed for speed, a priority that took precedence over the cargo-carrying capacity of a three-masted bark (or barque) that was shaped not unlike a shoe box.

9. It has not proved possible to verify H-B's voyage in the *Electric*, the first of the colourful yarns that punctuate the narrative.

and thirteen of the piccaninnies were to be my fellow-passengers.[10]

Oh ye gods of war, why had ye suffered your poor votary to land himself in such a mess? Only fancy, ye modern day sybarites, you who grumble at the fancied hardships you have to undergo on board a ten thousand ton mail boat, just think how you would have liked to contemplate a fourteen thousand mile trip, having to double Cape Horn in the depths of winter, cooped up in the tiny saloon, of a small six hundred ton wind-jammer, in company with three lachrymose women and thirteen squawking children? Augh, my heart was dark, very dark indeed. However, nothing could be done, the tug had hold of us, the last moorings had been let go and as soon as we were clear of the land we sheeted home the topsails, manned the halyards and bore away for the Horn. Nor were my misgivings to prove wrong, for I may here state that under no other circumstances, during my somewhat hard life, have I ever had to endure such misery as I underwent during that wretched voyage. The ship was a very good one of its kind and the crew were above the average of the class of men usually to be found in the fo'castle of a wool ship of that epoch. I had paid the full price for a first-class cabin passage and expected to receive the usual first-class fare, such as fresh meat, mutton, pork, poultry, etc., but there were neither pigs, sheep nor poultry on board, and although I messed with the captain and his mate, still, with the exception of bacon, cheese, salt butter and jam, we had exactly the same provisions as were issued to the crew, so that you may say, we made the voyage on bare navy rations. I should not however have grumbled at this, although I well knew I was being badly swindled, for the salt horse and pork were of good quality, and after a man has been through years of bush fighting and frontier life, with its attendant hardships, he is not, provided he is worth his salt, going to turn up his nose at wholesome though rough fare. The cuddy was also a snug enough place in which to abide, and although I was in bad health and much run down, suffering from an old wound in my chest,[11] still as I was well supplied with books, I should have got on all right, had it not been for my fellow-passengers—three women and thirteen children, the eldest of the latter not being more than ten years of age, while three of them were infants in arms.

Now it turned out, that these three women were widows, who with their families were being shipped home on the cheap, by some goody-goody society who, having more religion in their composition than common sense, had paid intermediate passage fares for them, leaving it in the hands of Providence to look after them *en voyage*. Providence not wishing to be bothered with them, had instigated myself to take passage, without

10. 'Piccaninny' was a derogatory term for a small African or Australasian child, and H-B deploys it to signal his disapproval of all the small children aboard.

11. *See* n. 9 above.

making inquiries, and so shuffling out of His task, had delegated it to Quin and myself. This may be so, but once while off the Horn, on giving one of the widdy women an extra tot of grog, she declared that it was Providence, who had guided us to ship in the *Electric* for the purpose of looking after herself and her kids. It may be so, though I fancied then, and still believe, the engineering faculty, of our misfortune, to have been Old Nick himself. It also happened, that when the contract aforementioned was made, that the usual intermediate passengers' quarters had been stowed chock full of wool, so that the shipping company (there being no demand at the moment for first-class passages) had put them into the cuddy to live, but allowing them only third-class rations and no attendance whatever.

Very many queer things were done at sea in those days, on board the old wind-jammers,[12] but I have never heard or read of a more heartless, brutal case than the one I am writing about. Just think of the facts. These poor people had their rations served out to them in bulk once a week, and were expected to do everything for themselves, store their rations in their cabins, prepare their food, carry it along the main deck to the galley, which was situated abaft the foremast, and then bring it back again when cooked, the said deck being often flooded with over two feet of icy cold water, which, rushing from side to side, owing to the motion of the rolling, plunging ship, made the journey one of danger, even to a bold hardy man not used to the sea and a matter of utter impossibility for a timid woman. There was no stewardess on board, and the dissolute-looking steward, and the still dirtier cabin-boy, seeing no chance of receiving tips from them at the end of the journey, absolutely refused to render them any service at all; a refusal that was backed up by the skipper, on the plea, that they were only third-class passengers. All this would have been bad enough had the mothers been capable women but they were far from that, as they were the most lackadaisical, useless bodies it has ever been my hard lot to meet, each and all of them asserting, they had seen better days, and so as to enhance their claims to a spurious gentility, absolutely refused to either help themselves or their wretched offspring. However it was too late for me to make any other arrangements, we were at sea, and I could only hope and trust we should be chased home by a gale of wind, but these hopes were doomed to be quickly shattered, as although we left port with a strong fair wind yet on the second day it drew right ahead, and we were on a bowline,[13] till we weathered the Horn, fifty-seven days after we had left Auckland, during the whole of which time the three ladies, in reduced circumstances, remained in their bunks, leaving it to

12. A windjammer was a commercial sailing ship with multiple mast and sails.

13. To sail on a bowline means stopping the sail from accidentally being forced backwards, in the direction of the masts, by holding the edge of the sail towards the bow of the ship and into the wind.

my servant and myself to wait on them and look after, as best we might, their squealing progeny.

True at times they managed to sing hymns of a doleful nature, but that did not recompense us, and long before we weathered the Horn, King Herod (I mean the one who made a name by infant killing) rose many points in my estimation,[14] as I was sorely tempted to launch an armful or two of howling kids over the lee rail every hour out of the twenty-four. The skipper was a grim old Scotch shell-back[15] who had crawled aft through the horse-pipe, bringing with him neither manners nor conversation; he was, I have no doubt, when sober a good seaman and navigator but was the most unpleasant table companion I have ever met, as his methods of eating would have disgusted a pig. He was, however, very partial to religion, which he took every night with rum, imbibing them both in equal quantities; as he used, after supper, to sit at the cuddy table with a huge Bible in front of him and a bottle of rum mighty adjacent on the swing tray.

Thus provided, following the text with his finger and spelling out the hard words, he would read, in an audible voice, a verse or two from any chapter at which the book might open and then gravely shaking his head, would absorb a stiff nip of rum and would so continue his devotions and potations until he became as drunk as old Noah (late commander of the Ark) when he would lurch off to his virtuous bunk.[16] It may therefore be easily imagined, that I did not get much pleasure or profit out of this old sea-dog's society and as the continuous yowls of the kids effectually prevented my reading, even when not engaged in feeding or grooming them, and as we were hove to, fore-reaching, off the Horn for twenty-one days, with everything smothered in ice, I may be forgiven, by even the tenderest-hearted matron, when I state that I frequently consigned the useless sluts of mothers, their tender though very dirty offspring, together with the skipper and the shipping agent to a far warmer latitude than Cape Stiff.[17]

Anyhow there is one thing certain, that had it not been for Quin and myself, things must have gone very hard with our miserable fellow-passengers, so perhaps after all it may have been Providence who sent me along to pay our passage money, without first of all making full inquiries, as to who might be going with us, though at that time I was fully convinced to the contrary. However, the longest voyage must end some time or other, so after losing our fore and main topmasts and being nearly cast away in the Channel, thanks to the old man having taken in an overdose of

14. For King Herod and the Massacre of the Innocents, see Matthew 2: 16–18.

15. 'Shellback' was a nautical term for an old sailor.

16. See Genesis 9: 20–3 for the drunkenness of Noah.

17. 'Cape Stiff' was slang for Cape Horn.

the book of Deuteronomy mixed with O.P. rum,[18] we dropped our anchor at Gravesend,[19] where I thankfully went on shore, after enduring one hundred and twenty-seven days of unsophisticated—(the word begins with an H).

On reaching London, I found my family were over in Paris, so left the following night for the gay city.

18. Deuteronomy is the fifth book of the Old Testament. O.P. (over proof) rum is very intoxicating at nearly 60 per cent alcohol by volume.

19. Gravesend was a mercantile town in north-western Kent on the south bank of the Thames, twenty miles from central London.

Chapter II

I Start Again on the Long Trail

FIVE weeks of civilization were quite enough for me, and as the doctors strongly advised me not to risk the winter in Europe, I determined to skip it, by taking a cruise round Africa. I was guided in this choice by the fact that one of my elder brothers, a lieutenant in the Royal Navy,[20] was stationed on the East African coast, and as it was expected, his ship would be shortly returning to England, to be paid off, I thought that perhaps if I picked him up at Zanzibar, he might be able to give me a passage home, failing which, I would find my own way through the Mediterranean and get back to England at my leisure. Perhaps I might get some shooting but I was then like the majority of Britishers, even at the present day, profoundly ignorant of Africa. I therefore booked passages for myself and Quin by the mail boat to Zanzibar, taking him with me because he sternly refused to be left behind. The voyage out to Cape Town was a pleasant one and I found life, on a first-class mail boat, very different to that which I had experienced on board the *Electric;* so that by the time we reached the Cape my health had improved wonderfully and I was again nearly fit.[21]

On arrival in Table Bay I discovered, that to reach Zanzibar, it was necessary for passengers, proceeding round the coast, to transship into a small coasting steamer that, stopping at all the intermediary ports, dropped the mails and passengers destined for those places, that had been brought out by the ocean boat; so that after bidding farewell to the

20. William Lecky Hamilton Browne (1848–1900) was Major George Browne's third son. He outlived his two elder brothers and became his father's heir. He entered the Royal Navy as a cadet in September 1860, and was promoted sub-lieutenant on 16 June 1868, lieutenant on 3 September 1872, commander on 30 June 1886 and captain on 1 January 1893.

21. According to his own statement of 25 September 1879 to the Colonial Military Secretary of the Cape when requesting a commission in the Cape Mounted Rifles, H-B arrived in the Cape Colony in February 1878. When would he have had to have left Auckland in New Zealand to reach Cape Town by that date? H-B says his initial voyage to Gravesend took him 127 days (100 or so days was the usual sailing time); he was then with his family in Paris another five weeks (or so he claims); and it would have taken just over three weeks in a Union Line or Castle Line steamship to sail from England to the Cape. So, if he left New Zealand in late August, soon after the last references to him there (see p. 14, n. 7) and his seemingly very swift failure as a publican, the time-frame would just about fit.

Cape Town crowd the rest of us, proceeding further, were transshipped and in a couple of days continued our voyage.

It was on a lovely afternoon that we steamed out of the dock, not a ripple on the water and every promise of a continuance of the fine weather, for which I was thankful, as the discipline on board, struck me as being very lax indeed, many of the crew being drunk and even some of the officers, slightly resembling teetotallers on strike. Moreover the ship itself was simply crowded with passengers. I did not however bother myself about this state of affairs, as in the bright sunshine it did not seem possible any serious disaster could happen and once out at sea both officers and men would quickly sober up. The afternoon passed away and I thoroughly enjoyed the splendid coast scenery, which was very distinct and when the first dressing-bell rang, went down into my cabin, to change into dinner kit.

I had been surprised, all the afternoon, at the closeness we had been keeping to the shore, but on making inquiries, had been informed, that it was customary for boats, proceeding up the coast, to hug the land, so as to avoid the strength of the great current that sets round the Cape and that on such a bright, clear evening there could be no danger. Well, I was just proceeding leisurely to remove my coat, when the ship gave a bump and I distinctly heard her tearing holes in her skin as she scraped over a reef; then came another bump and she sat tight. In a moment the shrieks of women and children, together with the shouting of men, plainly let me know something out of the common had happened.[22] Hastily opening my dispatch case, I grabbed a roll of notes, which with a few valuables I thrust into a waterproof sponge bag and made fast to my person; then with Quin, who had rushed to me, at the first alarm, tackled to to help a lot of women and children, who shrieking with fear, were trying to get on deck. Here for a time confusion reigned. The boat was crowded with passengers, among whom were many children of Israel, most of them foreign Jews, on their way to the diamond fields, and these beauties, what with their selfish cowardice and lamentations, made infinitely more row than even some of the most nervous women; in fact a lot of them had to be rather roughly handled, before they could be reduced into a state of quietude.[23]

22. A pity to ruin a good yarn, but there is absolutely no record of a coastal steamer being wrecked along the coast of the Overberg District in Cape Colony in early 1878 (*see* South African Heritage Resources Agency, *List of Shipwrecks*, pp. 1–5).

23. For H-B's brand of antisemitism, see the Introduction, p. xxi.

In his derogatory comments about the Jewish people he places aboard his fictional shipwreck, H-B is being anachronistic as well as antisemitic, and seems to have lost his sense of direction. If, as he says, they were on their way to the diamond fields in Griqualand West which were inland from Cape Town, then why would they be taking passage eastwards around the coast of South Africa? He insists there were many Jews, mainly foreign, but at that date it is unlikely to have been so. Under the British administration of the Cape after

Both Quin and myself had taken an active part in quelling the disturbance and as soon as this was done I was able to take a look round. It was still broad daylight, the sun not having yet set, and how on earth the officer of the watch and the quartermaster at the con, had managed to pile us up, where we were, the Lord himself only knew. One thing however was plain as a pikestaff, the ship was a hopeless wreck and the captain and crew, as a whole, were quite incapable of coping with the disaster. The skipper and chief officer, did wander around for a bit as if they were dazed, but, as far as I heard, gave no orders at all, though the second officer, a fine young fellow, kept his head and behaved, as all the world expects, a British seaman to do when faced with sudden danger; in fact, it was entirely due to his exertions that the bulk of the passengers were saved. As it was evident nothing could be done for the ship, he gave orders for the two quarter boats to be lowered and this, with some trouble, owing to the unhandiness of the half-drunken crew, was done but on reaching the water the port boat immediately filled, she being so sun-cracked as to be quite unseaworthy. The stewardess also did her duty well, as she procured and issued out to the women a number of life-belts, though the sight of these, necessitated our again having to knock down a few Jew boys, in order to prevent them from grabbing and annexing these useful articles. Nor was it only the children of Israel who showed such quite unnecessary anxiety for self-preservation; as a nasty, oleaginous missionary, belonging to some fancy religion or other and who weighed at least nineteen stone, made a most determined effort, to capture one of the belts from a diminutive German sheeny[24] who had surreptitiously sneaked

---

1806, a handful of mainly English, German and Dutch Jews had been allowed to settle in the colony. They played a significant part as *smouse*, or itinerant traders in the rural districts (*platteland*), accelerating the transition from a subsistence to a cash economy. The discovery of diamonds in 1867 introduced an entirely new element into the hitherto pastoral and agricultural life of southern Africa. A small trickle of Jews, usually from Britain or Germany, joined the stream of enterprising emigrants flowing in from all parts of the world to make their fortunes. Although few in number, Jews at the diamond diggings centred at Kimberley played a significant part in the rapid evolution of the industry. Along with Gentile magnates like Cecil Rhodes, Jewish capitalists such as Alfred Beit (born in Hamburg) and Barney Barnato (born in London) traded in diamonds, owned and operated mining claims, and floated mining companies both locally and in Europe, bringing new-found wealth to the Cape and energising the economy of southern Africa.

When H-B might have encountered many more Jews travelling in South Africa was a decade later than 1878. The assassination of Tsar Alexander II in 1881, followed by a wave of pogroms and antisemitic laws in Russia, prompted the mass emigration of Jews from the Pale of Settlement. Out of a total of about three million migrants, 40,000 Eastern European Jews chose South Africa where they were attracted by the economic opportunities created by the discovery in 1886 of gold on the Witwatersrand in the Zuid-Afrikaansche Republiek (South African Republic/Transvaal; henceforth ZAR).

24. 'Sheeny' is a derogatory term for a Jewish person.

it. The struggle was most diverting, for as the Puritan sky-pilot[25] tried to buckle the belt round his enormous corporation, Shylock, clinging to him like a limpet, tried to find protection within the same apparatus, while both of them vociferated and declared that he individually had the sole right to the life-saving girdle. It would have amused me greatly to have watched the tug of war between Jew smouser[26] and Christian soul-catcher to its bitter end but the plucky stewardess wanted the bone of contention for the use of a woman, so requested the worthy Quin to procure it for her; which he did in a summary manner as, on their refusing to part with it, he quietly knocked them both down and handed over the belt to its rightful owner. I may here state that the language of the bereaved devil-dodger, as he wallowed in the scuppers, was quite unfit for publication, being such as would have made a camp of mule-packers either blush or turn green with envy. In the meantime another boat had been got into the water, which with the serviceable one already lowered being filled with women and children shoved off for the shore on which they safely landed. The boats then returned to the ship, and although the sun had set and it was by now nearly dark, succeeded in taking off two more loads, which also reached their destination in safety; both boats however, were somewhat damaged, in fact so much so, as to render it impossible to make more trips that night, even had the darkness permitted the attempt to be made.

When the boats left for the last time, those of us who remained on the ship, saw we must pass the night where we were; there was no danger to be apprehended so long as the calm continued but should it come on to blow, or a heavy ground swell get up, the wreck would soon be knocked into scrapiron and all of us be summoned, to toe the line before Davy Jones. It however struck me, I might just as well parade before that potentate, in a well-fed condition as in a fasting one, so calling Quin, we dived down into the saloon, to see what we could discover in the way of rations. The saloon was half full of water but on the sideboard, and quite dry, were a ham, tongue, and other cold comestibles which, wrapping up in a table-cloth, I took on deck; Quin at the same time managing to get into my cabin, where he rescued my ulster and portmanteau undamaged and on our second trip, we burgled the bar-room door and brought on deck a good supply of bottled ale and spirits. These provisions were thankfully received by our brother unfortunates so we squatted down on deck and made a good square meal. All this time the captain had remained within his deck cabin and neither by word nor deed, had tried to do anything for the safety or encouragement of his passengers. Not that we, who had voluntarily remained on the wreck, wanted his condolence or sympathy, for we were

25. Protestant minister of religion.

26. In South African usage, a *smous* ('smouser') was an itinerant pedlar. But it is also a derogatory term for a Jew from Germany or Eastern Europe (*see* n. 23, above).

all men who had knocked about the world above a bit, knew the danger we were in and were quite ready to face it without squealing. One of our number, a man bound for Natal, and who had been a fellow-passenger on the ocean mail boat, I knew to have been a master in the mercantile marine, so as I handed him my tobacco pouch, I said, "Mr Jackson, you're an old shell-back and knowing the coast well, I think it would be better for the rest, if you were to direct us to take such steps, as you may deem fit, to give us a fighting chance for our lives, should it come on to blow." "Well," he replied, "you see it's this way, the ship's captain is still on board and it would be taking a great liberty on my part, should I issue any orders or in any way appear to take the command out of his hands."

Now this was quite right and, I had no doubt, was strict etiquette but then as the ship's skipper had shut himself up in his cabin, I considered, he had voluntarily abdicated the command and that it was our duty, to do the best we could for ourselves. These ideas, myself and some of the others urged on Mr Jackson, until at last he consented to give us the benefit of his experience. After he had taken a good look round he said, "I don't think we shall have any wind to-night but if a ground swell comes on, as it is quite likely to do, the boat will part amidship, just abaft the funnel and the fore part sink; so get as many ropes as you can and stretch them from the after bollards, round the mainmast and the companion hatch, in order that we can have something to hold on by, should the sea break over the stern part, which is firmly fixed on the rocks and will, I think, hold together for the night." This we did and as we were joined by the boatswain and two others of the crew, now fairly sober, we made a good job of it, completing just in time, for a heavy ground swell shortly set in when, as Jackson had prognosticated, before midnight, the hull of the ship parted, the bows disappearing in a whirl of foam, while the stern part on which we were, remained intact; and although we soon got drenched, by the seas that broke over us, still, thanks to the stretched ropes, there was but little danger of any of us being swept away. Morning came and as the sun rose, the heavy swell subsided, which was very lucky, for had it continued or increased, the remains of the hull would have soon been knocked to pieces and moreover the boats would not have been able to again get alongside. This however they did and we were all, eventually landed on the beach where we found the passengers, who had come ashore the previous night, in rather an evil plight. I had however come off fairly well, as I had saved my money and valuables and Quin had managed to bring on shore a portmanteau full of clothes. One individual had however fared even better than I (let us designate him as Smith). Well Mr Smith had been a fellow-passenger on the ocean boat, and on leaving Southampton had worshipped so devoutly at the shrine of Bacchus[27] that,

27. Bacchus was the Roman god of wine, and the inference is that Smith was a drunkard.

after we had been a few days at sea, the captain and doctor had forbidden him to be served with any more of his favourite potations, thereby reducing him to a term of enforced sobriety. Of course as soon as the boat reached Cape Town he made up for lost time and treated himself to a scrumptious bust but as he was booked through to Port Natal, where he resided, some friends had collected him and put him, very full indeed, on board the coasting steamer; when he promptly turned in so as to get a good snooze, which would render him fit to continue his devotion to the rosy god. He was therefore enjoying a refreshing siesta when the boat struck and peacefully slumbered through the subsequent turmoil. It was therefore only on the stewardess, who was, in the most plucky way, making a last survey of the cabins to see that none of the women or children passengers had been overlooked that he was discovered. "Get up, sir, get up at once!" cried the stewardess, shaking the sleeping beauty. "Eh what, oh mine's a brandy," grunted the bacchanalian relapsing into slumber. "But, sir, you must get up at once, the ship's ashore and wrecked," screamed the plucky woman. "Eh what, what's that, ship's wrecked is it, then go and tell the captain it's his business not mine, I'm a first-class passenger go night," and the imperturbable inebriate turned over to continue his rest cure. "But, sir, you must get up, indeed you must, the passengers are leaving the ship," and she shook and pulled him with all her strength. "Can't have got to Natal yet and I'm booked through," quoth Smith, but it was no use, the brave little woman stuck to him, pulled him out of his bunk and drove him up the companion way, before her, in the same way as she would have driven a marauding hen out of her back garden. On their arrival on deck, she busied herself getting the women and children into the boats, while he loafed about in a disconsolate sort of a way, not taking the slightest interest in anything that was going on and eventually, after the last boat had pushed off, he drifted out of everyone's ken and was not missed until next morning, when the question was passed round, "Where is Smith?" He was certainly not on deck, and as no sea, heavy enough to wash him away, had broken over us during the night, Jackson opined he must have gone below, and started off down the companion steps to look for him. On reaching the saloon he found the water to be up to his shoulders but by wading and swimming he managed to get into the state-room, which he shared with Smith, and there he found that philosopher comfortably asleep in his top berth, with the water only an inch under the bunk boards. Jackson quickly and I fear rather unceremoniously woke him up, when the delinquent, coolly taking his neatly-folded clothes, watch and cash, from under his pillow, tied them to the top of his head with the bed sheet, slid into the water and followed his rescuer on deck, where he carefully dried himself, then calmly dressing, went on shore, the only one, out of that ship-wrecked crowd, who had thoroughly enjoyed a night's repose. Now I leave it to you, my reader, to decide, whether his philosophical conduct was caused by hardihood or brandy or did he trust Old Nick to look after his own? anyhow, he scored. The wretched women and children, in fact all the people, who had landed the previous evening, had passed a miserable night camped out on the beach but during the day carts and carriages, sent from Simon's Bay,[28] arrived and took us all back to Cape Town. I have given a full account of this wreck, not because there was anything out of the common about it, but because it was responsible for my passing thirty years in South Africa, an idea that had never previously entered my mind. On reaching Cape Town I found I should either have to wait there a month for a boat, to take me on to Zanzibar, or proceed slowly up the coast, putting in time at Port Elizabeth, East London and Port Natal,[29] at the last of which ports the East Coast boat would catch me up and take me on. I chose the latter course of procedure, as I had already exhausted the sights of Cape Town and being unacquainted with any one residing there, I thought I might better kill time at one of the other ports, especially as the hotel accommodation at Cape Town was, at that epoch, vile. I therefore returned to the ocean boat and went in her as far as East London, which was her destination, and her port of departure for her return journey to England; so that on reaching there I had to land and wait for the coasting steamer that was to take me on to Zanzibar. This sounded bad, but when I got on shore I found it to be far worse than I had even anticipated, as I quickly discovered the place to be the protoplast of hell upon earth, tenanted by the scum and refuse of the seven seas. Let me explain. At that time the breakwater and the harbour works had just been begun and all ships, trading to the port, had to lie out in an open roadstead,[30] the dangers of which were very manifest, by the number of wrecks piled up along the beach. This being the case, all passengers and goods, consigned to East

28. Simon's Town, then the British naval station at the Cape, is on the western shore of False Bay.

29. Port Elizabeth (now renamed Gqeberha) was founded in 1820 at the conclusion of the Fifth Cape Frontier War on the western shore of Algoa Bay, and served as the main port for the Eastern Cape. East London was established in 1836 at the mouth of the Buffalo River after the end of the Sixth Cape Frontier War. It was the supply port for the British garrison at King William's Town, founded in 1835 as the administrative capital and military headquarters of British Kaffraria, forty miles inland to the north-west. Since June 1877 East London and King William's Town had been connected by a railway line.

   Port Natal, known officially since 1835 as Durban when it was named after the Governor of the Cape, Lieutenant-General Sir Benjamin D'Urban (1834–8), had been founded in 1824 in Zulu territory by hunter-traders from the Cape. It was the port of the British Colony of Natal.

30. Work on the harbour breakwater had begun earlier in the 1870s, but landing from ships anchored off the mouth of the river was still by lighter, and was indeed a hazardous operation.

SHIPWRECKED BUT UNCONCERNED.

London, had to be landed in cargo boats that were hauled over the bar and into the river along a huge hawser, leading from the wharf to a buoy moored out at sea, to which the tightly-battened-down barges were towed and from whence, having picked up the hawser, they were dragged along it by their crews. This was savagely, hard and very dangerous work and the men forming the crews, were perhaps the roughest and most abandoned toughs in the world; being chiefly composed of runaway sailors, of every nationality, so that, the East London serf boatmen were, at that time, the terror of the South African coast. Well it may be easily imagined that a small colonial seaport town having a large percentage of its population composed of such a type of mankind, drawing big wages, and who were able to buy vile brandy (known as Cape Smoke) for ninepence per bottle, besides obtaining other liquor by the unorthodox way of broaching cargo, was not the most reposeful nor pleasant haven in which to pass a fortnight; and before I had been an hour in the frowsy, boozing den, miscalled an hotel, I was thoroughly sick and disgusted with the place and longed to clear out. But where was I to go? I was as ignorant of South Africa as an English colonial secretary and knew not which way to turn, when happening to look out of the window, I saw coming along the road, a sergeant dressed in the uniform of the 24th Regiment and immediately went out and accosted him, asking for news of his corps, many of the senior officers of which I knew well,[31] and was delighted when he informed me, that his regiment was quartered at King William's Town and that many of my old friends were still serving in it. He also informed me that King was only a short journey by rail, that I could reach there the same day and that the hotel accommodation there was much better than at East London. This was indeed good news, so Quin bundled our traps across the river to the station and the same evening we found ourselves camped in King William's Town, where I obtained comfortable quarters.[32]

31. The 1st Battalion, 24th (2nd Warwickshire) Regiment had been stationed in India and Burma previous to seeing continuous service for eight years in various Mediterranean garrisons before beginning its South African tour of duty on 4 February 1877. It is inconceivable, therefore, that H-B could (as he claimed) have known many of the senior officers well, or indeed have had any 'old friends' in the battalion at all.

32. It appears that, throughout H-B's service in the Ninth Cape Frontier War, Quin accompanied him as his batman, or personal servant.

Chapter III

A South African Picnic

MY old friends in the first battalion of H.M. 24th Regiment, received me very kindly and I enjoyed for a couple of weeks the *bon camaraderie,* always to be found in the society of an English regimental mess, so was quite sorry when the date of my departure drew near. Now during the whole time I was located at King William's Town, rumours were afloat that the natives, especially the Gaika tribe, were in a state of great unrest and threatening to raid into the Cape Colony, so as to wipe out the Fingoe tribe, that had lived for many years under the regis of British protection.[1] These Fingoes, had originally been the slaves and helots of the Gaikas but now having waxed fat and consequently cheeky, were very much inclined to fancy themselves quite as good as their former masters. I do not wish to imply that they would have dared to stand up against the Gaikas in battle, no not for a moment but having lived for some years under the tuition of missionaries they had lost their pristine humility, so that at beer-drinkings and other native social gatherings, they were more than uppish in their manners and gave their whilom lords and masters to understand, that they considered themselves to be on a level plane of equality.[2] This impudence on the part

1. Between 1779 and 1878, first the Dutch, then the British colonial power at the Cape fought nine wars of conquest and dispossession against the Xhosa people. In these wars, regular troops of the Cape garrison were assisted by colonial paramilitary units, settler commandos and volunteer regiments, and African allies, most notably the amaMfengu. In the general settlement of the frontier in 1865–6 between the Eighth and Ninth Cape Frontier Wars, the defeated Ngqika amaXhosa were confined to an area north of King William's Town in the Ciskei, and the Gcaleka amaXhosa to a coastal location in the Transkei. Much of the former Gcaleka territory was made over to the Cape's African allies, the amaMfengu in Fingoland, and the abaThembu in Emigrant Thembuland. Deep resentments therefore simmered between the amaGcaleka and those who had supplanted them.

2. There is much scholarly debate over the origins of the 'Fingos', or amaMfengu. The current consensus is that they were amaGcaleka Xhosa who in the 1820s accepted missionaries and developed their own identity in Xhosa society, farming more intensively than their neighbours, participating eagerly in trade and resisting the traditional authority of chiefs. In May 1835, during the Sixth Cape Frontier War, the governor of the Cape arranged for nearly 17,000 of them to move west across the Kei River into the Colony, where they were settled around Fort Peddie between the Fish and Keiskamma Rivers. There they added to the colonial labour supply and were increasingly accepted into the colonial order

of the Fingoes, was extremely galling to the haughty Gaikas, who still regarded them as their dogs and chafed at the idea, that the absurd British law did not allow them (the Gaikas) to take big sticks and reason their one-time despised slaves, back again to their original subservience. Both tribes were rich in cattle, and each tribe longed to possess his neighbour's, and when a nigger languishes for anything,[3] be he so-called Christian or Pagan, he usually tries to obtain it by the simple method of thieving. Numerous stock robberies had therefore occurred, for some time, along the frontier, which helped to fan the embers of jealousy into the flames of war. For the last year or more, there had been bickerings and trouble on the border, though no one believed it would come to actual blows, as all white men, border traders and settlers as well as officials had a great respect and liking for old Kreli,[4] the paramount chief of the Gaikas, who together with the seniors of his tribe earnestly desired to maintain peace. Kreli had however a son named Segou,[5] a bitter hater of both white men and Fingoes, who was the head centre and leader of the young bloods and warriors, always the most turbulent faction among native tribes, and this fellow together with his tail, puffed up as all niggers become when they have waxed fat, determined to raid and loot the Fingoes, even at the risk of bringing on a war with the white man. These tribal frictions at length culminated during a big beer-drinking match, held by some Fingoes in British territory, but at which some Gaikas were present; a row started, blows were struck, blood was drawn and the Gaikas, few in number, had to bolt across the frontier, returning shortly afterwards in strength to revenge the insult. The Fingoes squealed loudly for British protection, the Gaikas made a big raid over the border and the war began.[6] Well to make a long story short, the news of

---

by becoming Christians, dressing in European clothes, building European-style houses, and sending their children to school. All this set them apart from the still-independent amaXhosa, against whom they were determined to protect their new identity and prosperity. Consequently, over the next three Cape Frontier Wars they would prove staunch military allies of the British authorities against the amaXhosa, fielding more men than any other colonial unit.

3. 'Nigger' is now an unacceptable derogatory term for an African or African-American, but in the nineteenth century could be applied to any person of colour. Even then, it indicated racist contempt, and H-B always employs it in that spirit.

4. Sarhili (1809–92) succeeded his father Hintsa, who was killed in the Sixth Cape Frontier War, as *nkosi* of the Gcaleka amaXhosa and as the titular Paramount Chief of the Xhosa nation. During his rule his people suffered woefully in the Seventh (1846–7), Eighth (1850–3) and Ninth (1877–8) Cape Frontier Wars.

5. Sigcawu (d. 1902), the belligerent son and heir of Sarhili, had in 1872 successfully raided the abaThembu in Emigrant Thembuland, and planned one day to drive the amaMfengu in Fingoland into the sea.

6. On 3 August 1877 a party of amaGcaleka gate-crashed the festive beer-drinking at a wedding feast being held by an Mfengu called Ngcayecibi because they resented that the celebrations were being held in Fingoland, on land that had once been theirs. Tempers

the Gaikas' raid and the declaration of the war reached King William's Town the night previous to my contemplated departure from there,[7] and of course, the chance of a scrap caused much pleasurable excitement among my kind entertainers; so much so, that their elation became infectious, spreading even to myself, the consequence being, that I at once offered my services to the General, Sir Arthur Cunningham,[8] and volunteered to join any irregular force it might be deemed necessary to raise. The General being pleased to accept my offer,[9] in a couple of days, I was again in the saddle, ready to play once more the game I loved so dearly. The disturbances in South Africa, during the years 1877 and 1878, are called the Gaika and Galeka Wars,[10] and I suppose it is right to speak of them as such, although there was but little hard fighting done, and as for privations they were entirely absent,[11] at least so it appeared to Quin

flared and the amaMfengu beat up their unwelcome guests, killing one. The amaGcaleka launched retaliatory raids, and the Cape authorities rushed to offer protection to their Mfengu allies.

Sir Bartle Frere, the High Commissioner, believed that the restlessness on the Cape Eastern Frontier was hobbling his freedom to act elsewhere in southern Africa to implement his plan to confederate the whole subcontinent under the British Crown. Therefore, when he arrived at the troubled frontier in early September 1877, he decided that was the moment to settle the Xhosa question once and for all, and commenced military operations.

7. This is fabrication for the sake of the yarn H-B is spinning, because when war broke out on the Cape Eastern Frontier, he was on the high seas on his way from New Zealand to Britain.

8. General Sir Arthur Cunynghame (1812–84) was General Officer Commanding Her Majesty's Forces at the Cape of Good Hope, Natal and St Helena from November 1873 until March 1878 when he was superseded by Lieutenant-General Sir Frederic Thesiger (from October 1878 the second Baron Chelmsford). Cunynghame was an amiable, conscientious general officer who had been appointed to what was initially a 'safe' command. However, when Conservative policy-makers began spurring on the confederation of South Africa, his command involved more military intervention than anticipated. His conduct of the Ninth Cape Frontier War was ploddingly conventional but he was superseded for political rather than military reasons, having become embroiled with the colonial government at the Cape over the question of command and the direction of operations against the amaXhosa.

9. General Cunynghame handed over his command to Lieutenant-General Thesiger in King William's Town on 4 March 1878, so it is just conceivable that the newly-arrived H-B could have offered him his services, posing as a veteran of the New Zealand wars.

10. The conflict is commonly known today to historians as the Ninth Cape Frontier War, while the amaXhosa still call it the War of Ngcayecibi.

11. From the British perspective it is possible to minimise the scale of the fighting because casualties among British soldiers and colonial troops numbered no more than 60 white and 133 African soldiers killed. The impact of the war was very different for the amaXhosa. An estimated 3,680 Xhosa warriors died on the battlefield, an appalling 50 per cent casualty rate among combatants. And this figure does not include those who died later of their wounds and privations, or Xhosa non-combatants who perished of starvation as a consequence of British scorched-earth operations. More than 45,000 Xhosa cattle were carried off by the victors. Some 4,000 starving Xhosa women who had taken refuge with

and myself, who had both of us experienced, what genuine hardships and bitter savage warfare really meant in New Zealand.[12] Of course there were some men who grumbled at the work and commissariat but they were creatures who, having most likely been brought up on scraps and meagre diet in their youth, would find fault with the cuisine and accommodation of the Savoy or Cecil hotels;[13] certainly they were not hall-marked lost legionaries.

Now I must confess to liking a good dinner and snug bed myself and blame no man for looking after his personal comforts, even in the field, but I thoroughly despise and have always had the utmost contempt for a thing, posing as a man, who whines about the roughness of his rations, so long as he has any to eat at all, or of having to bed down in the rain and mud, when the glorious game of war is afoot. Bad scran to a rotter of that sort, he is quite out of place at the front; he should bury his weapons and take the billet of head swab-wringer in a London cook-shop. Of course a soldier must be fed and should be well fed, but I assert and maintain that the mobility and usefulness of H.M. troops, both Imperial and Colonial, during all the wars in South Africa, were most unnecessarily hampered by the long lines of wagons, employed to lug along superfluous luxuries and kit that were never even dreamed of in the New Zealand wars.

As far as the fighting went, I was not fortunate enough to be present at any of the three engagements, that took place in the Transkei,[14] which by a stretch of considerable imagination might be called battles, though I had my share in many skirmishes and cattle-lifting operations. The major engagements were brought about by the natives attacking various patrols; in the first of which, they drove a party of the Cape Frontier Armed and Mounted Police off the field;[15] in the second they were badly beaten by the

---

the British were transported by sea from East London to earn a bare living in the environs of Cape Town, far from home and family.

12. H-B knew of the New Zealand wars only through hearsay and not through personal experience, having arrived in that country after their cessation. However, on landing in the Cape, he presented himself from the very outset as a veteran of this conflict, presumably banking on the unlikelihood of there being anyone in the Cape to gainsay him and expose him as a fraudster. It has not proved possible to ascertain whether Quin was a veteran of the New Zealand wars.

13. The Savoy Hotel in the Strand in London, which opened in 1889, and the Cecil Hotel nearby, which opened in 1898 (and was demolished in 1930), were both bywords for luxury when H-B was writing.

14. H-B was present at none of the battles in the Transkei for the simple reason that they were all fought before he reached the Cape.

15. At Gwadana on 26 September 1877, in the first encounter of the war, Inspector Chalmers and a mixed force, some sixty strong, of FAMP (Frontier Armed and Mounted Police [henceforth FAMP], the Colony's only regular military unit, which was stationed along the frontier) were routed by a Gcaleka war party.

Cape Volunteers;[16] and in the third a couple of companies of the 24th, a few of the Naval Brigade and a party of Carrington's Horse, drove their whole army, together with that of the Galekas, which tribe under their chief Sandilli had broken out,[17] helter-skelter off the field, a defeat which disheartened both tribes to such an extent that they retired into their most inaccessible fastnesses and refused to come out and fight again in the open.[18] True there were a few other skirmishes, and the troops were given the chance of showing their inaptitude at bush fighting, especially at the Peiri Bush,[19] some twenty miles from King William's Town, where

16. Ibeka, a trading store on the west bank of the Qora river, was fortified with a low sod wall and ditch and was held by Colonel Charles Griffith with 180 FAMP and some 2,000 Mfengu levies. On 29 September 1877, 7,000–8,000 amaGcaleka under their renowned war-leader Khiva attacked the post but were driven off. They renewed the attack the following day but were routed in a vigorous counter-attack. Victorious, Griffith then advanced in three punitive columns through Gcalekaland.

17. As a child, Sandile (1820–78) succeeded his father Ngqika (1778–1829) as chief of the Ngqika amaXhosa with his half-brother, the famous warrior Maqoma (1798–1873), as regent until 1840. It was Sandile's unfortunate destiny to rule his people during their defeats in the Seventh (1846–7), Eighth (1850–3) and Ninth (1877–8) Cape Frontier Wars. When the amaGcaleka refused to give up the struggle in the last of these wars, even after their defeat at Ibeka, Sandile reluctantly entered the fray in their support in late December 1877.

18. Captain Russell Upcher (1844–1937) of the 1/24th was in command at Centane (spelled at the time as Kentani or Quintani), a forward supply and operational base deep in Gcaleka territory twelve miles south-east of Ibeka. To defend his camp, he laagered his wagons and built a strong earthwork surrounded by trenches and rifle pits. The garrison consisted of two companies of the 1/24th, 24 Bluejackets of the Naval Brigade from HMS *Active*, 90 FAMP, and 70 Frontier Light Horse (about 600 white troops in all), supported by artillery and 560 Mfengu levies. On 7 February 1878 about 5,000 amaXhosa, consisting of the Gcaleka contingent led by Khiva and Sarhili's son, Sigcawu, and the Ngqika contingent led by Sandile, attacked Centane. The Xhosa assault was uncoordinated. The amaGcaleka attacked first and were repulsed and scattered; and the amaNgqika were checked in their turn and cut down in a remorseless pursuit. Centane was the last set-piece engagement of the war. The spirit of the amaGcaleka was utterly broken and they never again appeared in the field as an army. The amaNgqika were left to carry on the fight alone from their fastnesses in the Amathole Mountains.

H-B fails to mention two significant skirmishes that also took place. At Holland's Shop on 2 December 1877 the amaGcaleka fell upon an FAMP patrol; and on 26 December 1877 the amaNgqika attacked the Draaibsoch Hotel, a foray which signalled their entry into the war. He also ignores what must be considered a fourth battle. On 13 January 1878 about a thousand amaGcaleka and amaNgqika attacked Colonel Richard Glyn at Nyumaga, nineteen miles to the south-west of his headquarters at Ibeka. Glyn had under his command a company of the 1/24th and one of the 88th (Connaught Rangers) Regiment, two troops of the FAMP, fifty Bluejackets and some Royal Marines of the Naval Brigade from HMS *Active*, and a large Mfengu levy. In a brisk firefight they repulsed the Xhosa attack.

19. The Pirie Bush was a rugged region of the Amathole Mountains some twenty miles long, and a similar distance north-west of King Wiliam's Town. Its deep clefts and ravines were covered in impenetrable bush and dense forest; the Pirie Bush was the traditional fighting-ground of the amaNgqika.

some marvellous combined movements, as useless as they were elaborate, consumed time up to the middle of 1878,[20] when the death of Sandilli, killed by a chance shot, put an end to the Galeka resistance.[21] The Gaikas, had earlier in the year caved in,[22] and for some months all the work of the forces was devoted to the attempt of catching old Kreli, in which they were unsuccessful, as the poor old fellow was so popular, that neither white settler, official, nor native, would give him away.[23] The first field service I was called upon to perform, opened my eyes as to the impedimenta, thought necessary in South Africa, for a patrol or small war party to encumber themselves with. It happened in this way. At the moment I was in King William's Town, when one day Lieut. Colonel Pulleine,[24] at the time town commandant, sent for me and on my reporting said, "Oh, Browne, I want you to start off this morning with whatever spare men can

20. Lieutenant-General Thesiger who had superseded General Cunynghame on 2 March 1878, struggled to bring the campaign in the Amathole to a swift conclusion. He became bogged down in what amounted to counter-insurgency operations. He eventually adopted a ruthless, scorched-earth policy in which no prisoners were taken and which targeted civilians who were supplying their fighting-men. Remorselessly ground down, by the beginning of July 1878 the amaNgqika had given up the struggle.

21. On 31 May 1878 Sandile was mortally wounded in a skirmish near isiDenge Hill in the Pirie Bush and died on 5 June. A British patrol found his body on 7 June and gave it burial two days later.

22. Concurrently with his operations in the Amathole Mountains against the amaNgqika, in April 1878 Thesiger opened a new campaign in the Transkei to finish off any residual Gcaleka resistance. But conventional sweeps failed to trap those amaGcaleka still fighting, and Thesiger soon abandoned large-scale operations in the Transkei and instead deployed small mounted detachments helped by infantry to strike the amaGcaleka from fortified posts. With the withdrawal in early August of all British forces from the Transkei, the war was over.

23. Sarhili was still at large when hostilities ended, but with a reward of £1,000 (purchasing power today of at least £154,000) and 500 cattle on his head. He remained in hiding in an inaccessible refuge deep in Bomvana territory north-east across the Mbashe River. He refused to emerge even when offered a free pardon in 1881, and died in exile in Bomvanaland.

24. Lieutenant-Colonel Henry Burmester Pulleine (1838–79), 1/24th Regiment, was educated at the Royal Military College, Sandhurst. In 1855 he was gazetted to an ensigncy, without purchase, in the 30th (Cambridgeshire) Regiment, and in 1858 was appointed a lieutenant into the 2/24th Regiment. When serving in Mauritius he became a captain by purchase in 1860 and established a reputation as an able administrator in the commissariat department of the garrison. In 1871 he transferred into the 1/24th and served with it for three years in Gibraltar before accompanying it to the Cape in January 1875. In 1877 he was promoted brevet lieutenant-colonel. A short man lacking in dash and bearing, he was a genial and popular officer. He served with the 1/24th throughout the Ninth Cape Frontier War. In September 1878, with hostilities against the amaZulu impending, he embarked for Natal where he was first appointed to command Durban and then made commandant of Pietermaritzburg. With the invasion of Zululand imminent, on 17 January 1879 he rejoined his regiment, which formed part of No. 3 Column.

be scraped together and go by train to the railhead at the Kei Road Station, from whence you will have to get on, as best you can, to a railway bridge that is built across the Buffalo River, and some miles further along the semi-constructed line,[25] as the O.C. of the volunteers guarding the bridge earnestly demands help, stating he expects to be attacked by overwhelming numbers. I can't understand this, as I have never apprehended any danger in that locality, but must of course send the required assistance, as the O.C. at Kei Road has not a man to spare.[26] Of course you are fully aware, that I have no duty men to spare you, so I have given orders to collect every man in town fit to carry a rifle. You will have a queer lot, officers' servants not at the front, together with both tommies and volunteers dismissed from hospital, as fit for service, in fact they will be a scratch pack, but they are the only men I can send and I don't believe there is the least danger of your having to fight. You will draw rations at the Kei Road and assume command of the post on your arrival, and now as your train will start at noon you had better get ready." I was off to my quarters like a shot, where I extracted a wild howl of delight from Quin by the old days' magic words "swags[27] and haversacks, rail at noon, on foot." There was no need to say another word nor give any more directions, so I turned my pony and cantered away, being quite certain that, bar an earthquake or sudden death, the worthy man would be at the station with our two swags ready packed, together with four days' rations ready to be humped, at 11.45 to a minute. I was a bit rushed with work that morning and as it was a long march from the barracks to the station, my, somewhat motley, crowd had to fall in at 10 o'clock, so I had no time to ask many questions of the camp adjutant when I took them over. Now as I said before, this was the very first war party I had ever taken command of in South Africa, and I was much surprised to find them paraded without swags or even greatcoats, carrying nothing except their rifles, ammunition pouches and

25. At the outbreak of the Ninth Cape Frontier War, the railway line being constructed between East London and Queenstown had only got as far as its terminus at Kei Road, a short way from King William's Town. Kei Road was one of a line of frontier posts manned by the FAMP.

26. H-B's Kei Road assignment is something of a mystery. In Chapter IV which follows, he describes in his inimitable fashion how he was recruited into Pulleine's Rangers in February 1878, the same month he really did land at the Cape, and not the fictional date of his arrival some five to six months earlier. As recounted, this improvised mission – if it ever took place – would seem therefore to have preceded his joining Pulleine's Rangers. Most likely, H-B is spinning one of his yarns, incorporating what he had learned of the nature of such operations, and typically placing himself to the forefront in the role of commander. The object of the tale is to poke fun at the excessive commissariat arrangements expected by British troops in the field and the bureaucracy it entailed, and also at their lack of military initiative and derring-do.

27. 'Swags' in Australian usage are the bundles carried by tramps, miners or bush-travellers.

water bottles. True the Colonel had already informed me that we were to draw our rations at Kei Road, but how about blankets—were the men to draw them there also? I put the question to the camp adjutant who replied, "Oh, no, the blankets, packs, etc., have been sent on to the station in a wagon," and I marvelled. On reaching the station I found Quin with his own and my swags done up in the old New Zealand fashion. I at once entrained the men and after a short, though roundabout journey, arrived at Kei Road, the temporary terminus on the main line from East London to Queenstown, then under construction, though the work had been stopped owing to the war. Kei Road was also an important place, as it was the point from which the rations and stores, required for the use of the troops in the Transkei, were despatched by bullock wagon to the front. Our train was met by the O.C. of the place and a commissariat officer, the latter of whom, after the usual salutations, requested me to step into his office and sign receipts for rations, stores, etc. This I did, and was nearly struck dumb, when I cast my eyes over the long list of comestibles that it was evidently considered necessary, for a detachment of less than one hundred men, proceeding on an urgent though short expedition, to burden themselves. I had in my innocence and ignorance of South African methods of procedure, imagined that, as in the New Zealand wars, each man would have been served out with about four pounds of cooked meat or perhaps bacon, and four pounds of biscuits, which with a blanket and his private little odds and ends he would have to hump on his own back; in fact Quin had packed our swags with that idea but when I came to study that list, what did I see? I rubbed my eyes but there it was, written in a clerkly hand, so many pounds of fresh meat, sufficient for two days' consumption, so many pounds of bully beef enough for six days' consumption, with even quantities of flour, biscuit, baking powder, compressed vegetables, tea, coffee, sugar, split peas, lime juice, rum, pepper, salt, cocoa, and great Scott! could I credit my eyes?—jam! Nor was this all for as I was gasping for breath, up bustled a smart commissariat sergeant, with what he called a supplementary list of luxuries, which had been purchased for the benefit of the troops by kind-hearted, patriotic Colonial ladies, and of which a portion was to be issued to my party. Oh, ye gods of war! what was the noble game coming to? I glanced at the proffered document, and there plainly writ, was preserved milk, arrowroot, corn-flour and the Lord only knows what else. I was completely flabbergasted, and under the impression I had gone dotty or at least had got a touch of the sun, I turned to the commissariat officer and said as coolly as I could, "I think there must be some mistake here. I'm going on Active Service and, maybe, will have to fight in a few hours' time, so how in the name of all that's righteous can you expect my party to hump this grocery shop on their backs?" "Hump it on your backs!" quoth he. "Why, two wagons have been requisitioned for you, and as they are already packed, come over to the mess and have a drink and a mouthful of tiffin while they inspan the oxen."[28] The suggestion was a good one, absorbing tiffin,[29] would give me time to recover my equilibrium and I badly wanted a drink to soothe my ruffled nerves, so, was in the act of accompanying him, when up doubled a sergeant of the Ordnance Department, who requested me to sign another receipt, for tents, camp kettles, baking pots, tools and sufficient miscellaneous articles, enough to stock a hardware shop. "Sir," said he, saluting, "everything has been packed on the wagons, would you like to inspect them?" "No, thanks," I replied, "for if I do, I may find warming-pans and infant feeding-bottles, and by the great gun of Athlone,[30] I draw the line at them." I went to the mess and tried to eat tiffin but my meal was spoilt, as my brain buzzed with the list of stores I had signed for and I asked myself could this be war, or was it a big picnic I had shipped for? I could not make it out, and visions, rose before my mind's eye, of the dripping New Zealand bush, the snow-covered fern ranges and the icy-cold river beds, as they did also, of outfits of, gaunt, famished men, half clad in ragged shawls and jumpers, loaded like pack mules, who, with only a few mouthfuls of putrid salt pork and mouldy biscuits, twixt them and starvation, toiled on uncomplainingly to serve their Queen and flag. No matter, I mentally gasped, as I gazed out over the bright, sunlit, open veldt and swigged off a glass of ale, new countries new ways of doing things, and maybe, we will be able to serve our dear and gracious Queen and the glorious old Rag,[31] as well with our waist-belts tightened, with split peas, arrowroot and jam as we did in the old days, when the said belts hung loose, on a regimen of corrupt pig's flesh and decomposed biscuits. On the other hand, how we were going to catch a mobile enemy, lugging along, as we were about to do, food and ordnance truck, sufficient to stock Whiteley's Stores,[32] was beyond my comprehension, so I relegated the matter to Old Nick; maybe the niggers would come to our whistle and allow themselves to be killed in a decent manner, anyhow there's the fall in, so that I shall shortly ascertain how the oracle is worked in South Africa.

Of course, during tiffin, I had tried to gather all the information I could, about the road we were to travel and the nature of the fighting I might expect, either *en route* or on our arrival at our destination; and

28. To 'inspan' was to yoke the oxen to the wagons.

29. 'Tiffin' is an Anglo-Indian term, then commonly used in the army, for a light meal or lunch.

30. This is a Protestant Irish oath. In 1691, for ten days the forces of William III bombarded the strategic town of Athlone in central Ireland, a stronghold of the Jacobites, before storming it with great slaughter.

31. The 'old Rag' is the Union Flag.

32. Whiteley's was one of London's first department stores.

had been assured that the road was a very good one, running through bare open country, without any cover or bush, the whole way, that could give an enemy the remotest chance of forming an ambuscade; moreover that my spans of oxen were very good ones, in the fittest condition and that I should reach the bridge long before the sun set. So far so good, but when I spoke about the chances of a scrap, a badly-concealed grin ran all round the company and the O.C. said, "Ah, well, you must tell us all about the fighting when you come back, for my own part I don't believe you will see a hostile nigger." This was not cheerful news, nor could I understand it, as why on earth should a post commandant squeal so loudly for help, unless the said post was in the greatest danger; anyhow my orders were to go to his relief, so that when the bugle sounded the fall in, I thanked my entertainers for their hospitality and proceeded to my wagons.

On reaching them, I found the oxen inspanned and the men in their shirt sleeves ready to move off, but the worthy Quin was half daft with excitement at the novel outfit, for on seeing me he rushed up and babbling in his talk exclaimed, "Oh, be the holy piper that played before Moses, look at this, sor, sure they are sinding us to foight nagurs wid long carts, each cart wid a tint on its tail, propelled by bulls, sor, wid horns reaching from Hell to Galway and not a tail tween tin of thim, sor, and yer honour, sor, no man humps onything but his own four bones yer honour, and av he gits tired av thim, sure he puts thim in the tint of the cart he does, and sor, there's oat male an pay male, and the Blessed Saint Biddy only knows whot beside, an' be this an' be that, sor, av the foighting is only aqual to the ating Africy will be a hard place to bate it will." Cutting my faithful henchman's panegyrics short, I formed our small column of march and moved off.

The road I found to be a very good one, the wagons were light, the oxen in good fettle and as the men marched in their shirt sleeves, only carrying their rifles and belts, we slung along at a good pace, reaching our destination a couple of hours before sunset. As we approached the place, I was destined to receive another surprise; I could see the iron bridge spanning the river and noticed it had been sand-bagged at both ends, which had turned it into an impregnable fort, at least against savages unprovided with artillery, especially as no high ground commanded it in any way. The defenders were evidently on the alert, as the bridge simply bristled with bayonets, and the tents of the garrison had all been lowered by the simple plan of pulling the foot of the pole out through the doorway. Come, said I to myself, this looks as if there were fighting going on and I swept the veldt on both sides of the river with my glasses, but although the country was as open as a calm sea and for miles absolutely devoid of cover, still I could not see a vestige of any enemy so marched on till we reached the camp at the end of the bridge. After waiting a few minutes for a passage to be made through the sand bags, a big fine-looking, bearded man came out, evidently in a state of extreme nervousness, who after ejaculating, "Thank God you have arrived in time," introduced himself to me as the O.C. of the post. After he had read the written orders, I had received from Colonel Pulleine, I asked, "What is the matter? where are the niggers and when do you expect to be attacked?" "Oh," he replied, "I expect to be attacked every moment, that bush," and he pointed at one at least twenty miles away, "is chock full of them, but I have taken every precaution and have kept the men standing at their alarm posts." "Since when?" I queried. "Oh, since yesterday morning," he replied. "Then dismiss them at once to their ordinary camp duties, one sentry on the top of those sand bags is quite sufficient," and in a few minutes the camps were pitched and the men were comfortably making a lusty supper, off the sumptuous rations we had been provided with. Next day I started back to King William's Town, taking with me the officer who had caused the scare, where he was examined by a medical board, when it turned out the poor fellow had had a bad sunstroke in India. He was invalided to Cape Town where he died shortly afterwards, fully convinced to the last he was surrounded by hordes of niggers ravening for his blood.

Chapter IV

Pulleine's Lambs

They don't know much of soldiering, and nothing more of drill,
Their discipline is awful, and their language is worse still;
Sure, it's enough to dazzle you, to hear the blanks and d——ns,
That punctuate the sentiments, of Pulleine's ruddy Lambs.

QUIN.

ONE of my earliest commands, and certainly one of my most amusing and interesting was thrust upon me at very short notice. In February 1878 I was the guest of Colonel Pulleine of the first 24th Regiment (now the South Wales Borderers).[1] After dinner, over cigars he said to me, "Maori, I have raised a regiment of Rangers called after me.[2] I've no possible chance of looking after them myself and the men, though of magnificent stamp, require a taut hand, and to be knocked into shape. I want you to ride to their camp across the river to-morrow, and take command."[3] I hesitated and pointed out that I was a cavalryman and did not care to have anything to do with foot sloggers; but he insisted, saying I had already been put in orders for the post. I was by no means keen on the job, for the men had already made a name for themselves and Pulleine's Lambs, as they were called, were more feared by the citizens than the Kafirs.[4] But orders are orders and I obeyed. This is how Pulleine's Rangers had been raised.

A railroad was being constructed from Kei Road to Queenstown but the work had to cease when war broke out and it became a problem what

1. On 1 July 1881 the Childers Army Reforms divided the United Kingdom into regimental districts, each allocated a two-battalion regiment, usually bearing a 'county' title. The old regimental numbers were abolished.

2. It would seem that from the moment he landed in the Cape, H-B claimed he was a veteran of the New Zealand Wars. With none apparently to gainsay him, he was believed – and he would have had a ready fund of vivid yarns to back up his fraudulent assertion. It seems that the nickname 'Maori' was immediately accorded him, and it stuck ever after.

3. While not placed in command of Pulleine's Rangers (the commandant was Captain Hugh Edward McTaggart), H-B was appointed lieutenant on 26 February 1878. Typically, H-B has promoted himself.

4. The word 'Kafir' or 'Kaffir' has long been regarded as an opprobrious racial slur referring to indigenous, dark-skinned Africans. In the nineteenth century the British and other white

to do with the men employed thereon, huge English navvies of the old type. Other works had also ceased, so Pulleine's Rangers became a refuge for the rowdy, dissolute and the desolate. I had been told that a man brought before the magistrates, for a rowdy drunk, or other like offence, was often asked, "Will you go to gaol or join Pulleine's Rangers?" But it is only fair to say, that in the field, away from town and the canteens they were a very fine set of fellows.[5] I was not altogether happy when, at daybreak next morning, I rode across the bridge to the camp. Colonel Pulleine had told me that, as is usual in hot countries, the parade would take place before sunrise. Well, here was the camp, but where were the men? and above all where was the sentry?[6] Presently I saw a rifle leaning against a bush; I rode up and saw a man sitting under the bush. He had no boots or socks on, and wore only a tattered shirt and a pair of trousers, of which the less said the better. The most noticeable thing about him was a huge black eye, and I don't think you could have put your finger upon a sound spot on his face. He had no hat but in his hands he held a tin pannikin, which he turned round and round and gazed into its depths with his undarkened orb. I opened a conversation with, "Who on earth are you?" He replied, with much bad language, "I'm the —— sentry, and if I'm not —— soon relieved I'm darned if I don't go home. Who the Hades

---

settlers commonly employed the term, and in the Cape it came to be associated primarily with the amaXhosa. For that reason, the British often referred to the Cape Frontier Wars as the Kaffir Wars.

5. During the first phase of the Ninth Cape Frontier War, a counter-offensive was planned in December 1877 against the amaGcaleka, and Colonel Glyn was gazetted Commander of the Army of the Transkei. Reinforcements were required, but there was scant response among the colonists for volunteers to augment the regulars of the garrison and Naval Brigade. So, Sir Bartle Frere ordered Pulleine, who was popular with the settlers, to raise two volunteer corps. One, the Frontier Light Horse (henceforth FLH), initially under the command of Lieutenant Frederick Carrington (1844–1913) of the 1/24th, was mounted. It proved an efficient unit, invaluable for scouting and raiding, and saw service not only in the Ninth Cape Frontier War, but also in the Anglo-Zulu War and the Second Anglo-Pedi War, being finally disbanded in December 1879.

The other corps, Pulleine's Rangers, was more ephemeral. It was an infantry unit of six companies, 400 strong, and the men were under British military rather than colonial command, serving under Her Majesty's Regulations. The Rangers were noted for their rough and tough qualities and earned the sardonic nickname of Pulleine's Pups, or more usually, Pulleine's Lambs. They were drawn mainly from discharged road workers and British navvies working on the construction of the railway from King William's Town, but also included volunteers (some of them described as 'Coloureds') from among unemployed East London louts, drunkards from the diamond diggings and down-and-outs from as far west as Cape Town. The indignant *Grahamstown Journal* of 14 January 1878 characterised them as 'the very scum and off-scourings of the earth. The scenes of drunkenness and lawlessness in our streets are a disgrace to a civilized community.' The newspaper concluded that Pulleine's Lambs were fit for nothing other than to 'furnish food for powder'.

6. Here follows a typical H-B yarn.

are you anyhow?" I intimated as gently as seemed necessary that I was his new commanding officer but this information did not seem to strike him as a matter of any importance, for slowly finishing the contents of his pannikin, he said, "Just you ride up to the —— camp and tell that —— corporal o' the guard that I want to come home." Argument with this chap seemed useless, so I made my way sorrowfully up to the camp. I could not see a soul about. I looked into the guard tent, and found the guard, more or less battered, fast asleep. I struck the tent sharply with my sjambok but could get no answer, so I rode over to the officers' lines. I dismounted at the first tent. It was fastened up, so I thrashed it and shouted. A sleepy voice inquired, "Who the such-and-such a place was there?" I replied, "I'm the new commandant. Come out at once and speak to me." There were muttered ejaculations, with much scuffling and presently two dishevelled objects, who might have been anything, appeared. "Your name and rank, sir?" I said to the elder of the scarecrows. "Lieutenant So-and-So," he replied. Then to my inquiry, "Why are not the men on parade, sir?" he replied, "I do not think they care to turn out this morning." "Go and find the regimental sergeant-major, if you have such a person in this camp," I said, and he shuffled off. The other fellow I sent to wake the rest of the officers, and by this time I had determined, in my mind, to make more than one man's life miserable and to generally twist and cut the tails, of at least, that mob of Lambs. Presently there appeared a smart-looking but still rather drunk fellow, trying, as well as he could, to button his tunic. He was the sergeant-major and had served in the regulars. "I'll try, sir, but I don't think they'll come," he said when I had ordered him to turn the men out. "Have you any old soldiers, mounted police, or any men who have ever been under discipline before? If so march them here." He saluted and presently marched up twenty or thirty men to me. I told them I meant to have a change in the camp at once and ordered them to assist the sergeant-major in turning out the other men. The force of discipline remained strong and there were some brisk and lively minutes while they jumped into the tents and threw out the occupants head first, and so finally Pulleine's Rangers fell in. They mustered about two hundred in all and then I inspected them. Ye gods! what a crowd of drunken scoundrels they were. To the officers I said, "Go at once to your posts and proceed with the drill." Only one officer knew anything about drill and what he knew was immaterial, but at last I set the men lounging about, marching you could not call it, then sadly rode back to tell Colonel Pulleine that, until about seventy men had been discharged and some competent officers secured we could never form a corps. This was done, and so we raised Pulleine's Lambs, a terror to the country and a nuisance to myself.

A month to six weeks' hard work and the depot of Pulleine's Rangers, at King, presented a very different appearance to the fold of Lambs that

THE SENTINEL LAMB.

I had taken over in February; and one day General Thesiger (afterwards Lord Chelmsford) ordered me to take command at a farm, belonging to a big colonial pot who was difficult to get on with and who required much tact to handle. When I took over command, the garrison consisted of two companies of Pulleine's Rangers, two detachments of regular infantry and a body of Carrington's Horse.[7] Every morning the owner of the farm, who would not have been able to have lived there had it not been garrisoned, came to the orderly tent with complaints of the most frivolous nature, one of them I remember being, that the men sat down under the shade of his trees.[8] He owned a valuable old cock ostrich, and one day he came whining to me with the complaint that the bird had been stolen by my men. I said, "What rot! what could they do with it? It's only strayed away." But he argued on till in despair I ordered the bugler to blow the alarm, which meant that every man would go to his alarm post and leave the camp empty.

"Now," I said, "we will go round and search." We looked into every tent, in the water carts, in empty ammunition boxes, and to my annoyance, he even accepted my invitation to search my own tent. Then I took up my parable and told him some home truths. That night there was an awful row in the lines of the Rangers. Fighting went on at a high rate, the air quivered with language and more blood was spilt, in five minutes, than in the whole of a colonial action. I turned out the rest of the camp, got the rioters tied up to wagon wheels or pegged out and the next morning had the worst cases brought before me.

The first was a huge navvy known as Kentish Jim. "You are charged with creating a disturbance in camp and resisting the picket. What have you got to say?" He thumped a huge fist down on the table before me and said, "This is what I've got to say." The colour-sergeant on duty said, "Stand to attention." Again the huge fist shot out and a gigantic arm swept the astonished and horrified regular aside, with the words, "Get thee away, thee blooming militiaman, I'm a-talking to the commandant." Then he turned to me with "You're the gent as axed me a question and this is all I've got to say. I'll be durned if I'll have any of that ruddy duck cooked in ma pot." I gave the fellow three extra guards, though it was impossible to deal with men so lacking in any sense of discipline, and the next day he was brought before me again. While on sentry over two prisoners (regulars) he had handed his rifle to one of them and sent the other to the canteen. When I asked him what he had to say for himself, he launched out, "Look 'ere, mister, I calls this blooming rot. Yesterday morning, as ever was, sergeant comes to me and says, 'Jim, you're for extra guard this

---

7. The FLH.

8. There follows another of H-B's engaging yarns. How much of what he describes actually occurred is impossible to determine.

morning,' an' I says, 'Right, Sergeant.' So I togs up smart and gives me old gun a rub up and falls in. Then 'e puts me in charge of two prisoners, who were to dig a 'ole so wide and so deep by twelve o'clock. So I says, 'Right, Mr Luftenant,' an' marches off. Then I says to the prisoners, 'Now you Tommies, dig that 'ole,' and they only says, 'You walk about sentry.' And, sir, it 'ud give yer stomachache to sees them Tommies start to dig. So I says to them, 'Tommies, the gel'tmn says as 'ow the 'ole must be dug come twelve o'clock, thee knows more about gun than oi does, one of yer take the gun an' I'll shift the muck.' So one of the Tommies took the gun an' I soon dug that 'ole bigger than I was tole to. Then I says to t'other Tommy, ''Ere, lad, thee's doing nowt, take this crown to the canteen and get beer and smokes.' And 'e did so, and we was a-sittin' happy by the 'ole having our beer an' smokes, when up comes officer, an' told me I was a prisoner. Now I axes you, sir, wot the 'ell's the use of that?"

I forget how I punished the fellow, but not much could be done with a man whose ideas of soldiering were so lax.

Later on in the year I was ordered to proceed with my men to the Transkei and take command of a station, of considerable importance, called Quintani,[9] where among other details that I had under me was a detachment of mounted infantry belonging to that glorious old regiment, the Connaught Rangers.[10]

9. On 1 May 1878 H-B was promoted captain and commander of a company of Pulleine's Rangers stationed at Centane (Quintani) alongside a company of the 1/24th. On 14 June four companies of the 1/24th were ordered to vacate their fortified posts in the Transkei and return to King Willliam's Town, while the remainder of the regiment was concentrated at Ibeka under Pulleine in his first field command. H-B was left in command at Centane with his company of Pulleine's Rangers and a detachment of mounted infantry.

Centane, named after a neighbouring hill, was established as a camp by Colonel Glyn in December 1877 on a spur of land with a stream on three sides. It was positioned on the high ground to dominate approaches to the drifts across the lower Kei River from the east. Captain Russell Upcher of the 1/24th, who took command in February 1878, improved the defences, but they were not entirely complete when the amaXhosa unsuccessfully attacked the post on 7 February. Upcher was relieved in April by Captain Thomas Rainsford of the 1/24th who continued to improve the defences, so that when H-B took command of Centane it was described as a 'tight little fort'. It was by then a rectangular earthwork with a parapet two yards high with flanking bastions, surrounded by a ditch.

10. The 88th Regiment had arrived in Cape Town in July 1877 as part of the colony's garrison alongside the 1/24th Regiment.

Chapter V

Father Walsh

I THINK it was in June and July 1878 I took over the command of Quintani and there, as I said before, I found a detachment of mounted infantry belonging to the Connaught Rangers; they were a warm lot; fine fighters, but having no sense of *meum* and *tuum*. Nothing was too hot or heavy for them to steal.[1] If it were too hot, they would sit down while it cooled; if it were too heavy, they would fetch a bullock cart to carry it off. How they stole a mission bell, for instance, is a Transkei tradition but that is another yarn.[2] One morning soon after I took command they besieged my orderly tent, and intimated they all wanted to see me. I said, I could only see one at a time and presently the colour-sergeant ushered in a big Irishman with a mouth like a torn haversack. "Plaze, sor, we hear you do be an Oirishman." I owned up cheerfully and asked him what he wanted. "Sor," he said, "we do be onaisy about our sowls." "Sowls!" I exclaimed. "You can rest perfectly contented that every man in the detachment is irretrievably lost. You haven't got a sowl among the lot of you possible to be saved." He overlooked the remark, and said, "Sor, we do want to confess." "Better not confess to me," I said, "or I'll have to send every one of you down, to your headquarters, for a courts-martial." "But, sor," he begins again, "we do sadly want a praste." "A priest!" I exclaimed; "why, a whole college of cardinals could do you no good but I'll send down country and ask for a priest to be sent up." He thanked me, and the deputation went back to its lines with sighs of relief. The following Saturday, Father Walsh turned up and from the first I took a great liking to him. He was certainly one of the finest men I ever knew in South Africa, or anywhere else, as far as that goes. Father Walsh was a big, raw-boned, Irish priest, with a fund of droll stories, the courage of a lion, the tenderness of a woman, and a hearty laugh that was worth its weight in rifles, when the corps, he happened to be with, was fighting in a tight corner. A few years afterwards, in the first Boer War, he happened to be besieged in a lonely fort and in spite of the wishes of the young officer, in command, he refused point blank to consent to a surrender; and he so fired

1. Another of H-B's yarns follows.
2. See pp. 56, 60–4 below.

the little garrison with his own unquenchable courage that they held out till the war was over and made one of the few bright spots, in a long story of British disasters.[3]

All this is a matter of history, as South Africans know, and it is for me to tell of the man as I met him. Well, Father Walsh reached my camp on a Saturday afternoon and we had a pleasant evening. I had had a church rigged up with tarpaulins and next morning he set to work to try and ease the consciences of his parishioners. Knowing that he could not, as a Catholic priest, break his fast before saying Mass, I asked him "when he would have breakfast?" The holy Father hove a sigh, that nearly blew me out of the tent and said, "I shall be late, very late, as I shall have to hear the men's confessions first." "Father," I said, "before you have got half through those blackguards' sins, it'll be dinner-time and more, I recommend you, so as to expedite matters, to take them by sections; however, I'll have breakfast ready when you're through." The day was miserably cold and wet, when about noon the Father bustled into my tent exclaiming with unction, "Ah, ah, me boy, I want a drop of comfort before breakfast." The whisky bottle was brought out and saluted and then we went together to the mess tent. No sooner had we entered, when Quin rushed in with the principal dish, a steaming, savoury, game stew, the odour of which being tempting enough to make an anchorite break his fast during a black Lent. Unhappily, as Quin entered the tent, he caught his foot in the curtain and in a twinkling the boiling hot stew was pouring all down the wrong side of the holy man's neck.

Up jumped his reverence foaming. "Och, yer clumsy blaggard," howled he, "if I were Major Browne now,[4] I'd call ye a —— scoundrel, but as I'm Father Walsh, I only tell ye, ye potato-faced Irishman, don't ye do it agin. And seeing by the cut ov yer ugly mug you're Irish and knowing you didn't

3. The Revd Father Walsh served as a Roman Catholic military chaplain in the Ninth Cape Frontier War and subsequently with No. 1 Column during the Anglo-Zulu War when Fort Eshowe was blockaded by the amaZulu between 24 January and 3 April 1879. He and the Anglican Revd Robert Roberston alternated services at the garrison's Sunday church parade when his favourite hymn was 'Hold the Fort'. He once again acted as military chaplain in the Second Anglo-Pedi War in late 1879, and then settled in Lydenburg in the Transvaal Territory (formerly the ZAR, annexed by Britain in 1877).

During the Transvaal Rebellion (First Anglo-Boer War), undeterred by his experiences in Fort Eshowe, Father Walsh threw in his lot with the British garrison of the town when the improvised Fort Mary (which he blessed) was invested by the Boers between 27 December 1880 and 3 May 1881. By all accounts he was the mainstay of the defence and regularly helped stiffen the resolve of the commander, the young Second Lieutenant Walter Long, 94th Regiment. In 1884–5 he accompanied Sir Charles Warren's Bechuanaland expedition as chaplain when H-B ran across him once more. Father Walsh died shortly afterwards in Kimberely (see pp. 239–41 below).

4. Through the medium of Quin's peroration, H-B has promoted himself from captain to major.

come to yer divotions this marnin, I'll be after yer wid a kippeen as soon as I've broken this black fast, bad luck to ye."

Then we soothed and scraped the stew off the holy man and he settled down to his breakfast, when presently, being pacified and comforted he forgave the worthy Quin and the camp, purified by his past labours, rested in peace.

Towards the end of 1878 the regular troops moved back to the base and Colonel Pulleine commanding at Ibeka asked me to march down to King William's Town, a large party of his Lambs whose time had expired.[5] Some of the Lambs, who had been sent down previously, had given a lot of trouble, getting drunk, raising Cain, and roaming about the country to the consternation of the settlers, who had by this time begun to rebuild and re-occupy their ruined homesteads and who held Pulleine's Lambs in greater fear than they did the Kafirs. On the morning we started down, Pulleine by way of a joke, said he would bet me a dinner I didn't get my party down intact; which wager I laughingly accepted.[6] As my party marched on to our second night's halt, at the Kei River drift, I saw, to my annoyance, that the hotel and canteen had been re-opened, so I rode on to warn the proprietor, saying to him, "You may sell the men all the beer you like but no hard tack" (as we called spirits in that part). "If you disobey," I continued, "I will make it hot for you, and if you're fool enough, to let the men get drunk, they'll make it hotter still." He agreed. He knew Pulleine's Lambs by reputation and swore he would not sell them a drop of spirits. When the men arrived, I had the arms piled and before I dismissed them, I warned them, saying they could have all the beer they wanted but no spirits. Then hot with my long ride I went with my four officers, down to the river to bathe. We were all swimming about, enjoying ourselves, when suddenly there was a report and a bullet splashed up the water near my head. Then another whizzed past me and looking up, I saw three of my precious men, standing on the trestle bridge, that crossed the river, taking aim at me. I was exceedingly annoyed, I hope it was not wrong of me, and I swam ashore at a racing stroke, urged on by another bullet that whistled over my head. When I landed I did not stop to dry or dress, but rushed along, stark naked, to catch the fellows as they came from the bridge. On my way I caught up an ox-yoke and armed with this I met them and dealt out impromptu justice that soon squashed the mutiny, of which nothing more was said. I don't think the fellows wanted to kill me. Their idea was to give me a scare by way of protest against my temperance measure. They however got but little by it. One of them had gone down with a

5. In early August 1878 Colonel Glyn withdrew all the British forces from the Transkei. The Cape government set aside 1 August as a day of public thanksgiving throughout the Colony for victory over the amaXhosa.

6. Another of H-B's inimitable yarns follows.

broken jaw and another with a smashed shoulder, while I had difficulty to save the life of the third as my servant Quin was proceeding to batter his brains out when Kentish Jim seized him and dragging his prey from Quin lashed the bounder more dead than alive to the wheel of a wagon where I kept him all night.

Then as a female face at the hotel window was looking rather scared, I bethought myself of my clothes, and dressed.

I marched my party to the base, leaving the two injured men in the Koumgha Hospital and as by doing so I could not claim that the party was intact Colonel Pulleine won his bet and received his dinner.

Before I quite disband the Lambs I think I might say something more about some of the extraordinary men who formed the nucleus of the regiment and who as a class have quite disappeared from both England and the Colonies. Wonderful men they were. I had never met them before. I shall never meet their like again, so here goes for my last yarn about the Lambs although many of them served under me the following year in Zululand, showing that the spirit of the Lost Legion exists in the heart of the untutored navvy as well as in the heart of his better born and educated countryman.

Chapter VI

The Idiosyncrasy of the British Navvy on Field Service

IT WAS in 1878 I joined Pulleine's Rangers. The yarn of how I came to belong to the Lambs has been told and also how they were recruited, and in that yarn I stated, that the nucleus of the regiment was composed of some two hundred British navvies of the old type, that is now almost extinct.[1] They were mostly men of from thirty-five to fifty years of age, big, burly, powerful men who could work like horses when they were on the job and who could drink like the Sahara Desert when they were not.

To see those men shift muck, as they termed soil, was a treat and to see them shift beer was a marvel. They were not the kind of men whom you would make welcome to a tea-fight, or a muffin wrangle, but at any other sort of combat their company was to be desired and the stiffer and closer the engagement, the more would they have been appreciated.

They were a very fine lot of men, a class quite distinct to themselves and after the blue-jacket quite the handiest man I have ever met; of course I do not include the regular Frontiersman as he is in a manner born to bush and veldt work.

In town they were a nuisance to everyone, the military as well as the civilians hating the sight of them as it meant extra guards and pickets for the military and the civilian knew that his town would be painted a more vivid scarlet than even an upcountry colonial desires. Yet they never, to my knowledge, went out of their way to interfere with anyone and certainly never molested any inoffensive man, woman or child. But their drunken sprees were colossal, their drunken gambols elephantine, and as no law-abiding citizen can look on at and enjoy more than two fights at a time, it becomes somewhat monotonous when there are perhaps a dozen going on in each street, simultaneously, so Pulleine's Lambs were voted a nuisance and cordially detested.

The language of the navvy was in a marked degree free. True, he was somewhat handicapped as regards the number of adjectives he possessed,

---

1. See p. 41, n. 5, above.

but he tried to make up by repetition what he lacked in quantity. He was also in a sense colour blind, or rather I should say he only saw things in one colour, as he invariably described all things animate and inanimate a brilliant crimson. He did not use these two words but implied that colour by a shorter and perhaps more expressive term.

In town these men were a nuisance, as I have stated, but get them up country, away from the beer and vile Cape brandy, and they became quite different.

Of course, in one sense of the word, you could never make soldiers of them, yet once in the veldt with a little tact you could do anything with them. What Tommy called hard work, road-making, entrenching, and fort-building was to them child's play and as soon as the drink was out of them, they were most obedient and obliging. Their ideas of discipline were undoubtedly crude; no chicken ranch was safe and they were all born poachers, but then in the veldt, these slight failings did not matter, as hen-roosts are few and far between and the game laws such as they were did not hold good in war-time.

One of my greatest difficulties, up country, was how to punish them, not for crime, for where there is no drink and nothing to steal there is but little crime; but for such offences as being late, or dirty on parade, it was necessary to inflict certain small punishments, and these consisted for a time of doing the camp fatigue work, such as digging ash-pits and other holes in the ground for camp use. This sort of work is hated by Tommy but it did not do for my men and I had to change it, the reason why I will tell you.

Our camp was at Quintani, in the Transkei,[2] and we were a long way from any neighbours.

The work was all done. The camp safely entrenched and comfortable and there was little or no fatigue to be done in quarters when the men were not out on patrol.

One day, it had been necessary for me to punish two men for being dirty at inspection and they were ordered to dig an ash-pit, another man being put on sentry over them.[3] This man, I have yarned of him before, was a huge navvy called Kentish Jim. As I was strolling about round the fort I saw him in charge of the delinquents and walked past him. After he had saluted me to the best of his ability he said, "Beg pardon, sir. You are a gentleman and I can talk to you." I said, "Not now; if you want to speak to me you must do so when you are off duty." He looked unhappy but said no more. That evening, seeing him hanging round, I called him and said, "Now then, what do you want to say to me?" Quoth he, "Look 'ere, sir. This

2. *See* p. 45, n. 9, above.
3. An extended H-B yarns follows.

morning as ever was, just as I was a setting down to a game of banker, sergeant 'e comes to me an ses, 'Jim, you do sentry go over them two —— as got toko from commandant this morning.' I ses, 'Right, sergeant,' and I does it. Now what I wants to know is, who you were a-punishing of – me or them two ——? You ses to them, 'You two dirty —— I'll give you two —— fatigues coz yer can't keep yer —— selves clean, you did.'" I could have taken my oath I had never made any such remarks but I did not want to argue so I let it stand at that and only replied, "Well?" He continued: "Then the sergeant he tells me to take the two —— swine and make them dig that 'ole, and stand by while they did it, or walk about with a —— gun on shoulder to see they didn't run away. W'ere the 'ell are they going to run to? They wants their dinner come 12 o'clock they do. They don't want to run away and I wanted my —— game of banker I did and I had to play silly —— I 'ad, with a —— gun on my shoulder, and about that —— 'ole, call that punishment, do you? Why, to dig a 'ole like that wouldn't make a man sweat a pint o' ale out of him if he was lucky to 'ave one. No, by gosh, when you wants a ——'ole dug you tell me an' I'll do myself proud to dig one for ye, and you let them dirty swine play silly —— with their —— guns and Jim will get his game of banker and put a —— 'ed on the man as don't do as you tells him, there now."

I liked Jim, but had to tell him that that sort of discipline would be against the Queen's Regulations, but he was a sceptic. "Ah don't believe," said he, "the good old Queen, Gord bless her! ever regelated any such —— rot. No, it's old Gladstone's work, the old fule, with his Bulgan 'trocities and sich like, —— him."[4]

Jim was decidedly a Tory, but he had given me a hint and consequently punishment by fatigue was put on one side and pack drill or punishment guards, such as doing sentry go over the watercarts or the cook-house, were instituted instead; this they hated and in a very short time punctuality and cleanliness were amply enforced and practised.

I had no chance, unfortunately, of taking these men into a fight, worth speaking about, but I could see how keen they were for one. No march was too long and no shortage of rations ever stood in the way, but the Fates were not propitious and the niggers too broken to stand, so towards the end of the year I received orders that we were to be disbanded and that I was to take the last detachment, consisting of about 120 men, down country for that purpose. I had already taken down one big detachment about which I have yarned before. That party had been paid off in King

4. In April 1876 the Bulgarians rose up against Ottoman rule and were harshly suppressed with many atrocities against civilians. William Gladstone, a former and future Liberal prime minister, then in opposition, in his pamphlet 'The Bulgarian Horrors and the Question of the East' secured much sympathy for the southern Slavs and simultaneously attacked the Tory government for continuing to support the Ottomans against Russian ambitions in the region.

William's Town and had raised such ructions that it was determined to give another town the benefit this time, and Koumgha, a small town in the Ciskei,[5] and about half-way down to King, was selected, at which to give the Lambs a chance of blowing off some of their steam, blue some of their money, and quiet down before reaching King.

Koumgha was a small dorp[6] containing a F.A.M.P. barracks, three canteens, a few stores and a church. It was also garrisoned by some companies of the 88th Regiment and the Lambs could not do much harm there.

Well we reached the place near mid-day, piled arms and formed camp. The paymaster was there to meet us and after dinner the men received four days' leave and one month's pay.

I had had the arms, ammunition, etc., placed in store and the fun began.

Now it is not my intention to write about the gambols and the bust of the Lambs but only of a small section of them. Suffice it, they bought all the women's clothes in the stores, they dressed up in them, they danced unholy dances, they fought many fights and painted the dorp a very vivid red indeed. But there were eight men who took no part in these frivolous proceedings. They were quiet, staid men who had been mates for many years, always working together on the same railway construction, and having all things in common. They had occupied the same tent and had always, while with me, kept themselves apart from the other men, so they were known to myself and the other officers as the inseparables.

These men when they received their pay expended it on bread, cheese, bacon, beer, gin, tobacco, etc., and betook themselves with their stores and blankets down to the river bank where, in the most methodical way, they camped under some willow trees, running a rope round their camp to show that for the time being it was private property and would be defended as such by force of arms. After clearing the ground and making down their beds, they sat down to eat, drink and enjoy themselves.

Any visitor was welcome to food and drink, but after he had been entertained he must pass on. The following afternoon I was out for a ride with one of the officers of the 88th when we passed close to their camp and to my utter surprise we saw the finishing round of a tremendous fight between two of them.

Calling the eldest member of the party to me I said, "Sorry to see you chaps fighting; what is the row about?" "There ain't no row, sir, but we'll be proud if you and your friend will drink a drop of beer along with us." He then continued: "We be all mates as you know, sir, and we have got a big job on the road as soon as we get's to King."

5. Komga, forty miles north of East London, had been established in 1854 as a military camp and by 1877 had developed into a farming village.
6. *Dorp* (Afrikaans), a common South African colloquialism for a village.

My curiosity was aroused, so we dismounted and accepted their hospitality as far as having a glass of beer.

The other men after saluting, still sat, in a listless way, smoking their pipes and saying nothing. Presently one huge fellow got up and going over to another, who might have been his twin brother as far as size went, said to him (but without the least animus or ill-will in his voice), "Bill, I bees a better man than you be." The other looked up and leisurely taking his pipe from his mouth, wiping it on his sleeve and putting it carefully away drawled out, "No, you ain't, Dick." Then the two of them quietly and without any haste, stripped and set to to fight, two others without comment getting up to act as seconds. They fought four fast rounds but without the least bit of bad spirit and when at the end of the fourth round Dick was grassed by a tremendous cross-counter he was promptly helped up by the victorious Bill and after they had mutually assisted one another to wash and dress, they resumed their seats, their pipes and their beer without any elation on the part of the victor or depression on the part of the vanquished. As for the others they seemed to look on the whole incident as not worth talking about.

Just as we were mounting the same thing occurred again, one giant lounging up to another with the formula, "Alf, I bees a better man than you be." "No, you ain't, Jack," and they started another desperate fight without the slightest bad blood or more bad language than they commonly used in ordinary conversation.

My curiosity was now thoroughly roused and getting our host out of earshot of the others I asked him the cause of all this fighting. He scratched his head and said, "Well you see, sir, it's this way. We be mates. We be each man as good as the other, and we takes on contract on the line as soon as you discharges us. So we is just trying who is best man to boss the show."

"Why, will he get more money than the rest?"

"No fear, we keeps all money in the same bag, but us must have a gaffer and best man must be he." Now it seemed to me a long and painful way to try who was the best man. A spin of a coin might have decided it, but no, they had four days' leisure, and how could they put in those four days in a more genial or delightful way than in fighting with their best friends, solving the problem and enjoying themselves at the same time.

Of one thing I am certain, that men who could punch and take a punching from his pal without a murmur would be an awful fiend in a hand-to-hand fight with an enemy and I have always had a deep feeling of regret that I never had the chance of taking that gang into a real good scrap, as I am sure they would have exhibited a form that would have made that fight a record.

Chapter VII

Loot and Some Looters

THE word loot to a fighting man has a significance that renders it almost sacred. It has buoyed up many a weary and foot-sore warrior on a long and fatiguing march and has encouraged men, in many a deed of daring do, from the hour that Tubal Cain forged the first sword-blade till the present time.[1] For although, in these degenerate days, it is inveighed against by the Exeter Hall,[2] cum-kid-glove, anti-fighting, peace-at-any-price crowd, yet, it has been the incentive of nearly all the wars, great deeds of arms and conquests, that have ever taken place, since man first of all began to war against his fellow-man.

Nor are the days of loot over, in the super-civilized countries of the period. Only a few years ago the godly Germans looted China, of her ancient scientific instruments and everything else she could lay her claws on;[3] while even among the most sanctified in our own goody-goody country, does not a right honourable gentleman (!!) boast of robbing his neighbour's hen-roost? Why, therefore, should the poor, hard-fighting Tommy, be prevented from gathering a little of the fruit, that may come in his way, after he had run all the risks to win the battles for his nation, who pocketing the lion's share of the plunder, calls him a thief and marauder. The art of looting may be divided into many sorts. You can loot the enemy, you can loot the non-combatants, and the looter may be looted. What, may I ask, has become of nearly all the prize-money, earned by the army and navy for the last two hundred years, and who has looted our sailors

---

1. *Genesis* 4: 22: 'Tubal-cain, an instructor of every artificer in brass and iron'. A descendant of Cain, he is credited in the Bible as being the first blacksmith.

2. From 1831 until 1907 Exeter Hall, a large public meeting place on the north side of the Strand in London, was the venue for many great gatherings of activists for various causes in human betterment, such as anti-slavery. Its activities aroused strong emotions both for and against, and conservatives like H-B despised its spirit of humanitarianism.

3. H-B is referring to the Boxer Rebellion (1899–1901), which was an anti-foreigner and anti-Christian uprising in northern China. The German, Russian and Japanese troops of the international expeditionary force of the Eight Nations Alliance were especially noted for the atrocities they committed between September 1900 and March 1901 in suppressing the insurrection, but it was the British (and not the Germans) who were primarily responsible for the systematic looting of Beijing after its capture in August 1900.

and soldiers of their just share? I am going to spin you a yarn, the rights and wrongs of it you must, if you care to read it, decide for yourself, but it will point out how a poor, hard-working colonial commandant, through no fault of his own, nearly got into serious trouble through the anxiety of some kind-hearted Tommies who only wishing to please him started marauding. The facts are as follows.

In 1878 I was in command of an important post in the Transkei called Quintani, some twenty-five miles from the Headquarter Camp at Ibeka. About mid-way between these posts was a ruined mission station, that had, previous to the outbreak of the war, been a thriving concern. The enemy had however looted it, and burnt it down, but, as it afterwards turned out, had left the detached wooden belfry standing, and in it swung a scrumptious bell, which I believe had been the gift of some well-meaning but misguided English ladies.[4] Now among the different details of my garrison, as I have previously mentioned, was a small detachment of mounted infantry belonging to that gallant and distinguished regiment known as H.M. 88th Connaught Rangers. This glorious corps, during the Peninsular War, not only earned for themselves an undying fame, by their splendid fighting qualities, but they were also designated, by General Picton, for other qualities they must have possessed, as the Connaught Robbers, and the detachment that served with me had both these qualities largely developed.[5] Now these M.I.[6] were on the whole a very fine lot of men, for although, the Fates being against us, I had no chance of witnessing their undoubted courage in the field of battle, yet their cheery behaviour in camp, their good humour, their anxiety to oblige, and as soon as they discovered I was a countryman of their own, to render me any trifling service that lay in their power to offer, was quite enough to make me pleased and proud to have the honour of having them under my command. This good-will, or rather the ways they took of showing it, was at times very embarrassing to me and on two occasions nearly landed me in deep water.[7] *Par exemple*. First of all, in the Ciskei, where I originally

---

4. The only mission station halfway between Ibeka and Centane was the Wesleyan one at Butterworth founded in 1827. The resident missionary in 1878 was the Revd Ebenezer Joseph Warner. By 1878 the mission station had grown into a small settlement with a few European-style houses, a scattering of shops and a great number of Mfengu huts around the fringes of the village. The amaXhosa did not burn down the mission in the Ninth Cape Frontier War. However, they had destroyed it in the Sixth Cape Frontier War of 1834–5. It is evidently from recounted memories of this event that H-B weaves his extended yarn of the mission bell on pp. 60–4 below.

5. Lieutenant-General Sir Thomas Picton (1758–1815), a hero of the Peninsular War who was killed at Waterloo, was notoriously foul-mouthed. During the Peninsular War he dubbed the 88th Regiment 'The Connaught Footpads' for their incessant plundering.

6. Mounted Infantry.

7. There follows one of H-B's yarns.

made the acquaintance of the mounted company of the 88th, having, for a short time some of them attached to me the same boys placed me in what might be called, a very serious dilemma and through them I suffered a most unholy fright. I was at the time stationed, some miles from King William's Town, and in close vicinity to my camp were many farmhouses that had been abandoned by their owners, on the outbreak of the war, who had left most of their furniture and many of their belongings, as well as poultry and vegetables in the gardens, behind them. Some of the latter, I must confess, came in very handy for our mess, that consisted of myself, a sub belonging to the Rangers, and three colonial officers, all of them very good fellows, so we lived and dined well in peace and harmony. Of course there were strict standing orders against looting of any kind, or the destruction of property; and these orders had just been renewed by General Thesiger, on his taking over command, and were fairly well carried out. No Tommy however can understand why, he should not eke out his hard rations, with a few vegetables growing to waste, and as far as the poultry were concerned, I had the solemn assurance of our cook, Tim Muldony, as well as my own servant Quin, ably substantiated by Dennis O'Sullivan and Mike Doolan, henchman to the Ranger officer, "that the hins, poor craters, were that lonesome on the disarted farms, that they came into camp of their own free will and that, there was no way, at all at all of kaping the poor bastes from getting into the pots, God bless thim." So that of course after the hins had insisted on serving themselves up, of their own accord, I could have no further scruples against eating them. This was all very well, as long as no tell-tale feathers flew about the camp, but one lovely evening, after a hard day's patrol, dinner being over, and we squatting on ammunition boxes, yarned over our pipes, I was unfortunate enough to remark with a yawn and a stretch, "I wish to goodness I had the sofa, out of such and such farmhouse here; it would be awfully comfy to lie on and make one's tent look home-like, and if we only had the piano, you So-and-So could give us some music these glorious nights."

These careless words of mine, were, of course, regarded by my officers as empty talk but they acted far otherwise on Mike and Dennis who chanced to overhear them and who, in their kind-hearted,blundering fashion, sought to pleasure me. Next morning I started with the mounted men and some Fingoe levies on a three days' patrol and while returning was met by a mounted orderly, with a message, that the General would inspect my camp that afternoon.[8] It was a matter of hard riding to get there before him but we managed to reach the post as his escort crossed the ridge not two miles away. One glance round the camp to see it was

8. According to Major John Crealock, Thesiger's Assistant Military Secretary, on 1 June 1878 the general did indeed inspect Centane and would undoubtedly have encountered H-B. (Hummel, ed., *The Frontier War Journal of Major John Crealock*, p. 101)

all spick and span, then I rushed to my tent to try and make myself look pretty. The Ranger officer had reached his a moment before and I heard a wild yell of consternation rise from it, which was augmented by my own pious ejaculation of "Oh, Hades!" an exclamation that, under the same circumstances, might have been uttered with perfect propriety by the Blessed Saint Patrick himself. Yes and more, for there, right in front of me, in my very own tent, stood a splendid sofa covered with gorgeous chintz; while the Dead March from Saul, played in a minor key,[9] proclaimed the nature of the surprise packet that had reached my unfortunate and evidently despairing companion. There was no time for fuss or inquiries, we had to bolt on to the parade ground, to receive the General whose party was by now entering the camp. I had never met him before, but had a few days previously acknowledged a memo, directed to all post commandants, ordering them, to on no account allow the property of the refugee settlers to be interfered with. Well here was a pretty kettle of fish. He might want to stay the night at my camp, when naturally I must offer him the use of my tent until his own was pitched. He might want a meal and the Lord only knew what plunder had arrived in the rough mess hut during my short absence. Rumour reported him to be a very strict, stern officer and judging from my own tent, the whole camp might have become a repository for stolen property so that, as he rode up to the parade I was in a mortal blue funk, while visions of courts-martial danced before my mind's eye, and as I gave the order to "present arms," I devoutly wished that the ground would open and swallow me up. Had I only known then, what a kind-hearted, courteous and considerate man I had to deal with, I might have spared myself half my apprehensions, for directly he rode up to me he said, "Please dismiss the men at once, Commandant Browne, I see you have just come off a long patrol, I have no intention of troubling you to-day but will inspect you on my return." On my asking him if he would not dismount and have some tea, he answered, "Oh, no, thanks, I shall ride on to Haynes' mill,[10] but, before I go let me impress on you the absolute necessity of seeing that the General Order regarding the deserted farms is carried out to the letter, as so many complaints have come in from the owners, but I am sure you will do that. Good afternoon. Come, gentlemen, let's move on." With that the dear, good fellow rode gaily away, leaving me

9. The 'Dead March' from Act III of George Frideric Handel's oratorio *Saul*, composed in 1738, was regularly played at funerals, especially military ones. Music performed in a minor key is associated with melancholy sentiments.

10. Haynes' Mill, some seventy miles west of Centane as the crow flies, was a sawmill close to where the Buffalo River plunges down from its mountain source. On account of its strategic situation, during Thesiger's operations in the Amathole Mountains it was an important communications centre and for much of this time also his field quarters. Troops under his direct orders were always billeted there.

planted there, offering up praise and thanksgiving to the Blessed Saint Nicholas (patron of defaulters and worse) for my merciful escape. Then to interview the delinquents. So after dismissing the men, I went with the other officers to the mess hut, which was also used as the orderly room. On reaching it, I might have again broken out into preans of gratitude for my wonderful preservation; as the hut built of grass and covered with a bucksail, that had at the moment of my departure, only contained an old packing-case for a table, and empty ammunition boxes for seats, was now furnished with a fine hardwood dining-room table, eight chairs and two bent-wood American rockers, while round the flimsy, grass walls, through which the wind had beforetimes whistled, were now hung curtains of various patterns, to say nothing about lamps, and goodness only knew how much other gear now embellished our, at one time, sordid hut. If there was anything wanting to make the tableau complete, there stood the four sinners, all in a row, evidently expecting unlimited kudos and each with a suppressed grin of exaltation and self-satisfaction, spread all over his expressive mug; that tempted me sorely to take and knock their blundering heads together.

We entered the hut and sat down. For a few moments I said nothing but only regarded the quartette with as grim and stern a look as I could call up, until, I saw the complacent smirk gradually die out of each face and they began to get decidedly uncomfortable. Then I said impressively, "I am sorry for you men, but there is no hope for you. You will all be certainly hung in three days' time; so I should recommend you all, to turn to and make your sowls, for mercy you can't expect in this world."

A wild howl broke from the four miserables. "Och, willie waroo," whined Mike, "is it to be hung we are, sir? an' what for at all at all?" "Didn't we do it just to make your honour and our officers homelike and comfortable?" groaned Denis. "And me," yelped Tim, "wid the most lovely turkey in the pot, so tinder it's just falling to paices it is, an' divil a feather flying about to give it away at all at all. Och murther, Major, it's not thaives we are; sure did we not lave the illigint stove half-way, so heavy it was, it near bruk our backs, it did." "An' if we did drink wan bottle of whisky," chimed in Quin, adding more with sorrow than contrition, "didn't we lave tin bottles behind us?" Then all together in chorus: "Och, Major dear, sure it's yerself as will spake the good word for us, sure you'll not let that blaggard Provost hang us, och mille murther an' turf," etc. etc., and the laments of the sinners rose high.

"I should like to speak for you," said I, "but you have heard the orders read and you have broken them with your infernal marauding. No, I fear there's no hope for you." Then turning to the other officers I asked, "What do you think, gentlemen?" "No, sir," said one of them, "not the least hope in the world, the General is sure to hang them as an example to others." "Yes, sir," said another, "but perhaps if you spoke very hard for them he might let them off with twenty-five lashes apiece and ten years' prison; that is to say, if they have taken nothing that can't be replaced." "Och, och, by this and by that," roared Mike, "we'll take ivery bit ov it back, even the stove, if we do break our backs wid it, the black baste, may the cuss o' Crumell rest on it,[11] we will indade yer honour." But the humour of the whole show was getting too much for me and I also wanted to slake my thirst, so to cut it short I said, "Quin, get us something to drink and have a bath ready for me in ten minutes. The rest of you scoundrels get about your business, until the Provost and escort come for you; but here you, Doolan, run to the conductor and tell him to have a wagon inspanned to-morrow morning; and as for you, Muldony, if you give us a good dinner to-night maybe I'll spake the word that will save that fat back of yours from a scratching. Be off wid yer now." Exit the bandits, while we sat back in the luxurious chairs, laughed our fill, congratulated ourselves on our miraculous escape and drunk the General's health out of cut glass tumblers, instead of the usual chipped pannikins. A few minutes afterwards, I revelled in a big bath, instead of sponging myself out of a stable bucket, and for that night we all enjoyed, what the worthy Quin called "civoilized convaniences," even to the use of the piano. Next morning the wagon returned all these "convaniences" back to their proper places, even the stove, bad scran to it, so that the General when he inspected my camp, which he did three days afterwards, found it pure and clean in more ways than one and had only praise and good words to give me; which would not have been the case, had he done so, on the date he originally intended. But it was the mission bell I started yarning about, so let me try back and regain the spoor.[12]

Well the only thing of any appreciable value, left at the plundered and burnt-down mission, was the wooden belfry with the bell still slung aloft in it and this attracted the attention and excited the predaceous instincts among a party of the aforementioned M.I., who while acting as escort, to a ration wagon, had to outspan and camp near the mission for a night, on the trek from Headquarters to Quintani. Now the road ran some little distance from the mission and as the bell was not noticeable from it, neither myself nor officers were aware of its existence, but two of these Tommies, with the usual restlessness and inquisitiveness of their kind, must needs go and poke about where they soon discovered it. Of course the first thing to be done, was to pull the still attached rope, when the bell gave out a doleful clang. "Be gobs but that's a foine bell, Moike,"

11. Oliver Cromwell (1599–1658) ('Crumell') remains notorious in Irish popular memory. He led the forces of the Commonwealth of England in the ruthless re-conquest of Ireland, 1649–53, and the Cromwellian Settlement of 1652 was disastrous for Irish Catholics.

12. See p. 56, n. 4, above. Sadly, the entertaining yarn that follows about the mission bell must be a pure fabrication.

quoth Pat. "It's all that an' more, Pat," assented Mike. "Sure 'twould be an illigent thing to put up in camp an' bate the hours on," said the first villain. "It's a bhoy of discarnment ye are, Pat, but how'll we git it down? An' maybe it's sacrilege 'twud be." "Divil a bit," asserted the tempter, "sure it's only a nagur convinticle,[13] and thim black heretics at that, an' tell me, didn't they burn the church down thimselves, the black-advised divils; an' whose to know they didn't burn the bell down too, bad luck to the blaggards. Anyhow we'll have the blessed bell. Sure 'twill pleasure the Major, he's so proud of the camp, he'll be woild deloighted wid it."

There was no need of further argument; the brace of worthies promptly set fire to the long, thick, dry grass that had grown, in rank profusion, round the foot of the wooden edifice which, being sun-dried, quickly ignited and soon the pride of the late mission came down with a crash.

It took all hands and a couple of yokes of oxen to drag the fallen tinkler up to the wagon which had to be half unloaded before it could be stowed away, and then having made everything fast again, the sacrilegious gang, thoroughly pleased with themselves, ate their supper and slept, I have no doubt, the sleep of the just, without any twinges of remorse or conscience. Now it must have taken these fellows at least two hours' real, hard work, to carry out their nefarious act, which if they had been ordered to do as a fatigue, after a day in the saddle, they probably would have grumbled at, deeply if not loudly, yet here for sheer mischievous devilment they had imposed the labour on themselves and then retired to rest as contentedly as a pack of school-boys after a feast of stolen fruit.

Two days later I was sitting writing in my tent when, to my unbounded astonishment, I heard the hours of noon struck on a fine-toned bell and at once ordered the word to be passed for the sergeant-major who belonged to Pulleine's Lambs. On his arrival I demanded, "Where did the bell that has just been struck come from?" "I dinna ken," he replied; "'tis those wild Irish (he was an Ulster man himself) have just rigged it up, sir." "Go and fetch their sergeant-in-charge," I said, and presently as smart and trim a man, from West of the Shannon, as ever served Her Gracious Majesty, stood before me. "Sergeant," said I, "where did you get the bell from that I have heard struck?" "Oh, sor, we've just put it up, thinking 'twould be a convaniency to bate the hours on, sir, an' ud please yer, sir." "Yes, but where did you get it from?" "'Deed, sir, I didn't get it at all at all; sure 'twas Corporal Finacune an' the last escort as got it, sure 'tis a wee bit ov a bell, sir, and a convaniency to bate the hours on, yer honour, an' no use to them black nagurs at all at all, sor." "Here let me see your convaniency and go and bring Corporal Finacune to me." So leaving my quarters I walked to the guard tent and there in front of it, slung on

13. A Protestant non-conformist religious assembly of Africans.

strong poles, was a splendid bell that I knew, although no judge of the cost of musical instruments, must, with the transport, have cost a lot of money. But how the deuce could it have fallen into the clutches of these beauties? One glance was enough to show me it was a church bell, but there were no churches within a hundred miles of that part of the world and I did not know, nor could I conceive that a nigger mission should have ever possessed such an expensive article. Anyhow, Corporal Finacune might be able to throw some light on the subject; presently he hurried up. "Corporal," said I, "where did you get this from?" "Sure, sor, 'tis a bell, sor." "Yes," said I, "that I can see for myself, but where did you get it from?" "And we thought it wud be a convanience to bate the hours on, sor, and be a pleasure for ye's, sor." "Yes, but where did you get it from?" "Is it get it yer want to know, sor? Sure we didn't get it at all, sor, we just fetched it along, sor, as we thought it would be a convaniency—" "Yes, yes, but where did you fetch it from?" "Fetch it from, sor; sure we didn't fetch it at all at all, the wagon fetched it, sor, and we thought it wud be moighty convanient—" "Confound your convanient, how did it get on the wagon?" "Sure, sor, did we not near break our hearts, let alone our backs, lifting it in the wagon, an' we thought—" "Damn your thoughts, where did you lift it on to the wagon?" "Sure it was on the road from Ibaky,[14] sor; 'twas Pat O'Rafferty an' Mike Frinch as found it, lying lonesome on the felt, poor thing, and onable to bate itself at all at all, it was so we thought it wud be conva—" "Oh, bad luck to your convaniency; if you fellows don't take care, a courts-martial will find it convanient to put more stripes on your back than you will ever wear on your arms; now be off with you." Exit Corporal Finacune and the sergeant, the former trying to look dignified, but just as they passed out of earshot, I heard him mutter, "No matter, sergeant, we've got the bell and the Major's as pleased as if another boy's best girl had just kissed him." Now as I said before, I was quite unaware that the looted mission had ever possessed a bell and all my officers were in the same state of blissful ignorance, so that although the conversation, for the next few days, dwelt on the subject, of how the deuce a bell of that size had ever got into such a remote part of the world, yet, as none of us ever dreamt that it could belong to the mission we kept it in camp and made use of it as a convaniency to bate the hours on; moreover men belonging to the Lost Legion are used to finding queer things, in out-of-the-way parts of the world. I had once, myself, found the figure-head of a big ship on the top of a mountain in the centre of the North Island of New Zealand;[15] so that shortly we ceased to talk about it and with the exception of hearing the hours beaten on it forgot it altogether. I individually, I must

14. Ibeka.

15. It has not proved possible to verify this tale.

confess, delighted in it, as in more ways than one, it gave tone to the camp and I have always been very particular about the neatness, comfort and appearance of my temporary homes. Besides which it was safe where it was, should I be called on, at any date, to return it to its rightful owners.

Time passed, the boys of the 88th had rejoined their own regiment, when I was visited by Colonel Glyn, then in command of the Transkei, and on a tour of inspection.[16] I had known him many years and the inspection being over, we were sitting in my tent chatting, when the confounded bell struck the hours of noon. The Colonel, good man, was at the moment imbibing liquid refreshment, and as the clang of the first beat struck his ear, he gave a jump like a wounded buck. "Good God, Maori," he spluttered, in the midst of his coughing, for the liquor had gone the wrong way and nearly choked the dacent ould gentleman; "what on earth have you got there?" "Oh, it's only a bell, sir, we beat the hours on," I remarked innocently enough, surprised as I was at his flurry and heat. "Only a bell!" he howled; "only a bell. Oh, Maori, you sacrilegious beggar, you're in for a pretty scrape; here are all the dignitaries of the Church complaining to the General and raising Cain in the press, accusing the troops of being marauders and with sacrilegiously stealing some infernal bell or other. I have denied this, but here I find the beastly thing in your camp, sir. Why on earth can't you leave their wretched missions alone, sir? You'll find yourself in the wrong box, sir, if you interfere with these missionaries and their loot. What the—which the—where the—" and the dear old fellow bubbled away until I thought he would chuck an apoplectic fit. Then at last I took the chance of getting a word in edgeways and explained matters so as to somewhat pacify him, while a good lunch soon afterwards and a better dinner that night thoroughly restored me to his pristine friendship. Still, all that afternoon and evening I noticed the old fellow cock his ear whenever the bell was struck and several times I heard him mutter, "A very fine bell that, deuced good tone, handy to have in a big camp, thrown away here," etc., etc., and next morning after a good breakfast, just previous to starting off, he said, "Maori, have that bell put into my wagon, I shall take it into Headquarters and see that it is returned to the proper authorities; by doing so, I shall doubtless make your peace with them, especially as I shall tell them you will pay all expenses of having it re-hung, etc., and I think you will have got off very luckily. Good-bye, my dear boy, ride in and see me at Ibeka, if you have a chance and you might try to pick up a few partridges on the way; those we had last night were very good. And

16. Richard Thomas Glyn, CB (1831–1900), was Colonel of the 1/24th Regiment which had been stationed in the Cape Colony since January 1875. He had seen service in the Crimean War, 1854–5, the Indian Mutiny, 1857–8, and the Diamond Field Revolt of 1875 in Griqualand West. During the Ninth Cape Frontier War, 1877–8, he was gazetted Commander of the Army of the Transkei in December 1877 with the acting rank of brigadier general.

now then take care of yourself, and whatever you do, don't steal any more church bells. Good-bye," and with this parting benediction the dear old chap cantered gaily away in a heavenly temper and, I have no doubt, as full of good intentions, concerning the bell, as Hades is of nonjuring parsons. His parting order was obeyed, the blessed bell was sent into Headquarters and for some days myself and men missed, with regret, its silvery tones; but it was gone, and there was the end of it as far as myself and Pulleine's Lambs were concerned. Yet I was destined to hear it again and that not in its mission belfry. No, it was still doing better service in the world. For on my riding into Ibeka, a short time afterwards, not forgetting to take with me some partridges, as instructed by the Colonel, I was guest in the camp of his gallant corps and again heard and recognized those sweet tones I knew so well, announcing the hours as they had done for me.

"You have a fine bell there," I remarked to a pal. "Yes," said he, "a very fine one, and we're all very proud of it; the Colonel brought it back with him the other day. I wonder where the old boy picked it up—quite an acquisition to the camp, is it not?" "Yes, quite," said I, with a heavy sigh, and for a few moments I meditated on the dishonesty and looting propensities of some people in this world.

Many years have passed since then, but sometimes I wonder, whether that bell still records the hours for that gallant regiment, or if it has gone back, to summon greasy niggers to attend worship they don't understand; as it was originally intended to do by its benevolent though misguided donors. And now before I spin you grimmer yarns let me tell you a brace, that I trust will amuse you as during a war humour and pathos are often told off in the same half section.

Chapter VIII

Grand Rounds and the
Blue-Jacket Sentries

YES, I have often stated and still maintain that the gallant blue-jackets, who served Her late Gracious Majesty, were second to none, either as fighting men, during the stress of war, or when out for a frolic in times of piping peace and moreover that their quaint acts and remarks have often caused a hearty laugh to those, having a sense of humour, who have been lucky enough to serve in the same outfit with them in the field, or to have witnessed their high jinks during their well-earned hours of liberty. Let me spin you a yarn about a brace of them I came in contact with in the Kafir War of 1877.

It happened in this way and the scene was Ibeka, the Headquarter Camp of the British Field Force in the Transkei, and the date some time in December 1877. At the outbreak of the war, H.M.S. *Active*, then flagship on the South African station, had landed a strong party of blue-jackets,[1] who came up-country to bear a hand in twisting old Kreli's caudal appendage,[2] and on the day the occurrence I am going to tell you about happened, had marched into Ibeka and pitched their tents at some distance from the remainder of the camp, which was a very straggling one spread out on the crest of a long ridge.

Now at this time there were many shaves and picket-line yarns (rumours) flying around and on the day the blue-jackets joined up, it was reported that the enemy was going to make a night attack on the camp, so that although none of the senior officers believed this to be likely, still the O.C. considered it to be prudent to make arrangements, so as to give the Kafirs a warm reception should they attempt any such movement and in consequence sentries and pickets were doubled, while the remainder

1. 'Blue-jacket' is slang for a sailor. A Naval Contingent from HMS *Active* under the command of Commander H.T. Wright was landed at East London on 15 December 1877, two months after the start of operations in the Transkei on 9 October 1877. It consisted of 196 men (42 of whom were Royal Marines). Six 12-pounder guns, two rocket tubes and a Gatling gun were also put ashore.

2. In other words, twisting Sarhili's tail.

of the men were warned to hold themselves in readiness to turn out at a moment's notice. As it chanced, I happened to be field-officer on that night,[3] coming on duty at guard mounting, and of course a portion of my work consisted in visiting all the posts, pickets and sentries during the night.

This was rather a long and tedious job as the camps of the various units were much scattered and at a considerable distance from one another, so that it necessitated my making my rounds mounted and even then it would take me a long time to do the work thoroughly. The night turned out to be a very fine one, with a splendid moon, that shed so brilliant a light, that I could easily have read big print by it; not a breath of air, not even the smallest bit of mist in the sky, so that the whole country lay open like a book. The long grass round the camps had been all burnt away for a considerable distance, so that not a single man, much less a large body of the enemy, could possibly approach our lines without being immediately spotted. At 9.30 p.m. my orderly together with four other troopers and a trumpeter brought round my horse and I started my first tour of inspection. "Not much chance of any fun to-night, boys," I said, as I swung myself into the saddle and let my eyes range over the moonlit veldt; "this is not the sort of night a mob of niggers would select on which to rush a camp; but no matter, half sections right, walk march," and we moved off.

In due course of time, after visiting all the pickets and outposts of the main camp, I at last approached the lines of the Naval Brigade, which were on the extreme left and some little distance away from the other units. As I rode, towards their advanced post, I could plainly see the two men on sentry, one of whom was standing up, while the other, in accordance with orders, was lying prone on the ground, and of course they had not the slightest difficulty in both seeing and hearing my small party of horsemen as we approached them. We were still perhaps a hundred yards or more from them, when the man standing up brought his rifle to the port, emitting, at the same time, a bellow that boomed across the silent veldt and for a minute quieted the chirping of the astounded ground crickets. "'Alt, who goes there?" "Grand Rounds," I replied, wondering if his stentorian hail had alarmed the whole camp and fully expecting a general turn-out, or at least the pickets would stand to their arms. Of course I had brought my party promptly to the halt and for some moments waited patiently for the continuation of the challenge, viz., "Halt, Grand Rounds, advance one," etc., but somehow that blue-jacket did not seem to be fully conversant with military tactics or etiquette, for after shuffling

3. Since H-B did not arrive in the Cape until February 1878, he most certainly was not present at Ibeka in December 1877. This is another of his 'histories' into which he has spuriously inserted himself as the leading player.

about for a few moments and fumbling with his rifle he brought it to the order and, in what was evidently meant to be a propitiatory tone of voice, rumbled out, "Come on, Mr 'Orse Hofficer, I knows as 'ow you ain't no ruddy nigger." As this was evidently all the military ceremony I was going to receive, with a quiet chuckle to myself and a smothered guffaw from my troopers, we rode up to him, when I repeated to him the usual formal challenge and gently intimated that as in a short time I should be again passing his post I should expect to be challenged in a proper manner. This I did, not that I was a pedantic stickler for red book formula or ceremony and well knew that a sailor makes a sentry second to none in the world, still as I was forced to again pass his post on my return journey, approaching it from the other flank and being sure Jack would make an awful hash of the challenge, I was prompted by the imp of drollery to hear how he would mix up the instructions I had bestowed on him. To my gentle admonition he respectfully replied, "Ay, ay, sir," and I continued my rounds. After I had visited the other posts and made certain everyone was on the *qui vive* I wheeled about and returned towards the right of the camp, eventually reaching the one at which I had received the unorthodox greeting. As I rode towards the spot I could plainly see the same men were on guard though they had changed places, *i.e.*, the one who had been originally standing up was now lying down, so that our approach was challenged by another voice of perhaps not quite such a voluminous timbre, but still quite loud enough to wake a stone-deaf man, and again, "'Alt, who goes there?" rumbled across the moonlit veldt. Again my party halted and I answered, "Grand Rounds;" but again, notwithstanding my previous careful instructions, the sentry was evidently flummoxed; for after hawking and clearing his throat a few times, he turned to his recumbent companion and giving him a kick in the ribs, that was enough to stave in the plates of a battle-ship, he growled out in a voice, meant to be a whisper but which was audible at twice the distance we were apart, "Jack, Jack, rouse up, ye lazy swine, 'ere's that —— as calls hisself Grand Rounds come agin, git up yer waster and sling him 'is ruddy patter." Up jumped Jack and the earth shook with his bellow: "It's all right, Mr Grand Rounds, pass and all's well."

ARCADES AMBO[4]

There is no doubt that even in England itself, the country that boasts of being the birthplace of free parliamentary institutions, and of possessing the most ancient Parliament in the world, one that has existed for hundreds

4. *Arcades ambo* (Latin) means 'both Arcadians', *viz.* two people of like occupations or tastes, with the ancillary meaning of two rascals or fools. All these appellations apply to the two Cape parliamentarians H-B lampoons in the yarn that follows.

of years and has been the model from which all other nationalities have more or less copied their houses of representatives, that many queer fish are, even at this modern epoch, being returned as M.P.'s by the free and independent electors. Yet such queer fish, and so many of them, are returned as members that a looker-on, possessing no party politics, may often wonder what on earth ever induced human beings, outside a madhouse, to elect such utter rotters to represent them at the grave deliberations that frame laws for the guidance and safety of our mighty Empire.[5]

This being so, in the Mother Parliament,[6] it is not to be wondered at that in the Colonial houses of representatives some very strange species of bipeds, who emerging or being extracted from the back blocks or up-country constituencies, take their seats. It may be true that these creatures are cute and crafty men, in their own pettifogging line of business, and are quite capable of roping in their full whack of whatever is going worth having, yet so far as the knowledge of the Empire's history, let alone that of classic nations, are as ignorant as the beasts that perish. This being the case, at the present moment, it can be easily understood that years ago, when representative government was first granted to the various Colonies, the queerness of the politicians who attended them was more remarkable, and that very many of them were as unfit to legislate as they were to mix in polite society.

It was in the year 1878, when the Gaika and Galeka Wars were still in progress, that I was ordered to proceed from Cape Town to East London in command of a party of irregulars destined for the front,[7] and for that purpose we embarked on one of the Union Company's ships which was proceeding to Natal,[8] calling in at all the ports along the coast. At the time of which I am writing there were no railway communications between Cape Town, Port Elizabeth or East London, and any travellers journeying from the capital to the eastern provinces of Cape Colony, must proceed by ship, via one of these ports, so that many more passengers were sea-

5. H-B clearly entertains a snobbish prejudice against colonial parliamentary institutions and their elected representatives. The Cape had been granted 'Representative Government' in 1853, though the executive power remained in the hands of the governor appointed by London. However, in 1872 the Cape was granted 'Responsible Government' with the executive directly accountable to parliament elected by all males regardless of race who owned property valued at £25 (purchasing power today of about £3,850).

6. The British Parliament in Westminster

7. H-B was apparently stationed in the Eastern Cape throughout his period of service in the Ninth Cape Frontier War, and there is no record of his escorting irregulars from Cape Town to the front. Fabricated or not, this sea voyage provides him with a vehicle for venting his unbridled prejudices against both Jews and ill-educated colonial parliamentarians.

8. The Union Line was founded in 1853 as the Southampton Steam Shipping Company and renamed the Union Line in 1857. It won the contract to carry mail to South Africa, mainly to Cape Colony.

borne in those days than there are at present. The voyage also took longer time, as not only were the boats slower but the loading and discharging of cargo, at the various ports, were far more difficult, breakwater and harbour accommodation being then in their infancy.

Few people who travelled in those days will ever forget the horrors and dangers of the swinging basket, the foul stench and discomfort of the filthy serf boats, or the vile language and the brutal blackguardism of the ruffians who manned them: truly travelling in South Africa is luxurious in these days to what it was in the seventies. Well one fine afternoon we steamed out of Cape Town docks, the boat being fairly full of passengers bound up the coast, as well as my filibusters.[9] The passage was a very pleasant one and I enjoyed it thoroughly, laying in as much fun as possible so as to last out a long stay up-country as I knew my destination was the Transkei and there was no society to be got up there. In the saloon there was a typical South African crowd as well as a number of new chums transferred from the lately-arrived mail boat. Here you could see a group of over-dressed Hebrews, whose villainous faces and worse manners stamp them as denizens of Houndsditch and the various continental Juden Strausse returning from their home trip to their I.D.B. pursuits at Kimberley.[10]

Eyeing them with contempt and aversion are a few diamond-diggers returning from the Old Country. Then you have a handful of military men *en route* to join their various corps at the front, while merchants, returning from England, and Cape Town, together with bagmen,[11] interior traders, farmers and a sprinkle of Germans, Dutch and Portuguese collectively make up a polyglot gang rarely met with in other parts of the world. Acquaintanceship was very easily made on a South African coasting steamer and, before we had been twenty-four hours on the water most of the passengers, with the exception of the I.D.B.'s, who frequented the smoking saloon and liquor bar, were on speaking terms, so that the conversation became general and many a good yarn was spun and listened to with avidity. Now amongst the passengers were two men between whom no special amenity was exchanged; the rest of us soon tumbled to that fact and at first rather wondered at it, as there was no very striking difference to be observed between them either in breeding,

9. Filibusters are irregular soldiers or freebooters who act without official authorisation from their own government. This appellation did not apply to H-B's 'party of irregulars' which would have been raised by either the Cape or British military authorities.

10. H-B gives full vent to his antisemitism. Houndsditch was a poor area in the East End of London where many Jews had settled. 'Jude Strauss' is a German-Jewish name. I.D.B. is illicit diamond buying, the illegal trade in uncut diamonds by unlicensed persons. H-B infers that all Jews at the Kimberely diggings were involved in this criminal activity.

11. 'Bagmen' are travelling salesmen.

manners or conversation. They were both of them middle-aged, vulgar, ostentatious, ignorant cads who, having for some incomprehensible reason been returned as members to the brand-new Cape Parliament,[12] were on their way home after having misrepresented their constituencies in the deliberations of the Colony.

What their original quarrel was about none knew nor cared, but it was generally supposed that each man gave the other credit of having overreached himself in some piece of underhand jobbery, which as they were, both of them, upcountry canteen and winkel keepers was more than probable.[13] Be this as it may the brace of them were inordinately proud of being M.P.'s, and each man tried to run the other down and belittle him behind his back, while both of them bragged enormously of his own sterling qualities that had raised him to the proud pre-eminence of senatorial rank, of his visits to Government House and his own unrivalled knowledge.

Well, we reached Mossel Bay and anchored there for a couple of days and then steamed on to the Nysna where we again dropped our mud hook.[14] This latter place is celebrated for a forest containing a large number of elephants and is the only district in Cape Colony where these majestic animals still exist and in which they are strictly preserved by the Government.

This being the case the conversation, in the smoking-room, naturally turned upon elephants and as there were two or three interior traders and hunters among the crowd, elephant yarns were the order of the day. Now for various reasons this conversation greatly interested me. True I had only been a year in the country but had already gained sufficient experience to grasp the fact that, the great drawback to South Africa was the lack of sufficient transport. I had experienced the heart-breaking slowness of the ox-wagon for military purposes and had heard how difficult it was to convey heavy machinery to the diamond fields, so that hearing there were numerous elephants so adjacent to Cape Town, I asked the question why they were not captured, tamed and trained as is the case in India. To this query of mine an old settler answered that, it was an accepted fact, the African elephant was untamable but to this I disagreed, asking if the attempt had ever been made and arguing that the elephants used in Europe by the ancients, notably by Phyrus, were most

12. The Cape Parliament was not so new. Responsible Government had been in operation in the Cape since 1872.

13. A *winkel* is a shop in Afrikaans, so the two MPs were shopkeepers and purveyors of liquor and food in military camps. In other words, both were in the low-status retail trade. H-B contemptuously gives them lower-class accents with dropped and misplaced aitches.

14. Knysna, a settlement on the northern shore of an estuary between Cape Town and Port Elizabeth, had since 1858 been the commercial centre and harbour for the region.

probably African ones and that the Carthaginians certainly used them.[15]

Now, there were some dozen men in the smoking-room, at the time, imbibing their anti-tiffin bitters,[16] among whom was one of these obnoxious M.P.'s and the discussion became general each man giving his opinion.

One of the military men quite agreed with me, stating that it was an historical fact that Jugurtha had to pay a yearly tribute to Carthage of so many elephants[17] and that it was an indisputable fact that Hannibal imported them into Spain and took them across the Alps, with him, when he invaded Italy, these beasts being, in his opinion, African ones. Up to this time the M.P. had sat silent, none of us taking any notice of him, but it was contrary to the bounder's nature not to try and shove himself to the front, so he burst into the conversation with the remark, "Of course, 'e 'ad helephants with 'im, or 'ow could he have pulled 'is cannons over the 'ills, trek oxen could never have done it." For a minute we all stared at him in awe and silence, then a grizzled old interior man articulated, "Hannibal, you say, pulled his cannons over the Alps with elephants?" "Ja, how could 'e have pulled 'is big guns over with oxen or mules?" and it was only the thick upper deck which prevented the roar of ribald laughter, that burst simultaneously from all of us, reaching and disturbing the sweet little cherub that sits up aloft. Anyhow, if it did not disturb the aforesaid cherub, it considerably disturbed the M.P., who opened his little pig's eyes and glared at us, evidently shocked and surprised, that humble, insignificant mortals should dare to laugh at any remark made by a man of his rank and smell. But he could not overawe us, for the more he glared the more we laughed, until at last he wheeled about and stalked out of the port doorway with a look of indignant disgust on his face, that simply sent us into fits. Just as his back disappeared out of the port door, his hated rival entered through the starboard one, who looking round demanded, "Wot are all you gents laughing habout? Tell us the joke." As soon as one of us could

15. H-B is advertising his classical education. Pyrrhus of Epirus (c. 319–272 BCE) campaigned in Italy in 280–275 BCE against Rome, and Hannibal (247–c. 183 BCE), the leading Carthaginian general in the Second Punic War, invaded Italy and fought against Rome (218–201 BCE). The war elephants they both deployed were the now-extinct North African elephant (*Loxodonta Africana pharoahensis*) that lived north of the Sahara. They were smaller than the Bush (Savannah) elephant today, but probably the same size as the equatorial African forest elephant.

16. H-B means ante-tiffin, viz. before tiffin. 'Bitters' is one of the many varieties of herbal liqueurs in which bitter herbs, roots and plants have been infused in alcohol. It is drunk as an aid to digestion and as a health tonic for the stomach.

17. The military gentleman – or rather, H-B who put the word in his mouth – was confused. Jugurtha, King of Numidia (c. 160–104 BCE), did not pay tribute to Carthage which the Romans had finally destroyed in 146 BCE at the end of the Third Punic War, but was much later engaged in a long and ultimately unsuccessful war with Rome (112–106 BCE).

get his wind he informed the new-comer we were laughing at his brother member's assertion that Hannibal had made use of elephants to draw his cannon across the Alps. At once the second Solon broke out—" Ho, ho, ho, the ignorant ass, as if 'Annibal would 'ave tried to 'ave pulled his cannon over the Halps. Not 'e, why, he'd have loaded 'em up on the elephants' backs, just the same as I've seen pictures in the *Illustrated London News* of the Army carrying theirs in India and Hafghanistan. That's how 'Annibal got his big guns over the Halps, you bet." Again from sea to heaven went up a mighty roar, at which the bumptious rotter opened his mouth and stood speechless, glaring at us like a lion at bay, then turned his back and leaving his bitters untasted stalked out, in exactly the same way as his opponent had previously done. Of course the joke ran all through the ship, and up to the time they landed at Port Elizabeth they were pestered with queries as to the weight and number of Hannibal Barka's train of artillery.[18]

18. The point of this anecdote is that the two vulgar, puffed-up colonial MPs lacked a classical education, the hallmark of a gentleman (such as H-B) who had gone to a public school.

Chapter IX

The Zulu Army

TOWARDS the end of 1878 all the Imperial Troops in the Transkei and at King William's Town received orders to proceed to Natal as a dark thundercloud lowered over the garden colony of South Africa and that great and good, though in the future to be much maligned, statesman Sir Bartle Frere was taking,[1] with his usual acumen, such steps as he could, to guard against the threatened danger.

Earlier in the year the 90th Regiment under Colonel E. Wood,[2] one battery of Artillery under Colonel Tremlett[3] and the Frontier Light Horse (late Carrington's Horse) under Commandant Redvers Buller[4] had marched overland, so that by the end of October all the regulars had vacated the Transkei and the country was handed over to the care of Colonial officers and magistrates. I was myself still at Quintani, waiting

1. Sir Henry Bartle Edward Frere, Bart. (1815 –84), was a senior proconsul of empire with considerable experience in India. In 1877 he was appointed Governor of the Cape and High Commissioner for South Africa. The Conservative government had tasked him with effecting a confederation of the white-ruled states of southern Africa under Britain, and this required the pacification and disarming of all still-independent African polities in the region.

2. Brevet Colonel Henry Evelyn Wood, VC, CB (1838–1919), a gallant and intellectual soldier with a reputation as a military innovator, was also an astute operator in the politics of command. He served in the Crimea, 1854–5, the Indian Mutiny, 1858–9 (when he earned the Victoria Cross), the Third Anglo-Asante War, 1873–4 and the Ninth Cape Frontier War, 1878. On Special Service in 1879, during the Anglo-Zulu War he commanded No. 4 Column and the renamed Flying Column with the local rank of brigadier general.

3. Brevet Lieutenant-Colonel Edmund J. Tremlett commanded No. 11 Battery, 7th Brigade, Royal Artillery during the Ninth Cape Frontier War and the Anglo-Zulu War when he served with No. 4 Column and the renamed Flying Column.

4. Brevet Major Redvers Henry Buller, CB (1839–1908), 60th (The King's Royal Rifle Corps) Regiment, was a brilliant leader of irregular horse. He served in the Second Opium War in 1860, the Red River Expedition, 1870, the Third Anglo-Asante War, 1873–4, and in the Ninth Cape Frontier War, 1878, when he took command of the FLH on 22 April 1878. Promoted brevet lieutenant-colonel in November 1878, during the Anglo-Zulu War he commanded the FLH with No. 4 Column and the renamed Flying Column. He won the Victoria Cross at the battle of Hlobane.

to be relieved,[5] when it was my intention to return home, but the same day my relieving officer arrived, I received a letter from Colonel Glyn telling me, that he had not the slightest doubt, but that war was imminent with the great Zulu nation, that, in case it took place, he would command one of the columns intended to invade Zululand, and requesting me to come down country, for, as he was sure I should offer my services, he was making arrangements[6] for me to be appointed to his command.[6] This was very flattering and as I had no wish to arrive at home during a winter, although thanks to the splendid climate of the Transkei I had quite recovered my health and strength, I determined to comply with his wishes, especially as I was certain the Zulus would put up a fight well worth a Lost Legionary, out of employment, taking a hand in. I therefore packed my belongings into a mule cart and, with Quin, started hot-foot for King William's Town, which we reached on the morning of the same day, the 24th, entrained for East London; so that I was able to have an interview with Colonel Glyn who directed me to remain in King and assist Commandant Rupert Lonsdale to raise officers and non-commissioned officers, who were to form the staff of one of the regiments of Natal natives, the General contemplated organizing for the ensuing war.[7]

5. Since 14 June when the 1/24th had been recalled to King William's Town, Captain H-B had been left in command at Centane with a company of Pulleine's Rangers. When Pulleine's Rangers were disbanded, he transferred on 4 August 1878 to the Transkei Rifles, a Cape volunteer corps performing what were in effect frontier policing duties, with the rank of lieutenant. Still stationed at Centane, he served with this corps for the next three months.

6. Unfortunately, it has not proved possible to trace this letter.

7. Rupert laTrobe Lonsdale (1849–88) was Commandant of the 3rd Regiment, Natal Native Contingent. He was born in Melbourne, Australia, the son of an officer of the 4th (The King's Own Royal) Regiment who had settled there. Lonsdale entered the Royal Military College, Sandhurst in 1867. He was commissioned ensign in the 74th (Highlanders) Regiment in September 1868 and was promoted lieutenant by purchase in November 1871. He sold his commission in 1874 and wedded Katherine Russell in November 1875, this 'marriage on insufficient means' apparently forcing him out of the Army. The couple settled in the Cape Colony where Lonsdale had several relatives and he served as a special magistrate in the Keiskamma Hoek district. He and his wife were comfortably off on £300 a year, but he missed the Army and she, described by Fred Carrington as 'a pretty little girl' (Smith, *Wedding Feast War*, p. 180), was unfitted for a rough, frontier life.

Lonsdale volunteered for service during the Ninth Cape Frontier War. He was given command of a unit of Mfengu levies that made up part of Colonel Wood's Keiskamma Hoek command during the gruelling campaign in the Amathole Mountains against the amaNgqika. Wood recorded in his memoirs that he was 'the best leader of Natives' he had ever seen. Noting Lonsdale's 'slight but strong build', Wood remembered how he always led his Mfengu levy 'at a cracking pace' (Wood, *Midshipman to Field Marshal*, vol. I, pp. 301, 302). Lonsdale also impressed Major Crealock. In his journal he lauded the 'lithe active figure of the Keiskamma magistrate whose face is redeemed from boyishness by the square jowl that tells of the determination which will make his name an unforgotten one as long as the

On the completion of this work, which lasted only a fortnight, myself and Quin started as an advance guard to East London, so as to secure accommodation for the 60 officers and the 120 non-coms. that had been engaged,[8] should the state of the weather render the river bar uncrossable. I had just finished the business and was making for the hotel when, from out of a gang of loafing surf-boatmen rose the titanic roar, "Gord strike me lucky, if there ain't my old messmate and skipper," and in a moment

---

tales of this war are told' (Hummel, *Crealock Journal*, p. 59: 5 April 1878). With such an outstanding record and with the support of influential patrons such as Wood and Crealock, it is no surprise that Lonsdale was offered the command of the 3rd NNC when the regiment of Natal Africans was raised for the impending Zululand campaign. On 28 November 1878 a General Order was published naming him the commanding officer of the 3rd NNC.

Lieutenant-General Thesiger (after 5 October 1878 Lord Chelmsford), who on 9 August 1878 arrived in Pietermaritzburg, the capital of Natal, to prepare for a likely Zululand campaign, had been favourably impressed by the performance of the Mfengu levies in the Ninth Cape Frontier War. On 17 August he received a memorandum from Lieutenant-Colonel Anthony Durnford, RE, proposing a Native Contingent of five regiments of infantry for service in Zululand. Sir Henry Bulwer (1836–1914), Lieutenant-Governor of Natal, 1875–80, had the right as Supreme Chief to exact *isibhalo* (compulsory labour and military service) from Africans living in the colony. This meant in practice that Natal magistrates were empowered to require the African chiefs in the Native Reserves to raise levies from among their male adherents for military service. Bulwer and many of his colonial officials believed that these Natal African levies should be mustered and allowed to fight in their traditional manner akin to that of the Zulu foe, but Chelmsford and Durnford were determined that they must be organised along the British regimental system and placed under the command of European officers and NCOs. The military had their way, and on 23 November Chelmsford issued a general order setting out the regulations for the NNC. There were to be three regiments of seven battalions, each battalion consisting of ten companies, with an initial nominal establishment of 1,100 officers and men. Three white officers and six NCOs would lead each company which was to consist of one African officer, ten African NCOs and ninety men. The problem was finding suitably qualified white officers and NCOs.

H-B, after his service with Pulleine's Rangers and the Transkei Rifles, was better qualified than most of those seeking service with the NNC. On 9 November 1878 Major Crealock, Chelmsford's Acting Military Secretary, writing from Pietermaritzburg, appointed him as lieutenant in the NNC. It was Chelmsford who made the selection of NNC officers, but as a matter of courtesy their names were submitted to Bulwer (who would have had no personal knowledge of any of the Cape officers listed) and were approved by him before their appointments became official (see Laband, *Chelmsford's Zululand Campaign*, pp. 117–18: Chelmsford to Bulwer: Memorandum, PMBurg, 4 March 1879).

8. These were the officers and NCOs for the two battalions of the 3rd Regiment, NNC who left King William's Town for East London by train on 20 November 1878. H-B would have been acquainted with many of them because the unemployed roughnecks and adventurers from the disbanded Pulleine's Rangers were more prepared than most to sign up with the NNC. Like H-B, they were for the most part blatant racists, contemptuous of the Africans they were to train and lead in battle but whose language they could not speak. Tough cases all, they would make little attempt to gain the trust of their men and instead would impose their authority through harsh discipline.

Quin also joined the 1/3rd NNC alongside H-B, initially with the rank of corporal, subsequently being promoted to sergeant. He continued to act as H-B's batman.

my hand was nearly wrenched off by old Jack Williams, who had formerly been an old tent-mate of mine, when I had originally joined the Lost Legion, some years previously, in New Zealand and whom I had last seen as bos'n on board a brig, of worse than questionable morality, among the South Sea Islands.[9] I was very glad to meet the old pirate once more, while his delight was expressed so noisily, that it immediately attracted all the roughs in the vicinity who were thunderstruck to see one of their no class fraternity shaking hands with a smartly-uniformed officer and at once crowded round us in such a manner as to incommode and annoy me. This old Jack spotted and immediately started to remedy after his own fashion which was effectual if not polite.

"'Ere sling yer ruddy 'ooks, yer steamboat, makeshift, brass-polishing sodgers, who axed yer to shove yer blooming oars in? Do ye think as 'ow an hofficer as is a gen'leman wants to be lumbered up with the likes of ye? Yer rotten beachcombers, 'ere get." And they got, with the exception of one huge ruffian who demanded, "Who the 'ell was a-going to make 'im shift 'is kedge?"[10] Old Jack quickly set his mind at rest on that point, as without another word, he sprung at him, seized him by the collar and waist-belt, shook him as a dog shakes a rat and hove him, staggering back, until he collapsed into a muddy sluit,[11] which contained old-time fish heads and other decayed, unprofitable matter; where he lay vomiting language filthier than even the ditch in which he reclined. I fully expected that Jack's impetuosity would cause a row, as the cursing blackguard had evidently a following, but my surmises were incorrect as after hauling their mate out of his wallow, they retired uttering threats and maledictions, couched in language, sufficiently torrid as to have blistered off the white-wash from the inside of a newly-built Nonconformist conventicle. So it was evident to me, that Jack Williams had established a reputation, among the unhung blackguards of East London boatmen,[12] such as to make him feared and respected. Truly a man can thrive for a long time, in many classes of society, on his reputation, be it either for sanctity or high-toned blackguardism. As soon as we were alone, Jack demanded, "where I was bound for." And on my informing him I was *en route* for Natal he at once exclaimed with more cuss words than I care to recount or any printer would dare to set up, for if he did, they would most certainly

---

9. There is no record of H-B cruising among the Pacific South Sea islands. The inference is that the brig in question was engaged in smuggling or illicit trade, or even piracy. The episode with 'Jack Williams' is another exuberant H-B yarn.

10. To 'kedge' is a nautical term meaning to warp (haul) a ship by means of a hawser attached to a small anchor, or kedge. Colloquially, it meant to move over.

11. A *sluit* (Afrikaans) is a ditch or water furrow alongside a street.

12. The men who operated the surf-boats that brought passengers ashore from ships anchored beyond the bar at the port's river mouth. See pp. 27–8.

fuse his machine, "Wot, going up to fight ruddy niggers are ye and got Quin along with ye too, I'll bet, so be it as 'e's still alive and hearty. Well darn my rags if old Jack Williams don't sign on the same ship's articles, seeing as 'ow I 'aven't done a bit for the Queen and flag, Gord bless 'em, since we was up Taupo way.[13] Wot do yer say? don't throw up a good-paying, steady job? D——n jobs when there's fighting going on; I ships I do and so does my mate; you can trust 'im, we signs on to-night we do, and if ye want any more men there's a few 'ere about among this scum as I'll answer for. Yes, I'll 'ave a drink along of you and I'll be a proud man if ye'll let me pay for it; 'twon't be the first un we've 'ad together, old mess-mates as we are; though in course the likes of you can't be pals with the likes of me, I'm on the foke-sel head I am, and you're on the ruddy poop you are, so as I signs right on, just give us yer flipper and let's have a last hand-shake, God bless yer." Old Jack rambled on till we reached the hotel and had our drink, but he was wrong about the last hand-shake, that eventuated many years afterwards, as it was gripping my hand, in a far-off country that, world-wanderers as we both were, neither of us had at that time ever heard of that old Jack Williams one-time pirate, filibuster, sea-ruffian and loyal soldier to his Queen and country, took his last departure from land, mast-headed his top-sel yards[14] and set sail on a longer voyage than even he, tough old shell-back as he was, had ever previously signed on for. But that day was still far away in the womb of futurity and even had we been able to foresee the event it would not have spoilt our drink as Lost Legionaries learn, early in their career, to laugh at the nose of the grim monarch come he as he may. That evening Jack brought up and introduced to me Bill Conway (his mate) who had likewise used the sea all his life and possessed an unholy knowledge of the South Sea Islands; in fact it is my belief, though old Jack would never own up to it, that both of them were badly wanted in those parts of the world and had had good and sufficient reasons for transferring their persons from the romantic islands to the more prosaic continent of South Africa. Of course this was only conjecture on my part but I noticed once or twice, on my mentioning the Brig Karl and Bully Brag,[15] both of them wilted and seemed strangely uncomfortable, especially about the neck.[16] However it

13. Taupō is a town in the centre of the North Island of New Zealand situated on the edge of a large lake. In 1868, an Armed Constabulary post was established there and by the late 1870s the hot water pools around Taupō began to attract tourists. In July 1872 Hamilton-Browne had enlisted in the Armed Constabulary and was posted to the Taupō district. He took his discharge in October 1875 and joined the tourist industry in the area (see Introduction).

14. The 'top-sel yards' are the spars from which topsails are set on a square-rigger.

15. Presumably, these are the names of two ships.

16. In other words, both Williams and Conway were in fear of being hanged for piracy.

was no business of mine and I had seen many a man, whose departure from his country had simply been an act of injustice to the common hangman, die like a hero in the dense bush of New Zealand and sure it's much better and a heap more economical to let a real fighting man, who had run foul of his country's laws, die fighting for his flag, than to put the said country to the expense of judges, juries, sheriff, hangman and rope to ensure the same purpose. Next morning Commandant Lonsdale and his party arrived, the bar was propitious, the tug with the boats were ready and as the tide suited in less than an hour we were on board the Union Company's S.S. *Nubian*[17] and on the third morning, after leaving East London, dropped our anchor off Port Natal,[18] as Durban was commonly called in those days.[19] Here we also found the bar on its best behaviour so quickly landed and marched the men to the rest-camp at Durban.[20] The following day we entrained for Pine Town,[21] from whence we started to march to Pietermaritzburg,[22] but at a place called Camperdown[23] we found the General's mule cart, the driver of which handed Lonsdale a note, which contained the order that he and myself were to make use of the cart and report at Pietermaritzburg without a moment's delay. Of course we entered the cart and started gaily on our way, but before we arrived at our destination, and just as we had reached the bare top of a high hill, we were struck by the most terrific thunderstorm I ever have had to face. The driver lost his head, the six mules maddened by the

17. SS *Nubian* was a steamer built in 1876 and operated by the Union Line for the Cape mail service. She was used as a troopship in 1877–9. On 20 December 1892 she was lost in the Atlantic Ocean off Lisbon.

18. The *Nubian* arrived off Durban on 25 November 1878.

19. *See* p. 27, n. 29, above.

20. The sandbar across the entrance to Durban bay between the Point to the north and the Bluff to the south, meant that only small ships with a shallow draught could enter the harbour. Most oceangoing vessels consequently had to remain in the outer anchorage and passengers and cargo had to be brought through the surf by lighter. When the surf was high and stormy, lighters did not attempt to cross the sandbar.

21. Pinetown, in the hills ten miles north-west of Durban, was established in 1850. During the Anglo-Zulu War it was the main British military depot in Natal. Construction of the railway line between Durban and Pinetown began on 1 January 1876, and it was operational from 4 September 1878. The line between Pinetown and Pietermaritzburg was not completed until 1 December 1880.

22. Pietermaritzburg on the Msunduze River, fifty miles north-west of Durban, was the largest settlement in Natal. It had been laid out in 1839 by Voortrekkers who named it after two of their leaders, Pieter Retief and Gerrit Maritz. Since 1842 it had been the capital of the British Colony of Natal. The headquarters of the British garrison of Natal were at Fort Napier on a hill that overlooked Government House and the cathedral. Besides being the seat of government, Pietermaritzburg was also the commercial hub of the Natal midlands.

23. Camperdown is a small settlement laid out in 1865 thirty-five miles north-west of Durban.

vivid lightning and the lashing hail became unmanageable, we had to jump out and rush to their heads, the force of the wind overturned the cart, and for at least twenty minutes, if ever two men, on this earth, smelt h—ll it was Lonsdale and myself. I had experienced as heavy squalls of wind before, and since then have seen hailstones pierce corrugated iron roofs like rifle bullets, but I have never before or since seen such lightning and certainly never want to again. It seemed as if we were enveloped by continuous electric flashes that came so quickly one after the other as to be contiguous and so close to us that if one of us had let go his grip on the mules' head collars, he could have dabbled his hands in liquid flames. Nor could we use our hands to shelter our eyes as we had to hang on to the mules and the skin on my face seemed to grow hot and blister as if Ould Nick was shaving me wid the spear-head he wears at the end of his tail.[24] Well the storm like everything else came to an end, so that after we had righted the cart, straightened out the mules and harness, and administered toko to the cowardly driver, we again got into the cart and arrived, drenched through and plastered with mud, in Pietermaritzburg. Here I stayed a week and as the final arrangements, *re* the formation of the projected invading columns,[25] had not been definitely settled, by Colonel Glyn's desire I marched with Lonsdale's party through Grey Town[26] and the Thorn country to Sand Spruit where we formed a large camp on a flat and awaited the arrival of his native rank and file, who were to be handed over to him there, by the resident magistrate of the district.[27] While we are halted here I think I may tell you some few facts about the Zulu army we were to encounter and which was the most perfect organization ever completed by a savage race;[28] in fact Tchaka, the

24. 'Ould Nick' is the Devil.

25. The officers and NCOs of the 3rd NNC were paid in Pietermaritzburg on 7 December 1878. Many went on a drinking spree in the local canteens and got into fights.

26. The 3rd NNC began its march for Sand Spruit (*see* next note) on 10 December 1878. The thriving township of Greytown, named after the Governor of the Cape from 1854 to 1861, Sir George Grey (Natal was then a District of Cape Colony), was laid out in 1850 as the administrative centre of Umvoti County bordering the Thukela River. A stone laager, built in 1854 and improved in 1877, protected the magistrate's courthouse.

27. Sand Spruit, between Greytown and Helpmekaar, about eighty-five miles north of Pietermaritzburg, and close to the present village of Pomeroy, was the isolated seat since 1876 of the Resident Magistrate of the Umsinga Division of Klip River County, Henry Francis Fynn, Jnr. (1846–1915). His newly-built magistracy was on the slopes above the stream where the NNC were to encamp. The valley floor of the confluence of the Thukela and Mzinyathi (Buffalo) Rivers where Sand Spruit was situated is a region of dry thornveld and bush.

28. H-B's description below of the Zulu military system is accurate enough in some particulars, although not in many others. For corrections to his account, *see* footnotes in the remainder of this chapter.

founder of the Zulu nation,[29] planned and enforced universal conscription to its utmost limitations. I am therefore quite justified in stating that the whole of the Zulu people was really an army as both boys and girls had to serve in regiments and although I do not wish to infer that the women went on the war-path, still every girl was bound to join a female regiment (*ibuto*) and forced to parade when her *ibuto* was ordered to dance before the king or even to marry when the girls composing her *ibuto* reached a marriageable age.[30] The boy however went through a very severe course of training, beginning while still young to prepare for his military service and as no deformed children were allowed to exist and no peace-at-any-price fathers or radical orators were tolerated for a moment, the lad was very anxious, or at least had to pretend he was, to become a warrior.

As soon as a youth was ten years old he might be inspanned to carry the swag of his father, uncle or elder brother on the war-path; which would consist of a sleeping-mat, water-calabash, cooking-pot, docha-pipe, a few pounds of dried meat or mealies and perhaps a spare assagai and knob-stick.[31] When he reached the age of fourteen or fifteen he would be drafted with other boys of his own age to the nearest military kraal where he would have to do fatigue duties,[32] herd and milk cattle, fetch firewood, etc., at the same time being taught how to use his arms, how to fence with sticks, military drill and dances. During this period of his training, provided he wanted to eat, he had to skirmish around and find or steal the materials for his meal as the only provision for his sustenance, made by the kraal commandant, were a number of the wildest cows, drawn from the royal herd entrusted to the care of the regiment, and these unruly animals the recruit boys had to run down, hold and milk before they dined. This was very rough training and a boy had to be soundly constituted to survive the ordeal of his initiation into military life.[33] As soon as a lad was old enough to be considered fit for active service he

29. King Shaka kaSenzangakhona (r. 1816–28) created and consolidated the Zulu kingdom through wars of conquest and assimilation.

30. An age-grade regiment of Zulu men or women was called an *ibutho* (pl. *amabutho*). It was formed to undertake various kinds of military and economic service for the king. Women were formed into *amabutho* primarily for the purpose of marriage to male *amabutho* which had received royal permission to take wives and set up their own households.

31. Boys between the ages of five and twelve were put to work by their elders, herding, hoeing, harvesting and keeping watch for intruders or dangerous animals. Some of the more mettlesome would be sent off to serve as *izindibi* (sing. *udibi*), baggage-carriers for warriors. A 'docha-pipe' was for smoking *dagga* (cannabis or marijuana). An assagai (H-B's spelling; assegai is more usual) was a spear or *umkhonto* (pl. *imikhonto*).

32. A 'military kraal' was an *ikhanda* (pl. *amakhanda*), a royal military homestead where *amabutho* were stationed.

33. At fourteen or so, adolescent boys of the same age-grade from around the kingdom mustered as cadets at the *amakhanda* nearest their homes.

might be drafted into a regiment, or if there were enough boys fit for the purpose they might be all formed into a new regiment, each sub-tribe forming its own company, while warriors of repute were selected by the king to officer it. A Zulu regiment numbered from three to six thousand men and had its own kraal at which the men on duty lived, and a newly-formed regiment would have to build its own barracks, break up ground for cultivation, and when this was done it would receive a name from the king and be considered a unit of the royal army.[34] Should any individual soldier or number of soldiers greatly distinguish themselves in action, he or they might be drafted into one of the royal regiments and also be rewarded by receiving permission to marry—a reward highly thought of and much prized, as he then could mount the head ring (*kehla*), the mark of manhood, which would not otherwise have been granted to them until they were at least thirty-five or forty years old, nor would they have been permitted to marry till then.[35]

A warrior's war outfit consisted of a shield made out of dried ox-hide, oval in shape, about 2 feet 6 inches wide and long enough for the owner to look over, when he held it by the middle of the strengthening stick that ran up it lengthways. His offensive arms consisted of from two to three assagais, one of which would be the stabbing assagai (*bogwan*) that had a blade of at least a foot to 18 inches long fixed to a strong shaft of wood of about 2 feet in length. This weapon, as formidable as the short stabbing sword of the ancient Roman soldier, was never thrown but only used in hand-to-hand combat, while the others, if carried, being much lighter might be thrown, though the Zulu warrior was not encouraged to throw his assagai but was taught to rush in, defend himself with his shield and stab home with his bogwan.[36] He also carried a knobkerry and a plain

34. At about seventeen or eighteen, once they had passed puberty, the king would form cadets of the same age-grade into a new *ibutho* with its own *ikhanda*.

35. H-B is somewhat confused here. All the *amabutho* were 'royal regiments' and individuals (including the king) always remained members of the age-grade regiment into which they had been mustered. However, the king might favour certain *amabutho* above others and reward them accordingly, and individuals who had distinguished themselves in battle might be rewarded with a gift of cattle or have conferred on them a distinctive necklace, an *isiqu* (pl. *iziqu*), as a badge of bravery. The headring was the *isicoco* (pl. *isicoco*) – not a 'kehla' – a circlet of animal tendons or fibres sewn into the hair, coated with beeswax or gum, and then greased and polished. To *khehla* was to assume the *isicoco* as the indication of being a full adult no longer subordinate to elders and in a position to take a wife and become an *ikhehla* (pl. *amakhehla*), or married man. At intervals the king gave a male *ibutho* permission to *khehla* and to marry a designated and much younger female *ibutho*. The king never gave individuals permission to *khehla*, as H-B suggests, and permission was granted only to an entire *ibutho*, all at the same time. As a sign of royal favour, this might occur when the *ibutho* was slightly younger than was the norm.

36. The typical stabbing-spear, or *iklwa* (pl. *amaklwa*) – why H-B calls it a '*bogwan*' is unclear – had a tapering blade some eighteen inches long and an inch and a half wide. The shaft

stick both made of hard wood.[37] His food, carried for him by a boy,[38] consisted of a small bag of dried meat and grain, but as all the kraals, on the line of march,[39] had to contribute to the maintenance of the king's troops very little food was carried on an expedition. A force equipped, as above, could easily march 30 miles a day and put up a big fight at the end of their journey or if necessary cover 50 miles a day and continue to do so for weeks at a stretch,[40] so that an army opposed to them must always be on the alert as no cavalry could keep pace with them over rough and broken country. Their favourite time to attack was the early morning, their plan being to surprise and envelop their enemy, when they would rush in and kill everything with the exception of the girls and cattle.

The Zulu discipline was very strict, disobedience or neglect of duty being punished by death;[41] in fact death was the only penalty served out and the guilty one might not only bring death to himself but to all his family and friends; so it behoved a Zulu soldier to obey and obey smartly. He showed no mercy, he expected none, and when ordered on active service he well knew he must conquer or die for certain disgrace and death, probably torture, awaited a beaten army. A Zulu soldier, whether married or not, had to put in six months out of the year, under arms, at his military kraal; the balance of the year he might go home but was always liable to be called out at any moment, not only in case of war, for his regiment might be required to do duty at the royal kraal, also at certain feasts the majority of the army would be mobilized, before the king, for the purpose of showing off their capabilities in drill and dancing.[42] At

---

was about thirty inches long, as thick as a man's thumb, with a butt at the end to prevent the hand from slipping off. There were various light throwing-spears, or *izijula* (sing. *isijula*), with small tapered blades and shafts between four and five feet long.

37. The knobkerrie or *iwisa* (pl. *amawisa*) was a knobbed stick for clubbing an opponent in combat. Warriors might sometimes carry a short, thick knobless fighting stick, an *isikhwili* (pl. *izikhwili*), but not usually along with an *iwisa*.

38. An *udibi*.

39. A 'kraal' is really an enclosure for livestock, but the word was (and still is) commonly used in South Africa for an *umuzi* (pl. *imizi*), the circular family homestead of huts surrounding the livestock enclosure.

40. H-B was not alone among the British in greatly exaggerating the distance a Zulu army could march in a day. In 1879 the Zulu army averaged only about twelve miles a day by easy stages with halts for foraging.

41. That might have been the case in King Shaka's day, but by 1879 cowards and shirkers mere merely ritually disgraced and then given an opportunity to redeem themselves.

42. That was indeed one of the purposes of the military assemblies at the king's 'great place', especially when the army was mustering to go on campaign. But considerable ritual significance was involved, such as the ritual 'strengthening' of the army before it marched off to war, and the extensive ceremonies that occurred during the *umKhosi*, the 'first fruits' ceremony in late December, when the sacred bond between the king and his people was reaffirmed.

such times petitions might be presented to the sable potentate, who also took the opportunity of rewarding or punishing those brought before him. The most frequent petition was for permission to marry and at times the king would allow aspirants to holy wedlock to prove their right to be considered men and perhaps test their capability of managing a wife in the following way: A wild and savage bull would be turned loose into a large enclosed space and a dozen love-lorn young men sent in to kill it with no weapons except their bare hands; should they succeed in killing the bull the king granted their request and they were contented; while if the bull killed them they were also contented or at least never complained.[43]

There was great rivalry between the various regiments and even between companies of the same regiment and the king would occasionally allow, or even order, one corps to fight another, in which combat only sticks were permitted to be used, but as a shillelagh made of hard and unbreakable wood and handled by a man trained to use it, is by no means a despicable weapon very many on both sides would be maimed and killed.

The Zulu march was usually conducted in single file, the companies moving in parallel lines, while each regiment would take its own line for the objective point, and on reaching that point, or rather some given spot a few miles short of it, the leading files of each petty column would halt and the rear close up, until each company formed a dense mass of men in a ring formation, as the Zulu was quite incompetent to form or advance in line.

The regiments having converged together the chief *induna* (General) would give his orders for the attack and the regiments be formed up to carry them out. In case it should be a laager, camp or village to be stormed, the youngest regiments would be placed on the flanks whose first duty was to surround and completely envelop the enemy, thereby preventing the escape of any fugitives and these men were called the horns of the army. The main body, called the chest of the army, never moved until the flankers had taken up their positions. Then a combined attack would be made but always the junior regiments were first engaged.

The Zulu well understood the utility of a flank attack and should the position of the enemy be so extended or their numbers be so great that the Zulus could not surround them they would still try to out-flank them, but all attacks, whether frontal or flanking, were first made by the youngest regiments and should these be beaten back then the more matured and veteran soldiers moved forward to do the work. The oldest veterans

43. H-B misunderstands the significance of the killing of several bulls with bare hands, for their flesh, cut into strips and smeared with *imithi* (sing. *umuthi*), occult medicines, played an essential part in the ritual strengthening of the army. The practice had nothing directly to do with marriage.

formed the reserve which encouraged the fighting line and killed any combatant who turned tail.[44]

The Zulus had no field ambulances, so after a fight the wounded were examined by their *indunas* and if found to be unable to march or to be otherwise seriously hurt were put to death, usually by drowning, provided a river was close at hand, otherwise he was put out of his misery by his nearest relation.[45] After the fight at Rourke's Drift[46] we found on the banks of the Buffalo nearly one hundred blood-stained shields on which their wounded owners had been carried down to the river so as to be drowned. The Zulus were very superstitious, being great believers in omens, witchcraft, divinations and bone-throwing and also believed that the moon exercised great power for good and evil and that at certain phases of the luminary it was lucky or most unlucky to undertake any important act especially that of war.

The numerical strength of the Zulu army has always been disputed but I am of opinion that it must have been near sixty thousand men at the declaration of the war and these men,[47] trained as they were and as mobile as monkeys, were not an enemy to be sneezed at, much less to be treated lightly. Now I have told you something about the Zulus I will go on with

44. H-B is not far off in his description of the Zulu army on the march and of its tactics, but he saw action only in skirmishes with Zulu irregulars and never faced the main Zulu army in battle. He is therefore relying on descriptions in British sources, whereas historians can now draw on a great deal of recorded Zulu oral testimony for a more accurate account.

   After extensive ritual preparation over several days, a Zulu army marched out in one large column. Once it neared the enemy, the column split into two or more divisions marching parallel to each other and preceded by scouts. Once the enemy had been located and the decision taken to engage, the whole army was drawn up in a circle, an *umkhumbi* (pl. *imikhumbi*), to be ritually strengthened for combat and to receive its orders. The Zulu tactical intention was to outflank and enclose the enemy. While the 'chest' of the bull's-head formation, which consisted of the veteran *amabutho*, advanced slowly, the 'horns' of younger, fleeter *amabutho* were sent out to rapidly enclose the enemy. The 'chest' then charged and engaged the surrounded foe, while the 'loins', or reserve, either gave support where necessary or pursued the defeated enemy. The amaZulu advanced in lines of skirmishers in open order several ranks deep, coming on in short rushes. They only concentrated when close to the enemy and about to engage in hand-to-hand combat.

45. There is absolutely no evidence, either in other contemporary accounts or in Zulu recorded oral testimony, that the amaZulu drowned their wounded or otherwise killed those who could not make it home after combat. The Zulu fallen were disposed of in dongas, antbear holes and grain-pits by friends or relatives, or might be allowed to lie where they had fallen, covered with their shield.

46. The battle of Rorke's Drift, 22–3 January 1879. James (Jim) Alfred Rorke (d. 1875) – not 'Rourke' – was the son of an Irishman from County Galway, Ireland, who emigrated to the Cape Colony. In 1849 he acquired a farm in Natal on the middle Mzinyathi River abutting a ford that came to be known as Rorke's Drift. H-B persists in spelling Rorke as Rourke.

47. H-B doubles the size of the army the amaZulu put into the field in 1879 which, all told, never exceeded 30,000 men, including irregulars. The army engaged at Isandlwana

my yarn. Two days after our arrival at Sandspruit, some two thousand five hundred natives reached us who had to be formed into battalions and companies and put through such drill as it was possible to teach them in less than a fortnight. Of course to try and teach a mob of savages, who did not understand one word of English, in such a limited space of time, the intricacies of company drill or battalion movements was absurd and I was far from pleased,[48] after we had been at the game for a week, when the General, as he passed through on his way to Helpmaker,[49] told me I was to take command of the 1st Battalion of this nigger regiment. However the eve of war is not the time to grumble and I remembered what slashing good fun I had had in days gone by with the native contingents in New Zealand,[50] so although I had been looking forward to having the command of a troop of mounted scouts still I made the best of it and set to with redoubled energy to knock my battalion into shape. Three days after my appointment to the 3rd Natal Native Contingent we were ordered to strike camp, proceed to Rourke's Drift and remain there till the arrival of the rest of No. 3 Column, to which we belonged.[51]

---

numbered about 24,000, and that engaged at Khambula about 20,000; between 15,000 and 20,000 fought at Ulundi.

48. On 21 December 1878 their officers began sorting the 3rd NNC into companies and giving each company a name. The men, who wore the same traditional dress as the amaZulu, were issued with red puggarees to wind around their heads to mark them out from the enemy, and were also supplied with cooking pots, belts and blankets: blue ones for the 1st Battalion and grey ones for the 2nd Battalion.

The majority of the levies making up the 3rd NNC had been raised in Weenen County of Natal. Three companies of iziGqoza, four companies of abaThembu and one company of amaBhele formed part of the 1st Battalion, and six companies of amaChunu the 2nd Battalion. To make up the remaining companies of ten in each battalion, men were raised in the Klip River Division of Klip River County from six small chiefdoms.

49. Helpmekaar (meaning 'help each other' in Afrikaans), and not 'Helpmaker'. In early December 1878 the main depot for No. 3 Column was established at Helpmekaar on the rolling escarpment that overlooks both the plain around the Umsinga magistracy and Sand Spruit to the south, and the valley of the Mzinyathi River to the north. Three galvanised-iron sheds and large huts were erected to hold the accumulating stores for the imperial and colonial troops concentrating there in late December 1878 and early January 1879.

50. This is a fabrication on H-B's part.

51. On 6 December 1878, while in Pietermaritzburg, H-B was promoted to the rank of captain in the 1/3rd NNC. The 3rd NNC moved forward on 2 January 1879 from Sand Spruit to a position on Knostrope farm halfway down the escarpment from Helpmekaar to Rorke's Drift. It would seem, therefore, that Lord Chelmsford, on his way to establish his headquarters at Helpmekaar, appointed H-B as Commandant of the 1st Battalion on 30 or 31 December 1878. On 5 January 1879 all the troops of No. 3 Column encamped in the vicinity of Helpmekaar, including the 3rd NNC, began to move down to Rorke's Drift. By 9 January all of No. 3 Column (except for the Helpmekaar garrison) were concentrated at Rorke's Drift for the invasion of Zululand on 11 January when the ultimatum expired.

Chapter X

Advance into Zululand

BEFORE daylight on the morning of the 10th January 1879,[1] the head-quarter column of the Zululand Field Force began to cross the Buffalo River at Rourke's Drift and enter Zululand.

I had a few days before been appointed Commandant of the 1st Battalion of the 3rd Regiment of the Natal Native Contingent, composed of ten companies. Each company consisted of three white officers, six white non-com. officers and one hundred or more Natal natives. The exact number of natives I never knew but I had about twelve hundred of them in all.

The officers were chiefly a smart lot of young Colonials, most of whom spoke Zulu, all of them good shots and fine horsemen.

The non-coms. were a motley crowd, a few of them old soldiers and ex-clerks, the majority of them runaway sailors, ex-navvies, and East London boatmen. They were an awful tough crowd, but they looked a hard-fighting lot and though their language was strong, and they were evidently very rough, they looked also very ready, and I afterwards found that most of them did not belie their looks. The greater number of both officers and non-coms. had served through the Gaika and Galeka wars of 1877 and 1878,[2] and many of them had been under me before.

The column was commanded by General Lord Chelmsford and was composed of both battalions of the 24th Regiment, one battery of Royal Artillery, two companies of Mounted Infantry, the Natal Mounted Police, the Natal Carbineers, and the 3rd Regiment of Natal Native Contingent, of which Commandant Lonsdale was commandant-in-chief, I commanding the 1st and Commandant Cooper the 2nd Battalion.[3] Of course we had

1. With the expiry of their ultimatum to the Zulu king on 11 January 1879, the British commenced their invasion of the Zulu kingdom. No. 3 (Centre) Column crossed the Mzinyathi River that same day, and No. 1 (Right) Column crossed the Thukela River on 12 January. No. 4 (Left) Column had already crossed the Ncome River on 6 January into the Disputed Territory, and jumped the gun on 10 January when a flying column began to advance down the left bank of the river.

2. Ninth Cape Frontier War.

3. Commandant A. W. Cooper, 2/3rd NNC, late of the 95th Regiment.

doctors, ambulances, commissariat officers and the usual miles of wagons, without which no column can march in Africa.[4]

The morning was very cold, the dense morning fog, for which Zululand is famous, hung close to the ground, and although it was midsummer the cold bit, causing us to shiver in our thin khaki clothing, whilst the naked natives turned blue, their teeth chattering like stone-breakers at work.

There were four crossing-places to the river, a very rapid one and on that day in flood.

Two of these were fairly practicable drifts (fords), and two ponts that had been put together by the Royal Engineer officer and some of my non-coms. These drifts were above and below the ponts and my orders were that I was to cross at the lower drift, line the ridge on the other side and hold it while the 24th, the guns and the wagons were got across by the ponts.

The Mounted Infantry were to cross after my men and the mounted volunteers were to cross after Commandant Cooper at the upper drift.

Well before daylight in the bitter fog, we came down to the drift. The river was full, rapid and very cold and looked far from tempting. However orders must be obeyed so we hardened our hearts and dashed at it, the natives all locking arms and rushing in *en masse*. My horse was nearly carried off his feet but having been used to crossing bad rivers in New Zealand, I kept him up and over we got. I do not know how many of my natives were lost.[5] I had never received a long roll of them when I took over the command, and but few returns were ever sent in.

A most dashing act was done at the drift by Captain Hayes who was in command of my rear company.

One of the Mounted Infantry, a poor horseman, lost control of his horse, and horse and man were swept down the river. Captain Hayes who had crossed, dashed in and saved both. This was done under the eye of the General who mentioned it in dispatches, and who rode that night to my camp to thank Captain Hayes personally.[6]

Now we were in Zululand, cold, wet through and shivering with our tempers short and crisp. The Colonial can grumble just as well as an old Tommy, and he has, as a rule, more command of language. However it did

4. No. 3 Column of 4,709 men was made up of N Battery, 5th Brigade, RA, the 5th (Field) Company, RE, the 1/24th Regiment, the 2/24th Regiment, Nos 1 and 2 Squadrons, Mounted Infantry, the Natal Mounted Police (henceforth NMP), units of the Natal Mounted Volunteer Corps, the 1/3rd NNC, the 2/3rd NNC and the Natal Native Pioneer Corps (henceforth NNPC).

5. At some places the water came up to the men's necks, but there are no reports in official documents, newspaper articles or memoirs of any having been drowned.

6. Captain P.W. Hayes, 1/3rd NNC whose name appeared in Column Orders for his act of bravery.

not take me long to get my men into line, and we pushed on, up the rise, and took possession of the top of the ridge, which we lined.

Just then the sun came up and away went the fog. For the first hour or so we enjoyed it. But when our clothes were dry we began to get dry ourselves and I may say we dried very quickly and soon began to scorch.

There was no shade and as the sun increased in heat, there we lay on that bare ridge and roasted all that live-long day. Certainly we had plenty of water nearly as warm as ourselves, but that scorching sun would have been less intolerable had we been on the move.

There was no enemy in sight, nothing to do, conversation died away, it was too hot to sleep, even the East London boatmen could not curse, and the only thing I could do was to stick four assagais into the ground,[7] rest a shield on them, lie with my head in the shade of the latter and think of iced drinks.

How we white men longed for the enemy or anything to break this monotony, but no enemy came. Although Serhio (one of Cetewayo's principal *indunas* (chiefs) and one of the chief causes of the war) had his kraal only a few miles off, he refused to call on us for afternoon tea, but we called on him for early coffee next morning.[8]

However the longest day must have an ending and at dark the pickets were posted, and we were ordered down to the camp that had been pitched in a long line on the Zulu bank of the river.

Now I do not want to rake up old stories or say anything unkind about men, most of whom are dead. But in the book of Standing Orders, issued to all commandants, the first order was that no camp should be pitched without being laagered. Yet here was a camp, stretching away in a long line, without any attempt at a laager or any other defence.[9]

After a feed of bully beef and biscuit washed down by a pannikin of muddy coffee, the first food that day, I had just finished my pipe and was rolling myself up in my blankets when the orderly officer arrived with the order that I was to parade eight companies of my men before daylight and join the party that was to attack Serhio's kraal next morning.

It seemed I had hardly been to sleep, when the faithful Quin roused me up with a pannikin of coffee and it was a case of turn out and get my men

7. These would have been commandeered from the NNC who carried traditional weapons.

8. Sihayo kaXongo (c. 1824–83), the *inkosi* of the Qungebe people in south-western Zululand and *induna* of the iNdabakawombe *ibutho*, was an especial favourite of King Cetshwayo and a member of his council. His kwaSogekle *umuzi* was in the valley of the Batshe River just north-east of Rorke's Drift. A cross-border incident led by several of his sons in July 1878 had been seized upon by the British as one of their justifications for their invasion of the Zulu kingdom. On 12 January 1879, No. 3 Column destroyed kwaSogekle *umuzi* in the first action of the war.

9. H-B is referring to the extended bivouac of No. 3 Column along the Zulu bank of the Mzinyathi River on the night of 11–12 January.

together. We had some trouble in turning out the natives but it was done at last and we marched off, being ordered to take post in rear of the mounted advance guard, the sun rising as we crossed the ridge and advanced on the precipitous Krantz where Serhio had his stronghold.[10]

As we got nearer we could hear the lowing of cattle, the sound coming from a deep cleft running into the precipice. Just then the screen of mounted men moved away to the right and left and I received orders to advance to the front.

It may be as well here to say something about the arming of my motley gang. My officers and non-coms. were each armed with M.H. rifles[11] and each carried seventy rounds of ammunition. Fifty more M.H. rifles were distributed amongst the natives, but as they were quite ignorant of the use of rifles, and the M.H. is not a rifle to be played with by a duffer, we were ourselves in far greater danger of our own men than the enemy were. Fifty more old muzzle-loading rifles were provided but I did not fear these so much, as the natives usually forgot to tear off the end of the paper cartridge or placed it in ball part first, so that the rifle refused to go off. We certainly had no time to instruct them in musketry but as only five rounds, per man, was issued, I trusted, with luck, to get through the job without being shot by my own niggers.[12]

The rest of the force had shields, assagais and knobkerries and I made up my mind that the closer the action was the safer it would be for me. I therefore determined to charge the first moment I could. But alas! I did not know then, in what an awful funk the Natal Kafir was of the real fighting Zulu.

Anyhow the mounted men cleared my front and I pressed on, passing Lord Chelmsford and his staff who up to that time had accompanied the advance guard. The General returned my salute and calling me over to him said, "Commandant Browne, those Krantzes are full of cattle; go down and take them but on no account are you to fire before you are fired at." He also said, "I shall hold you responsible that no women or children are killed."

He then wished me luck in the most kind and courteous manner – a manner that endeared him to all of us. No General that I ever served under

---

10. A 'krantz', 'kraantz' or 'krans' is a rocky ridge or cliff. Sihayo's *umuzi* called kwaSogekle was at its base with defensible caves in the krans above.

11. Martini-Henry rifles.

12. About 300 breech-loading Martini-Henry rifles (either Mark I or Mark II), the standard British infantry weapon, were issued to the 3rd NNC, most of them being distributed to the 2nd Battalion. In addition, 205 obsolete percussion-cap, muzzle-loading Enfield rifles (introduced in 1853) were divided equally between the two battalions. They seem to have been given little, if any, practice in using these firearms, with the result that they were ineffectually handled in combat.

in South Africa, was so respected and liked as he was, and certainly, no Colonial officer ever said a word against him or blamed him for the awful disaster that came later on.

Well I got my men into line and advanced to the first fight in Zululand.[13] Previous to moving off I repeated the General's orders to my captains, at the same time telling them to impress on their men that any man who hurt a woman or a child would be shot at once. I then gave the order to advance, and we moved on to the Krantz in what might be called a line, but a very crooked one, as a South African native cannot walk in a line, draw a line, or form a line, and if placed in a line will soon mob himself into a ring.

The Krantz was a precipitous mountain about 500 feet high, and where the enemy and the cattle were located was in a deep cleft running in V shape, the foot of the hill being covered with boulders and bushes.

My men advanced leaping and jumping, singing war-songs, sharpening their assagais, and looking so bloodthirsty that I feared they would kill every woman and child we came across. But as we drew nearer the scene of action, their zeal for fighting—like Bob Acre's courage—oozed out of them.[14] Their war-songs dwindled away and they seemed indisposed to come on. In fact some of them suddenly remembering they had important business to transact towards the rear had to be encouraged with the butt of the rifle or the ready boot of my non-coms. As the native must be led, myself and all the officers were in front. This being the case, and we being far more in funk of our playful savages armed with M.H. rifles than of the enemy, I gave orders that there was to be no firing but that we must trust to the steel.

As we neared the place I observed I could send a party to the right and left of the V-shaped entrance. I therefore detached the two flank

13. Chelmsford, in his letter of 12 January to Sir Bartle Frere, described the skirmish as follows. 'I ordered Colonel Glyn with 4 Companies of 1/24th & 1/3d Native Contingent to work up under the Kraantz where some of Sirayo's strongholds were said to be in skirmishing order – On the approach of this force near the Kraantz, fire was opened upon them out of the caves [at 8.30 a.m.] for half an hour & ended in our obtaining possession of all the caves . . . Colonel Degacher [Lieutenant-Colonel Henry J. Degacher, CB (1835–1902), who commanded the 2/24th throughout 1879] who had been sent for from Camp when we found that the Kraantz was occupied by the enemy came up towards the end of the affair with ½ battn. 2/24th and about 400 2/3rd Native Contingent – This force went forward to Sirayo's own Kraal [kwaSogekle] which is situated under a very steep Kraantz which is filled with caves – The British soldiers & natives skirmished and entered all the caves which were found empty – I ordered Sirayo's Kraal to be burnt but none of the other huts were touched – The Native Contingent behaved very well & not a native touched a woman or child or killed a wounded man' (Laband, *Chelmsford's Zululand Campaign*, pp. 60–1).

14. Squire Bob Acres is a cowardly character in Richard Brinsley Sheridan's comedy *The Rivals* (1775).

companies, and when they had moved off to their assigned places I again advanced.

A voice hailed us asking by whose orders we came. My interpreter and right-hand man (Capt. R. Duncombe) answered "by the orders of the Great White Queen" and the enemy, or those of them who had exposed themselves, at once ran back to cover. I again ordered the advance; a few shots were fired at us, and I immediately gave the word to charge and led it, followed splendidly by No. 8 Company, commanded by Captains R. Duncombe and O. Murray.[15] A ragged volley was fired at us by the enemy, but we charged on through it and up the rising ground to the mouth of the V which we found to be full of boulders. I had gained the mouth when I looked back. Ye gods of war, what a sight for a commandant! No. 8 Company, led by two of the best Colonial officers I have ever met, were on my heels, but the rest. I saw their backs in a mad stampede while among them raged their furious officers and non-coms.

Above the rifle shots rang out their wild imprecations while with butt, fist and boot they tried to instil courage into that awful mob of cowardly Kafirs.

Now I must say a word about No. 8 Company. Among my 1200 men I had 300 real Zulus. They were the remains of a young Zulu regiment that had been destroyed by Cetewayo's orders the year before. He had ordered a fight to take place, with sticks, between them and his own royal regiment. The youngsters had beaten their seniors, and this so enraged the king that he turned Serhio's regiment, armed with shields and assagais, on to them who had decimated them. This was not cricket, as the boys had only their sticks, however some of them had escaped to Natal with Esikota, the king's youngest brother, and these 300 men were quite game to return and play another match, backed up by white men, with their destroyers. Their contempt for the Natal Kafir was unbounded, and they were splendid fighting men.[16] They formed three of my companies, Nos. 8, 9 and 10. No. 9 was in camp. No. 8 was with me and No. 10 was one of the companies I had sent to work round the enemy's flank.

15. Captain Orlando E. Murray, 2/3rd NNC. He was later killed in the battle of Isandlwana.

16. H-B's account of the iziGqoza contingent in the 3rd NNC is misleading. The true facts are that Sikhotha ('Esikota'), Mkhungo and Mbuyazi were sons of King Mpande and were full brothers. Their half-brother Cetshwayo was Mpande's heir presumptive, but Mpande favoured Mbuyazi to succeed him. Mbuyazi's supporters were known as the iziGqoza and Cetshwayo's rival faction as the uSuthu. The succession struggle was decided in 1856 at the battle of Ndondakusuka when Mbuyazi was defeated and killed. Mkhungo and Sikhotha took refuge in Natal with their surviving followers, the iziGqoza. The two brothers were educated at Bishop Colenso's school for the sons of chiefs. In 1879 these two Zulu princes, who represented a dynastic threat to Cetshwayo, were living in Weenen County, Natal. The iziGqoza, who were anxious to avenge themselves against King Cetshwayo, contributed 273 men to the 1/3rd NNC, making up three companies (Nos 8, 9 and 10) led by Sikhotha.

I left off, as our charge swept into the mouth of the V. Here the Zulus, who had up to this time been firing at us from under cover, met us and for a time we had a sweet hand-to-hand fight. Shield clashed against shield, assagai met assagai and the hissing word "Guzzie," as the stab went home, was answered by the grunt or yell of the wounded man. I had my hands full and had to use freely both sword and revolver. The enemy fought splendidly but my men would not be denied. Had not Serhio been the *induna* (chief) of the Impie who had killed their brothers, and would they not have their revenge?

My white officers and non-coms. also fought like fiends and we drove them back over the rocks and round the rocks until at last they took refuge in rear of the cattle jammed into the narrow end of the V. These had to be driven out before we could get at them again and it was done; also a lot of women and children were brought out. Thank the Lord none of them hurt, and they with the cattle were removed to the open. We now found that the enemy had retreated by a narrow path to the top of a cliff about 60 feet high and had blocked the path by rolling big boulders into it.

They opened fire on us, which although hot was very badly directed and my officers and non-coms. returned it with interest.

Just then Lieutenant Harford of the 99th Regiment, who was acting as S.O.[17] to Commandant Lonsdale, came up to me. He was a charming companion, one of the very best, but he was a crazy bug and beetle hunter, and would run about on the hottest day with a landing-net to catch butterflies and other insects. He moreover collected and treasured snakes, scorpions and loathsome beasts of all sorts.[18] He had never been under fire before and had on two or three occasions talked to me about a man's feelings while undergoing his baptism of fire, and had expressed hopes he would be cool and good while undergoing his. Well we were in

They held themselves aloof from the other African levies. Mkhungo did not accompany the iziGqoza to war and was represented by his son. Sikhotha was later present at the battle of Isandlwana. He escaped, but 54 of his men perished.

H-B is confusing the story of the iziGqoza with an incident that took place on 25 December 1877 at oNdini during the *umKhosi* festival. A fight broke out between the iNdluyengwe, a young *ibutho* incorporated with the uThulwane, and the youthful uVe who formed the vanguard of the iNgobamakhosi *ibutho*. King Cetshwayo was deeply angered by the fracas, but no refugees fled to Natal as a consequence. Nor was Sihayo, who was an *induna* of the iNdabakawombe *ibutho*, involved.

17. Staff Officer.

18. Henry Charles (Charlie) Harford (1850–1937) spent his adolescence in Natal where he learned to speak isiZulu. He was gazetted ensign in the 99th Regiment in 1870, and lieutenant in 1871. Keen to see action in Zululand, he proceeded on Transport Service to Natal. He landed in Durban in December 1878 and Lord Chelmsford immediately appointed him Adjutant to the 3rd NNC. He had a keen interest in zoology and entomology, and collected specimens avidly. For a full account of his life and career, see Laband, *Charlie Harford*, pp. 5–10, 12–15.

CHARGE AT SERHIO'S KRANTZ.

rather a hot corner and he was standing to my right rear when I heard an exclamation, and turning round saw him lying on the ground having dropped his sword and revolver. "Good God, Harford," I said, "you are hit!" "No, sir," he replied, "not hit but I have caught such a beauty." And there the lunatic, in his first action, and under a heavy fire, his qualms of nervousness all forgotten, had captured some infernal microbe or other, and was blowing its wings out, as unconscious of the bullets striking the rocks all round him as if he had been in his garden at home. He was just expatiating on his victory and reeling off Latin names—they might have been Hebrew for all I knew or cared—when I stopped him, and told him to get as quick as he could to the right flanking company and hurry them up. He looked at me with sorrow, put his prize into a tin box and was off like a shot.[19]

All this time my bold runaways had been absent, but now they returned in this manner.

There was in the second 24th a major (Wilson Black by name), and Commandant Lonsdale having been knocked over by sunstroke during the previous day, Major Black had been placed, for the time being, in full command of the 3rd N.N.C.

He was a Highlander, brave as his own sword, tender-hearted as a woman, hospitable as a Maori, but with a temper well, may I say it, just a little peppery. He had served through the Crimea and Mutiny with, I think, the Black Watch, and I had only met him the night before.[20]

Up to this time he had been with the 2nd Battalion of the 3rd, but when he saw the undignified retreat of the greater part of my men, he drew his sword, and quickly bringing forward a strong party of the 24th, with fixed bayonets, he rode right at them. They were now between the devil and the

19. It would seem that, to spin another good yarn, Hamiliton-Browne is combining Harford's collecting mania (which he and some of the other NNC officers evidently found a trifle absurd) with Harford's own admission in his memoir of the skirmish that he had thrown his jammed revolver away and that he had earlier lost his cumbersome sword in the thick bush. For Harford's full account of the skirmish, see Laband, *Charlie Harford*, pp. 45–52. Whatever the true facts, it is H-B's account of Harford's beetle-mania in the midst of battle that has been perpetuated, initially by Donald Morris in *The Washing of the Spears*, p. 325.

20. Major Wilsone Black (1833–1909), 2/24th Regiment, had seen service in the Crimean War, 1854–6, serving with the 42nd (The Royal Highland) Regiment of Foot (in 1881 renamed the 1st Battalion, The Black Watch [Royal Highlanders]). He then transferred to the 24th Regiment and fought in the Ninth Cape Frontier War, 1878. In 1879 he initially commanded the Lines of Communication, Greytown and Middle Drift, and was then attached to Chelmsford's personal staff. On 9 January 1879 Commandant Lonsdale was badly concussed – he was not a victim of sunstroke – when his pony threw him (see Harford's detailed description of the incident in Laband, *Charlie Harford*, p. 39; and the report dated 13 January 1879 by the Special Correspondent, *Natal Mercury*, 20 January 1879) and the following day Major Black was appointed to the temporary command of the 3rd NNC until Lonsdale was sufficiently recovered to return to duty on 20 January.

deep sea. They were already catching toko badly from their own white officers and non-coms.,[21] and as if that was not enough here comes a man on horseback followed by a lot of those red soldiers, who with flashing steel, were rushing right at them. It was too much. They had to turn back and with their officers trying to get them into some sort of shape they were driven at the point of the bayonet back to me. When they arrived Black burst through them and joined me. At once they halted. Forward they would not come, back they could not go, for there was that awful line of the red soldiers with fixed bayonets, and among them raged their own white men. So they did just what I expected they would do; every man of them who had a gun let it off, quite regardless as to the direction the business end pointed, and they fired away as fast as they could load.

In vain their officers ordered them to cease fire, in vain their non-coms. kicked and cuffed them; fire they would and fire they did so long as they had a cartridge left.

Well that was a very sultry spot indeed for the time being but there is an end to most things in this world and, thank the Lord, their fire-play soon ended.

Some of them rammed their cartridges down bullet first so they became harmless as their rifles refused to go off, and as it does not take a raw savage long to let off five rounds of M.H. ammunition when he aims at nothing the firing died away and we were again able to pay attention to the Zulus. We also counted our dead and wounded and I found that my beauties had bagged thirty-two of themselves, but I could well spare them.[22]

I do not believe that the enemy were responsible for a single one, their fire having been kept down by my officers who perforated every head that was raised to fire at us, so the firing ceased. Yet we were at the base of a 60-foot perpendicular cliff and could not get at them and I saw at once that we must wait for the flanking companies to work round. They were having a hard job getting at the spot on account of the roughness of the ground but there was nothing else to do.

Major Black thought otherwise. How he expected to scale the cliff I know not, but he got to the foot of it and shouted for rifles to come on. He was standing with his back turned to the rock and was waving his sword when the Zulus hearing him rolled over some stones; one struck the gallant Major on the—well, not on the head—and he fell on his knees and poured out a volume of Gaelic that filled my non-coms. with delight.

21. To 'catch toko' is nineteenth-century slang for receiving a thrashing.

22. In giving these figures, H-B again reveals his deep prejudice against the men he commanded. The official casualty returns for the skirmish in fact listed three black NNC soldiers killed and twelve wounded, along with the wounded Corporal Meyer and Lieutenant J. Purvis of the 1/3rd NNC.

It might have been prayers he was letting go, but the volubility and unctuousness forbid that idea, and they all thought, though they could not understand one word of his orison, that he was using very bad language indeed and all the more they admired him.

A few minutes before Colonel Glyn and Major Cleary had come up and were standing by me.[23] We were unable to restrain our laughter and burst into a roar as Black limped up to us cursing, in good Anglo-Saxon, the Zulus for wounding a gentleman in a place he could not show to anyone but the doctor.

However he was not much hurt and soon recovering his temper joined in the laugh.

The flanking companies had by this time worked round and Lieutenant Harford who had joined one of them shouted to the Zulus that if they surrendered they would not be killed.

This they did, and the fighting, as far as I was concerned, was over for that day.

The mounted men who had gone to the top of the hill had a sharp skirmish with a large party of the enemy, these being joined by the Zulus who had escaped from me. But they were easily routed, the troopers pursuing some distance and killing a good few.[24]

Leaving one company behind me to collect our own wounded, I joined the main command with the rest of my men and we returned to camp for the night. Serhio had been well punished, his big kraal had been burned, two of his sons were among the dead, some of his daughters among the prisoners, and his pet herd of cattle had been captured.

If you wish to know the cause of the war I must refer you to Blue Books for the information.[25] It was no business of mine and my opinion was not asked on the question.

Next day (the 12th) we rested in camp, and my natives asked for an ox, to medicine themselves with. This I gave them hoping the ceremony

23. Major Cornelius Francis Clery (1838–1926), 32nd (Cornwall) Light Infantry. He was Instructor of Tactics at the Royal Military College, Sandhurst, 1871, and Professor, 1872–5. In 1875–7 he was DAQMG on the HQ Staff, Dublin, and then at Aldershot, 1877–8. In 1878, as a Special Staff Officer, he served briefly in the Northern War in Griqualand West, and in the First Anglo-Pedi War. In 1879 he joined No. 3 Column as Principal Staff Officer to Colonel Glyn.

24. During the skirmish in which H-B was engaged, Chelmsford ordered the mounted men of No. 3 Column to swing around in support to the high ground to the north above kwaSogekle. As they neared the top, they were fired on by about sixty of Sihayo's men from about a hundred yards away. The Mounted Infantry and NMP dismounted and commenced a frontal attack, while the Natal Mounted Volunteers moved out to the right to attack the Zulu left flank and eventually drove the amaZulu back over the side of the mountain. Chelmsford estimated that during the day's fighting the amaZulu lost about thirty men.

25. The 'Blue Books' are the *British Parliamentary Papers*, the printed collections of official correspondence presented to both Houses of Parliament

might instil some courage into them, as they swore it would, but I had no idea of the diabolical cruelty they were going to practise on the poor beast or I would have seen them in Hades first. Anyway, something must have gone wrong with the performance as their courage did not increase but rather diminished. However I will not touch on the subject of Kafir witchcraft, but pass on.[26]

During the day the General visited my camp and kindly thanked me for the work of the day before. He also requested me to present to him Captains Duncombe and Murray.

The same evening I received orders to strike camp, and at daylight to move out to the scene of the late fight, and camp there with the object of making a road over a swamp, so as to allow the heavy wagons to advance.

We moved out and camped, but when it came to road-making trouble began.[27]

The Colonial officers turned sulky. They had come out to fight not to make roads.[28] None of the natives had ever used pick or spade before, and it took me all my time to get them turned to. Certainly it is not a pleasant job to make roads in Zululand during the summer-time, the sun hot, flies bad, and men sulky. The Colonial officers were not at their best, and men who would willingly stand up to their middles all day long in the drift of a river plugging oxen over, grumbled and swore. It required no small amount of tact to get them started, but when they saw me off shirt and turn to, they could not hang back and once started we soon made things hum and the road grew apace.

In this manner things went on till the 19th of January. On that morning I was visited by the General and his staff. He informed me that news had been received that the Zulu army was to leave Ulundi that morning to attack us,[29] and ordered, in case he was attacked, I was to move down and

26. The men of the NNC wished to sacrifice an ox to the shades of the ancestors, or *amadlozi* (sing. *idlozi*), and would have stabbed it to death slowly so that its agonised bellowing would alert the ancestral spirits to the ceremony. Strips of the beast's flesh, smeared with *imithi*, would have played their part in the ritual for 'strengthening' the men for war.

27. On 14 January four companies of the 2/24th, the 1/3rd NNC and some NNPC encamped in the Batshe valley some four miles from Rorke's Drift and stayed there until 20 January. Working parties laboured at making the track passable for the convoys of wagons bringing up supplies.

28. As the *Times of Natal* correspondent (Charles Norris-Newman) reported on 20 January (*Natal Mercury*, 28 January 1879), many of the 1/3rd NNC officers harboured a number of 'so-called grievances, as to work, and rations . . . and threats of resignation have been rife'.

29. Nowhere else do we find that on 19 January Chelmsford had intelligence that the Zulu army was on the march, having set out from the kwaNodwengu *ikhanda* on 17 January. Indeed, on 19 January he wrote to Colonel Anthony Durnford, the commander of No. 2 Column, that his immediate intention was 'to operate against the two Matyanas', that is, against Matshana kaMondisa, the Sithole *inkosi*, who lived in the Qudeni bush south-east

attack the right flank of the enemy. I suggested that as I lay in their road, they would eat me up long before they reached him. He thought not, but I requested the chief of the staff to allow me to take my men off work and laager my camp.

This he refused, but as soon as the staff left I altered the position of my wagons, told off my white men to their respective posts and made what preparations I could in case of a fight. I took no precautions, for my natives, with the exception of the Zulu companies,[30] as I knew that the Natal Kafir would bolt at the first onset.[31]

That afternoon I received a note from Captain Duncombe who was in command of the picket on the top of the hill, informing me that there was a large number of cattle in the valleys on his right, and requesting me to come up at once. This I did, taking with me two companies of my Zulus,[32] the other one being on picket with him. On joining him on the top of the pass we moved carefully to the edge of some very rough ground consisting of deep valleys, and on looking into these we saw a large number of cattle herded by a few unarmed Zulus, who called to us to come down, as they wished to surrender themselves and the cattle. This was a temptation, a very nice bait indeed, but I saw through it. I had matriculated in ambush work in New Zealand,[33] had had more than my share of it and with all my faults I have never been deemed a greedy or covetous man, so directed Captain Duncombe to shout to them ordering them to come up and surrender on the top, but this they refused to do. Captain Duncombe then at my request called Umvubie,[34] the head fighting *induna* (chief) of my Zulus and asked him what he thought of it. He at once replied, "That is a trap, those bushes are full of Zulus. If we descend they will kill every one of us, but we shall have a good fight first. I and my brothers are ready to descend with the chief."

---

of the British camp, and Matshana kaSitshakuza, the Mchunu *inkosi*, who dwelt in the valley of the Mzinyathi River nearby. Both posed the danger of a potential flank attack on No. 3 column when it resumed its march on oNdini (Laband, *Chelmsford's Zululand Campaign*, p. 73).

30. The iziGqoza companies.

31. In his newspaper report of 20 January, Norris-Newman wrote that the situation of the rough encampment of the 1/3rd NNC under H-B beyond the Batshe River 'is not only a regular swamp, but is also in a very exposed position'.

32. That is, two companies of iziGqoza.

33. In fact, having served in New Zealand only for a short time with the peacetime Armed Constabulary, it is doubtful whether H-B had previously ever been involved in such operations.

34. H-B makes frequent reference to Mvubi (see p. 10, n. 2, above) during operations in January 1879, but it is impossible to determine whether he was a real individual or a stock character deployed to represent the martial spirit of the three companies of iziGqoza in the 1/3rd NNC.

Now this was startling. I had no doubt that what Umvubie stated was true, and if so a large body of the enemy—how large I knew not—must be on the General's right flank.

I immediately sent off a runner to the H.Q. camp, with a note to that effect, and, as it was approaching sunset, retired to my camp, leaving Captain Duncombe with a few good men (well hidden) to keep watch for any moves they (the Zulus) might carry on.

The Zulus, seeing I had retired, came out of their ambush, some 1500 strong, and started towards a large military kraal which we knew to be several miles down the river. I partook of early coffee at that kraal later on.[35]

Seeing they left the cattle behind, Duncombe and his men, as soon as they lost sight of the enemy, descended into the valley, captured some 150 head of them and brought them into my camp.

On reaching my camp I found Major Black had arrived, bringing with him two companies of the second 24th. I reported to him what I had seen and Captain Duncombe coming in shortly afterwards, Major Black at once sent a report into the H.Q. camp.

The night passed quietly, but my natives were very restless and evidently in a great funk.[36]

Next morning Captain Hallam Parr, one of the staff,[37] came out with orders to Major Black and myself that we were to get ready to march as the whole column was to move forward, so we struck camp and packed wagons. On the General reaching us, he questioned myself and Duncombe as to what we had seen and we reported fully. This interview being over, I was ordered by the C.S.O. to move my men on and clear the road, a

35. No such *ikhanda* is known to have been situated in the vicinity or to have been occupied by the British.

36. This entire episode on 19 January as recounted by H-B is problematic. For one thing, as late as 21 January Chelmsford was consistently reporting that patrols were finding the countryside quite deserted with no sign of the amaZulu or of their cattle. True, Norris-Newman, reporting on 20 January from the 'Bashee River Camp', stated that: 'Rumours have been rife since yesterday that we are to have a night attack upon us by a large Zulu Impi under Usirajo [Sihayo], and therefore . . . small entrenchments are being erected just outside the exposed parts of the camp.' However, there is no hint in his account that this false alarm was the consequence of a report by H-B on Captain Duncombe's supposed encounter with a Zulu force. Tantalisingly, Norris-Newman went on to report that on 20 January, the day No. 3 Column advanced to Isandlwana, a company of the 1/3rd NNC was despatched to some *imizi* nearby where guns and cattle were confiscated from the occupants, all old men, women and children, adherents of Gamdana kaXongo, a brother of Sihayo, who had surrendered the previous day. Was this raid the germ of H-B's yarn about Captain Duncombe's exploits on 19 January?

37. Captain Henry Hallam Parr (1847–1914), 13th (1st Somersetshire Prince Albert's Light Infantry) Regiment, had since 1877 been Sir Bartle Frere's Military Secretary. Frere gave him permission in January 1879 to join Colonel Glyn's staff.

rough wagon track over the pass, of any boulders and stones that might be lying on it and was to be supported by a party of the second 24th, under Lieutenant Pope.[38]

Away we went and after a few miles came to a queer-shaped mountain that looked like a sphinx lying down,[39] by the same token I have never seen the beast depicted standing up, anyhow the road ran between this mountain and a kopje when we at once came out on a big plain.

I had just reached here when Major Cleary [Clery] rode up, who directed me to move to my left so as to be ready to encamp, he riding with me, and pointing out the ground on which my camp was to be pitched, which would be on the extreme left of the line.[40]

The column came up, and the camp was arranged in the same form as it had been on the bank of the river, only it was much more extended. As soon as the tents were pitched, and we had had some food, I was joined by Commandant Lonsdale, who had that day come out of hospital. I was talking to some of my best officers when he joined us and his first words to me were, "My God, Maori, what do you think of this camp?" I replied, "Some one is mad." The Colonial officers were loud and long in complaint, and Duncombe said, "Do the staff think we are going to meet an army of school-girls? Why in the name of all that is holy do we not laager?"[41]

38. Lieutenant Charles D'Aguilar Pope (1849–79), 2/24th Regiment, served in the Ninth Cape Frontier War in February–August 1878 and was present at kwaSogekle on 12 January. He commanded G Company at Isandlwana, and was killed in the battle.

39. The mountain was Isandlwana, and ironically resembled the Sphinx, which was portrayed on the badge of the 24th Regiment, so many of whose members perished at its base on 22 January. The amaZulu perceived the mountain differently, and in isiZulu the name means 'something like a small house or hut'.

40. The camp extended along a line parallel to Isandlwana, some 200 yards from the base of the mountain and 200–300 yards from a donga which ran off to the south-east in front. The camp consisted of a series of smaller camps with the infantry battalions, the artillery battery and the mounted force (the Natal Mounted Volunteers, the Mounted Infantry and the NMP) each having their own. Ordinarily, the NNC camp would have been placed 'downstream' at the southern end of the line because of what the British considered their incurably insanitary habits. But that was where the track back to Rorke's Drift crossed a low rise of ground, the 'saddle', or 'neck' between Isandlwana and a stony knoll to its south. Since the line of communication had to be secured, the camp of the 1/24th was pitched there, and it was believed that the northern end of the camp where the NNC were placed (the 2/3rd NNC at the northernmost extremity with the 1/3rd NNC to their right) was less likely to be attacked. The men of the NNC began building shelters for themselves from wood found nearby.

41. Despite standing field regulations, the camp was secured neither by a laager of wagons nor by a shelter trench because Chelmsford and his over-confident staff did not think that necessary since they intended to resume the advance at once, and the camp was only a temporary one.

In the evening I strolled over to the 24th lines to have a chat with the officers, all of whom I knew well.[42] Whilst there, I had a yarn with Colonel Glyn who was acting as Brigadier-General, and would have had command of the column had not the General and staff decided to join us at the last moment. He was a very old friend of my family's and had served as a Lieutenant under my father.[43] He did not seem to be in good spirits, but said nothing about the camp and on my remarking it looked very pretty though rather extended, he looked hard at me, shook his head and said "Very."

That night Lonsdale came to my tent and told me that myself and Cooper were each to parade eight companies before daylight, and to clear the rough broken valleys to our right front. He would take command, and that Major Dartnell,[44] with the Natal Mounted Police and volunteers were to act in concert with us, keeping on the high ground.[45] I inquired if any orders had been given to laager the camp. He answered "No," adding language not very complimentary to certain members of the staff, which I fully endorsed.

42. By this stage, after serving alongside many of them in the Transkei during in the Ninth Cape Frontier War, H-B would have been on friendly terms with officers of the 24th Regiment.

43. Glyn was commander of No. 3 Column, but his authority was effectively dimmed by Chelmsford's decision to accompany the column with his Headquarters Staff. The assertion that Glyn served under H-B's father, Major (retired) George Browne, is another of his fabrications. Glyn was commissioned by purchase in 1850 in the 82nd Regiment (The Prince of Wales's Volunteers), and served with it until 1867 when he purchased the lieutenant-colonelcy of the 1/24th Regiment. Major Browne was commissioned by purchase first in the 36th (Herefordshire) Regiment and then in the 44th (East Essex) Regiment.

44. Brevet Major John George Dartnell (1837–1913) retired from the 27th (Inniskilling) Regiment by sale of commission in 1869. He had seen service in the Indian Mutiny, 1857–9, and in the Anglo-Bhutan (Duar) War, 1865. In 1874 he was appointed Commandant of the NMP and Inspector of Volunteer Forces, Natal. He was Commandant of Natal Colonial Defensive District No. 1 from December 1878 to July 1879. He was with No. 3 Column on Chelmsford's Headquarters Staff as commander of the NMP and the Natal Mounted Volunteers.

45. A hundred NMP and half (fifty troopers) of the Natal Mounted Volunteers under Dartnell were to move out ahead of Lonsdale and sixteen companies of the 3rd NNC (1,600 men) at 4.30 a.m. on 21 January. Their mission was a reconnaissance in force to the south-east where Lord Chelmsford had been led to believe by his scouts that Matshana kaMondisa was gathering a force in the region of the Qudeni bush and Mangeni River to interrupt No. 3 Column's line of supply once that column advanced further into Zululand.

Chapter XI

Coming Events Throw Shadows
Before Them

BEFORE daylight we moved out of camp, and while doing so I saw and spoke to Lieut.-Col. Pulleine of the first 24th. We were old friends, and he chaffed me, saying, "A lot of you nigger leaders will be knocked over to-day." I answered, "If that is so, when I return to camp I shall not find one of you alive." We laughed and parted. Which prophecy was to come right you shall hear.[1]

At the head of my men I crossed a donga to join up with Lonsdale who was with the 2nd battalion, and on doing so he instructed me to make a detour of a hill and descend into some valleys, he working round the other side in such a manner so as to catch anything or any one who might be between us.[2]

This movement was carried out and we captured some hundreds of head of cattle, though all the kraals we passed contained only old men, women, girls and children.

To a girl, I returned some goats which one of my men had taken from her and, through Duncombe, questioned her as to the movements of all the men. She replied, "That they had been ordered to join the King's big army." We again asked "where that was." She pointed with her chin over to the N.E., at the same time saying, "They would attack us in two days' time." This bore out the opinion I had formed, after hearing the news on the 19th that the army had left Ulundi.

In our next drive I captured two young men and questioned them. They had no goats to be given back to them, but there are more ways than one of extracting information.

---

1. Are we to take this morbid banter, made tragically prescient in hindsight, with a grain of salt?

2. The two NNC battalions advanced in skirmishing order up the valley of the Ndweni River and swung to their right up the flat-topped Malakatha Mountain. The 1/3rd NNC moved along the top of the mountain while the 2/3rd NNC advanced in parallel along the difficult terrain of Malakatha's northern, western and southern slopes. They joined up again at noon to the east of Malakatha to rest and eat.

They were led apart and well questioned. War is war and you can't play at savage war with kid gloves on. The information amounted to this. They had both left the big army and had come over to see their mother. We inquired, "Where is the big army?" They pointed in the same direction as the girl had done. "When was the attack to take place?" They did not know, but the moon would be right in two days' time.

This information tallied with the girl's and Lonsdale, Cooper and myself discussed it.[3]

The day wore on. The valleys became as hot as furnaces. We captured more cattle. So towards evening we left the low country after the most trying day and made for the high land.[4]

On reaching it, I at once suggested we should return to the camp and inform the General of what we had learned. This was decided on and as we were then seven miles from camp Captain O. Murray was immediately dispatched, with two companies, to drive the captured cattle there.[5] The remainder of us rested; as the white non-coms., most of whom were on foot, were very tired after their rough day's work in the stony, rugged valleys.

Poor Murray! I never saw him again. He was one of the very best stamp of Colonials, brave, loyal and true, always ready for hard work, a splendid shot and horseman. I know before he went down in the awful hell of the 22nd that he did his duty to the last, and that very many of the enemy fell to his rifle.

Evening was drawing on. We had fallen in and were preparing to return to camp when two mounted men rode up, informing us that Major Dartnell had sent them to find us, and to ask us to come and support him as he had 300 Zulus in front of him, the ground in rear of the enemy being so rough, he was unable to use his horses to advantage.

I requested Lonsdale not to think of doing such a thing, pointing out at the same time that we had no food or reserve ammunition, also that we were seven miles from camp, our white men worn out and that it would be night before we could reach Dartnell, who was over three miles from us and at least that distance further away from camp than we were.

3. The advancing Zulu army had bivouacked the night of 20 January at Siphezi mountain, only some ten miles north-east of H-B's position. To avoid detection by British mounted patrols, during the evening of 21 January it would begin moving west in small groups to the Ngwebeni valley north-east of the British camp at Isandlwana which it intended to attack. It is therefore more than likely that H-B extracted the intelligence he records from the captive Zulu girl and two young men.

4. After their midday meal, the two battalions continued their sweep of Malakatha and then proceeded east up Hlazakazi Mountain, reaching its eastern end by late afternoon.

5. Several hundred captured cattle were sent back to the camp at Isandlwana, escorted by one company (not two) under Captain Orlando E. Murray, 2/3rd NNC, who thus had the misfortune to be caught in the battle the next day and killed.

Again was not this party of Zulus the advance guard of the big army? a trap to catch us or a small party of men on their way to join the big army who would clear out directly they saw Dartnell reinforced.

Duncombe who was asked to give an opinion fully agreed with me, but Lonsdale, who had not got over his sunstroke,[6] was simply spoiling for a fight, so orders were given for us to advance, and away we went.

I regret to say that as we moved off four of my officers left me without leave and returned to camp. Their punishment came quickly, they were all killed next day.[7]

Well on we went till we came to an open valley and saw the mounted men drawn up at one end of it, while at the other end were from 200 to 300 Zulus with very rough ground just in their rear and at this moment the sun set.

I again pointed out to Lonsdale the folly of our joining the mounted men. If it was a trap and we descended, our men, or rather our white men who had been on foot all day were too much exhausted to put up a good fight.

If it was not a trap, the enemy would never stand and allow about 1400 more men to join the mounted forces but would fall back into the rough ground where it would be impossible to follow them in the dark.

However Lonsdale decided to descend, so down we went. As we advanced, the Zulus drew off into the rough ground and the night fell.[8] There is no twilight in Zululand.

Here we were at least eleven miles from camp, no food, no spare ammunition, well knowing that a huge army of Zulus must be in our close vicinity. Well I was not in command, but I begged Lonsdale even at that hour to return to camp. I said, "We know the camp is going to be attacked, every cock fights best in his own yard. When the General hears our news he will order the camp to be laagered and we can put up a fight there against the whole Zulu nation, whilst out here we shall be stamped flat in a minute." But no, Lonsdale would not grasp the situation, and decided to stay where we were, with the intention of going for those few Zulus in the morning.[9]

6. Lonsdale had in fact been concussed. See p. 94, n. 20, above.

7. Two, not four, officers absconded without leave. They were Samuel Avery and Frank Holcroft, both lieutenants in the 1/3rd NNC, and both perished at Isandlwana.

8. The 3rd NNC was supposed to rendezvous with Dartnell's mounted force at the eastern end of Hlazakazi before returning to the camp at Isandlwana. During the afternoon some 2,000 amaZulu under Matshana had skilfully retired eastwards before them, and by late afternoon were massed on the Magogo heights, 2½ miles north-east of Hlazakazi. When Dartnell attempted to approach them from the valley of the Mangeni River below, the amaZulu proficiently deployed into two horns in skirmishing order, and the mounted men had to withdraw to avoid being enveloped.

9. We cannot know if H-B's conviction that the Zulu army was going to attack the camp at Isandlwana was really expressed to Lonsdale at the time, or whether his words were written

Major Dartnell concurred with him. They decided to form two squares, our men in one, Dartnell's in another, and we were to bivouac there for the night.[10]

My Colonial officers were furious. Colonial officers are given to speaking their minds. Even Captain Duncombe came to me and asked me if everyone had gone mad. "What in God's name are we to do here?"

The squares were formed.[11] We had in our square about 1400 natives armed as I have before mentioned, with their complement of white officers and non-coms., but few of the officers had brought their rifles, and very many cartridges had been lost while scrambling over the rocks and rough ground during the day. I of course disarmed the natives, who had M.H. rifles, and gave them to the officers but the ammunition was very short.

The natives were made to sit down in a square, two deep, the white men being inside. Ye Gods of war! as if Natal Kafirs in a formation two deep would stand for a moment against a rush of Zulus. Sick with disgust, as soon as the square was formed, I lay down and, strange to say, fell asleep. I had loosened my revolver belt for a minute, meaning to buckle it again, but went to sleep without having done so. I do not know how long I slept when I felt myself rushed over and trampled on. I tried to get to my feet, but was knocked down again. I then tried to find my revolver, but was unable to do so. I never let go of my horse's bridle which I was holding in my hand, and at last staggered to my feet.

The square was broken,[12] natives rushing all ways mixed up with plunging horses, while the night was horrible with yells, shouts and imprecations. "My God," I thought, "why am I not assagaied?" as half-mad natives rushed by me jostling me with their shields. In a flash I saw it was a false alarm. To wrench a knobkerry out of a native's hand, and to

------

with hindsight. Either way, they express his oft-voiced contempt of the ineptitude of those in command.

10. Evening was approaching, and to forestall an advance by Matshana's force towards Isandlwana, Dartnell and Lonsdale decided to bivouac in a single hollow square (not two squares) for the night on the eastern eminence of the Hlazakazi heights, westwards across the valley from Magogo and the Zulu watch-fires. Dartnell sent back two ADCs of Chelmsford's personal staff to report to the General at Isandlwana. There was nothing in their report to alarm Chelmsford. All he did was to order Lieutenant Henry Walsh, 1/13th Light Infantry, who had served with the Mounted Infantry in the First Anglo-Pedi War of 1878 and who commanded a troop of No. 1 Squadron through 1879, to proceed with a detachment of Mounted Infantry to Dartnell's bivouac with provisions. Walsh carried Chelmsford's orders that Dartnell should attack the amaZulu on Magogo when he thought fit.

11. Harford, as Lonsdale's Adjutant, oversaw the posting of four companies of the 3rd NNC as outposts surrounding the bivouac, while Lonsdale and Cooper formed the remainder of the NNC along three sides of the square. Dartnell's mounted men formed the fourth side.

12. It seems that No. 1 Company, 1/3rd NNC, at one of the corners of the square, first gave way and fled, initiating the stampede.

lay about me, was the work of a moment. My white men fought their way to my shout and backing me up splendidly we soon quelled the uproar and thrashed the cowardly brutes back to their places.

To pick up my revolver and buckle the belt did not take long, and then it was time to inquire the cause of the row. It seems that one of the natives had gone to sleep and had dropped his shield and assagais, and this was enough to frighten the bold Natal Kafirs into a stampede.

Yet with *these curs* I was expected to stop a rush of the finest fighting savages in the world!

As soon as I met Lonsdale I again urged him to return to camp even at this hour, and perhaps he might have done so, when Major Dartnell came over to us and informed us that he had sent an orderly back to camp to request the General to reinforce us.[13] This would be worse and worse, with a force of men barely strong enough to meet 30,000 to 40,000 Zulus, even when in laager. It certainly was not the game to break up that force into two parts at a distance of quite eleven miles and just before a big fight was expected to take place.[14]

Again I sat down, sick to the very heart, but of course I could say no more. Lonsdale was my chief, and it was my duty to loyally back him up and obey his orders.

About an hour afterwards, one of the horses shook himself, and immediately the cowardly hounds of Natal Kafirs again stampeded, but

13. In fact, rather than an orderly, Dartnell sent Lieutenant Walsh (who had only just returned from Isandlwana with Chelmsford's orders) back to the General to request reinforcements. Major Clery received Dartnell's note from Walsh at 1.30 a.m. and woke Chelmsford up. The General believed that Dartnell's message confirmed that the main Zulu army was pushing down the Mangeni valley and threatened to invade Natal downstream of Rorke's Drift. He swiftly decided that he would move out immediately with half the force still encamped at Isandlwana, not simply to reinforce Dartnell as requested, but to intercept the Zulu army and force on the decisive battle he had always sought, and which he was confident he would win. He accordingly ordered Colonel Glyn to be ready to march out at daybreak at 4.30 a.m. with a flying column accompanied by no wagons, consisting of about half the force encamped at Isandlwana: four out of the six 7-pounder guns of N/5 Battery, RA, six companies of the 2/24th Regiment in light marching order, a detachment of No. 1 Squadron Mounted Infantry and men of No. 1 Company, NNPC. Chelmsford and his staff were to accompany the flying column.

Their departure would leave the camp with its stores, oxen and wagons under the protection of a reduced garrison consisting of a division of two 7-pounder guns, five companies of the 1/24th Regiment and one of the 2/24th, the balance of the mounted troops not already deployed, two companies each from the 1/3rd NNC and the 2/3rd NNC and small details from other units. Chelmsford put Lieutenant-Colonel Pulleine in command of the defence of the camp.

14. It is not inconceivable that H-B saw the folly of Chelmsford dividing his force in the face of the enemy, and that was certainly the burden thereafter of the widespread criticism of the General's conduct of the Isandlwana campaign. But the likelihood is that in his account H-B is employing hindsight to express misgivings he did not necessarily harbour at the time.

we were ready for them this time, and thrashed them back to their places. I then informed them that the next man who moved would be at once shot and that the two Zulu companies should charge and kill off the company to which the delinquent belonged. This threat put the fear of the Lord into them, and for the rest of the night they sat tight.

The weary night dragged on, no chance of sleep, no chance of rest, as we had to watch our wretched niggers, and I was very pleased to see the east lighten and grow pale.

Chapter XII

The Day of Isandlwana

JUST after daybreak, to my unbounded surprise, the General, staff, four guns, the Mounted Infantry and I think six companies of the second 24th reached us.[1] Colonel Glyn rode over to me and drawing me aside said, "In God's name, Maori, what are you doing here?" I answered him with a question, "In God's name, sir, what are you doing here?"

He shook his head and replied, "I am not in command." And fine old soldier as he was, I could see he was much disturbed.

As we were speaking, I received orders to get my men into line and advance into the rough ground, into which the enemy had retreated the night before. We were now going further away from the camp; but orders must be obeyed, so getting my crowd under way, we advanced.

After moving forwards about two miles I found a party of the enemy in caves and behind a good cover of rocks and stunted bush. They appeared to be well supplied with firearms, and opened out on us, making fairly good practice.[2]

1. Chelmsford and Glyn's flying column reached Hlazakazi at about 6.30 a.m. As in any fluid military situation, the precise moments when events took place on 22 January are difficult to fix. Participants subsequently differed in their estimations or failed to take specific notice of the time. Chris Peers, *Rorke's Drift and Isandlwana*, pp. 27–95, 107–9, 114, 117, 123, 125 and 129, has recently attempted to create a detailed timetable, but in the footnotes below I have made a number of adjustments to it based on my own reading of the evidence and on other factors such as the time of sunset that day.

2. The amaZulu on Magogo had broken away by 9.00 a.m., some withdrawing south-east to the Phindo heights where Matshana had his stronghold, and others north to Silutshana mountain. Their strategic intention is still a matter of debate, but it seems both groups planned to pull back to Siphezi mountain, drawing the British forces on Hlazakazi after them, away from the camp at Isandlwana which the main Zulu army was going to attack.

Chelmsford took Matshana's bait, and his forces in the field were dissipated during 22 January as they were drawn further eastwards. At 9.15 a.m. he ordered the 3rd NNC to advance in skirmishing order north-east from Hlazakazi to take Silulwane hill to the west of Magogo while Dartnell's mounted men advanced up the Mangeni valley towards the Phindo ridge with its dense bush and cliffside caves. There Dartnell became involved in a heavy skirmish with Matshana's men. The 2/3rd NNC moved forward to give assistance while the 1/3rd NNC under H-B's command remained on Silulwane in support.

I was just going to try to kick a charge out of my beauties, when a mounted orderly rode up with orders for me,[3] which were that I was at once to report myself with my battalion to the General, and that he was to guide me to the place where the General was waiting for me.

Getting my men together and advising Lonsdale of my orders, I requested him to take over my skirmish,[4] and on his relieving me with the 2nd battalion I moved down a valley and found the General and staff quietly at breakfast.[5]

Never shall I forget the sight of that peaceful picnic. Here were the staff quietly breakfasting and the whole command scattered over the country! Over there the guns unlimbered, over the hills parties of Mounted Infantry and volunteers looting the scattered kraals for grain for their horses, a company of the 24th one place, and another far away, and yet I knew that an army of from 30,000 to 40,000 of the bravest and most mobile savages in the world were within striking distance of us,[6] and that our camp was some thirteen miles away; left with but few horsemen and only two guns to defend, and it a long straggling camp, hampered with all the wagons and impedimenta of the column.

As soon as I halted my men, the General rose and kindly greeting me asked me if I had had any breakfast. I replied, "No, nor had any of my men had any." I might have added "and no dinner or supper the night before." Of course he understood, that as commandant, I could not eat in presence of my fasting men.

I said, "Are you aware, sir, I was engaged when I received your order?" He said "No," and turning to the C.S.O.,[7] said, "Crealock, Browne tells me he was engaged when he received the order to come here." Colonel Crealock came to me and said, "Commandant Browne, I want you to return at once to camp and assist Colonel Pulleine *to strike camp and*

Meanwhile, Glyn and his flying column were ordered to clear the area around Silutshana where some Zulu forces had withdrawn north from Magogo, and then to wheel south to the rear of Dartnell's operations, sweeping along the Nondweni River valley between Magogo and the Phindo heights.

3. Chelmsford's messenger located H-B at about 9.45 a.m.

4. H-B cannot resist pushing himself to the forefront. Rather than the 2/3rd NNC taking over his skirmish, it was they who had been engaged on the Phindo heights while H-B's 1/3rd NNC had been kept in support on Silulwane (see n. 1, opposite).

5. H-B reported to Chelmsford soon after 10.00 a.m.

6. These numbers are exaggerated. Nearly 20,000 amaZulu assaulted the camp at Isandlwana, while an uncommitted reserve of between 3,000 and 4,000 went on to attack Rorke's Drift.

7. The 'C.S.O.' (Chief Staff Officer) H-B is referring to was Brevet Lieutenant-Colonel John Hope Crealock (1837–95), 95th (Derbyshire) Regiment. He had served in the Indian Mutiny, 1857–8, and in the Ninth Cape Frontier War, 1878. In 1879 he was a member of Chelmsford's personal staff and his Assistant Military Secretary.

come on here."[8] I nearly fell off my horse. Could these men know of the close proximity of the enemy? Were we all mad or what? However I was only a poor devil of a Colonial Commandant and as a simple irregular not supposed to criticise full-blown staff officers, so I saluted and said, "If I come across the enemy?" Oh," said he, "just brush them aside and go on," and with this he went on with his breakfast.[9]

So I kept on down that valley which presently opened out into a big plain, and on the far side of it, about thirteen miles off, was a queer-shaped mountain, the ground gently rising to the base of it. With my glasses I could discern a long white line which I knew to be tents. The name of that mountain was Isandlwana and the time was then 9 a.m. on the 22nd January 1879.

We marched very slowly on, the day was intensely hot, and my white non-coms. who were on foot very fagged. They had had a very hard day the day before. They had had no sleep and no food, and somehow over the whole command there seemed to hover a black cloud.

However push on was the word, and at 10 o'clock myself and Adjutant-Lieutenant Campbell,[10] who were riding some distance in front, flushed two Zulus. They bolted and we rode them down. Campbell shot his one, but I captured mine and on Duncombe coming up we questioned him.

He was only a boy and was frightened out of his life so that when asked where he came from, he pointed to the line of hills on the left flank of the camp saying "he had come from the King's big army." "What are you doing here?" we asked, to which he replied "that he and his mate had been sent by their *induna* to see if any white men were among the hills" we had just left, "but as they were sitting resting under the shade of a rock they did not hear the white men and were caught." "What was the size of the

8. Chelmsford had concluded that he could not bring on a major engagement in the vicinity of the Phindo heights. He consequently had sent word to Pulleine at Isandlwana to remain in the camp, and to send forward tents and supplies of food. H-B and the 1/3rd NNC, accompanied by Lonsdale, were to march back to Isandlwana to assist in bringing up the camp equipage and supplies to the troops in the field.

9. Lieutenant-Colonel Crealock subsequently stated that: 'The 1st battalion Natal Native Contingent had been ordered back to camp, and to skirmish through the ravines in case any Zulus were hanging about near the camp' (*British Parliamentary Papers* [*BPP*], C. 2260: enc. 2 in no. 12: Chelmsford to the Secretary of State for War, 9 February 1879: Statement of Lieutenant-Colonel J. North Crealock, Acting Military Secretary).

Having given his orders to H-B, Chelmsford rode off with his staff and a small escort to scout for a suitable campsite for when the whole of No. 3 Column moved forward from Isandlwana. He selected level ground just east of Hlazakazi on the Mangeni River above its spectacular horseshoe falls, and in the early afternoon, at about 12.30 p.m., ordered all the troops operating in the vicinity to concentrate there.

10. The identity of Adjutant-Lieutenant Campbell is unclear. The Adjutant of the 1/3rd NNC was W. C. R. Higginson, late lieutenant of the Dublin City Militia.

army?" He answered, "There were twelve full regiments" (about 30,000 or perhaps 36,000 men).[11]

Now here was the fat in the fire with a vengeance.

The big Zulu army within four miles of the left flank of the camp, Colonel Pulleine without mounted men, or only a few, only two guns, not more than 900 white men in all, the camp not laagered and the General away on a wild-goose chase, at least thirteen miles from him.

I was unaware, at the time, that Colonel Durnford, R.E., had, that morning, reached Isandlwana; he had some hundreds of natives and a rocket battery with him.[12]

I at once wrote a note to the following effect:

"10 a.m.—I have just captured a Zulu scout who informs me the Zulu army is behind the range of hills on the left flank of the camp. Will push on as fast as possible. The ground here is good for the rapid advance of mounted men and guns."[13]

This note I sent by a well-mounted officer with orders he was to ride as fast as possible.

The next thing was to try and advance as fast as I could. I rode forward and used my glasses, but everything so far was peaceful.

11. Thirteen *amabutho* were present at Isandlwana. The chest: uKhandempemvu and uMxhapho; the right horn: uDududu, iSangqu, iMbube, and uNokhenke; left horn: uMbonambi, iNgobamakhosi and uVe; reserve: uThulwane, iNdluyengwe, iNdlondlo and uDloko.

12. When Chelmsford moved out from the Isandlwana camp in the early hours of 22 January with Glyn's flying column, he was conscious that Pulleine's depleted garrison ought to be augmented against what he nevertheless considered an unlikely Zulu attack. He therefore summoned Colonel Anthony William Durnford (1830–79), RE – who had served disastrously during the Langalibalele Rebellion of 1873 and was now commander of No. 2 Column and anxious to retrieve his reputation – to bring up what troops he had available at Rorke's Drift to reinforce the camp. These comprised a detachment of 11/7th Brigade, RA (a rocket battery of three 9-pounder Hale's rockets), five troops of the Natal Native Mounted Contingent (NNC) and two companies of the 1/1st NNC. When Durnford arrived at Isandlwana with his reinforcements at about 10.30 a.m. on 22 January, this brought the garrison up to sixty-seven officers and 1,707 men, of whom approximately half were African.

13. This message was most likely sent an hour later than the time H-B states. Lieutenant Archibald Berkeley Milne, RN (1855–1938), one of Chelmsford's ADCs, reported on 3 February 1879 that 'Commandant Brown had observed the great numbers of natives at Isandulwana [*sic*] and sent three messengers to the General, but none of these reached him' (*BPP* (C. 2454): Sub-enc. in enc. in Appendix: Letters from the Admiralty to the Colonial Office, p. 184: 'Report on Proceedings of 21st, 23rd, and 24th January 1879', Lieutenant Archibald R. Milne, RN, 3 February 1879). Throughout the course of the morning and early afternoon, increasingly urgent messages were sent to Chelmsford that the camp at Isandlwana was under serious attack, but they either failed to find him since his whereabouts were unpredictable, or were discounted by the General and his staff who were utterly over-confident after their successes in the Ninth Cape Frontier War and, most recently, at kwaSogekle.

Just then I met two boys loaded with food. They had been sent out to me by the kind forethought of Lieutenant Beuie of my battalion.[14]

They also brought me a note from a great chum of mine, Lieutenant Anstey, first 24th, who told me he and Lieutenant Dailey had gone to my tent the night before,[15] and as they had found a good dinner spoiling, they had eaten it, but sent in return a couple of bottles of whisky. I was never fated to see any of these kind-hearted men again but it is the fortune of war. Well these loads were indeed a godsend, and I divided the food and drink among my non-coms. who were on foot and it just bucked them up and gave them heart for further exertions. I would not have minded having some myself, but I was mounted, and they were on foot, so after a ten minutes' halt I again gave the word to move on.

At about 11 o'clock I was on ahead and looking through my glasses when I saw a puff of smoke rise from the hills on the left of the camp. It was followed by another. They seemed to come from a huge black shadow that lay on the hills. Presently another puff and in a moment I knew they were bursting shells. Not a cloud was in the sky, and I knew that the black shadow resting on the hills must be the Zulu army moving down to attack the camp.

At once I dispatched the second message:

"11 a.m.—The Zulu army is attacking the left of the camp. The guns have opened on them. The ground here still suitable for guns and mounted men. Will push on so as to act as support to them."[16]

This I dispatched by a mounted officer, and at the same time my first messenger returned. He informed me he had delivered my note to a S.O. who had read it, and told him to rejoin me, and that I was to push on to camp.

But now my brave barbarians, with their wonderful eyesight, had seen the dreaded foe, and they refused to march. They could not run away as the Zulus were between them and safety, but it took all the muscular persuasion of my officers and the dauntless blackguardism of my non-coms. to kick a crawl out of them.

Umvubie of No. 8 Company helped me at this juncture to solve the problem. He said he and his men would march in rear and kill everyone who lagged behind, so at last I got a crawl out of them. I rode on and used my glasses.

14. It is unclear who Lieutenant Beuie might be. The only lieutenants recorded with names beginning with 'B' in the 1/3rd NNC were H. Baker and J. Brice.

15. Lieutenant Edgar Oliphant Anstey (1851–79) and Lieutenant James Patrick Daly (1855–79), both of F Company, 1/24th, were killed in the battle of Isandlwana.

16. More likely, H-B sent this message off at about 12.30 p.m., rather than at the time he states.

I could now see the troops lying down and firing volleys, while the guns kept up a steady fire. The Zulus did not seem able to advance. They were getting it hot, and as there was no cover they must have suffered very heavy losses, as they shortly afterwards fell back. The guns and troops also ceased firing. At about midday I was looking back anxiously to see if the mounted men and guns were coming up, when I heard the guns in camp reopen again; and riding forward, we were then about four miles from the camp. I saw a cloud of Zulus thrown out from their left and form the left horn of their army. These men swept round and attacked the front of the camp, and I saw the two right companies of the 24th and one gun thrown back to resist them. There was also plenty of independent firing going on within the camp, as if all the wagon men, servants, and in fact everyone who could use a rifle was firing away to save his life.

I at once sent another messenger with the following note:

"The camp is being attacked on the left and in front, and as yet is holding its own. Ground still good for the rapid advance of guns and horses. Am moving forward as fast as I can."

My second messenger joined me shortly after this and told me he had delivered my note to a staff officer and had received orders for me to push on to camp.

At 1 o'clock the camp was still holding its own and the Zulus were certainly checked. The guns were firing case and I could see the dense mass of natives writhe, sway and shrink back from the steady volleys of the gallant old 24th.

I had given orders to my men to deflect to their left so as to try to get into the right of the camp, and the officers and non-coms. were forcing the brutes on, when about half-past one I happened to glance to the right of the camp. Good God! what a sight it was. By the road that runs between the hill and the kopje, came a huge mob of maddened cattle, followed by a dense swarm of Zulus. These poured into the undefended right and rear of the camp, and at the same time the left horn of the enemy and the chest of the army rushed in. Nothing could stand against this combined attack. All formation was broken in a minute, and the camp became a seething pandemonium of men and cattle struggling in dense clouds of dust and smoke.

The defenders fought desperately and I could see through the mist the flash of bayonet and spear together with the tossing heads and horns of the infuriated cattle, while above the bellowing of the latter and the sharp crack of the rifles could be heard the exulting yells of the savages and the cheers of our men gradually dying away. Of course I saw in a moment everything was lost and at once galloped back to my men.

There was no time to write, but I said to Captain Develin, a fine horseman and a finer fellow, "Ride as hard as you can, and tell every officer you meet, 'For God's sake come back, the camp is surrounded and must be taken.'"[17]

Then getting my officers together, I said to them, "Our only chance is to retreat slowly," and ordered them to form their companies into rings, after the Zulu fashion, and retire, dismounting themselves and hiding all the white men among the natives. This we did, and although there were large parties of the enemy close to us, they took no notice of us, and we gradually retired out of their vicinity. When we had got to a place, about five miles from the camp, where I thought my white men and Zulus could put up a bit of a fight in case we were attacked, I halted and determined to await the course of events.[18] During the retreat I had often looked back and seen that the fighting was over in the camp, but that one company, in company square, was retreating slowly up the hill surrounded by a dense swarm of Zulus. This was Captain Younghusband's Company.[19] They kept the enemy off as long as their ammunition lasted, then used the bayonet until at last overcome by numbers they fell in a heap like the brave old British Tommy should.

Well here we were. The white men worn out and hungry, but most of them determined and I had the satisfaction to read on the grim, dirty faces of my roughs, that no matter what they had been in the past, they meant to stick to their work, do their duty like men and if necessary die game.

Curses not loud but very deep, went up for a time, and one or two of Lord Chelmsford's staff must have felt their ears tingle.

We sat and lay where we were. There was nowhere to go, nothing to be done, we had no food, and very little ammunition, but we had some water and tepid and muddy as it was it was thankfully used as there was no shade and the sun shone like a ball of fire. As soon as I had made what few arrangements I could I told the men to get some rest, as I was convinced that later on, we should be called upon to retake the camp, as through that camp was the only possible retreat for the General's party and ourselves.

After a time Captain Develin rode up to me. "Well," said I, "who did you see?" "I first saw Major Black with the second 24th and repeated your message—he at once turned back. Then I saw Colonel Harness with the

17. At about 1.30 p.m., from his position with the 1/3rd NNC four miles from Isandlwana, H-B ordered Captain R. Develin to ride in Chelmsford's direction and deliver this verbal message to every officer he met.

18. H-B withdrew the 1/3rd NNC for about a mile and halted at a defendable rocky position. He ordered each company to form a defensive circle, and waited on developments.

19. This was C Company, 1/24th, commanded by Captain Reginald Younghusband (1844–79), which made a last stand between about 2.25 p.m. and 2.45 p.m. It would have been

guns—he at once turned back. Then I saw the mounted men, and they turned back." "Well," said I, "where are they?" "Why, sir," he replied, "as we were marching back we met the staff and the troops were ordered to go back again, so I came on alone."[20]

Why had this been done? Those who want to know had better get the book Miss Colenso wrote in defence of Colonel Durnford, and if they study the evidences recapitulated in that book, especially that of Captain Church, they may find out. I am only writing of what I actually saw myself, and have no wish to throw mud at anyone. [21]

Some time later I saw the M.I. come out from the hills on to the open ground, form up and dismount. I at once sent an officer to their O.C. to tell him that if he would support me I would again advance. He acknowledged my message but sent no reply, and shortly afterwards he again mounted his men and returned to the hills.[22]

The long afternoon passed slowly away, and towards evening I saw a small body of horsemen riding towards us. On using my glasses I discovered it was the General and his staff and I at once mounted and rode to meet him.[23]

He looked very surprised when he saw me and said, "What are you doing here, Commandant Browne? You ought to have been in camp hours ago." I replied, "The camp has been taken, sir."

He flashed out at once, "How dare you tell me such a falsehood? Get your men into line at once and advance." I did so and led my 700 miserables supported by the staff against the victorious Zulu army.[24]

---

impossible at such a distance to have identified the company as Younghusband's, and H-B. is clearly employing hindsight.

20. Captain Develin encountered Colonel Harness at about 2.00 p.m.

21. Develin relayed H-B's message to Lieutenant-Colonel Harness, who was slowly moving towards the Mangeni campsite with his four 7-pounder guns and an escort of F and H Companies, the 2/24th. Harness immediately turned back towards Isandlwana. He had covered two or three miles when Chelmsford, who was not yet convinced the camp was under Zulu attack, ordered him to turn around again and join Glyn and the flying column at the Mangeni campsite. *See* the corroborative account by Captain H.B. Church of F Company, 2/24th, in Durnford, *Soldier's Life and Works*, pp. 14–15. H-B is mistaken in presumably attributing Church's account to Colenso & Durnford, *History of the Zulu War*.

22. These were the Mounted Infantry under Lieutenant-Colonel J.C. Russell, 12th (Prince of Wales's Royal) Lancers. At about 7.00 a.m. Chelmsford had ordered them on a reconnaissance to the north-east of Hlazakazi and they were now returning without encountering significant enemy forces. H-B sent his message to Russell at about 2.20 p.m. but Russell decided to ride to the Mangeni rendezvous to report.

23. Still incredulous, at about 2.35 p.m. Chelmsford had at last decided to return to Isandlwana with his staff and an escort of eighty Mounted Infantry and Natal Mounted Volunteers to investigate, and reached H-B's position at about 3.45 p.m.

24. In his statement, Crealock declared: 'The Lieutenant-General appeared to think that he would be able to brush through any parties of Zulus that might be in his road to the camp

We moved on about two and a half miles until we had opened out a good view of the camp,[25] when he called me to him and said, in a kindly manner, "On your honour, Commandant Browne, is the camp taken?" I answered, "The camp was taken at about 1.30 in the afternoon, and the Zulus are now burning some of the tents."

He said, "That may be the Quartermaster's fatigue burning the debris of the camp." I replied, "Q.M.'s fatigue do not burn tents, sir," and I offered him my glasses. He refused them, but said, "Halt your men at once," and leaving me, rode back to the staff and dispatched an officer to bring up the remainder of the column.[26]

I had just halted my men and placed them in the best position I could, when to my utter astonishment I saw a man on foot leading a pony, coming from the direction of the camp, and recognized him as Commandant Lonsdale.

He came up to me and said, "By Jove, Maori, this is fun; the camp is taken." "Don't see the humour," I said, "but go and tell the staff; they won't believe me."

He had had the most wonderful escape. As I have said before he was still suffering from sunstroke and having somehow lost the battalion he was with, had ridden towards the camp.[27] More than half stupefied by the great heat, he rode into it, and all at once awoke to the fact that the camp was full of Zulus, some of them wearing soldiers' tunics, and that the ground was littered with dead men. He then realized the situation at a glance and in less time than words can tell, he turned his pony's head and rode as hard as he could away. He was pursued, but the ground was good-going, and his pony "Dot" a very smart one, so he got clear away and joined us.[28]

Well, again a weary halt.[29] As we lay we could see long lines of Zulus marching along the hills on our right flank. They had with them many of

without force further than that referred to, viz., 1st battalion Native Contingent and some 80 mounted white men.'

25. It was now approximately 4.30 p.m.

26. Chelmsford sent Major Matthew Gossett (1839–1909), 54th (West Norfolk) Regiment, a member of his personal staff, galloping back to the Mangeni camp five or six miles in his rear. He ordered Glyn to concentrate his troops and march immediately to join the General.

27. Lonsdale, who was recovering from concussion, not sunstroke, had ridden ahead of the 1/3rd NNC to deliver Chelmsford's order to Pulleine to prepare to move camp and to arrange for supplies to be brought up to the forces in the field.

28. For details of Lonsdale's escapade, see Lieutenant Milne's report, p. 184. At the same moment that Lonsdale rejoined the halted 1/3rd NNC, Crealock, according to his statement, galloped forward from the General to order H-B to resume the advance. Crealock continued: 'I met Commandant Lonsdale, who remarked to me as I accosted him, "The Zulus have the camp." "How do you know?" I asked, incredulously. "Because I have been into it," was his answer.'

29. Chelmsford, after ordering Glyn to bring up the troops concentrating at Mangeni, advanced another mile or so towards Isandlwana with the 1/3rd NNC deployed in three

our wagons, most probably loaded with their wounded men, or plunder out of the camp.[30]

At last just as night fell, we were joined by the remainder of the column that had been sent for and we were then formed into line of attack. The guns were in the centre, flanking them parties of the second 24th, my battalion in line on the left, Cooper's battalion in line on the right, and the mounted men in front and on the flanks.[31]

The General spoke a few words to the men and then ready once more,[32] away we went to recapture the camp, or as Umvubie would say, "To die, but have a good fight first."

The night, as we were nearing the camp,[33] became very dark and I received orders that I was to retake the kopje at all costs being at the same time warned that if my men turned tail the party of the 24th (under Major Black) who supported me, were at once to fire a volley and charge. This was pleasant for me but of course I recognized the necessity.[34]

---

ranks with the white officers and NCOs and those levies with firearms to the fore. The Natal Mounted Volunteers and Mounted Infantry rode on either flank with scouts ahead of them.

30. In his report (p. 184), Lieutenant Milne wrote: 'We advanced until within five miles [of the camp], then halted until reinforcement came up. [We] could see the enemy going over the hills to our right in thousands, also a good many waggons.'

31. As the sun began to sink, Glyn finally came up some time around 6.30 p.m. (sunset on that date was at 7.04 p.m.) with the men of the flying column formed into fighting order, and with the apprehensive men of the 2/3rd NNC making up the rear.

For his resumed advance on the camp, Chelmsford arrayed his united force in regulation fighting formation. The guns in the centre were in column on the track with room to form line for action. There were three companies of the 2/24th Regiment on either flank of them. To their right were the 2/3rd NNC in line of column and beyond them the Mounted Infantry and Natal Mounted Police. To the left of the British infantry were the 1/3rd NNC flanked by the Natal Carbineers, the Buffalo Border Guard and Newcastle Mounted Rifles. Skirmishers were thrown out in front and a small guard was detailed to look after the wagons and ambulances in the rear.

32. Chelmsford's words, as reported by Major Clery were: 'Men, the enemy has taken our camp. Many of our friends must have lost their lives defending it. There is nothing left for us now but to fight our way through – and mind, we must fight hard, for we will have to fight for our lives. I know you, and I know I can depend on you' (Clery to Colonel G. B. Harman, 17 February 1879, in Clarke, *Zululand at War*, p. 85). Lieutenant Milne (p. 185) reported that Chelmsford's speech 'was answered by three hearty cheers, which were taken up by the Natives'.

33. In the gathering darkness of a moonless night Chelmsford's force cautiously advanced on the stricken camp. At about 7.30 p.m. it halted 900 yards from the camp and the artillery opened fire with several shrapnel shells on the neck. When there was no response, the advance resumed to within 300 yards of the camp.

34. Once again, H-B cannot resist putting himself putting himself in a leadership role in the centre of the action. In fact, the 1/3rd NNC did not storm the knoll on the left of the road that commanded the line of retreat to Natal. That critical role was assigned not to untried African levies but to professional British infantry. The three companies of the 2/24th on the left of the guns under Major Black's command were ordered to fix bayonets and take

The word was now given to move on. At the same time the guns opened fire so as to clear the ground in front of us of any large bodies of Zulus who might be there.

I dismounted and made for the kopje, dragging with me the principal Natal *induna,* whom I had clawed hold of by his head ring, swearing I would blow his brains out in case his men turned tail. He howled to them not to run away, but behind them came the 24th with fixed bayonets so that no matter what funk the natives were in, they had to come on.[35]

It was as dark as pitch, and soon we were stumbling and falling over dead men (black and white), dead horses, cattle, ruined tents and all the debris of the fight. But up and up the kopje we had to go, for every now and then Black's voice would ring out, "Steady the 24th—be ready to fire a volley and charge." Up and up we went as the shells came screaming over our heads; the burning time-fuses in the dark looking like rockets. Every time one came over us my wretched natives would utter a howl and try to sit down, but bayonets in rear of them will make even a Natal Kafir move on, and they had to come.

At last we arrived at the top, no living man was there and as the shells just passed over us I told my bugler to sound the "cease fire." He could not sound a note, so I shouted to Black that we were on the top and asked him to have the "cease fire" sounded. This was done and up rushed the 24th, who, when they reached the top of the hill, broke out into cheer after cheer. My Zulus to keep them company rattled their shields and assagais, for had not we retaken the camp; or rather perhaps I ought to say, reoccupied it. Anyhow we were there.[36]

Dear old Black came up to me, and on shaking hands, lamented we had not had a fight. He then poured me out a cup of sherry from his flask. I wanted it badly as it was over forty hours since I had tasted food, and

the knoll 'at all risks' with supporting fire from the artillery (Lieutenant Milne, p. 185). Chelmsford, in his report to the Secretary of State for War on 27 January, also unequivocally stated that the left wing of the 2/24th under Major Black seized the koppie on the left to secure his left flank. It is likely that the 1/3rd NNC gingerly advanced in support of the three companies of the 2/24th on their right, but it certainly was not the other way around as H-B claims.

35. As ever, in retrospect H-B misses no opportunity to denigrate the men of the NNC under his command. This should be compared to Crealock's statement in February 1879: 'I consider it but just to the Native Contingent to state that it was my belief that evening, and it is still the same, that the two battalions would have gone through any enemy we met, even as our own British troops were prepared to do. I noticed no signs of wavering on their part up to sunset, when I ceased to be able to observe them.' It is not unreasonable, however, to suppose (as H-B relates) that they were reluctant to push home an attack on the camp in the dark.

36. The victorious Zulu army had retired, and Black's men, and H-B's too, met no resistance in the camp except for a few stragglers. With the strategic knoll secured, the rest of the force then went forward and had reoccupied the camp by about 8.30. p.m.

my throat and mouth were parched and dry with shouting, mingled I fear with cursing.

However the Zulus could not have removed all the food from the camp and we were bound to find some. So I called for my trusty Irish servant, who was a past master in the art of looting.

He was serving as senior sergeant of No. 8 Company and I told him to take some good men and see what he could find. The remains of the hospital lines were close to us so down he went. He was soon back again with plenty of bully beef and biscuits and drawing me aside, slipped into my empty haversack a bottle of port and a bottle of brandy, also a large packet of tobacco. I said, "What have you got for yourself, Quin?" He replied and I know he grinned, "Troth, sor, is it so short a time your honour has known me that you can't trust me to look after meself." Well the bully beef went round, so did the biscuits and the brandy. And so did not the port, for Black and I drank most of that. However there was enough for everyone, and we had a rough but a square feed.

Just as we officers had finished and were sitting smoking, I looked across the Buffalo Valley. By the road it was a long way, but as the crow flies quite a short distance,[37] and in the direction I knew Rourke's Drift to lie I noticed a lot of tiny flashes. I called Black's attention to them, saying, "Those flashes must be musketry." He looked in the direction indicated and said, "Yes." I told Duncombe to call Umvubie and ask him. Umvubie at once said, "Yes, the Zulus are attacking the white man's camp by the river." I said to Black, "Do you know if the store camp was laagered?" He talked in Gaelic for a few minutes. He might have been praying but it did not sound like prayers, and just then all along the Natal bank of the Buffalo huge fires broke out and Duncombe exclaimed, "By God, the Zulus are in Natal! Lord help the women and children." There could be no doubt about it. The fires we saw were the friendly kraals and the farmhouses burning, and all we could do was to echo Duncombe's prayer, "God help the women and children." In a few minutes we saw a great flare over Rourke's Drift, and thought that the base hospital, the store camp and all our supplies were in the hands of the enemy.[38] We had not been very joyful before, but now we felt very sick indeed. If the Zulus chose to raid Natal there was nothing to stop their doing so. Our retreat, also, would be cut off. What was to become of us did not bother me. No one

---

37. About six miles.

38. The Zulu reserve had commenced their attack on Rorke's Drift at around 4.30 p.m. Their final assault on the perimeter petered out at about 10 p.m. when the flames of the hospital, set ablaze at about 7.30 p.m., flared up for the last time. H-B and his companions would have seen the flames from their bivouac at Isandlwana and also those of burning farmhouses and *imizi* set alight by parties of amaZulu scouring the countryside between the Mzinyathi River and the Helpmekaar heights.

depended on me, so I was like Umvubie, expected to be killed but hoped to have a good fight first.

Well the night wore away. We could get no sleep as we were too crowded to lie down and the kopje we were on was all covered with stones.[39]

39. The troops were ordered to bivouac on the ground, and a large hollow square was formed on the neck across the track back to Rorke's Drift. The three right-hand companies of the 2/24th formed two ranks deep in front with the guns pointing to the rear and defended by the mounted men. The two battalions of the 3rd NNC were on each flank. Major Black's three companies of the 2/24th remained on the stony knoll. It is odd that H-B, who can never resist a dig at the NNC, makes no mention of their behaviour during the dreadful night encamped on the battlefield. Lieutenant Milne (p. 185) mentions that 'Several times during the long hours of that night a false alarm was given, the Native Contingent rushing through our ranks. Fire was opened by our men, but no enemy came.' Harford, who was with the 2/3rd NNC (Laband, *Charlie Harford*, p. 74), recollected that during the night the men of his battalion attempted to slip away and had to be rounded up and driven back into the square where sentries of the 2/24th were placed over them to prevent a repetition.

Chapter XIII

The Morning after Isandlwana

JUST before daybreak orders were given to fall in and as soon as I got my men into their places I galloped across the camp to my tent to try and save some papers, medals, etc.

My God, in the grey dawn, it was a sight! In their mad rush into the camp, the Zulus had killed everything. Horses had been stabbed at their picket lines. Splendid spans of oxen were lying dead in their yokes, mules lay dead in their harness and even dogs were lying stabbed among the tents. Ripped open sacks of rice, flour, meal and sugar lay everywhere. They had even in their savage rage thrust their assagais into tins of bully beef, butter and jam. Among all this debris singly and in heaps, or rather in groups of two or three, lay the ripped and mutilated bodies of the gallant 24th,[1] showing how, when their formation was broken, they had stood it out, and fought back to back or in groups until they had been run over and destroyed. That they had fought to the last gasp could be seen by the number of dead Zulus who lay everywhere in amongst them, the bayonet wounds on their bodies telling of the fierce, though short combat that had taken place after the right horn of the Zulus had swept round the hill. I had just time to get to the door of my tent, inside of which I saw my old setter dog, dead, with an assagai thrust through her. My two spare horses were also lying killed at their picket rope, with my Totty groom dead between them.[2] As I said before, my camp was on the extreme left of the line, and the best part of the fighting had taken place there. I saw the bodies of two of my officers lying dead with heaps of empty cartridge shells by their sides. Both had been splendid shots and I bet they had done

1. The British were appalled to discover their dead partially stripped of their clothes and with their bellies ripped open and their intestines hanging out. They did not understand that both these actions were Zulu religious rituals for the removal of supernatural evil influence, or *mnyama*, that followed on the shedding of human blood. Disembowelment ensured that *mnyama* did not cause the killer to swell up like the dead; while it was necessary to exchange some of his clothing, ritually contaminated by his victim's blood, for his own, and to wear it until ritually cleansed on his return home.

2. By 'Totty' H-B presumably means that his groom was a 'Hottentot' (a now unacceptable term replaced by Khoisan) who had accompanied him from the Cape.

plenty of execution before they went under. As I reined up I glanced out to the left and left front of the camp, and saw heaps and heaps of Zulu dead. Where the volleys of the 24th had checked them, they lay in lines, and the donga I had ridden over on the morning of the 21st was chock-full of them. Surely the 24th had died game, but bitter as I felt, a thrill of admiration passed through me when I thought of the splendid courage of the savages who could advance to the charge suffering the awful punishment they were getting.

I had not time to dismount as I heard the bugle sound the advance and I galloped back to my men as fast as I could without trampling on the bodies of my poor comrades. On my way I reined up my horse sharply, for there lay the body of my old friend Lieut.-Col. Pulleine; I could do nothing for him, and it at once flashed through my mind our last words of chaff, so I saluted the poor remains and passed on as quickly as I could to my men.[3]

When I reached them I asked the Adjutant if any orders had reached us. He replied, "No, sir. Everyone has moved off except ourselves and the rear-guard of M.I. which Major Black has taken command of." Good old Black, I thought, always at the post of honour. Well he rode up to me and asked me "What I was doing there?" I said, "Waiting for orders." He made a few remarks in Gaelic and then said, "Come on, old fellow. Move off just in front of me, and if these black devils come after us we will have a nice little rear-guard action of our own."[4]

I did so, and sorrowfully returned by the same road we had so gaily advanced along three days before. A few shots as my officer picked off scattered Zulus was all that happened. But as we crossed some high ground we saw a large party of Zulus away to the left.

They stood still for a few minutes when they saw us, then broke up and fled all over the country. This was their beaten army retreating from Rourke's Drift. We afterwards heard that they did not know that we had been out in front of the camp, but thought they had killed all the white

3. It has never been established conclusively where and when on the battlefield Pulleine died, and his corpse was subsequently never positively identified. We can only take H-B's word for it that he came across Pulleine's body. But where precisely it lay is not clear since H-B was traversing the length of the camp from its left where his tent was pitched to its right where the 1/3rd NNC were drawn up, ready to march off from their bivouac.

4. Chelmsford gave the order at 4 a.m. to march back to Rorke's Drift, hoping in the pre-dawn light to spare as many of his men as possible the grisly sight of the sacked camp and the mutilated dead. In his haste to be gone, Chelmsford left the British dead unburied, a decision that raised a storm of indignation in Natal and Britain.

The 2/3rd NNC at the head of the column, marching four abreast, indeed saw little of the devastation, but the 1/3rd NNC, with H-B leading them, were the last foot soldiers to quit the ground. By then the sun was up, and they saw it all, as did the Mounted Infantry, NMP and Natal Mounted Volunteers who formed the column's rearguard and flankers.

A LAST SALUTE.

men. They therefore imagined that we were the dead men come to life again, that we were ghosts, and in superstitious terror fled away from us.[5]

We descended the steep pass to the Bashie River, halted for a few minutes to let the men and horses drink, then moved on to the high ground.

As we came to the top of a ridge, we saw the advance guard on the top of another ridge signalling.[6] I said to Black, "Who on earth can they be signalling to?" "The Lord only knows," he answered. But all at once a tremendous cheer broke out in front and ran along the column towards us, and Lieutenant Harford galloped back with the joyful news that there were white men signalling from the ruins of the base camp, and that the camp must have held out and beaten off the attack.

Our men began to cheer, and everyone was delighted. We had been very sick the night before when we thought the camp at Rourke's Drift had been taken and destroyed. Now we knew it was safe the reaction was very pleasant.

Yes; it was true a deed had been done by one company of the second 24th, assisted by a few irregulars and civilians, that has never been surpassed in the annals of British warfare. They had beaten off an attack of 4000 Zulus. True, they had an improvised laager of biscuit-boxes and mealie sacks and behind these they had done wonders. But how about the camp at Isandlwana? How about those 900 white men lying exposed to the vulture and the jackal in the camp a few miles behind?[7] How would that fight have ended if they had had a laager, and why had they not one? In another hour we were back at the Buffalo and again lined the same ridge we had sweltered on during the 10th, but this time we only had to wait while half the 24th crossed and only four guns. That long line of wagons that had taken such a tedious time to cross, where were they? They were stranded only a few miles away with two guns and 900 good officers and men.

Well everyone crossed and Black and myself rode down to the drift last of all. Giving him the post of honour as he was entitled to it I rode in front of him, as we came to the water, so that he was the last man of

5. When the retreating British column had crossed the Manzimnyama stream and were within three miles of Rorke's Drift, they came in sight of the amaZulu retreating after their failure to capture the post. The two forces passed by each other close enough for some provocative verbal exchanges, but the British were almost out of ammunition, and both they and the amaZulu, who had been heavily repulsed at Rorke's Drift with over 600 casualties, were exhausted, hungry and demoralised. Consequently, neither side fired a shot and all continued on their separate ways.

6. Chelmsford's column came in sight of Rorke's Drift at about 8 a.m. on 23 January.

7. British casualties along the firing line at Isandlwana, in the camp and along the line of flight down to Sothondose's (or Fugitives') Drift across the Mzinyathi comprised 52 officers and 739 troops.

No. 3 Column to leave Zululand—that is to say he was the last living man but there were plenty lying unburied, exposed to the sun, wind and rain, the beasts of the field and the birds of the air, and who was to blame? Who promulgated that book of orders the first of which was that no camp should be pitched without being laagered?

In writing this I have only stated facts that I personally saw, and I have tried to hurt no man's feelings who may be alive nor throw a stone at the memory of any man who may be dead.

The 3rd N.N.C. lost 18 officers and 36 N.C.O.'s, only 3 officers escaping. I do not think we lost many men as I am sure the Natal Kafirs bolted very early in the day.[8] I must however make exception of the one Zulu company left in camp. They sat tight until the enemy closed in. Then they charged and were killed to a man. But as Umvubie would have said, they had a good fight first.

It must have been about half-past three on the afternoon of the 23rd of January 1879 when Major Black and myself rode across the drift out of Zululand and proceeded at once up to the base camp.

My men, who had crossed before me, had sat down on a small flat to the right rear of the store and I joined them. They were not in a pleasant frame of mind, most of the officers slack and despondent, the non-coms. hungry and savage, while the natives clamoured to be allowed to go home. It therefore behoved me to buck them up and the first thing was to get the white men to make the cowardly niggers hold their row. Both the battalions had clumped together and it was absolutely necessary to enforce order and discipline. Getting the officers together I soon talked them into a better humour. I pointed out to them that one defeat had not ended the war and that, as we all must want to play a return match with the Zulus, we must do our duty, bide our time, and hope for better things. This quite satisfied them and they expressed their intention of backing me up.

I then turned my attention to the non-coms. I have already told you what sort of men they were, the majority of them being the driftweed of the seven seas—runaway sailors and East London boatmen with a sprinkling of ex-navvies and old soldiers. For the last three days they had been overworked, underfed and had had no sleep or rest at all and as they were a wild, lawless crowd they were inclined to be mutinous. However I knew them and they knew me, and I wanted to keep them for future service, as I was sure that, tough as they were, it would be hard to collect a more reckless or pluckier lot north of Hades.

8. According to official records, eight officers of the 1/3rd NNC and nine of the 2/3rd NNC perished at Isandlwana, along with 67 white NCOs of the 3rd NNC; 471 black troops (including non-combatants) were recorded as killed, although the number was probably closer to 500.

They all sat or lay in a clump some 100 in number belonging to both battalions, and as I approached them they looked as ugly a lot as any man would care to face without having iron bars between you and them.

As I came to them only a few stood up but a smart "shun" brought all to their feet.

I opened fire with: "Now then, my lads, how many of you are fit for duty? I want you to turn to at once, and help your officers to quiet those howling niggers. Those of you who are fit fall in, in rear of me." My servant Quin and all the old soldiers at once fell in, but the others stood muttering and grumbling in their throats.

Then I let them have it hot and strong. First I pointed out to them the fact, that the 24th and the guns were alongside, and it wanted very little of that sort of talk and behaviour to make me go to Colonel Glyn and get him to turn them on to such a set of mutinous scoundrels, and after I had called them by the names they most understood I turned to the leader of the sea pirates and singled him out.

This man—Jack Williams—was an old shell-back of the stamp that is now as rare as the dodo and as he had served with me in New Zealand we knew one another.[9]

He was a man of past middle life, grey and grizzled, about 5 feet 9 inches in height but of enormous width and strength. His face, arms and breast, nearly burned black with the sun, were all covered with the marks of ancient knife and bullet wounds. He had been to sea nearly all his life and had passed most of it in the South Seas and on the Pacific coast. A sandal-wood trader (*i.e.*, pirate), a black-bird catcher, a filibuster and blockade runner, with Walker and Garibaldi,[10] in Central America and there were but few scenes of bloodshed on that lively coast that old Jack had not played a part in. Yet I could not help liking the old buccaneer. His wide-open blue eye and fearless expression of face always made me think of the old Elizabethan sea-dogs which was strengthened by his kindly ways (when not roused) and his homely Devonshire speech. He could neither read nor write but was a born leader of men and I knew if I could get him on my side all the other pirates would follow like sheep.

Well I had given them their dressing-down so it was now time for me to give them their spoonful of jam. I told them there was plenty of good fighting in front of us and that none of them need repine because we had

9. H-B had previously encountered Williams in East London and recruited him to the NNC. *See* pp. 76–8, above. Whether he was a real person or H-B's creation for the sake of a yarn is uncertain.

10. William Walker (1824–60) was a mercenary and revolutionary leader born in Nashville, Tennessee, who made himself briefly President of Nicaragua, 1856–7. Giuseppe Garibaldi (1807–82) was an Italian revolutionary and republican who contributed to Italian unification. Between 1835 and 1848 he fought in revolutionary wars in Brazil, Uruguay and Argentina.

got one licking, but they surprised me, insomuch that although they had behaved, during the last three days, when our lives had not been worth a rotten orange, like men, yet now we were in comparative safety with food and rest before us they should turn to and begin their monkey tricks, and I wound up by saying that their mixed conduct made me look on them as nothing more nor less than a lot of bally conundrums, and "as for you, Jack Williams," turning sharply to the old buccaneer, "you are nothing more or less than an Ornithorhynchus Platypus."[11]

The old sea-dog broke into a broad grin; never before in all his long and wicked life had he ever been called by such a name.

He had served under many a Yankee skipper and many a blue-nose mate, but none of them had ever coined such a cuss word as that. It was medicine to him and he hugged himself enraptured.

Stepping out from among the men, he made me his very best sea-bow. Then turning to them and slapping one huge fist into the palm of the other enormous hand he harangued them.

Quoth he, "See 'ere, mates, when a hofficer, as we know to be a hofficer, and a hedecated genelman to boot, speaks you fair like as man to man, and goes so far as to call you uns a lot of blankety-blank comumrums and me, Jack Williams, a ruddy horni-korinky palibus, I say as how that's the hofficer I stands by and sticks to. Ain't I right, Bill?"—this to his chum. "In course ye are, Jack," came back the ready answer. "Then fall in astarn of the commandant, yer bally comumrums!" and the whole of the pirates fell in ready for anything. It is written somewhere that a soft word turneth away wrath. In this case a hard word stopped trouble.

In a very short time the niggers were reduced to silence and sorted out into their respective companies. Just then Lonsdale came up, he had been making arrangements for rations. I made my most despondent officer quartermaster so as to give him something to think about and a ration party having been told off to go and draw them, I went with Lonsdale round the laager to have a look at the debris of the fight. He told me that three of our officers had escaped and got into Rourke's Drift. Two of them, however, he was sorry to say, had ridden on, the other, a Dutchman, named Ardendorph [Adendorff], had remained, had fought bravely and was well spoken of

He also told me that the company of the second 3rd, who had been left in the base camp to help the commissariat officers, had behaved shamefully, that they had bolted, officers and men, and that though they had been entreated to stay and fight had run like curs and that the garrison had with difficulty been prevented from firing on them.

11. *Ornithorhynchus anatinus*, the duck-billed platypus, is a semi-aquatic, egg-laying mammal endemic to eastern Australia.

I will not mention the officers' names although I remember them. They rejoined, were promptly kicked out, and were slated in all the Colonial papers. Let them rip.[12]

And now I must give you a short description of the place, the defence of which not only saved us, but, I think, in a great measure saved Natal.

It had been a frontier trading post,[13] and consisted of a comfortable bungalow with a store some 15 yards from it; both buildings stood in line some 200 yards from a steep hill and were about 1000 yards from the drift across the Buffalo River. Both buildings were built of brick and thatched. In front was a fine orchard and between the orchard and the houses ran a natural step or ledge of rock 3 to 4 feet high so that the buildings stood that height above the ground in the orchard. Along this

12. Lieutenant Harry D. Davies of the Edendale Troop and Lieutenant Alfred F. Henderson of Hlubi's Troop, both of Durnford's No. 2 Column, escaped the Isandlwana battlefield. Henderson's troop maintained its coherence in the retreat, and assisted in preparing the defences at Rorke's Drift. However, Hlubi's Troop fled to Helpmekaar when the Zulu approached. Likewise, a company of the 2/3rd NNC, stationed at Rorke's Drift under the command of Captain William Stephenson, abandoned the garrison and bolted towards Helpmekaar. Lieutenant W. C. R. Higginson, the Adjutant of the 1/3rd NNC, escaped down the Fugitives' Trail and once across the Mzinyathi River disgracefully abandoned Lieutenants Coghill and Melvill to their fate (see p. 138, n. 8, below).

Both Stephenson and Higginson subsequently rejoined the 3rd NNC at Rorke's Drift on 31 January, but on Lonsdale's orders were promptly put under arrest for absenting themselves without permission or cause. Because both were colonial – not imperial – officers, it transpired that they could not be court-martialled for desertion. Instead, on 19 February 1879 they were officially informed that their services were dispensed with, being no longer required.

Gert Wilhelm Adendorff (1848–c. 1914), the grandson of a German surgeon, served with the Kaffrarian Rifles in the Ninth Cape Frontier War and subsequently as a lieutenant with the 1/3rd NNC. He escaped the Isandlwana battlefield, attaching himself to Hlubi's Troop, but, unlike Lieutenant Henderson, stayed on at Rorke's' Drift to take part in its defence. There have always been doubts that Adendorff fought at Rorke's Drift, but the preponderance of evidence singles him out as the only Isandlwana survivor to have been engaged at Rorke's Drift as well.

13. In 1849 James (Jim) Alfred Rorke acquired a farm in Natal on the middle Mzinyathi River abutting a ford that came to be known as Rorke's Drift. There he built a dwelling house and store. He died in 1875 and his widow sold the farm to John Surtees who, in turn, sold it in January 1878 to the Lutheran missionary Otto Witt (1840–1923), who bought it on behalf of the Lutheran Church of Sweden. In January 1879 Witt rented the mission station to the military, and No. 3 Column converted the church into a commissariat store and Witt's eleven-room house into a hospital.

When No. 3 Column advanced into Zululand, the depot was not fortified or entrenched, and the troops of the garrison were encamped nearby. Improvised defences were thrown up around the post just before the Zulu attack on 22 January by the defenders who numbered 8 officers, and 131 men, 35 of whom were sick in the hospital. The defenders lost 17 men killed, and 1 officer and 7 men wounded in the battle. An estimated minimum of 600 amaZulu died in the attack.

step of rock was placed a line of biscuit-boxes and on the top of these sacks of mealies (Indian corn). These formed a breastwork of about 3 feet or 3 feet 6 inches, giving a height from the ground in front of about 6 or 7 feet. The breastwork was therefore low enough to enable the defenders to use their bayonets over and was high enough to cover them when firing, from behind it, in a crouching position. There is no need to describe the rest of the work as the principal fighting took place here. The hospital (bungalow) had been roughly loopholed, so had the store. Just in the rear of the latter were large stacks of forage but there had been no time to remove them nor the heavy, dry thatch on the buildings. Had the Zulus set fire to these stacks the thatch on the store must have been ignited and our men burned out. But they did not, for although they attacked from the right and rear, they got such a pasting, during their advance, that they swept round the buildings, took cover in the orchard and attacked from there.

They certainly did set fire to the hospital but that gave the defenders light to sight their rifles by while it blocked their own chance of entering from that side.

However those who want to know about the defence of Rourke's Drift must read other accounts. I am only writing about what I actually saw myself and I had not the honour to be one of the defenders.

Well Lonsdale and myself went round to the front and there saw what a tremendous effort must have been made by both sides.

The dead Zulus lay in piles, in some places as high as the top of the parapet. Some killed by bullets and the wounds, at that short range, were ghastly but very many were killed by the bayonet. The attack must have been well pushed home and both sides deserve the greatest credit. The hospital was still smouldering and the stench from the burning flesh of the dead inside was very bad; it was much worse however when we came to clear the debris away two days afterwards. Some of our sick and wounded had been burned inside of the hospital and a number of Zulus had been also killed inside of the building itself.

In front of the hospital lay a large number of Zulus also a few of our men, who had been patients, and who when the hospital had been set on fire had, in trying to escape, rushed out among the enemy and been killed, their bodies being also ripped and much mutilated.

A few dead horses lay about, either killed by the assagai or by the bullets of the defenders, and I wondered why they had not been driven away before the fighting began.

One thing I noticed and that was the extraordinary way in which the majority of the Zulus lay. I had been over a good many battlefields and seen very many men who had been killed in action but I had never seen men lie in this position.[14] They seemed to have dropped on their elbows and knees and remained like that with their knees drawn up to their chins.

One huge fellow who must have been, in life, quite 7 feet high lay on his back with his heels on the top of the parapet and his head nearly touching the ground, the rest of his body supported by a heap of his dead comrades.

Well we went into the laager. No one seemed to know what to do and certainly no one tried to do anything. I spoke to several of the seniors and suggested that the thatch should be taken off the store and more loopholes made, also that the stacks of forage should be removed, but until I came to Colonel Harness, R.A., no one would pay the least attention. He at once saw things in the same light as I did and said, "I will send my gunners to remove the thatch if you will get the forage away." This we did and in a short time the place was secure from fire.[15]

No sooner had I seen my part of this work done than I began to feel as if I was rather hollow and I rejoined Lonsdale and Harford. Rations had been served out and we had bully beef, biscuit, tea and sugar in plenty but no cups, plates, knives, forks or spoons – not even a pot or kettle to boil water in. However we made shift to eat the bully and biscuits with our fingers, then boiled water in the empty bully tins, added tea and sugar and drank it with gusto.

During the afternoon it was discovered that a large number of wounded and worn-out Zulus had taken refuge or hidden in the mealie fields near the laager. My two companies of Zulus with some of my non-coms. and a few of the 24th quickly drew these fields and killed them with bayonet, butt and assagai.[16]

14. In fact, H-B's experience of battlefields had been confined to those in Zululand between 12 and 23 January 1879.

15. Not knowing Zulu intentions and fearing another attack, during 23 January the British forces at Rorke's Drift set about improving the defences. The barricades were rebuilt and strengthened and the four 7-pounder guns of N/5th RA were mounted at the corners of the post. The half-burnt thatch was pulled off the roof of the storehouse (previously the mission church), and the brush and trees were cleared away all around the perimeter.

16. The British buried 351 amaZulu who had been killed close to the post, a grisly operation that took two days. Some 200 additional Zulu bodies were found over the following weeks further off from the battlefield. Many of these supplementary 'dead' were Zulu wounded whom British patrols, conserving their ammunition, apparently despatched as H-B describes.

H-B was not alone in recording these killings. Private Henry Hook of the 1/24th, Lieutenant John Maxwell of the 2/3rd NNC, Trooper Harry Lugg of the NMP, Trooper Fred Symons of the Natal Carbineers, Gunner Abraham Evens and Lieutenant Nathanial Newnham-Davis of the Mounted Infantry, all had tales to tell of summary shootings and lynchings by hanging (see Stevenson, Knight and Baynham-Jones, *Rorke's Drift*, Vol. II, pp. 165–83). Captain Hallam Parr, in his *Kafir and Zulu Wars*, pp. 263–7, with the honour of the British Army at stake, was at pains to deny the widespread rumours in colonial circles

It was beastly but there was nothing else to do. War is war and savage war is the worst of the lot. Moreover our men were worked up to a pitch of fury by the sights they had seen in the morning and the mutilated bodies of the poor fellows lying in front of the burned hospital.

The evening drew on and Lonsdale went into the laager for orders. He returned and told us that the white troops were to hold the laager and that we were to remain outside. This was as absurd as it was shameful; not only were our white officers and non-coms. to meet, unprotected by the laager, the first rush of the Zulus, in case of an attack, but we should have been swept away by the fire of our own friends inside it.[17]

We were also to find the outlying pickets and the advanced sentries. Our natives, with the exception of the Zulus, were quite useless for this service. In fact they had all taken refuge in the caves and among the rocks of the mountain, and sternly refused to come out. And now there was a row. Of course the roster was lost and I regret to say that the officers and the non-coms., furious at what they considered their unfair treatment, refused to tum out. Lonsdale, Cooper and myself talked it over with them and at last we said we would take the outlying picket ourselves. Harford at once chipped in, so the most dangerous picket that night was formed by three commandants and a staff officer.

Quin, my servant, swore that I should not go on picket while he was to the fore and Captains Duncombe, Develin and Hayes volunteered for the other picket.[18] Of course when we were moving off everyone wanted to come and the cuss words and recriminations flew like hail. We quieted them down. We took one picket, Captain Duncombe and three other officers formed the other; there was not much choice between them. Inlying pickets were told off and as soon as it was dark we took our posts, extending the Zulus in a chain between them. The night was very dark

---

about the killing of the Zulu wounded. Yet, the brutality of the British troops towards those amaZulu who fell alive into their hands is understandable after the night spent among the disembowelled corpses of their comrades at Isandlwana; while – as Hallam Parr admits – the NNC were routinely let loose after every victorious battle in the war to finish off the Zulu wounded, and on this occasion were only too eager to revenge their dead comrades. In the event, only three wounded amaZulu were taken prisoner at Rorke's Drift.

17. The two battalions of the 3rd NNC were positioned at the south-eastern side of the post below Shiyane Mountain (also known as the Oskarsberg) to guard the valley up which the Zulus had made their attack from the south-west the previous day, and also on Shiyane itself, both to prevent the enemy from occupying it and to keep guard on the river to the north. Their wavering morale was sapped further by being posted in this exposed position rather than within the fortified post with the British soldiers. During the night there was a groundless alarm, after which a fair number of the NNC sneaked away.

18. Captains R. Duncombe, R. Develin and P. W. Hayes of the 1/3rd NNC. Hayes had distinguished himself on 11 January during No. 3 Column's crossing of the Mzinyathi when he had jumped into the swollen river and rescued a trooper of the Mounted Infantry who had been swept off his horse (see p. 87 above).

but passed off quietly although there was a false alarm at the laager, and most of our white men who had remained there got inside. I don't blame them. What was the use of staying outside to be shot down by their own friends?

Chapter XIV

Life at Rourke's Drift

IN the morning on our return to camp we heard that the General, staff, guns and mounted men were leaving for Helpmaker.[1] Previous to his departure the General sent for me and kindly asked me, "What I should like to do?" I told him, "I should like to remain with Colonel Glyn if he had any use for my services." Colonel Glyn, on being asked, was good enough to say, "He would be very sorry to lose me and hoped I should remain."

During my interview with the General I asked him, "If he had received my messages on the 22nd?" He told me, "That he had never heard a word about them," and was very much surprised when I told him what they were. He also asked me what I thought ought to be done with my natives and I told him the majority were worse than useless. I should like to keep the Zulus but the others were quite impossible and recommended that they should be at once disbanded.

He shook hands with me, said some very kind things about my services, mounted his horse and rode away. Lonsdale went with him, leaving me in command of the 3rd N.N.C., and I at once set to work to disband them.[2]

1. At 9 a.m. on 24 January Chelmsford and his staff with a small escort of NMP set off for Helpmekaar. They were followed by the artillery and most of the mounted men. Colonel Glyn was left in command at Rorke's Drift with Major Clery as his Chief Staff Officer.

2. As ever, H-B cannot resist pushing himself to the fore. In fact, when Lonsdale departed, it would have been Lieutenant Harford, as his Adjutant and the only regular British officer with the 3rd NNC, who would have been in command of the regiment, and not H-B who remained the commander of the 1st Battalion, nor Commandant Cooper, the commander of the 2nd Battalion. Furthermore, it was Lonsdale himself who ordered the 3rd NNC to be disbanded, and not H-B. What occurred was that Chelmsford, before leaving for Helpmekaar, ordered Lonsdale to find out which men of the 3rd NNC were willing to re-enter Zululand when he resumed the offensive, and to disband those who were not. Lonsdale addressed the regiment and concluded that only the iziGqoza were prepared to fight on, and that the rest were hopelessly demoralised. He thereupon took the decision to disband the entire regiment (although he subsequently gave Chelmsford the impression that they had deserted).

Lonsdale then proceeded to Helpmekaar to receive further orders, leaving H-B and the other white officers and NCOs to carry out the disbandment. During the afternoon, they took in the men's firearms along with the red puggarees that identified them as members of the NNC. At the whim of their officers, some companies were allowed to take their flags home.

First I sent for Umvubie and his Zulus and through Duncombe made them a speech. I told them they had behaved like men and that the Great White Queen would hear of their courage.

It was true, I was going to send all the other Kafirs home, as they were cowards and women, but I wanted the Zulus to stay with me. Umvubie talked to the other head-men for a few minutes and then said, "If you let these common low Kafirs go home and we remain, they will raid our women and cattle. We should like to stop with you. You white soldiers are men and fear nothing. If you did you would not stop here, but if you want us to remain march us and those dogs to the back of the hill, we will kill them all and then we will remain, otherwise we must go home to protect our property and wives."

Umvubie's idea of solving the problem was sound. He and his 200 men were quite ready to attack the 1200 Natal Kafirs and I firmly believe would have killed them off, but it would not do, so I had to tell them, with regret, that they must go. They formed up, called me their father, which was not true, gave me the royal salute, to which I was not entitled, and moved off to their camp.

Umvubie paused for a minute to beg my permission to be allowed to kill only a few of the Natal Kafirs, who he was sure had annoyed me very much. Alas! I could not grant his modest request, so again saluting he sorrowfully departed after his men. In the meantime the other natives had fallen in and had gathered round me in a ring.

I told them in a few plain words what I thought of them. Of course I spoke through Duncombe and I guessed from his vehemence and impassioned gestures he was emphasizing my remarks with a few of his own. I told them that the Great White Queen would send them women's aprons when she heard of their cowardice and that they had better go home and dig in the fields with their wives. This is the greatest insult you can offer a warrior and they hung their heads in shame.

But when I told them to go, and advised them to continue their journey to a country even hotter than Natal,[3] they waited not for pay nor rations but those of them who had guns threw them down and the whole of them breaking ranks bolted each man for his own home. The Zulus, forming themselves into solid rings, marched past our group of officers, raising their shields in the air, in salute, and rattled their assagais against them;

Not all the men understood what was happening, and had to be driven out of the camp. The iziGqoza companies left in good military order, but the other companies simply bolted for home in small groups, sowing panic wherever they went through northern Natal. Their departure precipitated the desertion of the black hospital bearers and NNPC at Rorke's Drift and left the British garrison without any black auxiliaries for outpost duty and other more menial military tasks.

3. That is, to go to hell.

UMVUBIE REQUESTS TO BE ALLOWED TO KILL JUST A FEW NATAL KAFIRS.'

then breaking into a war-song marched proudly away, every one of them a man and a warrior. So exit the rank and file of the 3rd N.N.C.

Now what was to be done with the officers and non-coms.? All the former and some of the latter had horses, so with Colonel Glyn's sanction I formed them into a troop and we took on ourselves the duties of scouts and other things.[4]

But there was lots of work to do besides. The dead to be buried, the smouldering hospital to be cleared away and the laager to be strengthened and made defensible, so officers and men turned to and worked like niggers, when driven by a strong armed overseer.

We had by this time learned our lesson and there would be no more camping without laagering.

Everyone was pretty sick; the first 24th had lost their Queen's colours,[5] their band instruments and had been fearfully cut up both in officers and men. The second 24th had lost both their colours, their band, and a lot of officers and men. We had lost everything except what we stood up in. We had neither tents, blankets nor greatcoats; not a spare shirt or a spare pair of socks to our names. I had a tooth-brush but I believe it was the only one in the crowd and I was selfish enough to keep that to myself.[6] We had however plenty of food and drink (vile Natal rum),

4. Once again, H-B is promoting himself. It was Harford, as the senior officer of the disbanded 3rd NNC, who was ordered to remain for duty at Rorke's Drift in charge of the white officers and NCOs of the Contingent until they had all been drafted off to other columns. In February 1879 many volunteered to form a new unit of irregular cavalry named the Natal Horse. It consisted of three troops totalling 158 men wearing their old NNC uniforms with a hackle in their hats. No. 1 Troop (de Burgh's Horse) of 48 men, was recruited from the 3rd NNC. For the time being, as H-B writes, its former officers and NCOs took on the duties at Rorke's Drift which he describes.

5. Every British battalion of infantry (excluding Rifle regiments) carried two Colours (or identifying flags) embodying the regiment's individuality and traditions, namely, the Sovereign's (King's or Queen's) Colour and the Regimental Colour. When No. 3 Column advanced into Zululand, the 1/24th Regiment carried the Queen's Colour with it, but left its Regimental Colour with the two companies of the 1/24th garrisoning the camp at Helpmekaar. The 2/24th carried both its Queen's Colour and Regimental Colour into Zululand. To lose a Colour to the enemy was considered a deep disgrace.

6. In the second week of February the garrison at Rorke's Drift consisted of B Company of the 1/24th that had defended the post, the six companies of the 2/24th that had not been engaged at Isandlwana, ten troopers of the NMP, a small detachment of Royal Engineers and the officers and NCOs of the disbanded 3rd NNC. Circumstances were indeed tough. The British regulars were encamped outside the fort during the daytime, but at sundown all came inside where conditions were very cramped. The officers slept on the verandah of the former commissariat store, but their men lay on the bare ground with only tarpaulins to cover them.

When Norris-Newman visited Rorke's Drift on 10 February, he found that the situation was worst for the officers and NCOs of the 3rd NNC who since 23 January had been 'bivouacked out on the ledges behind the fort, without tents, tarpaulins, clothes, and even in some tobacco (Boer)—splendid it was but at that time I had not learned to appreciate its good qualities—lime juice, soap, tea, coffee and sugar in abundance but we were short of ammunition. The reserve ammunition had, for some extraordinary reason, not been brought up to the base and many an uneasy glance was cast at the small pile of ammunition boxes. There is a good story about the reserve ammunition. It was being brought up to Helpmaker and had reached Sandspruit at the foot of the hills, when the O.C. of the wagon escort heard the news of the disaster. It was night and he had it all buried so as to prevent the Zulus getting possession of it in case he was overpowered. After reaching Helpmaker in safety a party was sent to find it and bring it in, but the rain had removed all marks and traces and although lines of soldiers were formed who advanced prodding the ground with their cleaning rods no ammunition was ever found during my stay at Rourke's Drift. We were therefore miserably short of ammunition and not at all comfortable in our minds until somehow we received a wagon load from somewhere and then we prayed for the enemy to come on.[7]

The next day the two officers who had escaped on the 22nd, but who had not remained at Rourke's Drift, returned, and one of them informed

---

cases no blankets. They had lost all their baggage and effects at Isandhlwana; and the stores for their re-equipment, by some mischance, had never reached Rorke's drift' (Norris-Newman, *In Zululand*, p. 118).

7. H-B's yarn about the lost ammunition has a basis of fact. Colonel Edward William Bray, the commander of the 4th (The King's Own Royal) Regiment and the officer in charge of the line of communications between Helpmekaar and No. 3 Column, was on the march to Helpmekaar on 22 January with 28 wagons of stores – fifteen of which held reserve ammunition – and an escort of twenty-two men. Learning of the disaster at Isandlwana, he halted at the courthouse at Umsinga and attempted to improve its defences while local settlers and missionaries came in for protection. On the evening of 24 January two Border Guard levies of jittery and unreliable Natal Africans came up to help defend the post. Their parlous situation improved on the evening of 24 January with the arrival of the 2/1st NNC under the command of Brevet Major Harcourt Mortimer Bengough.

On 19 January Chelmsford had ordered the 2/1st NNC, which formed part of Colonel Durnford's No. 2 Column, to take up position downstream from Rorke's Drift at the Mazongweni (KwaMahamba) Drift, six miles south-west of Malakatha mountain. This disposition had left the 2/1st NNC uselessly stranded during the battles of Isandlwana and Rorke's Drift. On the following day (23 January) they hurriedly moved up from the river to Helpmekaar, but on 24 January Chelmsford ordered them south to Umsinga to help Bray defend the courthouse.

There Bengough found the situation confused and the defenders demoralised. He therefore decided to abandon the magistracy and on 25 January took up position on a rocky knoll to the west of the road between Umsinga and Sand Spruit, where his NNC began constructing a stone-built redoubt called Fort Bengough. Meanwhile, four companies of the 2/4th came up from Greytown and on 29 January proceeded with Bray and the wagons of supplies and ammunition to Helpmekaar where Bray took up the command of the fort. No hastily buried ammunition was ever lost – but that does rather spoil H-B's yarn.

me that he had got away in company with two of the officers of the first 24th, one of whom carried the colours of his regiment.

The story he told me was that they all three reached the river and plunged in. One, Lieutenant Coghill, got across safe. The other officer, who carried the colours, Lieutenant Melville, had his horse shot in the middle of the river where he lost the colours which were swept away by the current.

Lieutenant Coghill at once re-entered the river and went to his friend's assistance and they got him to the bank; here Lieutenant Coghill's horse was shot and my officer's horse turned turtle over a boulder but got out safe. The three officers scrambled out unhurt and my officer ran after his horse, caught it at the top of the hills and got away.[8]

I immediately reported the story to Colonel Glyn and Harford and myself determined to go down the river-bed and look for the colours. Major Black was also very keen on the job. A few days afterwards the river went down and a party of my officers started off to try and find the lost flag. I was awfully disgusted, for just as I was mounting, Colonel Glyn called me and told me I could not go as he wanted me.

The party left however under the command of Major Black. They found the remains of poor Melville and Coghill and buried them. Then Harford and a few of the officers entered the river bed and found the colours some way lower down.

They returned to the laager and as Black handed the old flag over to Colonel Glyn the excitement was tremendous, the Tommies and everyone cheering like fiends. The following day Colonel Glyn, Major Black and the colours were escorted by the officers of the defunct 3rd N.N.C. to Helpmaker where they were handed over to the keeping of the two companies of the first 24th stationed there.[9]

8. The two NNC officers were Captains Stephenson and Higginson (*see* p. 128, n. 12).

Lieutenant Nevill Josiah Aylmer Coghill (1852–79), 1/24th Regiment, was Orderly Officer on the staff of Colonel Glyn. He did not accompany Glyn on the reconnaissance-in-force on 22 January because of an injury to his knee on 20 January, and remained in the camp at Isandlwana. He escaped from the battlefield down the Fugitives' Trail and (despite his injured knee) turned back at the Mzinyathi River, along with Lieutenant Higginson, to assist Lieutenant Teignmouth Melvill (1842–79), the Adjutant of the 1/24th, who had ridden down the Fugitives' Trail with the battalion's cased Queen's Colour, but was then unhorsed in the flooded river. Melvill lost the Colour in the swirling waters, and the other two lost their horses. All three nevertheless made it to the steep Natal bank and continued on foot. Higginson cravenly abandoned the exhausted Coghill and Melvill and made his way to the top where he made good his escape by holding on to the tail of the horse of one of four men of Hlubi's Troop (Mounted Basutos) passing by. He implausibly tried to excuse his action by insisting that when the two lieutenants stopped and he carried on, that none of them imagined that the amaZulu were in close pursuit.

9. The search party found Coghill's and Melvill's bodies on 3 February and the Colour in the river the following day. On 5 February the Colour was returned to the 1/24th at Helpmekaar.

The reason I had been unable to take a hand in the finding of the colours was, that Lieutenant Chard, R.E., had been taken very ill,[10] and as I was a bit of an engineer I was used to superintend the building of the fort. But shortly a company of the R.E. turned up and I was once more able to be in the saddle with my boys.[11]

The rains now came on with fury—rain, hail, thunder and lightning, such as is never seen in England, and we had on an average about four heavy storms during the twenty-four hours. There we were without tents, blankets or greatcoats and we had just to grin and bear it. True, the storms only lasted a short time and then the sun would shine out and dry as quickly, but we usually had one storm at least during the night and then as the sun was absent we had to lie wet through the remainder of the night and shiver in the mud or sleep as best we could. We did everything possible to keep the laager clean but notwithstanding all our efforts it got very muddy.[12]

It was not so bad when you were once down in the mud but it was very nasty to have to get up and then lie down again as would be the case if we had a false alarm. Of these we had but few and that notwithstanding the awful strain to their nerves the men had suffered by the disaster at Isandlwana, yet it speaks volumes for the second 24th and my filibusters to be able to state that during the whole time we garrisoned Rourke's Drift not a single shot was fired in the way of a false alarm. The same cannot be

---

For Harford's detailed account of the proceedings in which he participated, see Laband, *Charlie Harford*, pp 94–5, 104–14.

10. Lieutenant John Rouse Merriott Chard, RE (1847–97), was attached in January 1879 as extra subaltern to the 5th Company, RE. He was the senior officer present during the unsuccessful Zulu attack on Rorke's Drift and was awarded the VC. Soon after the relief of Rorke's Drift he succumbed to the strain and disease, and was sent to the hospital in Ladysmith to recover.

11. Where H-B learned to be 'a bit of an engineer' is unclear, as is whether as he claims, he played any significant part in supervising the rebuilding of the fort. What is certain is that on 29 January half the 5th Company, RE, arrived at Rorke's Drift, and it was they who set about properly fortifying the post. They replaced the improvised barricade with a strong, stone-walled rectangular enclosure without flanking bastions, loopholed all around. The new wall took in the storehouse (now roofed with tarpaulins) and the cattle kraal, and was just under eight feet high except where it faced the Oskarsberg. There it rose to two stories with a banquette made of planks.

The new fortification was sometimes known as Fort Bromhead, named after Lieutenant Gonville Bromhead (1845–91), 2/24th Regiment, who had seen service in the Ninth Cape Frontier War in 1878, and in January 1879 was in command of B Company, 2/24th, during the defence of Rorke's Drift. Awarded the VC, he remained with his regiment on garrison duty throughout the rest of the war.

12. Conditions in the fort caused much sickness, predominantly dysentery and fever, aggravated by the lack of medicines. By early March there would be on average between forty and fifty men in hospital, and between forty and sixty additional men attending it for treatment. By 10 March eight men of the garrison had died of disease.

said of the relieving forces when they reached the front, when disgraceful false alarms, such as at Fort Funk, became common.[13] However I will now tell you of the great and only false alarm that took place at Rourke's Drift.

We had attached to us a civilian doctor, a very good fellow, who had seen much service and who had distinguished himself in the Russo-Turkish War.[14] He however had had a bad go of fever and his nerves had gone all to pieces though he still did his duty. Well one night I was lying down fast asleep in the angle of the laager I was in charge of; the aforesaid angle, having been the ancient pig-kraal of the farm,[15] was by no means a pleasant bedroom although airy enough, and we had just had our usual rain-storm, when I was suddenly woke up by the doctor who in an excited tone said, "For God's sake, Commandant, get up, the Zulus are on us." I was up in a second and the muttered order, "Stand to your arms," was answered by a rustle as the men rose from their mud beds and manned the parapet. The pig-kraal angle was the most exposed portion of the laager and being nearest the river was most likely to be attacked first. A sharp click as the breeches of the rifles were opened and shut, a sharper rattle as the 24th stood to arms and fixed bayonets and every man was at his post.

Not a further sound, not a word spoken.

I got into the most advanced spot and peered out into the darkness but could see nothing.

A bit of a moon and the stars gave a glimmer of light that would have flashed on the Zulu spears and given them away had they been there, but I saw not a spark nor flash.

I could see the white range marks that I had had put up and had any large body of men been between them and me they would have been obscured, so evidently my corner of the laager was not in danger of immediate attack.

Just then Colonel Glyn (the O.C.) came round. "What is it, Commandant Browne?" he said to me. "I don't see anything, sir," I replied; "there can be no large number of the enemy on this front." "Who gave you the alarm?" "Doctor ——" The Colonel turned sharply round. "What is it, Dr ——? Why did you give the alarm, sir?" "Good God, don't you hear them, sir?"

13. The Eshowe Relief Column and the 1st and 2nd Divisions of the South African Field Force were partly made up of recently arrived reinforcements who were untried and jittery, and several false alarms occurred, most notably that on 6 April at the eMvutsheni Mission soon after the relief of Eshowe, and at Fort Newdigate (nicknamed 'Fort Funk') on 6 June when the 2nd Division fired off thousands of rifle rounds and six rounds of canister in the dark against non-existent assailants.

14. The 'civilian doctor' was likely Surgeon-Major William Geoghegan, MB, of the Army Medical Department who was stationed at the Cape of Good Hope, the same Geoghegan mentioned by Harford (Laband, *Charlie Harford*, p. 102) as joining the Rorke's Drift garrison.

15. H-B means the cattle kraal, the projecting north-eastern section of the fort's perimeter.

said the medico, excitedly. "Hear them? Hear what, sir?" snorted the enraged Colonel. "Why, the frogs, sir," ejaculated the doctor. "The Zulus are waking them up as they advance."

A dead man could have heard the frogs. Anyone who has ever been in Natal or further north knows the diabolical row the frogs kick up, after rain, and the frogs round Rourke's Drift were like a strong-voiced crew at a chanty.

Curses not loud but very deep saluted the doctor from all sides and he retired in disgrace after an unpleasant *tête-à-tête* with the O.C., while the rest of us sought our mud beds again in disgust and disappointment. Rome was saved by the cackling of geese and they received great kudos.[16] But the frogs lost their chance of similar worship at Rourke's Drift owing to the absence of any enemy. Anyhow the only thing expended was cuss words and they, at Rourke's Drift, were too plentiful to be missed. No ammunition was wasted as would have been the case later on in the war.[17]

And now my messmate Harford got into disgrace. He was a gallant officer, a splendid companion, but, and the but is a very big one, he was a mad naturalist. He caught bugs and beetles both in season and out of season. I told a tale about him before in this yarn, but the awful tale I am going to relate now is one that even after a period of thirty years makes my blood run cold. For he committed a sin that in comparison made the seven deadly sins look trivial beside it. The crime was this, but I must give a short prelude so that it may be understood in all its hideousness.

The 24th had a small amount of reserve mess stores at Rourke's Drift, we had nothing, and although there was plenty of Natal rum I could not face the filth; vile stuff it was and hot enough to burn the inside out of a graven image. This being so the 24th, like the rattling good fellows they were, always asked me over to their corner whenever they opened a bottle and I had my tot.

Well just about this time a Natal man rushed through a wagon load of stores and asked leave to sell them.[18] I happened to have about £2 in my pocket at the time of the disaster and after buying two night-caps and some spoons and forks for Harford and myself, I asked the man if he had any liquor. He said he had a big square rigger of gin for his own use but

16. In 390 BCE, according to Roman tradition, when invading Gauls were besieging Rome, their night attack on the Capitol was thwarted when the cackling geese sacred to the goddess Juno alerted the defenders.

17. Whether or not this false alarm took place is unverifiable since there appears to be no corroborative evidence. In any event, it makes for a good yarn.

18. Harford (Laband, *Charlie Harford*, p. 120) gives a description of the traders who periodically appeared both at Rorke's Drift and Helpmekaar when the lines of communication were free from any chance of attack, and details the exorbitant prices they were charging for their goods.

not for trade.[19] I offered all the money I had left and an equal-sized bottle of Natal rum for it and we traded. Well now there was corn in Egypt and I could, in a small way, return the hospitality of the 24th so I at once sent round to my friends to come to my corner, that evening after inspection, and partake of the plunder. They had run out of spirits and the news was joyful.

I handed the bottle over to my servant Quin and told him to guard it with his life, and he swore he would do so. I was called away and I left Quin on sentry go over that precious bottle; he placed it carefully between two sacks and sat down on it so I thought it safe and attended to my duty. That afternoon we had our usual rain-storm and when it was over Harford came to me and asked me if he could have some gin. I was very busy at the time and said "Certainly, ask Quin for some."

Now it struck me it was strange that Harford should ask for it as he never touched spirits, but I thought he might feel chill after the rain and want a tot to warm himself.

Well the retreat was blown, the men manned the parapet, the O.C. inspected, and the men fell away. In a few minutes round came my friends, anxious for the tot they fondly expected to be in store for them.

"Hoots, Maori, where's the drappie?" said Black. I turned to Quin, who was standing stiffly at attention, and at once saw the worthy man was disgusted, sulky, almost mutinous. "Give me the bottle, Quin," I said. "Better ask Mr Harford for it, sir," he answered, with a grin on his expressive mug like an over-tortured fiend. "Harford," said I, "where is the gin?" and at once my heart darkened with apprehensions. "Oh, Commandant," quoth he, "I have caught such a lot of beauties," and he produced two large pickle bottles filled with scorpions, snakes and other foul creeping beasts and reptiles. "Do look at them." "But the gin, Harford?" I murmured, so full of consternation that I could hardly articulate. "I've preserved these with it," said he, utterly oblivious to his horrid crime. "What!" yelled I. "Oh yes," said he, "this is a very rare and poisonous reptile indeed"—pointing to a loathsome beast and beginning to expatiate on its hideousness and reel off long Latin names. "I don't care if it is a sucking devil," groaned I, "but where is the gin?" "In these bottles," said he, and so it was, every drop of it. Ye Gods! The only bottle of gin or any other drop of decent drink within 100 miles of us had gone to preserve his infernal microbes, and a dozen disgusted officers, who were just beginning to grasp the awful situation, were cursing him and lamenting sadly, oh, so sadly, his pursuit of Natural History, while dear old Black had to be supported back to his angle making remarks in Gaelic.

---

19. So-named after the shape of the bottle. A square rigger is a sailing ship where the four-cornered sails are carried by horizontal yards slung at right angles to each mast.

THE CRIME OF THE NATURALIST.

He was such a good fellow he was soon forgiven, but I do not think the dear fellow ever quite understood what an awful sin he had committed or realized what a wicked waste of liquor he had perpetrated.[20]

20. H-B clearly regards Harford's beetle-mania as irresistibly funny and cannot resist another yarn at his expense. As always, the appearance of Quin in the tale signals that we are not to take it too seriously.

Chapter XV

Collecting Information and Other Things

BUT now the weather cleared up, the flooded river went down and the days passed joyously and profitably in scouting down it.

My orders were that I was not to cross the river unless I considered it was fairly safe to do so or unless I considered there was something to be gained by my running the risk in crossing it. Well of course there was a great deal to be gained by doing so. The Zulus had kraals on the other side of the river—were they not hostile? and therefore to be plundered and destroyed. They had cattle, goats, fat-tailed sheep and fowls—were not these something to be gained?

They had our big camp to plunder—might we not have a little loot to repay us?[1]

No matter, my reader, what your ideas are, as regards plunder, you would have agreed with us if you were living on bully beef—everlasting bully beef. Yes, bully beef for breakfast, bully beef for lunch, bully beef for dinner—yea, and if you were peckish, during the night, bully beef for supper! *Tout jour,*[2] bully beef! I am willing to allow that bully beef is an excellent substitute for food but at the same time beg to assert it very soon becomes monotonous and we became desirous for a change. So our friends the enemy possessing all the toothsome dainties I have enumerated above we were very often tempted to cross that river and help ourselves to them and at the same time play old gooseberry with their owners.

So we used sometimes to cross that river, before daylight, and beat the Zulus up in their kraals when blazing huts, cracking carbines and revolvers would make them understand that we were still alive and kicking and then all the Zulu men having been killed or escaped, each one of us jumped what he could, one man a sheep, another a goat, others pots of Kafir beer;[3] the fowls stupefied by the smoke of the burning huts would

---

1. During the weeks following the relief of Rorke's Drift, endemic small-scale Zulu raiding and British counter-raiding took place across the Mzinyathi River by the garrisons at Rorke's Drift, Helpmekaar, Fort Bengough and Fort Pine. The British regularly patrolled the border and sent in scouting parties to gather intelligence.

2. H-B's bad French for *tout le jour*, the whole day.

3. *Utshwala*, sorghum beer.

be caught, have their necks wrung and be tied to the Ds. of our saddles[4] and then off we would go driving the cattle before us like a lot of jolly old Border moss troopers.[5]

Troth myself and my pirates lived high and I always took care that the O.C.'s mess had a good joint or a pair of fowls.[6] "Maori, where on earth do you get these things from?" he would inquire. "Find them down the river, sir," I would reply, and he would go away, shaking his head and muttering to himself biblical remarks about Ananias,[7] d——d thieves, will get themselves all killed, must put a stop to this, etc., etc., but he dined well and no stringent orders were promulgated.

One evening the O.C. sent for me to dine with him. I had sent him a pau (bustard) I had shot with my revolver and as he had also received some small stores from Helpmaker we fared sumptuously.[8] After a tot and a smoke he looked at me and said quietly, "Maori, do you think you could catch me a live Zulu?" I said, "I don't know, but I will try, sir." He said, "Don't hurt him too much as I must question him. I am very anxious to obtain information on certain matters and it is the only way I can obtain it." I said, "Had I not better question him outside, sir?" He said, "No, I'll have none of your Spanish Inquisition tricks. You bring him into camp, I will question him myself." I was not at all sure the dear old man knew how to extract information out of a native but I always obey orders, that is, if my inclinations are not too strong the other way. So talking the matter over with Captains Duncombe and Develin we determined to cross the river during the night and lay an ambuscade for any man who might be travelling from kraal to kraal.[9] This we did and hiding our horses among some bushes and rocks we lay dogo by a footpath and waited.[10]

4. A saddle D-ring on a military saddle was used to attach item such as canteens and ammunition pouches.

5. Moss-troopers were small bands of brigands, often disbanded or deserting soldiers, raiding across the border country between England and Scotland during the period of the English Commonwealth (1649–60). They were finally suppressed in the 1690s.

6. The O.C. was Colonel Glyn.

7. Presumably, Glyn was referring to Ananias and his wife Sapphira who were struck dead after lying to the Holy Spirit about money (Acts 5: 1–11).

8. The grey and brown kori bustard (*Ardeotis kori*), or pauw, is the largest flying bird native to Africa, with a length of up to four feet and a wingspan of over seven feet. It is a ground-dwelling bird that avoids flying on account of its weight, which can be as much as 40 lb. At the first sign of danger its response is to crouch motionless. H-B evidently shot it most unsportingly while it was cowering on the ground. It is unlikely he would have brought it down in flight with the Webley Royal Irish Constabulary pattern revolver carried by officers of the NNC, and which was accurate at no more than twenty-five yards.

9. Duncombe and Develin were evidently H-B's two closest companions from among the officers in the 1/3rd NNC and took part in many of his escapades.

10. To lie doggo (not dogo) is to remain motionless and quiet to escape detection.

About 6 a.m. along came a native and we were on him before he could let a yell out. I had him by the throat and threw him. Duncombe had him by the arms and Develin tied them. In a few seconds we were mounted, a rheim[11] was passed round the Zulu's neck so that he must run or hang and we were just starting when a lot more natives appeared. Duncombe had the prisoner, so at once cantered off while myself and Develin turned to cover his retreat. We were both dead shots and the party of the enemy were so surprised and astonished that they stood stock still. Crack, crack went our carbines and over rolled two of them. We loaded again. Both our horses were trained shooting horses and stood like rocks. We let rip and over went two more; again we fired and browned them, the M.H. bullets at 100 yards range would go through two or three men, so they let go a yell and bolted.[12] So we turned our horses and cantered after Duncombe, who was riding as fast as he could get the prisoner to move. A little persuasion from the butt end of a carbine made him mend his pace so that we reached and crossed the river without being cut off and brought our capture to the laager in triumph.

Our prisoner turned out to be a seasoned warrior instead of a young man so Colonel Glyn could get nothing out of him and gave orders that he should be taken down to the drift and let go.

He was also unkind in his remarks to me and blamed me for bringing him such a man as if I could pick and choose, besides he had only requested me to catch him a nigger and had not specified what sort of a one he wanted, but then this world is full of injustice and a scout must not be cast down if he gets his whack of it.

Now we had a picket on the top of the hill at the rear of the fort and they reported that they daily saw a Zulu at the top of another hill, overlooking the fort, who evidently took stock of everything that went on. After a few days this bounder, evidently thinking he was quite safe, began to send up smoke signals and this piece of cheek roused the bile of the O.C. Several parties were sent out to catch him, but he could see them leave the camp and he would disappear into some very rough ground. One night the O.C. sent for me and said, "Maori, I want you to put a stop to that fellow, it is simply disgraceful you have allowed this kind of thing to go on so long." Here was more injustice; he had entrusted the suppression of the Johnnie to others and now blamed me, but I have found it sound policy never to argue with or point out his faults to a choleric or liverish senior so I wisely said nothing but accepted the rebuke and the contract with equanimity.

11. A *riem* (pl. *rieme*) is a raw-hide thong.

12. The carbines H-B and his two companions would have been firing would most likely have been Swinburn-Henry .45 breech-loaders, the standard issue to colonial units, since Martini-Henry Mark II carbines were not shipped to South Africa until late February 1879.

It was evident that the Zulu must cross the river somewhere and I had noticed while scouting down our side of it a spoor leading in the direction of the hill from which he carried on his observations. At this spot there was a large mealie field abutting on the rough ground on the bank of the river, then some open ground and then some small patches of mealies. I had noticed that the spoor ran from the big field to one of the small patches and I determined to try for him there. Taking my two officers, Captains Duncombe and Develin, with me, we left the laager a couple of hours before daybreak and rode down to the spot, hid our horses and lay dogo. As soon as it was light we observed carefully the far bank of the river, the near bank we could not see, and the open space between the big field of mealies and the patch. Develin looked after the bank, Duncombe watched the open ground and I let my glance wander everywhere. One of us, therefore, if he came, was bound to spot him. It had not long been daylight when Develin whispered to me, "There he is." There was no morning mist and I just spotted him slide down the far side of the river bank, where we lost sight of him. We could now all concentrate our attention on the open ground and presently Duncombe spotted him crawl from the mealies and start squirming towards one of the small patches for fresh cover. I must say he did it splendidly; his naked body blended with the colour of the ground and would have been unseen by an untrained eye. He was evidently paying most attention to his right flank on which side was the camp from whence he might expect danger but we were on his other side and well concealed. We could easily have shot him but I wanted to capture him alive. My last capture had not been a lucky one and I wanted to take a prisoner to the O.C. as I knew he was most anxious to obtain information. Well we watched our friend gain the small patch. We could hunt him out of that if he tried to hide there, so we mounted and went for him. He must have been well on the *qui vive*[13] for we had not gained the open when he burst out of his cover and was running like a scared cat, for the big field, to try and regain the rough ground by the river bank, where he, at all events, would be safe from capture. But it was not to be. He ran well and was within thirty yards of his refuge, when my horse, the fastest of the three, overtook him and a tremendous smash, between the shoulders, from the butt of my carbine sent him rolling over and over like a shot rabbit. Before I could pull up my horse, the others were up to him and had tied his arms so that when I rode back to them he was sitting up looking very cheap. As he was still a bit sick I gave him some water and looked him over.

I was out of luck again, for instead of being a young fellow as I had hoped, he turned out to be a fine old war-dog, so it was good-bye to any chance of getting any information out of him. His field kit consisted of the

13. To be on the alert, or lookout, from a sentry's challenge in French.

COLLECTING INFORMATION FOR THE O.C.

usual Zulu outfit, one skin apron in front and one behind with the usual charm, etc., but there was one etc. he had no right to wear and that was a piece of turkey-red cloth bound round his head. This was the uniform of the Natal Native Contingent and on Duncombe demanding why he wore it, he answered, so as to deceive the red soldiers if he chanced to meet any. This was a fatal admission as it at once turned him into a spy.[14]

I almost felt sorry for the poor chap, but a scout must have no feelings and years of savage warfare had blunted any I might have ever possessed, so as soon as he had recovered his wind a rheim was passed round his neck and we trotted back to camp. On our arrival there we handed over the prisoner to the main guard, which during the day used a wagon outside the laager for a guardroom, and I at once reported to the O.C.

He ordered me to return to the prisoner, question him and then to report anything I might find out. This I did but of course could get nothing out of him, though he owned up readily he was a spy and that he wore the piece of red stuff round his head as a disguise. I was turning round to return to the O.C. when I struck my shin, which I had badly bruised a few days before, against the boom of the wagon. The pain was atrocious and I had just let go my first blessing when the Sergeant-Major, a huge Irishman, not seeing my accident, asked, "What will we do with the spoy, sor?" "Oh, hang the bally spy," I ripped out and limped away, rubbing my injured shin and blessing spies, wagons and everything that came in my way. On my reporting to the O.C. that I could get no information, but that the man owned up to being a spy, he ordered the Camp Adjutant to summon a drum-head courts-martial to try him.[15] Paper, pens and ink were found with difficulty; true, there was no drum but a rum keg did as well.

The officers, warned, assembled and the Sergeant-Major being sent for was ordered to march up the prisoner.

He stared open-mouthed for a few seconds, then blurted out, "Plaze, sor, I can't, shure he's hung, sor." "Hung!" exclaimed the O.C., who was standing within earshot. "Who ordered him to be hung?" "Commandant Browne, sor," replied the Sergeant-Major. "I ordered him to be hung?" I ejaculated. "What do you mean?" "Sure, sor, when I asked you at the guard wagon what was to be done with the spoy did you not say, sor, 'Oh, hang the spoy,' and there he is," pointing to the slaughter poles, and sure enough there he was. There was no help for it. It was clear enough the prisoner could not be tried after he was hung, so the court was dismissed and there was no one to blame but my poor shin.[16]

14. The captive became a spy, rather than a combatant, because he was masquerading as one of the other side.

15. A drumhead court-martial is a type of summary trial held during military operations.

16. Harford (Laband, *Charlie Harford*, pp. 102–3) gives a rather different version of the same incident:

By this time myself and my boys had made ourselves decidedly unpopular on the other side of the river. No decent kraal could retire to rest and be sure they would awake in the morning to find themselves alive or their huts and cattle intact.

The Zulus also could not understand, as my servant Quin expressed it, our field manœuvres.

Had they not beaten us at Isandlwana? Had they not taken our camp, killed all the defenders and captured all the camp contained? Were not the bodies of 900 white men lying unburied there, a feast for the asvogel[17] and jackal? and yet we who ought, by all the rules of the game (according to their ideas), to have run away to the sea, were not only sitting tight in a miserable camp, close to the scene of our disaster, but were sending parties of white devils across the river who killed men, burned kraals and swept away their cattle but who would not wait to be surrounded and killed. In vain they laid ambuscades and displayed tempting baits of cattle; on those occasions, it would seem, the white men did not hanker after beef and the traps were of no avail. Yet something must be done to put a stop to the nuisance so they appealed to the powers of Hades and sent for two first-class, up-to-date witchdoctors and explained their troubles to them. Could they drive us away? Why of course they could, provided they were well paid for the undertaking, so preliminaries being fixed on a satisfactory and business-like basis, the devil-dodgers started in to work the oracle.[18]

'In front of the Fort and some 600 or 700 yards down the slope of the hill, a scaffold had been put up by the Commissariat Department on which the carcasses of the cattle were hung up previous to issue, and one morning Major Black and I were sitting outside, warming ourselves in the sun and chatting, when we saw a most extraordinary-looking object suspended on the scaffold, and wondered what on earth it could be. Presently, a Private of the 24th came up from that direction, and Black asked him what the thing was, and he said that it was a Kaffir spy that had been hanged. "Good Heavens!", said Black, "By whose orders was he hung?" "Captain Harford, sir", was the reply, so we went down at once to look into the matter. The poor wretch, who was an old, wizened-up, grey-headed Native, had apparently been dead for some hours, and must have been hung sometime during the night, but by whom it was never discovered. Every possible enquiry was made, but not a soul knew anything about it and nothing was known of the Native or where he could have come from.'

It would seem that H-B felt guiltily compelled to write about the hanging but could not bring himself to admit that he and his two hard-bitten fellow-NNC officers had lynched the old Zulu man during the night, so concocted the extenuating (and gruesomely amusing) yarn about the dim, literal-minded sergeant-major and the aborted drumhead court-martial.

17. Vulture.

18. 'Witchdoctor' is a slippery term. In the Zulu world of medicine and magic, there were *izinyanga* (sing. *inyanga*), or traditional healers/herbalists; *izangoma* (sing. *isangoma*), or diviners, inspired by the ancestral spirits who unveiled the occult reasons for disease or disaster, warded off lightning and brought rain; and *abathakathi* (sing. *umthakathi*), or wizards/witches, who worked in secret and used their powers of evil to injure people's health, destroy life, prevent rain and cause all manner of misfortune. *Izangoma* had

Now the wind in Natal usually blows two ways during the twenty-four hours and most days it would blow across the river towards the camp all the afternoon. Accordingly one day we saw two natives appear on the bare ridge on the Zulu side of the river (the same ridge I wrote about in the first part of this yarn) who lit a fire and began to dance and gesticulate round it, the wind blowing the smoke towards us. We could not make out their game on the first day, but when the same thing happened the second day I inquired of some friendly Kafirs what these bounders were up to. They informed me, with awe, that the two natives were very powerful witch-doctors, that they were burning mutti (medicine) and parts of the dead body of a white man, so that the smoke should blow across to us, frighten us and make us run away to the sea.[19]

Now this was, clearly, not cricket; moreover it was against my principles to allow the remains of one of my comrades to be subjected to heathen rites, so I determined, although not a very religious man, to assert the powers of Christianity over Paganism.

I spoke to Develin on the matter. He had been a very well brought up young man, before he had joined the Lost Legion, and although his morals had somewhat deteriorated since that period yet he fully agreed that these cantrips must be put a stop to and expressed his feelings in pungent words.[20]

But how was it to be done? There was no bush nor stones on that infernal ridge that would afford cover to a cat and everything of that kind was far out of rifle-shot of the spot where these brutes carried out their unholy rites. However I bethought myself of a natural fold in the ground I had noticed during the 10th of January when we had lined that ridge all day and I mentioned this to Develin. He thought this would do provided we got there in the dark and lay perdu all morning. If they came again we should have them at about 400 yards range and both of us were certain for a much longer distance than that. Warning Develin to say nothing to anyone, so as not to cause unnecessary jealousy, and telling Colonel Glyn I was going out for an early scout, I forgot to tell him the purpose lest he should forbid the movement.

---

the ability to detect ('smell out') *abathakathi* and bring them to justice. Since the two 'witchdoctors' H-B refers to in his quite plausible yarn were working openly and at the people's behest, they would have been *izangoma*.

19. The two *izangoma* were burning *imithi* (sing. *umuthi*), occult medicine, to waft the smoke over the British in order, with the supernatural assistance of the ancestors, to induce them to quit the area. Usually, it was only *abathakathi* who included human body parts in their malignant *imithi* intended to harm people, although on occasion *izangoma* are known to have added human parts to their *imithi* on account of their enormous occult power against a hostile army.

20. 'Cantrip' is a word of Scottish origin, meaning a magic spell, a trick by sorcery.

We left the laager some two hours before daybreak, on foot, crossed the river, got into the fold of ground and lay low. We had plenty of food and drink with us and we determined to stay there all day. We were going to pit M.H. carbines against Satan and we felt like Crusaders at their very best and holiest moments. The day dragged a bit and it was very hot, but we meant to make it hotter for those bally rain-makers if they came and at last they did. They came up the Zulu side of the ridge and went to the same place where they had built the fire before and lit another upon which they threw a lot of stuff that made a big smoke which the wind blew in the direction of the laager. Then they began to dance round, point their sticks at the camp and utter cuss words and incantations. Disgusting-looking beasts they were and no doubt were more revolting in morals and manners than they were in person and field-kit.[21] Troth they looked fit and proper servants for the Evil One, at least I am ready to bet that no one else would have had them in their service and although they were not aware of the fact they were very soon to join their master. For by this time we had them covered. "Take the small one," I whispered to Develin. "Right," he replied. "Are you ready?" "Yes," said he and we both let go. My man spun round and round and then fell into the fire, getting a taste thereby of what was in store for him later on.[22] Develin's one collapsed in a heap and never moved.

We strolled up to them. My fellow had been hit through the throat, as I had taken rather too full a sight, but kicked the bucket when we reached him. Develin's one had been shot through the heart and on turning the body over we found it was a woman. We neither of us expressed any regret as a she witch-doctor is at least ten pieces of pork worse than a he one and as we walked back to the laager we patted ourselves on the back to think that we had put out of mess two of the foulest monsters that Providence allows to cumber the earth. *Vive la carbine à bas Satan!*[23]

21. *Izangoma* dressed differently from ordinary people, and would be recognised by their weird appearance. Their hair was worn in plaits over the face, their bodies were often painted white, black and red, and charms and *imithi* would be strung in baskets and pouches about them.

22. In other words, the fires of Hell.

23. H-B's French for 'long live the carbine and down with Satan'.

Chapter XVI

Under Orders for the Cape

BUT the good times were drawing to a close, for one evening two orderlies arrived from Helpmaker with dispatches and shortly afterwards Colonel Glyn sent to ask me to dinner. We dined and as soon as we were alone, he said, "Maori, I have had bad news." "Good God, sir," I replied, "not another disaster?" He said "No, but orders have come for you and four of your officers, Captains Duncombe, Develin, Hicks and Hayes to proceed to Capetown to assist Lonsdale to raise a regiment of Irregular Horse."[1]

I was dumfounded, I could not even cuss. I did not want to go, I was quite happy where I was, I was at the front; if I went back to the base I might be kept there, besides I wanted to remain with Colonel Glyn. He was a sportsman, a good soldier, had seen many years of colonial service, valued Colonial Irregulars, understood myself and my band of filibusters and would look over our little eccentricities provided we did our duty and fought well. I might even be attached to some Staff College man, far too highly educated to have any common sense or knowledge of savage warfare and this I dreaded. In fact I was in the deuce of a stew. All this and more I pointed out to the dear old man and begged his aid to extract me from the soup. He said, "I have wired to the General requesting him to allow you to stay. I cannot receive an answer for two days; you can stay till then."

Seeing I was very downhearted he said, "Maori, you may go down the river to-morrow, and if you cross I may look over it for once," and he winked a wicked wunk.

1. General Order No. 29, 8 February 1879 (*Times of Natal*, 10 February 1879) ordered Commandant Lonsdale, H-B., and Captains Develin, Duncombe, Hayes and W. Massey-Hicks of the 1/3rd NNC to Cape Town to recruit for a newly proposed mounted corps under Lonsdale's command, to be known as Lonsdale's Mounted Rifles (henceforth LMR), sometimes called Lonsdale's Horse.

Lonsdale preceded the other officers to Cape Town where he was reported by the *Natal Mercury* on 24 February to be already raising troopers for service in Natal. His intention was to make the Cape western districts – rather than the Eastern Cape where the Frontier Light Horse and Baker's Horse had already swept up most likely volunteers – his recruiting field.

I left him and went to my angle disconsolate but hopeful. After the evening's inspection I summoned my officers and told them I intended to take early morning coffee at a military kraal some miles down the river. One or two of them opined it was rather a big order. I allowed the fact and pointed out that everything depended on our surprising them, and to enable us to do that orders must be implicitly obeyed. They agreed, and Duncombe and I made our plans. We both knew the place as we had scouted it well. My plan to which Duncombe agreed was this. He was to take half a dozen men and to ride to the windward side of the kraal, they were to take with them a number of rope torches well covered with tar; these we had by us.

Just as daylight came they were to light them and throw them over the palisading on to the huts. The last few days had been very hot and dry and the thatch would burn like wild-fire. The gate of the kraal—and there was only one—was on the leeward side and I was to take up my position there, with the rest of the men (54 in number), and knock the stuffing out of the Zulus as the fire burned them out.[2]

This was very simple. The native sleeps heavily during the early morning and we knew our ground. Just after midnight we moved out of the fort and proceeded on our way, crossed the river and took up our positions without being discovered. A small ridge of stones about 150 yards from the gate afforded my men splendid cover; it also concealed our horses and enabled us to keep them just in our rear so that we could mount and bolt at once if the Zulus proved too strong for us. Half a gale of wind was blowing from the right direction, which drowned any sound our horses made and we waited impatiently for the dawn. Presently it came and I could distinguish the gate of the kraal and also see the foresight of my carbine. This was the right moment for Duncombe to begin. Suddenly a glare of light, then a burst of fire as torch after torch was thrown onto the huts. His bugler sounded as loud as he could and then galloped round the kraal sounding. My bugler did the same. Duncombe at once joined up with his men. Wild yells rang out as the flames, before the strong wind, swept over the kraal. The huts were close together and in far less time than it takes me to write it, the whole place was burning and flaming like the mouth of Tophet.[3] The gate was burst open and out rushed a swarm of Zulus mad with surprise and terror, to be met by a steady volley from my men. Every bullet told at that range and it staggered them, but they had to

2. A raid on this scale from Rorke's Drift into Zulu territory in the second week of February would normally have been reported in the Natal press, but H-B is the only source we have for this operation. The possibility of such a raid cannot be ruled out, but whether it really took place, or whether it is another of H-B's yarns to spice up the narrative, must remain an open question.

3. 'Tophet' is a term for Hell.

get out or burn. The flames were behind them and above them, the bugles were sounding, they must get out somehow and escape somewhere, so they broke through the fences and thorns and ran for the hills. Volley after volley was poured into them but go they must and a lot broke away to the flanks and escaped.

Oh, but we got a bit of our own back that day!

"Stand to your horses" was the order quickly given, a hurried glance over the men to see no one was left behind, then mount. In a moment we mounted and started at a canter and time it was to go. The Zulus had recovered from their surprise, the war-cry was being shouted on all the hills and crowds of natives were pouring down after us to cut us off. But we had the start of them, the ground was good-going for our horses and we were over the river before they could get up to us.

On our own side I halted, dismounted my men and gave them a taste of long-range shooting which surprised them, making them shake their shields and spears in impotent anger, but at last tired of losing men, without being able to hurt us, they drew off and we went home to breakfast, well pleased with our little jaunt, not a man or horse wounded.

The next day passed and during the evening orderlies turned up with the General's wire, and I heard with deep regret that I and the officers named must proceed at once. This order being imperative, we were to start next morning at daylight and make the best of our way direct to Pietermaritzburg without any delay.

I called my officers and non-coms. together and broke the news as gently as I could and then the row began. They swore I should not go or that they would all go with me, that I was their commandant and they would be all blankety, blankety, blanked before they served under any other. Dear old Glyn and Black came out and spoke to them. They liked the Colonel but they admired Black immensely. Could he not swear in a language simply heavenly, and although they understood it not, was it not all the more to be admired? So that when Colonel Glyn promised them that Black should command them during my absence they became pacified though the air of the pig-sty angle was very sulphurous that night with muttered oaths.

Now my man Quin, with all his good qualities, was a bad horseman, so I told him I must leave him behind as the ride would be a very hard one. It took the worthy man quite ten minutes to grasp the fact, then when he had done so he saluted me gravely and said, "I'll be blanked if I stop, I'll desert and follow you down on foot." I tried to argue with him but it was no good, go he would and go he did. I had a good strong, quiet horse, so I mounted him on it, but what he suffered on the journey only the Lord knows. He never complained but I saw the blood running down his saddle-flaps before the first day was over. Next morning at daylight we started and I said goodbye to Colonel Glyn and all the officers of the 24th with deep sorrow. Colonel Glyn expressed his regret at my departure, told me to hurry up with the recruiting and promised me that in the event of his commanding a column in the new campaign, I should have a command of Irregular Horse under him. This comforted me. Then I had to say good-bye to my officers and non-coms. This was very painful for all of us. Had I not fought with them, starved with them, lain out in the rain and hail with them and above all had I not twisted their tails for them when they required it?

The feeling towards a comrade is very strong in the Lost Legion, and as I rode away after a handshake all round the air seemed to burn blue and smelt like a cart-load of Tandstickor matches on fire.[4] However the last hand-grip, the last cheer, in which the men of the 24th join, is given and we ride away. I with a hump on me as big as a baggage camel's.

But we are used to partings in the Lost Legion, and though we are heading for the base instead of for the front, yet we soon bucked up. A pipe in the delicious morning air, a good horse between your knees, and good trusty pals with you, would make the most pessimistic misanthrope who ever croaked buck up, chuck his chest and sing.

We reached Helpmaker, where Captain Uptcher, first 24th,[5] a very old friend of mine, gave us a good breakfast. Then our horses having finished their water and feed we started again for Greytown. It was a hot and long trek through the Thorn country, a bit of rough desert no good to man or beast, and a hot, dreary ride it was even for us officers, trained and hardened horsemen as we were, while poor Quin must have suffered awfully. We soon began to pass lots of outspanned, loaded wagons; these had been abandoned by their owners and drivers the moment they heard the news of the disaster,[6] and there they remained, unguarded, for weeks. We helped ourselves when we required anything but pushed on as quickly as we could. Evening came on and our horses began to get very jaded and knocked up but they carried us through the thorns and at last we were on the borders of civilization. A large farmhouse attracted my attention and I determined to camp there for the night. When we reached it, we found it deserted. It must have been left in a hurry, some calves lay dead in a pen and ducks, hens, pigs, etc., roved about at their own sweet will. The stable door lay open so we soon had our horses watered, groomed

4. Säkerhets Tändstickor were a Swedish brand of wood-stick safety matches that usually came in small cardboard boxes.

5. Brevet Major Russell Upcher, with whom H-B had served in the 9th Cape Frontier War (see p. 33, n. 18, and p. 45, n. 9, above), was commander from 23 January to 11 May 1879 of the companies of the 1/24th stationed at Helpmekaar.

6. The supply wagons on their way to Helpmekaar from Greytown were abandoned by their drivers in fear of a Zulu invasion following Isandlwana.

and fed and then entered the house to look after ourselves. It was a fine, nice place well furnished and must have belonged to very well-to-do people.[7]

In the dining-room we found the table had evidently been just laid for breakfast, when the owners received the news of the disaster. The coffee-urn was on the table, while the food, dried up and mouldy, still on the dishes, was soon thrown out. Quin and Develin started a fire and made free with a splendid ham, hanging up. Hicks and Hayes found plenty of eggs and wrung the necks of a few ducks. Duncombe and myself had a look round. In the principal bedroom a gold watch and chain had been left on the table also a handful of gold and silver coins. There was plenty of spirits and bottled ale in the pantry and as by this time the cooks had prepared a sumptuous feed we were soon enjoying it. Then for bed.

I decided that we five officers should split the night into equal watches and said I would take the middle one, the worst, then threw myself on a bed and was asleep before I had time to think where I was.

Quin was exempt from guard as he was cook, and would have to get early breakfast ready, but when he awoke me before daylight, I found my kind-hearted officers had made another arrangement for sentry-go, leaving me out. They argued that if Quin was exempt through being cook I was also exempt as O.C. therefore they had done it all themselves. They had also groomed and fed the horses so that after we had finished a good though rough breakfast we were ready to start. My officers by acting as they had done were only acting in accordance with the way we have in the Legion and nothing more was said about it.

We reached Greytown before noon and I reported myself to a Major of the 4th King's Own who was Town Commandant.[8] He said his orders were that I was to go on at once by post-cart, but that it could only carry two and would not be ready to start for three hours, when it would call for me at the hotel.

I decided to take Quin with me, as he had had quite enough of the saddle, and that the officers should stay the night in Greytown and ride through with the horses next day. But how about money? We none of us had any. Quin hearing my remark produced from his pocket a handful of gold and silver. I also caught the glimmer of a gold watch and chain. "Here you are, sor," said he with a grin, "here's my savings." "Your stealings you mean, you d——d marauder. I've a good mind to hand you over to the

7. Local settlers between Rorke's Drift and Greytown forsook their farms in the wake of Isandlwana and took refuge in government and private laagers.

8. Brevet Major Augustus Charles Twentyman (1835–1913) of the 2/4th (King's Own Royal) Regiment was Commander of Imperial Forces in Colonial Defensive District No. VII. His three companies of the 2/4th were in garrison in Greytown where they had improved the defensibility of the town laager on receiving news of Isandlwana.

Provost Marshal.[9] Hand over that plunder." "I scorn the imputation, sor," said he, "sure I'm only saving the people's goods from them bloodthirsty scuts of savages." However before I left I found the rightful owner who thankfully receiving his watch and chain, returned Quin the money for his trouble in saving it and refused any offer of recompense from me for having made use of his house and food.

Well we reached the hotel and I informed the landlord of our plight and requested him to cash a cheque for me. He received us with open arms. "Cash a cheque for you? I'll cash fifty bally cheques for you, but no money of yours or your officers is to be taken in my house. No, you've been fighting for Natal you have. Come right in." Then to his wife: "Bet, open some champagne and get the best lunch going you can." Then bustling to his safe he took out £25 and said: "Here you are; if this is not enough I'll send to the bank for more.[10] Now drink up. Here's to you. Sit right down and tell us all the news from the front."

I divided the money between my officers and myself. Quin was already provided for and was coming with me, but the others would have to pay their way down with the horses and the days of loot were past.

We had a good lunch, drank a few bottles of fizz with the hospitable landlord and others who had flocked to hear the news. Then the post-cart drawing up Quin and myself got in and drove off followed by a rousing cheer.

What a glorious drive it was, up-hill and downhill, round corners with a precipice on one side and the hill on the other. The six mules galloping with their ears back as if Old Nick was after them and the cart swinging and bounding behind them as if it was an air balloon. Risky it looked but the old-time Natal post driver was as fine a whip as any the world could produce and knew his work and the road to perfection so the actual danger was very small.[11]

I had been through it often before, and enjoyed the pace and the rush through the air but not so the worthy Quin. He was new to it and it fairly astonished him. "Hould fast, your honour," he would yell, as we turned a sharp corner. "Just look at that now. We'll be wanting wings to fly through the air, like birds, just now. Holy Moses, that was a squeak. Oh, wirra, wirra, what are we here for at all, at all."

Then his conscience, or what he wore for one, would prick him. "Holy Mary, I wish I had left that watch and chain alone," he muttered. "Sure it's to a priest I'll confess as soon as I see one, by this and by that I will." "Do

9. H-B is threatening to hand Quin over to the Military Police who were under the command of the Provost Martial.

10. Purchasing power today of about £3,850.

11. The unpaved Greytown–Pietermaritzburg road was kept in reasonable repair by gangs of African labourers.

so to the Provo-Sergeant,[12] Quin," said I. "I will not, sor; he would not understand me good intentions, and sure it's bad the likes of them think of the likes of you and me, sor." There were plenty of relays of mules and the miles flew past, while the time passed quickly, shouting at the racing animals and listening to Quin's pious ejaculations, so that we reached Pietermaritzburg before evening after a most pleasant drive.

We found the town all laagered up and every one very nervous.[13] As we drove through the streets men and women came rushing out and shouting the usual silly questions: Will the Zulus be here to-night? Is there any danger? etc., etc.

Dropping Quin at the Crown Hotel with orders to get my traps, that had been left behind,[14] out of store, I drove straight to the Headquarter Office and reported myself. The General and most of the staff were away, but the senior staff officer took me up to the gaol to report my arrival to Sir Bartle Frere and Sir Henry Berkley.[15] Queer place of abode (I thought) the gaol, for H.M. High Commissioner and the Governor of Natal but it was the safest spot in the town so they roosted there.[16]

That being over, Captain Grenfell, the S.O.,[17] said to me, "Have you saved your dress clothes?" "Yes," said I, "they are here." "Then as it is guest night at the club come and dine with me."[18] "Right," said I and we parted. On reaching the Crown Hotel I found Quin had got a hot bath ready for me, shaving kit and dress clothes already laid out.

12. A provost sergeant is an appointed member of the regimental police (not the Military Police).

13. When news of Isandlwana reached Pietermaritzburg on 24 January, the white citizens hastily improvised a defensive laager in the middle of the city. In mid-February when H-B would have seen it, the laager consisted of several large buildings connected by barricades. Fort Napier, begun in 1843, the headquarters of the British garrison in Natal, overlooked the city but was held by only a small detachment of troops. When H-B stopped in Pietermaritzburg the level of alarm and tension was still very high and a Zulu incursion was anticipated daily.

14. The Crown Hotel, which opened in 1850, was on Commercial (now Chief Albert Luthuli) Road in central Pietermaritzburg. The site is now occupied by Liberty Liquors.

15. H-B means not Sir Henry Barkly (not Berkley), the Governor of the Cape and High Commissioner, 1870–77, but Sir Henry Bulwer, the Lieutenant-Governor of Natal (see pp. 74–5, n. 7, above).

16. To the west of the Pietermaritzburg laager, the substantial gaol on Burger Street, built in 1861, was also prepared for defence, and officials from nearby Government House took shelter there.

17. Brevet Major Francis W. Grenfell (1841–1925), 60th Rifles, a Deputy Assistant Adjutant and Quartermaster-General on Chelmsford's Headquarters Staff.

18. The Victoria Club on Longmarket (now Langalibalele) Street in Pietermaritzburg was founded in 1859. Its members always made officers from the garrison at Fort Napier and visiting officers welcome. The club closed its doors in 1996.

I had a look at myself in the glass, for the first time, and I did not feel proud of myself, but after a shave and a wallow in a hot bath, and oh, the enjoyment of it! self-respect again returned and then the comfort of being clean and dressing once more. *Figurez-vous* the easy dress suit, the clean boiled shirt with the polished front to a man who for over a month has lived day and night in breeches, boots and a tattered patrol jacket.

"Sor," said Quin, when he had finished dressing me, "will your honour be getting drunk tonight?" "No, Quin," said I. "Then with your honour's lave I will, sor." Of course I had noticed that he had already laid a good and solid foundation for a big bust. "Quin, have you confessed yet?" "I have not, sor, I will wait till I get to Cape Town; maybe there will be more to confess and I'll make one job of it." "Mind the Provo-Sergeant, Quin," said I. "I will, sor," said he. "I have seen him, he is a townie of mine, and if he is sober at tattoo it won't be my fault." So I left him and went to the club and enjoyed a good dinner. Serviettes, spoons and forks, finger glasses! By Jove, I was in a new country and I who had that morning picked the leg of an underdone, tough duck, held in my fist, enjoyed all these. Then the news. We had heard nothing at Rourke's Drift for weeks and everyone had plenty to tell me and plenty of questions to ask me, so a very pleasant evening was passed and I returned to my hotel and to bed.

What a night I was having! Fancy, clean sheets, clean pyjamas, mosquito curtains, how I luxuriated in them all but fell asleep before I had time to thoroughly enjoy them. Next morning Quin woke me and brought me early coffee. "Well, Quin," said I, "did you enjoy yourself?" "I did, sor. I had two fights I remember well and two more I misremember but they were good, and with your lave, sor, there is a man waiting now for me at the bathing-place. He's a fine hefty lad and they do say he is a boy with hands on him he can use. When your honour can dispense with me I'll be with him and it will be the father and mother of a fine fight; sure the others was only Rookies and of no account." "And the Provo-Sergeant?" I asked. "Faith we put him to bed as drunk as David's sow, by ten o'clock last night, but I've sent to wake him up so as not to miss the diversion this morning." "All right, Quin, lay me out some white clothes and you can go." I believe the fight was everything that could be desired. The fine hefty lad proved to be good with his hands, for although Quin was the victor, yet he had his work cut out for him and I did not see him any more that day.

Next morning my officers arrived and it was settled that we were to leave for Durban next day by post-cart. We sold our horses to the Remount Department, got our traps ready and about 10 a.m. the cart turned up but no Quin. We could not wait so Captain Grenfell kindly offered to have all the police-stations, guard-rooms, and other places of refuge searched for him and send him on if found so we started without him and reached Durban that night. On the way we passed the General and his staff and

I paid my respects to him. On reaching Durban we went to the Royal Hotel,[19] and next morning, to my unbounded astonishment, who should walk into my room but the missing Quin. How he got down the Lord only knows. Quin fenced with my questions when I asked about his journey but I have always been under the impression that he must have stolen two or three horses *en route*. Anyhow he was there and strangely anxious to get my traps on board ship. This was done and at midday we crossed the bar and with our bow pointing S.W. said *"Au revoir"* to Natal and steered for Cape Town.[20]

19. The Royal Hotel in Smith (now Anton Lembede) Street opened its doors in 1845 as McDonald's Commercial Hotel, the first hostelry in Durban. After Prince Alfred (1844–1900), Queen Victoria's second son, dined there in 1860, it was renamed the Royal Hotel in his honour. Still with the same name on the same site, today's luxury hotel is an entirely new building.

20. The *Natal Mercury* of 22 February reported that H-B and his four fellow-NNC officers arrived in Durban on 21 February, and that on 25 February they were due to sail for Cape Town on the steamer *Venice* to assist Lonsdale in recruiting and organising LMR. Quin also sailed with H-B.

PART II

Lonsdale's Horse

WE had a very pleasant though slow trip to Cape Town and one I thoroughly enjoyed as it was such a complete rest,[1] not that my health required repose and I was naturally burning to get back to the front but there was much satisfaction, on a dark stormy night, to listen to the howl of the wind, the wash of the waters and the splash of the rain on deck and be able to say, "Thank the Lord I've not got to visit outlying pickets to-night," or coiled up in my comfortable bunk grunt to myself, "This is better than a wallow in the mud on the lee side of a wet bush." But such selfish and sybaritic meditations were however subject to rapid change and I would fret and harass myself with the questions—"Are they having any fun at the front?" "Are the Zulus on the move and hostile?" May be they are attacking Rourke's Drift or Helpmaker at the present moment and my late comrades are fighting for their lives and the honour of our grand old Queen while I am snoring like a fattening ox in his litter, or gorging myself at a luxuriously-spread table, drinking iced drinks, while they, grimy with sweat, dust and blood, are facing death and the devil, playing men's parts in the most honourable of all games, namely, that of war, and doing it on bully, biscuit and muddy tepid water. Faith and when these thoughts entered my brain I would fret and worry, for my vivid imagination pictured the scene of a Zulu attack and I could plainly see with my mind's eye the long lines of rushing, yelling, whistling savages, note their flashing assagais and waving plumes, hear the clatter of their red, white or black shields, but above all the gallant, bronzed skinned warriors themselves as they charged madly home to victory or death. On the other hand I could see the stern faces of our noble Tommies, in whose eyes shone the British lust for battle as they calmly emptied their rifles, on the muzzles of which glanced the silvery bayonets so soon to be dappled red. I could see the calm, collected officers giving their orders and the gallant old Colonel standing in the midst of the turmoil as cool as if in his garden at home. All this I could see but my thoughts dwelt more on my own particular crowd, the reckless lost

---

1. The voyage from Durban on the *Venice* took five days, and H-B and his four companions landed in Cape Town on 2 March 1879.

legionaries I had so lately commanded, and I seemed to hear their wild cheers and imprecations and noted their savage eagerness to get to hand grips with their foes. Oh, but at such moments the longing to get back to my Lambs, at the front, seemed to be almost more than I could bear and I would pace the deck like a caged lion, cursing the luck that had sent me away from the game I so fondly loved and the boys who might be playing it. Quin at such times would try to comfort me. "Sure, sor," he'd say, "there's devil a bit of fun going on up there at all at all, nor there won't be till the rainforcements come out.[2] The Gineral, dear man, can't move, sor, and the black hathen, bad luck to them, will be busy waking their dead, licking their wounds and witch-doctorin' their dirty sowls.[3] So rest aisy, sor, sure we'll soon raise the men and be back again in toime to take the floor when the new divarsion starts and it's thin it's ourselves who'll be better for a few weeks' good aiting and drinking and soft lying and thin yer honour has not cologued with a lady for years; troth we'll both be more civilized after a little famale society, God bless thim." "Yes, Quin," I'd chip in, "and there's that long-deferred confession of yours you have to make. Sure if you let it stand over much longer you'll have to get relays of priests to hear it all, and by gad, if it's Father O'Connell who has to hear all about your villainies, troth it's myself as will speak the word to him that will put a stop to your aiting, drinking, debauchery and philanderings. I know your little ways, Quin my boy, it's the morals of an old tom cat you're acquiring. Faith it's another jaunt up into the Uriwera country you are wanting to cool you off,[4] for it's too fat and lusty you're getting." At the receipt of this broadside the worthy faithful fellow would retire with a broad grin on his expressive mug, muttering, "Maybe the holy man would say to yer honour—'Troth, Mejor, 'tis yerself and yer man that makes a foine half section, for there's a pair of ye's as the divil said to his horns'— but sure, sor, it's not my place to know what his riverence says or thinks." On my way down the coast we took on board, at East London, a middle-aged American gentleman who turned out to be a splendid companion, chock-full of dry humour and yarns of the late Civil War,[5] in which he had seen much service. His arrival on board, inside a swinging basket, was by no means dignified,[6] as he was shot out on deck like a bag of monkey's rations and sat there for a minute or two tenderly rubbing certain portions of his human corpus while his spirit-guided

2. The reinforcements Chelmsford had requested after Isandlwana began arriving in Durban in very late March and early April from the United Kingdom, Ceylon, St Helena and Mauritius.

3. Quin is referring to the ritual cleansing *amabutho* underwent after combat.

4. Te Urewara is forested, sparsely populated rugged hill country in the North Island of New Zealand.

5. The American Civil War (April 1861–May 1865) between the Union ('the North') and the seceding Confederacy ('the South').

6. See pp. 26–8 for the conveyance of passengers on board at East London.

language wandered into flowery realms of quaint though very sincere invocations against the ship, the surf boat and the sea, while his peroration anent the man at the steam winch was so sublime that it made the donkey-engine manipulator, an artist himself in cuss words, turn green with envy and open his mouth in awe and astonishment. Much amused I tendered a helping hand, which he accepted and regained his feet, whereupon, after he had subjected me to a close scrutiny, he said with great solemnity, "Sir, I am indebted to you for your courtesy, please accept my thanks." I bowed and he continued: "I guess, sir-re, judging from your dress and appearance you are a British fighting man, is that so?" Again I bowed and he went on: "Wal, I calculate, that the weather signs your face shows, you air just down from the front, on duty. Yes, sir-re, men resembling yourself and these other gentlemen don't have no urgent private business, family or otherwise, as to make you howl for leave, when thar's a dog and monkey time, with bullets flying up on the frontier. No, sir-re, I've been there some and know." Again I acquiesced, and he drawled on with such enhanced gravity, that had it not been for the burst of supernatural eloquence which he had let fly a few minutes before I should have thought that he was a fancy religion sky-pilot about to give tongue. "Wal, gentlemen, that being so, I should like to take up my parable and tell you, that you Britishers deserve all the Hades that the tarnal niggers gave you the other day, yes, gentlemen, and more, you strangers can take my word for it. Providence never intended this d——d country for anyone bar Niggers, Flies, Missionaries and Jews. No, God Almighty never wanted you Britishers nor any other civilized white man to enter South Africa and did his best to keep us out or why in thunder did he place a damned bar across every harbour mouth? Yes, sir-re, he did it, to keep us white men out, and as we lack gumption not to take his hint, you Britishers get your gruel from a lot of d——d Ethiopian minstrels[7] and I, Colonel Cyrus P. Stanwood,[8] late of the Confederate Army, comes nigh to breaking my darned crupper bone, busting my pants and using profane language boarding this packet.

"And now, sir-re, if you'll add to your courtesy by pointing out the direct trail to the bar saloon I suggest we, and these other gentlemen, make a bee-line for it and imbibe cocktails to the health of the great and good Queen, the President of the United States, a lost cause,[9] and all fighting men. Say, strangers, shall we get?" We got.

7. The minstrel show was an American form of theatre, developed in the early nineteenth century. The actors were mainly whites wearing blackface make-up for the purpose of comically portraying racial stereotypes of African Americans.

8. 'Colonel Stanwood' has not been traced, and appears to be H-B's invention for the sake of his yarn. 'Stanwood's' rampant racism might be expected of a former Confederate officer, and certainly expresses H-B's own views.

9. The 'lost cause' was that of the Confederacy in the American Civil War.

The advent of Colonel Stanwood was indeed a Godsend to us, as the coasting boat on which we travelled put into every port *en route* and we also were delayed by heavy weather, so that his quaint yarns and dry humour helped to pass the time which otherwise would have hung heavily on our hands. The boat was, moreover, crowded with the widows and orphans of the 24th Regiment, who had been embarked at East London, and very many of these forlorn creatures benefited largely by his open-handed generosity; he was a wealthy man who, not being goody-goody, believed in relieving distress with dollars and not with good advice, tracts, and red tape, which so many people in England believe in. Faith he was a white man and one who acted up to the maxim that "blood is thicker than water."

We reached Cape Town,[10] where I found that Lonsdale had already started to form the nucleus of a regiment. He had taken down with him from Rourke's Drift a captain named Gordon[11] and had inspanned a fine young Englishman—Kynnersley Gardner—whom I had been messmate with at Kei Road and who had seen service with the 88th and 24th, during 1877 and 1878, as Adjutant and Paymaster.[12] These officers had already recruited one troop which was despatched to Durban under Gordon a few days after my arrival.[13] Our office was within the castle and I was soon busy at work passing and attesting men,[14] Quin acting as a most efficient recruiting-sergeant, and Gardner giving me great assistance. We had no difficulty in getting men but when it came to clothing and equipping them it was quite another pair of shoes. There was no spare clothing or equipment in the Government stores,[15] so Lonsdale had to employ local Hebrew contractors who not only broke faith with him as to the date the

10. On 2 March 1879.

11. Captain Allan Gordon, 1/3rd NNC.

12. *Hart's Army Lists* for 1879 and 1880 make no reference to a Kynnersley Gardner serving in either the 24th or 88th Regiment. There is a Captain Smith Hannington Gardner with the 88th, but he served with his regiment throughout the Anglo-Zulu War.

13. On 14 March 'A' Troop, the first detachment of LMR under the command of Captain Gordon, sailed from Cape Town aboard the *Roman*. Their destination was Durban where they would undergo training and be fitted out with horses and saddlery.

14. The Castle of Good Hope is a bastioned fortress in Cape Town begun by the Dutch East India Company in 1666. Since 1806 it had been the headquarters of the British garrison at the Cape.

During 4–28 March Lonsdale and his officers (including H-B) were engaged on a recruiting drive through fourteen towns of the Cape as far east as Humansdorp near Algoa Bay, some 400 miles from Cape Town. Their objective was to recruit 450 whites and 360 Khoisan. In the event, Lonsdale eventually raised four troops of irregular cavalry, 236 men strong, many of them very young. Three of the troops went on in late April and early May to serve with the 1st Division, South African Field Force.

15. The LMR uniforms were made up from yellow/brown corduroy. Officers wore blue patrol jackets, cord breeches and either Foreign Service helmets or smashers (soft felt hats with wide brims).

goods were to be delivered on, but also eventually robbed the Government of a vast sum of money.[16] I have no space to descant in this book on the shameless robberies perpetrated by civilians and others on the Imperial Exchequer during the Zulu and subsequent wars in South Africa, nor to animadvert on the folly, if not worse, of officers placed in high authority who made contracts with and confided in men well known to be the most infernal rogues in the country, but this I hope to do in a following work, when I think I shall open the eyes of my readers as to how their money has been spent. But now to continue. There was great trouble after Isandlwana in getting Totty or native wagon-drivers and voerloupers,[17] as all the coloured people in South Africa dreaded the name of the Zulus, so that no sooner had I recruited a considerable number of men for Lonsdale's Horse than I was dispatched into the Caledon, George[18] and other outlying districts to buy horses and recruit Cape bastards,[19] as it was fondly hoped that the latter, having a strain of white blood in them, might not be so nervous as Colonial or Natal Kafirs. I however obtained but few and was sadly hampered by the missionaries, at the various mission stations myself and Captain Develin visited. *N.B.*—I shall give my experiences with missionaries, I.D.B.'s[20] and Army contract swindles in the book I have already mentioned it is my intention to publish. As regards the horses, I obtained a considerable number fairly cheap and of good quality and sent them down to Cape Town, where they were grabbed by the Imperial Remount officers for the regular regiments, so Lonsdale's Horse went short.

I was therefore very pleased when I received orders to return to the front though my joy was tempered by being directed to call in, *en route*, at East London and King William's Town so as to take on the men recruited at those places.[21] This I did and reached Durban with some sixty

16. H-B's antisemitism is unrelenting.

17. By 'Totty' H-B means Khoisan (*see* p. 121, n. 2, above). A *voorloper* is the leader of a span of oxen yoked to a wagon

18. Lonsdale had, as he stated on 27 February to Captain Mills (Simpson, 'Imperial and Colonial Officers'), 'settled a plan for Commandant Browne, who is to get the Hottentots together'. Caledon, sixty miles east of Cape Town, had its origins in the late eighteenth century and was named after the Earl of Caledon, Governor of the Cape (1806–11). George, proclaimed in 1811 and named after King George III, is 200 miles further east.

19. Technically, a *bastaard* was a man whose father was a slave and his mother Khoikhoin, but H-B uses the term more loosely to describe the Khoisan ('Coloureds') of his day who were of mixed descent, often including a white progenitor.

20. IDB: Illicit Diamond Buyer.

21. Lonsdale set up a transit camp in Papendorf (now Woodstock on the southern outskirts of Cape Town), where LMR recruits were processed before detachments embarked periodically for Durban. Captain Duncombe arrived with one on board the *Olympus* on 22 April; on 2 May Captain Massey-Hicks embarked with another on the *Manora*; and

tatterdemalions, without either arms or uniforms as there were no stores to be obtained in King.[22] On landing in Durban I found everything in an absolute state of chaos. Store-ships and troop-ships began to arrive and no provision had been made to receive or distribute the stores, equipment or clothing, etc., as it was landed. The Durban wharves, much smaller in those days than they are now, were soon covered and cumbered with mountainous heaps of all sorts of goods which the single rail on to the town vainly tried to reduce;[23] nor when the trains were loaded could the stuff be handled at the small town station so that in order to clear the trucks, for fresh loads, all their contents had to be dumped down along the line, where they were piled up in inexorable confusion, no one knowing or seeming to care where any stated supplies were or how they were to be come at. On my reporting myself to the General commanding the base of operations,[24] he was good enough to thank Providence for my advent, stating as his reason that the hundred or more men, recruited in Durban, for Lonsdale's Horse,[25] were lawless banditti, a menace and terror to the town and a cussed nuisance to himself and that he must detain me at Durban to curl their tails. He was certainly very kind about my detention and asked me to dine with him the following evening, provided that in the meantime I had not been butchered by my men. This was by no means cheering news for me who had fondly hoped to get on to the front next day, and recollections of poor Pulleine's Lambs flashed through my mind while my heart grew dark with apprehensions of a long detention at the base. Nor were my misgivings unfounded for on proceeding to the camp of Lonsdale's Horse I found the men all the General had described them to be, and worse, in fact he had been most charitable in his description so

<hr>

Commandant Lonsdale himself, with five officers, followed on 3 May on the *Olympus* with the last two companies of LMR.

22. At this point, H-B's narrative becomes increasingly opaque as he massages it to accommodate his bogus presence at the battle of Gingindlovu fought on 2 April (*see* next chapter). All the detachments of LMR, except for Captain Gordon's troop which had sailed from Cape Town in mid-March, embarked in Cape Town weeks *after* Gingindlovu (*see* previous footnote). H-B is careful not to specify the date he landed in Durban, and leaves us to infer it was well before the battle. In fact, he and his long-time associate, Captain Develin, with eighty-five members of LMR, sailed from East London on board CRMS *Lapland* and arrived beyond the bar at Durban on 24 April. That same afternoon they were landed by the *Fox* (*Natal Mercury*, 25 April 1879).

23. The steam railway that ran from the Point at the entrance to the harbour to the centre of Durban opened in 1860 and was the first public railway in South Africa.

24. H-B is presumably referring to Major-General the Hon. Sir Henry Clifford, VC (1826–83), Inspector-General of Lines of Communication and Base, who first stepped ashore at Durban on 9 April, seven days after Gingindlovu had been fought. H-B could well have reported to Clifford as he recounts, but only in the weeks after the battle, and not, as he implies for the sake of his misleading narrative, before it.

25. The men for LMR were recruited in the Cape, not in Durban.

that I had to buckle to and knock them into shape. My word it was a job; Lonsdale advised me he had forwarded uniforms and equipment for two hundred men. Where the cases were the Lord only knew and as He would not tell us we had to prospect and overhaul the miles of jumbled-up stores heaped along the railway lines to find those that belonged to us. After days of searching we found some, and with great trouble I managed to get two more troops equipped and sent to the front[26] while I also got the remainder of the condottieri out of Durban to a place called Saccharine,[27] where they could do but little harm and their vagaries not be criticized by an unappreciating public. All this was a fearful nuisance to myself, longing as I was for active service, but I did however manage to get a few hours at the front and had the great good luck to just drop in for and take a hand in the battle of Ginginhlova. I had had to make a flying trip up to the base camp at the Tugela River reaching there three days after the relief column had started in to succour Pearson's men beleaguered in Etchowe [Eshowe],[28] and while I was talking to Colonel Hopton of the 88th, who was in command there,[29] an important dispatch arrived for Lord Chelmsford who had gone on with the relieving force.

This was my chance, and I begged the Colonel to allow me to carry it on, which after some demur he consented to let me do.[30] Overjoyed at my miraculous luck I was soon in the saddle and by riding hard overtook the column as evening came on and they were forming laager or trying to do

26. On 19 May the headquarters and two troops of LMR left Durban by train for the encampment at Saccharine while one troop remained in Durban. They were then to proceed to join the 1st Division at the Lower Thukela. This forward movement of LMR therefore took place in late May and not (if we follow H-B's chronology) in late March and before the battle of Gingindlovu.

27. The Saccharine Hill sugar estate, some six miles north of Durban, was founded by Stephen Gee in 1855, and in 1879 was owned by A. de Chazal.

28. The Eshowe Relief Column of 3,390 white and 2,280 African troops, under the personal command of Lord Chelmsford, set out on 29 March from Fort Tenedos to relieve the garrison of Fort Eshowe which the amaZulu had blockaded since 23 January.

Precisely why H-B had to make his 'flying trip' to the Eshowe Relief Column's base camp at Fort Tenedos (which had been built by No. 1 Column between 13 and 17 January 1879) is left unexplained because it is a fabrication for the sake of the yarn that is to unfold about his unlikely presence at Gingindlovu.

29. Brevet Lieutenant-Colonel E. Hopton was in command of three companies of the 88th Regiment where, following Isandlwana, they remained in reserve at Fort Tenedos on the Zulu side of the Thukela until after the relief of Eshowe, when they formed part of the 1st Division, South African Field Force.

30. Fort Tenedos and the Eshowe Relief Column were in communication by heliograph and it was no longer necessary to send dispatches by messengers who were likely to be intercepted by Zulu patrols. This mysterious 'important dispatch' which had to be delivered to Chelmsford, and for which there is no corroborative evidence, is clearly a device on H-B's part, deployed to explain why he otherwise unaccountably joined the Eshowe Relief Column and was fortuitously present at Gingindlovu.

so,[31] for when I had delivered the dispatches, I looked about and marvelled at the confusion going on.[32] At that time I had never before seen a laager formed, no more had any other English officers then present, and in my humble judgment it would have been sound policy for the Chief Staff Officer to have pointed out the position on which he wished the work to be formed and then to have left the detail of the movement to be carried out by the Dutch and Colonial conductors, most of whom had probably been born in laagers, or at all events knew how to bring up and swing the long teams of oxen, so as to ensure each wagon reaching its proper place. Had this been done the laager would have been formed in a very short space of time and the troops would have had ample opportunity to eat their suppers and make themselves comfortable, but this plan would have been

31. Fort Tenedos was twenty-one miles from the slight knoll on the south bank of the Nyezane River where the Eshowe Relief Column was constructing a laager on 1 April. The route H-B would have taken was initially over open, undulating country that became increasingly covered in thick bush. After days of incessant rain, the column's wagons had turned the track into a churned-up quagmire. On the way, H-B would have had to cross the Nyoni River with its steep banks and the Matigulu, which was in spate. In his memoirs, *Campaigning in South Africa*, p. 126, Captain William Molyneux, Chelmsford's Senior ADC, described the Matigulu as 'forty yards wide and four feet deep . . . [with] the current running like a mill-stream'. Even so, with hard riding H-B might well have travelled the distance in one day. However, the numerous dongas, high grass and bush *en route*, where Zulu parties were likely lurking to cut off stragglers, made the journey extremely hazardous, and H-B implies that he rode alone, without an escort. Never one to be reticent about his exploits, is it likely that he would have failed to detail the many obstacles and dangers he would have had to overcome or avoid if he had really made the journey? It is not inconceivable that H-B borrowed the idea for his ride from Guy Dawnay, the brother of Viscount Downe and a gentleman-adventurer, whose memoirs were privately printed *c.*1886. With two companions, Dawnay rode on from Fort Tenedos on 29 March to reach the Eshowe Relief Column's first laager at the Nyoni River, ten miles away, where he joined the 5th Battalion NNC (Dawnay, *Campaigns*, pp. 8–9).

32. H-B's description of the chaos he witnessed at the laager on the night of 1 April is further proof that he was not actually there. Captain Molyneux, whom Chelmsford had appointed laager-master, admitted in his memoirs, *Campaigning in South Africa*, p. 124, that on 29 March, when the column halted for the first time at the Nyoni River, 'that night the waggon-drivers, who had had no practice in laagering, got so out of hand that the laager was made anyhow, and would hold only one third of our oxen'. However, when the halt was made the following night at the Matigulu River, Molyneux believed that 'the laager this time was large enough and fairly well made' (p. 124). The column, which took all day to cross the Matigulu River, laagered again on 31 March. On the fourth night of its advance, when H-B purportedly arrived while the column was establishing its laager, there had been a further, considerable improvement in its construction that belies H-B's description. Chelmsford and his staff had decided that to simplify the procedure the laager would be exactly 130 yards square with thirty wagons or carts to a side. The shelter trench would be dug fifteen yards in front of the laager, leaving enough space for 2,000 men in close order two ranks deep in the space between. Molyneux prided himself that on the evening of 1 April 'the laager was finished and the shelter trench marked out in no time' (p. 128), with no confusion as there had been on 29 March.

far too simple for the British Staff College man of that epoch, so instead, excited staff officers and Aldershot-trained transport conductors who, until a few days previously, had never seen, much less handled, a South African bullock wagon and who could not speak one word of Dutch or Kafir, took the contract in hand and of course tied the long teams of oxen into knots and made such a mess and confusion as would have delighted any old mummy ever embalmed in the War Office.[33] Three times these energetic, zealous, but, for laagering purposes, utterly incompetent officers essayed to form laager and three times they ignominiously failed, and it was not until hundreds of soldiers had been employed to pull and haul on the wagons that at length a formation was completed which although it might gratify a Staff College man would have excited derision in a dopper boy of tender age.[34] No sooner were the wagons in position than the troops were set to work to dig shelter trenches,[35] which when completed were at once manned, the Tommies being kept in them all night, and continuously on the alert, a very bad precedent for youths of immature nervousness, especially as, during the whole night, excited officers wandered to and fro fussing and worrying their men with such exhilarating warnings as "Close up, men, close up, close up, be ready men, be ready, the Zulus might break through here," etc., etc., until the wretched, town-bred conscripts shivered with apprehension in their wet jackets, for as we had heavy rain during the night and as some wiseacre thought it might spoil the laager to unpack the men's greatcoats and blankets the miserable lads were subjected, unprotected, to the wet. Also for the same reason, the majority of the troops went without food,[36] which was a very bad preparation for youthful street arabs to undergo just on the eve of being introduced to an enemy.[37] It must be remembered that the regiments sent out to Natal, after the disaster of Isandlwana, were the first products of the then newly-invented short service system;[38]

33. H-B takes the opportunity to fulminate against the inefficiency of hidebound, regular officers, one of his pet peeves. It should be noted, however, that in preparation before leading the Eshowe Relief Column into Zululand, Chelmsford composed a pamphlet for use by his officers titled *Special Instructions Regarding the Management of Ox Transport on the Line of March . . . and for Forming Wagon Laagers*.

34. *Doppers* were the adherents of a particularly conservative and fundamentalist Calvinist sect that in the 1830s had caught on in Boer frontier communities. They had a principled and uncouth resistance to refinement of manners, and for H-B represented obscurantist country bumpkins.

35. On the contrary, Molyneux states that the men 'went to their dinners before digging the trench' (*Campaigning*, p. 128).

36. *See* the note above.

37. A 'street Arab' is an offensive term for a homeless child living by begging and stealing.

38. The introduction of short service in 1870 was part of the wide-ranging British army reforms carried out under Edward Cardwell, Secretary of State for War, 1868–74. Short

that their ranks denuded of seasoned men were for the most part filled with boys and that the majority of the non-commissioned officers, the real backbone of the fighting line, were of such tender age as to be utterly valueless, so far as giving confidence to their squads on the field of battle, this in itself being a great source of danger. Again, the men being chiefly recruits, drafts from the linked battalion,[39] or volunteers from other regiments did not know their officers and, for the same reasons, the officers did not know their men, while the total absence of old and tried soldiers in the ranks left the youthful conscripts without the steadying leaven so absolutely necessary in an untried body of men going into action for the first time in their lives.

It is therefore not to be wondered at, that some of the troops employed in South Africa during the latter part of the Zulu War, acted in such a way as might well make their old regimental ancestors squirm in their bloody graves and on several occasions filled their officers with consternation. Strange as it may appear, still it is, alas, nevertheless true, that Englishmen are quite incapable of learning a lesson, for the salient faults and mistakes made in a campaign, although animadverted on at the time by the Press and fully acknowledged by the authorities, are quickly forgotten or ignored, especially so when this country is engaged in savage warfare, for the absurd blunders made by our ancestors in the American forests one hundred and fifty years ago[40] I have individually seen perpetrated in New Zealand and South Africa. There is an old quotation that reads somewhat in this way, "Those whom the gods mark for destruction they first drive mad," and in my humble opinion the great majority of the British nation are rapidly qualifying for lunatic asylums; for here are a people who having been taught, by bitter experience in the past, the utter inutility of putting young and insufficiently-trained troops into the field, deliberately shutting their eyes and ears to the lessons we received in South Africa

---

service, whereby recruits spent six years in the regular army and six in the reserve, was designed to create a large reserve of trained reservists, reduce unhealthy service abroad, and save money. However, in practice, short-term enlistment meant that experienced soldiers left the ranks earlier and the number of younger, inexperienced men rose proportionately. Consequently, in 1879 many of the soldiers sent out to Zululand were young, inadequately trained, unused to combat conditions and susceptible to disease.

39. Cardwell's Localisation Bill of 1872 created sixty-nine brigade districts with two linked battalions attached to each depot. The battalions alternated in recruiting at home and serving abroad with the intention that the Empire would be guarded only by seasoned troops. But as colonial commitments increased, a growing number of home-based and imperfectly trained battalions were required to serve overseas, as in Zululand in 1879.

40. Presumably H-B is referring to the French and Indian War of 1754–63 or to Pontiac's War of 1763–66.

and Egypt,[41] and pinning their faith on mobs of semi-organized youths, known as territorials,[42] and that, not for a war of conquest but for the very existence of the homeland. There is no excuse for the callousness of the English nation, *re* their safety, for they have not lacked warnings; these they have had in plenty, and to a knockabout Frontiersman like myself it is more than incomprehensible why such warnings should be disregarded especially when emanating from such a man as Lord Roberts.[43]

Surely his frequent speeches and letters, noted as they are by the public Press, should be attended to: for he is a man grown old in the practice of warfare and has studied his noble profession from A to Z— yet notwithstanding these his most solemn warnings are either taken no notice of or treated with unmerited contempt. Yes, the population of these islands are content to allow the safety of their nation to slide as if it were no business of theirs to bear a hand for the protection of their own homes and firesides. Nor will they wake up until they see the scuppers of the roads run crimson and the red cock crowing over their own homesteads.

Then by the Lord Harry[44] it will serve them right; for when a people are so sunk in sloth that they will not learn the use of arms, so as to protect their flag, country and personal property, they deserve to be kicked into a more healthy frame of mind. And now you may say, "What is this outsider talking about? He is not a Staff College man, nor has he ever held a Royal Commission." Both remarks would be quite true, but then the writer has experienced many years of rough warfare and, on several occasions, has had to face the music in the company of semi-trained, unreliable men, so that he can speak from bitter experience.

41. H-B is presumably referring to the Second Anglo-Boer War 1899–1902, to the Anglo-Egyptian War of 1882, and to the Mahdist War (1881–99) in the Sudan which was under Egyptian rule.

42. H-B is using the opportunity to sound off against the Territorial Force created in 1908 during the military reforms following the Second Anglo-Boer War. It was a part-time volunteer component of the British Army intended to augment British land forces without resorting to conscription. The Territorial Force consolidated the nineteenth-century Volunteer Force and the Yeomanry into a unified auxiliary, commanded by the War Office. It was not a success. Fewer than 40 per cent of the men in the previous auxiliary institutions transferred into it, and at the time when H-B was writing, it was consistently under strength. The regular army did not consider it to be an effective military force, and it was persistently denigrated by the proponents of conscription.

43. In retirement, Field Marshal Earl Roberts of Kandahar (1832–1914) was a fierce critic of the Territorial Force and a strong proponent of conscription as a better alternative.

44. Early twentieth-century euphemism for 'by God'.

Chapter II

Ginginhlova

THE morning of the 2nd of April 1879 dawned damp and misty, and the men looked haggard, depressed and far from lively, but as it was the General's intention to halt where we were for the day, so as to give the oxen and men a much-required rest, preparations were made for breakfast. These, however, were quickly interrupted, the alarm was given, and at 6 a.m. two strong columns of Zulus came in sight who fording the Inyezani [Nyezane] River advanced to the attack, both columns throwing out clouds of skirmishers to the right and left, so as to surround the laager, and while they carried out this movement two other dense columns appeared from the direction of the Amatikulu [AmaTigulu] bush whose horns rapidly thrown out quickly joined hands with those already mentioned.[1] The celerity and precision with which these movements were carried out was simply beautiful, for, in less than ten minutes after the heads of the columns had appeared, the laager was completely enveloped; a signal was given and the gallant savages started a charge that for very many of them was to be their last on this planet. The engagement was commenced by the Gatling guns[2] at the range of about one thousand yards but the enemy closed in very quickly and soon everyone who could use a rifle was banging away for all he was worth so that the enemy paused when about four hundred yards distant and opened a tremendous fire which was however so badly directed that but few casualties occurred among our men.

I was at this time greatly amused at the tactics of an immensely big and fat old Dutchman, one of the grand old Trek Boers, who although he had not seen his knees for ages was as full of fight as an old buck goat.

1. H-B's second-hand description of the battle is based on the official reports, newspaper accounts and memoirs readily available at his time of writing, He would also have gleaned details from veterans of the battle. He evidently relies on his own imagination for some of the more colourful passages. For a recent, evidence-based account of the battle of Gingindlovu, *see* Laband, *Shadow of Isandlwana*, pp. 318–29.

2. The Gatling gun, an early version of the machine gun, came into service with the British Army in 1871 and was first employed in the Third Anglo-Asante War of 1873–4. Regarded primarily as a defensive weapon to be sited at prepared positions like the laager at Gingindlovu, it was highly effective up to 1,000 yards. However, it was an unreliable weapon because of its tendency to jam.

Troth and he fought comfortably, for sitting on the padded driving-box of his wagon with a case of ammunition on one side of him, and a big square rigger of gin mighty convanient, he picked off Zulu after Zulu with the rapidity of a boy looting a cherry tree, while every time he made a shot he deemed worthy to be commemorated he would treat himself to a klein soupje[3] of gin, chuck a chuckle and rub with gusto the elephantine protuberance that occupied the locality of his anatomy which in his youth he had called his waist. Faith, he was a broth of a boy and did honour to his parents' and tutors' upbringing.[4]

The enemy did not pause long for presently they must have received some order, or, more likely, seen some signal, for a tremendous whistle and yell went up and simultaneously they launched themselves at the laager. It must have been about 6.20 a.m. when the Zulus made their first great effort to storm the front, right, and rear faces of our defences, and their advance was indeed a splendid sight, as just at that moment the sun came out and shone full on the lines of plumed warriors, who, with their arms and legs adorned with streaming cow-tails and each brandishing his coloured ox-hide shield and flashing assagais rushed forward to what he fondly hoped to be an orgie of blood, with a dash and elan that no civilized troops could have exceeded.[5] This magnificent charge, beautiful as it was as a spectacle, was a trifle too enervating for the over-worried, unfed and somewhat nervous youths who had to face it, very many of whom more than wobbled in the shelter trenches. In fact it was only the frantic efforts of the officers of one regiment that, on the death of their Colonel, prevented their men from making a clean bolt of it, and that just at the most critical moment when the charging Zulus were within one hundred yards of the shelter trenches.[6] Troth it was a near call and for a few minutes it was a toss-up whether the laager at Ginginhlova was not to

3. A small sip.

4. H-B evidently bases this fanciful description on the published account by John Dunn, a Zululand hunter-trader who joined the Eshowe Relief Column to organise reconnaissance and advise on laagering procedures, who, in his own account, settled himself with his rifle on an ammunition wagon and picked off numbers of the attacking amaZulu with deadly accuracy (see Moodie, ed., *John Dunn*, p. 102). See also Norbury, *Naval Brigade*, p. 271, who wrote: 'The tops of the waggons being occupied by conductors and others who possessed firearms, and among them was Mr. Dunn who is celebrated as a marksman, who did much execution from this elevated position.'

5. This description of the advancing Zulu *amabutho* is another indication that H-B was not present at Gingindlovu. While some of the amaZulu, especially commanders, wore elements of their festival regalia such as feather headdresses, the great majority were stripped for action and wore only their loin-covers. They carried their spears and shields, and a large number also had firearms of varying quality.

6. The wavering battalion was the 3/60th Rifles, made up primarily of raw recruits aged between 19 and 23. Their morale was badly shaken when their commander, Lieutenant-Colonel Francis Northey (1836–79), was mortally wounded.

be a second shambles like Isandlwana. Now the blue-jackets, or rather a portion of them, had taken charge of the right front of the laager, and in their usual make-yourself-at-home, handy sort of way had constructed, out of their kit-bags and anything else they could get held of, a rough sort of bastion in which they had planted a Gatling gun, and as I had no men to look after and had never before seen a machine gun in my life, I went over to their post to watch it work,[7] and was much struck by the cool, dare-devil bearing and splendid self-reliance of my old friends whom the Maoris years before had called the Ngati Jacks,[8] who were as they always have been in the past, and please God always will be in the future, when in action thoroughly enjoying themselves as it is only a right and proper frame of mind for men to be in when they are doing work for King and Flag.

Comparisons are, I know, odious, but no impartial looker-on that day could have been present without being strongly impressed with the difference between the conduct of the mature blue-jacket together with that of the stalwart jolly and the half-baked nervous boys in whose company they were fighting.

When I reached the Gatling the Zulu skirmishers were beginning to close in and the cool, staid old shell-back in charge of the gun was simply pop-popping at them in a quiet leisurely sort of a way, a proceeding that did not seem to meet with the approbation of a youthful ordinary seaman who was assisting him, and who, as I came up, said in rather an excited manner, "Fire quicker, Quartermaster, for Gawd's sake, fire quicker." "Fire quicker," growled the ancient mariner, pausing to expectorate a much-chewed quid. "Fire quicker, yer young scupperling, fire quicker be d——d, wait till the black —— come thicker," and for a few moments he continued his deliberate manipulations. Presently came the rush, the before-mentioned Colonel was shot, his regiment became worse than wobbly and the ordinary seaman had no longer need to exhort his senior to expedite the juice distributor which, fortunately not jamming and being backed up by the steady fire of the blue-jackets and jollies,[9] in my humble opinion, saved the whole outfit from being cut up both physically and morally.

---

7. H-B purports to have joined two companies of the Naval Brigade from HMS *Boadicea* (the 'blue-jackets'), who, along with some Royal Marines, were holding the front right (north-eastern) corner of the laager and manning a Gatling gun. The rest of the Naval Contingent from the *Boadicea* was stationed at the front left (north-west) corner of the laager.

The Naval Contingent from HMS *Shah* held the other two corners.

8. *Ngāti* is the prefix for a Māori tribal group, here referring to the 'tribe' of sailors, or 'Jacks'.

9. A 'jolly' is slang for a Royal Marine. Detachments of a hundred Royal Marines from HMS *Boadicea* and *Shah* fought at Gingindlovu.

The Zulus' rush was only checked when they were within twenty yards of the laager, some of them falling shot dead at even a closer distance, while one small boy, a mat-carrier,[10] crossing by a miracle the zone of fire, reached the Naval Brigade bastion, where one of the blue-jackets spotting him, leaned over, grabbed him by the nape of the neck and collected him, kicking and squirming, inside the work, where after he had been cuffed into a state of quietude his captor kept him prisoner by sitting on him till the end of the engagement. This youthful corner-man,[11] preserved alive as a *spolia opima*,[12] was adopted by the crew of H.M.S. *Boadicea* as a mascot and, if I remember rightly, was subsequently entered into the Royal Navy, a proceeding that reflects great credit on the handy men, although I have sometimes thought that considering the manner in which he was first of all captured and detained, that the Exeter Hall gang would have wailed over him as a brutally pressed boy.[13] After enduring considerable punishment, which would have been heavier had the troops' shooting been better, the Zulus fell back, but only to try and come on again. This effort, however, was a failure, being quickly checked, and large numbers were seen leaving the field, whereupon Captain Barrow's Mounted Infantry[14] and every man in the laager, who could raise a horse, dashed out in pursuit.[15] Of course I joined in the fun, fondly expecting the

10. An *udibi* (see p. 80, n. 3, above) or baggage boy of between five and twelve, did not accompany a warrior into battle. This story, for which no corroborative evidence has been found, is inherently unlikely.

11. In boxing terms, a 'cornerman', or second, must remain outside the combat area.

12. *Spolia opima* (Latin) means rich spoils, and is technically the armour and arms taken by the victor from a slain general.

13. See p. 55, n. 2, above for Exeter Hall.

14. Captain Percy H. S. Barrow (1848–86), 19th Hussars, went out on Special Service in March 1878 to form a squadron of mounted infantry during the Ninth Cape Frontier War. During the Anglo-Zulu War he served with No. 1 Column in command of No. 2 Squadron, Mounted Infantry and fought at Nyezane. He then commanded the Divisional Troops with the Eshowe Relief Column and fought at Gingindlovu where he was wounded. He subsequently commanded the mounted men of the 1st Division, South African Field Force, and then the Mounted Infantry with Clarke's Column.

For lack of regular cavalry until the final stage of the Anglo-Zulu War, Chelmsford had to call upon mounted infantry drawn from volunteers from infantry regiments. Mounted infantry retained their regimental tunics and replaced their blue trousers with brown cord breeches. They were routinely armed with carbines. Like Boer commandos, they usually fought dismounted when contact was made with the enemy and were not normally required to charge home like regular cavalry. But Chelmsford envisaged them taking on this role as well, and on his insistence they were issued with cavalry sabres.

15. Barrow sortied out of the laager's eastern face and wheeled right with one troop of the Mounted Infantry in the leading line and with Jantze's Native Horse and No. 2 Troop, Mafunzi's Mounted Natives in a second line in support to rescue any of those in front who were unhorsed. At the same time, the second troop of Mounted Infantry and the Natal Volunteer Guides wheeled left out of the laager.

PRESSED INTO H.M. NAVY.

fugitives, of whom there were several thousands still in the vicinity, either on the tops of the hills or running in front of us, to make another attempt to put up a fight, but this they did not do, as those on the hills remained there until dispersed by the shells and rockets,[16] and those in the valley simply ran on till they were either shot or sabred, without making any combined attempt to retaliate on their pursuers.

Personally I was very busy. I had lost very many dear friends at Isandlwana, so wanted *utu* (Maori for payment or revenge)[17] and, as I was well mounted and had used a sword from childhood, I took it, but I had time to notice the sole attempt at resistance that, to my knowledge, was made by one of the fugitives. The Mounted Infantry had been raised by Captain Barrow and was composed of men drawn from every regiment, the only test as to efficiency being the individual's statement that he was able to ride; of course some of them could do so, but the majority, when mounted, looked as uncomfortable as a lot of moulting devils squatting on icebergs, and it certainly would have been much safer for themselves, comrades, and especially horses, as well as rendering them more dangerous to the enemy, had they been served out with shillelaghs instead of swords.[18] Be this as it may, as there was no cavalry in the country, two hundred foot soldiers were clapped into the pig-skin and issued with carbines and swords in lieu of their rifles and bayonets. The carbine was all right, as it is a much handier weapon for a mounted man to use than a rifle, and of course the men, having been trained to the use of a rifle, could use the shorter weapon just as well, but when it came to *l'arme blanche* it was quite another thing.[19] They sadly wanted another hand, for you see, being human, they only had two and when mounted these were both fully occupied; one holding the reins so as to try and guide the horse, the other being required to hold on with so as to retain their seat in the saddle. A sword was therefore to the majority of them more of an encumbrance than a useful lethal weapon.[20] It however had to be used, when the pursuit took place, and although but few of the men had the slightest idea how to

16. Two 9-pounder guns and four 24-pounder rocket tubes fired on the retiring Zulu army.

17. *Utu* is the Māori concept of reciprocation or balance. For a person to retain *Mana*, or the spiritual ability to perform effectively, both friendly and unfriendly actions require an appropriate response, and *utu* covers both the reciprocation of kind deeds, and the seeking of revenge.

18. A shillelagh is a thick stick of blackthorn or oak used in Ireland, typically as a weapon.

19. A cutting or thrusting weapon, as opposed to a firearm.

20. However, in his official account of the battle to the Secretary of State for War, Chelmsford wrote that Barrow 'reports the sabres of the Mounted Infantry to have proved of the greatest service, some 50 or 60 men having been sabred' (*BPP*, C. 2367: enc. 1 in no. 42: Chelmsford to Colonel Stanley, 10 April 1879). Since it was Chelmsford's idea that the Mounted Infantry be armed with swords, Barrow's report to his commanding officer could be taken with a slight pinch of salt.

handle them, still they drew them and gaily followed their flying enemies and of course by doing so they required their right hands to grasp the sword-hilt instead of the cantle of the saddle, thereby throwing on the left hand the double duty of holding the reins and gripping the gullet plates[21] of their saddles which sadly interfered with the menage of their horses. Again, although a South African horse is as a rule most tractable and one very easily trained, still, like most other quadrupeds, he objects and maybe kicks, should his rider all of a sudden require him to gallop after a mob of howling niggers and at the same time lop his ear off, slog him over the head, or amputate a steak from his hind quarter with a long flashing thing he has never seen before but which he finds out cuts worse than a sjambok.[22] Nevertheless and notwithstanding these manifold drawbacks both men and horses did very well, both being actuated by the highest possible motives, viz., the soldier to do his duty, the steed, because the rider using his spurs as accessory grappling irons kept them firmly fixed in his quivering flanks, and so the gallant Mounted Infantry rode hell for leather after their foes. Now it came to pass as I, riding my own line and being very busy using only the point,[23] chanced to notice a big fine Zulu louping[24] along through the long grass, and had half a mind to go for him, but at the same moment he was charged by a M.I. man, who galloping recklessly past him made a most comprehensive cut at him, which however, although it failed to annihilate or even wound the Zulu, still drew blood, as it lopped off the ear of his own horse, a proceeding that the animal resented by promptly kicking off its clumsy rider. The Tommy was however true grit, for in a moment he regained his feet and hanging on to the reins which, good man, he had never let go, he turned on to the astonished Zulu and discharged on to the latter's hide shield such a shower of blows that the noise sounded like a patent carpet-beater at work and effectually prevented him from using his assagai. Again, I was on the point of going to our man's assistance and had swung my horse ready to do so, when up from the rear galloped another Tommy who, holding on to the pommel of his saddle with his left hand, flourished his sword and shouted, "Let me get at the bleeding blighter, Dick," and then delivered a terrific cut which in this case missing the crow etched the pigeon as it nearly amputated poor Dick's sword hand, who might well have ejaculated, "Lord save me from my friends." This, nor any other pious cry he did not use, as his remarks, on receiving the wound, were of a decidedly declamatory

21. In a saddle, the gullet plate governs the width of the tree from the waist to the tree points.

22. A sjambok is a long stiff heavy whip.

23. H-B's picturesque yarn that follows about his part in the pursuit at Gingindlovu is manifest fiction.

24. 'Louping' is Northern Irish or Scots for 'leaping'.

nature and were sufficiently comprehensive so as to embrace not only his enemy and his rescuer but also all things animate and inanimate within the district. The blighter had however come off badly for he had been knocked end over end by the rescuer's horse, and before he could regain his feet the rider, whether voluntary or involuntary, was precipitated on to the top of him and without further delay, discarding his sword, grabbed the Zulu's knobkerrie with which he proceeded to bash its owner over the head, so seeing they were all right I devoted my attention to my own work.

The battle of Ginginhlova was most decidedly a victory, the Zulus having been beaten off and their army pursued for over seven miles with very heavy loss,[25] while it enabled Lord Chelmsford to immediately relieve Colonel Pearson's beleaguered column at Etchowe which was the objective of the expedition. Yet it caused every officer, of any experience, who witnessed the action grave anxiety, as the conduct of the young troops engaged was far from creditable and their behaviour did not improve. I have no wish to rake up old scandals, which some apologists declare ought to be forgotten, but I assert and maintain that the nation who, after the experiences of Zululand and Egypt, still rely on young and green troops for their preservation, while they ignore the solemn monitions of their most experienced men, deserve to lose their nationality and become slaves. Of one thing I am sure, and that is, it was the conduct of the young troops and the folly of very many of the senior officers that encouraged the Dutch Boers to declare their independence and subsequently to fight for it.[26] The remainder of the 2nd of April the troops rested, and on the following day the General relieved Etchowe and I made the best of my way back to my Lambs fairly well pleased with my outing though if possible more anxious to get back to the front than ever.

25. It seems probable that the amaZulu lost nearly 1,200 men in the battle compared, on the British side, to two officers, seven white troops and five black troops killed.

26. H-B is seemingly referring to the Transvaal Rebellion, or First Anglo-Boer War, of 1880–1.

Chapter III

Detained at the Base

THE battles of Kambula and Ginginhlova had secured the safety of Natal.[1] Troops were rapidly pouring in and were being as quickly as possible dispatched to the front. A very strong column was being formed under General Crealock to advance into Zululand from the coast and all hands looked forward to the culminating fight that, in the natural course of events, must take place near Ulundi, so that it was a moot point as to which column would first reach the goal and enjoy the big battle.[2] It was about this time I received a letter from Colonel Glyn advising me to try and join him with as little delay as possible and it tried my patience sorely when I received orders to remain at the base and continue to act as shepherd to Lonsdale's Lambs.[3] However there was no help for it and I had to conform to the admonitions of the Catechism "by doing my duty in that state of life in which it had pleased Providence or the Devil but mainly, I think, the Officer Commanding the Base of Operations to place me,"[4] though I fear the language I used very often in communing with myself, for I was never

1. The battle of Khambula was fought on 29 March 1879. No. 4 Column under the command of Colonel Evelyn Wood routed the main Zulu army (only subsidiary Zulu forces were engaged at Gingindlovu four days later). Khambula was the decisive turning-point of the war, and in conjunction with Gingindlovu it threw the amaZulu entirely onto the defensive.

2. The 1st Division, South African Field Force, under Major-General Henry Hope Crealock (1831–91) advanced slowly northwards up the coast towards oNdini while the 2nd Division, led by Chelmsford, advanced on the same objective from the west. On 3 June the 2nd Division was joined by No. 4 Column, renamed the Flying Column under Brigadier-General Wood. The 1st Division had advanced no further than Port Durnford when, on 4 July, the 2nd Division and the Flying Column conclusively scattered the Zulu army at the battle of Ulundi.

3. Colonel Glyn commanded the 1st Brigade, 2nd Division, which had been massing during May at Landman's Drift. On 31 May it crossed the Ncome River into Zululand and commenced its march on oNdini. It has not proved possible to trace Glyn's purported letter to H-B. It is in any case unclear in what capacity H-B could have joined Glyn's brigade, which consisted only of British troops, namely the 2/21st (Royal Scots Fusiliers) Regiment and the 58th (Rutlandshire) Regiment. If H-B had joined the 2nd Division it would have been the Divisional Troops under Lieutenant-Colonel Arthur Harness, RA, which included colonial mounted troops and the 2nd Battalion NNC.

4. This was Major-General Clifford (*see* p. 170, n. 24, above). During May H-B remained in Natal training the arriving detachments of LMR.

a grumbler, a thing I despise, is not to be found in a catechism or other goody-goody literature promulgated for the benefit and enlightenment of youthful niggers.[5]

While in Durban, previous to the relief of Etchowe, it had been the custom for all officers not on duty to go down to the docks, so as to meet and welcome the reinforcing regiments when they landed, and I happened to be present on the landing of a portion of the crew of H.M.S. *Shah,* who were to serve with the Naval Brigade.[6] The General, together with the fine old Commodore and the staff,[7] were all there, and very many civilians had gathered for the same purpose, everyone standing at the town end of the wharf, so as to allow the landing party room to form up. The blue-jackets came ashore in boats, and as the landing-steps were narrow, only one boat-load could be disembarked at a time, the men on landing being formed into squads and moved forward so as to make room for those following.

Well, the first squad landed, formed, and, in charge of a huge petty officer, came tramp, tramp along the wharf to take up their position where they were to wait for the remainder of their shipmates, and when they reached a point, just opposite the staff, the petty officer considering he had allowed sufficient room for the remainder of the landing party to form on, bellowed out "'Alt," but there was no halting in that squad as, perhaps owing to their novel surroundings or peradventure not knowing the meaning of the word, they continued their steady tramp, tramp, tramp. Again the petty officer bellowed "'Alt," with a volume and tone of voice sufficient to have arrested the flight of a runaway comet, but again no response from his contumacious or heedless men, who still continued to gain ground with their ceaseless tramp, tramp, tramp. Thunder and turf, this was too much for the equanimity of that petty officer. Nelson may have disobeyed orders but *his* squad might not, so after one more ineffectual bellow of halt he rushed at the leading file and landing him a punch in the ribs that would have stove in a pulpit howled out, "Heave to, you —" and the convoy promptly hove to.

The incident was so comical that all us lookers-on, including the General and staff, burst out laughing while the grand old Commodore turning to the General remarked, "My men may not be very conversant with military tactics but you will find them all right when the fighting

---

5. H-B's ingrained prejudices are only too transparent.

6. H-B was not there to witness the landing in Durban of the Naval Brigade from HMS *Shah* that came ashore on 7 March – a date when he was most definitely in Cape Town. H-B would have found all the details in the *Natal Mercury* of 6, 7, 8 and 10 March 1879 and he embroiders them to spin a yarn about the bluejackets' lack of parade ground training.

7. Rear-Admiral Francis William Sullivan, RN, Commodore, South Africa Station, was in command of the naval flotilla in Durban.

begins." And true enough we did. Lonsdale had sent up plenty of officers all of them very good fellows and fine recruits for the Lost Legion, though unfortunately they were only recruits, knowing nothing about drill, or any other military work, so they were of but little use to me as I had the trouble of training them as well as inculcating the rudiments of drill and decorum into an unruly gang, composed chiefly of runaway sailors and unrighteous surf-boatmen. I was therefore glad when there arrived a real live adjutant, one who had served several years in a crack hussar regiment.[8] He reported himself ready for duty one morning at daylight and accompanied me to the early drill parade, where he turned to and worked like a horse, yet, although he was very smart, both in his drilling and appearance, there was still something in his manner that led me to believe that early as it was in the day he had been kissing the baby (imbibing over-proof rum), nor as the morning passed could I disabuse my mind that he was not rather more than half-seas over, still he did his duty well and relieved me of a lot of hard, tiresome work, so I was duly thankful. Lunch-time came and cool drinks were in demand; we had had a morning's real hard work under a blazing sun, and what with drilling, giving instructions and a powerful lot of denunciations my throat resembled a lime-kiln, and not doubting he must be also equally parched I said to him, "Have a drink, Captain So-and-So." Quin had at that moment brought me a glass, that at a pinch might have been used as a stable bucket, full of iced ginger-beer in which was concealed a liberal soupçon of gin (the very best drink I know of for a thirsty man who has been overtaxing his voice in a very hot climate), that under the same circumstances would have tempted the Grand Worshipful Master of any band of red-nosed teetotallers to break his pledge, pawn his sash and go on the bust. I was therefore more than surprised when my new friend replied, "No, thank you, sir, I never touch liquor except when at meals." Here was a paragon and one to be treasured especially as at tiffin he only consumed a solitary glass of claret, and discoursed the while on the evils of imbibing numerous and mixed drinks, giving his hearers to understand that he was a staunch supporter of a moderation that he carried nearly to the extreme of total abstinence. All this was very nice; I was a most modest consumer of alcoholic beverages myself and, as the rest of the officers rather resembled the Sahara, I hoped the virtue of the new adjutant might be contagious and that they would all go into training so as to qualify themselves as candidates for a Zulu Band of Hope.[9] Yet, still, somehow, his abstemiousness was a trifle too ostentatious and

8. It has not proved possible to identify this officer – if he ever existed, that is, and was not invented by H-B for the sake of one of his typical yarns.

9. The Band of Hope was a non-denominational movement founded in 1847 with membership open to all children who pledged to abstain from drinking alcohol.

certainly could not account for attacks of shakiness, very perceptible at the daylight parade; but then he had served in India, and everyone knows that dingai fever is prevalent in India,[10] and perhaps such early rising did not suit his constitution. Yet as he was wont to retire to the privacy of his tent the very moment he could do so without the fear of being disturbed, I opined he ought to rise fresher in the morning than was the case. However, as he did his duty remarkably well and was always ready for hard work my suspicions died away and he became very popular right through the corps. So things went on smoothly till we shifted camp to Saccharine[11] where for over sixty hours we could get no stimulants at all, so that perforce Lonsdale's Lambs, *nolens volens*,[12] were quite sober for the space of some forty hours.

Now as our officers and non-coms. carried swords and, inasmuch as none of them, on joining, had the remotest idea of how to use them, I had made it a practice to give them an hour's instruction every evening, and on the second day of our enforced sobriety they had fallen in for their accustomed drill.

Coming on to the parade ground I missed the adjutant, so thinking that, indulging in a short siesta, he had not heard the bugle, I dispatched a non-com. with my compliments and a request that he should forthwith attend the drill. And by the Lord Harry he immediately complied with my command, for no sooner had the non-com. entered the tent than he reappeared running like a scared cat, yelling, "Wille willoo, blue murder," and faith I for one could not blame him, for, in close pursuit, running with big leaps like Satan chivying a fancy religion minister, followed the adjutant who, drawn sabre in hand and clad in his native modesty, plus a cholera belt,[13] devil a rag more, unless you count a tin helmet case, worn in lieu of a *chapeau*,[14] and a pair of jack spurs buckled on to his bare shins,[15] as clothing, gave tongue to the most blood-curdling threats and denunciations. The fugitive shot past me with the quite superfluous announcement, "'E's a-comin', sir, 'e's up the ruddy pole 'e is," and at once dodged round the nearest tent while his pursuer charging up to me

10. Dengue fever is a viral infection spread by mosquitoes that causes flu-like symptoms: high fever, headache, pain behind the eyes and nausea.

11. *See* p. 171, n. 20, above.

12. *Nolens volens* is Latin for 'like it or not'.

13. A cholera belt was a cloth waistband (usually red) about six inches wide and six feet long made of wool or flannel and worn wound around the stomach. The belief was that a cold abdomen could lead to cholera and other stomach ailments. Cholera belts were standard issue for the British Army, and were worn for decades even after it was established that cholera is a bacterial disease caused by drinking contaminated water.

14. French for hat.

15. A jack spur has a revolving rowel at the end of the spur with sharp points.

halted and made a most formal salute, at the same time remarking, "It is hot enough to make a moulting devil sweat snow-balls." His statement might be true, but neither time nor place were suitable for a discussion on climatic heat, so I quietly ordered him to hand me his weapon. This, the habit of discipline still being strong, after a moment's hesitation, the poor fellow did, and I sent him back to his tent under the escort of two powerful officers where he rapidly lapsed into a state of dangerous dementia, which the surgeon-major declared to be D.T.'s,[16] and on making strict investigation I found out that my abstemious adjutant was a hopeless secret dipsomaniac and had acquired his dose of the rats by being suddenly cut off from his regular tonic. Well, poor chap, he was invalided and I applied to Major W. F. Butler, C.B., at that time Assistant Adjutant and Quartermaster-General at Durban,[17] for another and as there was a plethora of ex-military men in Natal, at the moment seeking employment, he kindly dispatched one to me the following day. In my application I had intimated that I should prefer one who was not a secret absorber of alcoholic beverages, and in the chit the orderly brought back the A.A.Q.M.G. informed me that although he knew but little about the officer he was sending, still he could guarantee that he did not ambuscade his liquorish propensities. So far so good and I retired under my mosquito netting at bedtime feeling at peace with the world.

Next morning, *sans* an adjutant, I was very busy indeed, so much so that it was near tiffin-time before I got back to the lines when I at once asked Quin, "Has the new adjutant arrived?" "Begorra he has, sor, and he's the only cool spot in camp this blistering day, sor," replied the worthy man with such a note of admiration in his tone that it quite puzzled me, so I continued, "Only cool spot in camp, what do you mean?" "Mane, sor, why sure, sor, whin he dismounted out of an impty truck he swaggers up to the tent, sor, an' sez he to me sez he, 'Me man,' sez he, 'is it the Commandant's man ye are?' 'I am,' sez I, 'at this moment;' for sure, sor, it's putting a stitch in your honour's pijammies I was; 'but there are toimes,' sez I, 'whin I'm drill-instructor, recruiting-sergeant, provost-marshal, squadron-leader and the divil only knows what else besides in this camp, glory be to God.' 'Ah,' sez he, 'it's plinty av work ye have to do in this camp,' sez he. 'You're right, sor,' sez I, 'but as I suspicion it's the new adjutant yer honour is, and as I'm doing duty, for the moment, as the Commandant's man, sure it's the head he'd knock off ov me if he knew I was discoursing yer honour widout askin' ye av it's a mouth ye've got on ye, for maybe it's a drink, or some breakfast, or a bath ye may be wantin'

16. Delirium tremens.

17. Major Butler, late 67th (South Hampshire) Regiment, was on Special Service and served during the war as Assistant Adjutant and Quartermaster -General on Lines of Communication and at Base.

an' me cologuing here,' sez I. Wid that he laughs an' sez he, 'It's a bath an' a drink,' sez he, 'ye may give me an' I don't care a tinker's damn if the one's as dape as the ocean an' the other's as long as a priest's conscience,' sez he. So there he is, sor, in the bath-hut, yer honour, settin', as much av him as he can get in the tub, sor, wid a stovepipe hat full of ice on his head, sor, an' he's giv' me strict orders, sor, to bring him an iced gin sling ivery fifteen minutes,[18] sor, an' troth he's a punctual man, sor, for listen to the tares av him, an' av yer doubt him being a cool spot jest step into the hut, sor, an' judge for yerself. Oh, holy Saint Bridget,[19] jest listen to him." There was no need to strain my ears, for the shout, "Hi, bring along that swizzle,"[20] boomed along the lines and made many a thirsty old shell-back jump, as if he had been bit on a tender spot by a Gally Nipper.[21]

Inquisitive to see the man who could make himself at home in such a debonair manner I walked up to the bath-hut, a rough-built grass structure in which was the half of an old sugar puncheon that served the purpose of a bath, and rapped on the door with my sjambok. "Come in," roared a stentorian voice, and entering I discovered the tub to be full, of a portion, of a huge red-faced man, on whose head was set an old-fashioned high hat from which ran large drops of moisture resembling gigantic tears. In his dexter hand he held a long sleever[22] full of some cunningly-mixed drink, while his sinister claw gripped and gracefully waved a black cigar that was long enough and strong enough to make a jury dessle-boom for a buck wagon.[23] "Good morning, Captain West" (which was not his name), quoth I, "I am very glad to see that you have arrived and that my man has made you comfortable. Is there anything else you would like before tiffin?" "No thanks, sir," the monster replied. "My wants are few, trivial, and easily satisfied, but if your man were to add another glassful of gin and double the allowance of Angostura Bitters to my next glass of swizzle it will improve it and I shall be quite ready to join you at tiffin." "Cool card," said I to myself, as I walked away to our mess tent, "and most certainly not a secret imbiber, but we shall soon see how he shapes." Presently he joined us at tiffin and consumed sufficient bottled ale as would have floated a jolly boat,[24] and knowing

18. A gin sling is a long drink of gin and water, sweetened and flavoured with lemon or lime juice.

19. Saint Brigid (or Bridget) of Kildare is the patroness saint (or 'mother saint') of Ireland.

20. A swizzle is a long alcoholic drink, especially a frothy one, of rum or gin and bitters.

21. A 'Gallinipper' is a large mosquito or other insect that can bite or sting painfully.

22. A 'sleever' was a measure of beer, equal to about three-quarters of a pint.

23. A 'jury *disselboom*' is a makeshift wagon shaft; while a buck wagon is an open, flat-bottomed, four-wheeled carriage.

24. A jolly boat was a large ship's boat in use during the eighteenth and nineteenth centuries to ferry people to and from a ship anchored off-shore.

the quantity of swizzle he had imbibed before, I marvelled greatly at his capacity to carry it without turning a hair; for I am certain that if the amount of moisture he had absorbed, with impunity, had been spilt in the centre of the Great Thirst Land it would have formed an oasis, and that by no means a small one. Troth he was a powerful drinker and mighty draughty, but his worst enemy could never have accused him of being a sly boozer. During lunch he discoursed on the West Indies, where he had seen several years' service in the Royal Artillery, and spoke highly of the climate, assuring us, that among the islands an active man might acquire a thirst that necessitated considerable ingenuity to quench. He also quoted certain insular tipples, that required to be drunk on the spot to be thoroughly understood and appreciated, but which he promised to concoct, on the morrow, for our edification; in fact he waxed so eloquent that he would have afforded great amusement and instruction to a blue ribbon army in a state of mutiny. In person he was gigantic, being over six feet two inches in height, broad in proportion, and possessed a hold-all that would have done credit to a city alderman, so that it certainly required a considerable quantity of liquid to irrigate his frontiers. Yet at the same time he was a smart soldier, who knowing his work did it well and during the whole time he was with me I never saw him a least bit the worse for drink. Of course there were some very queer fish in the ranks, most of their prototypes I had met before, but one day there joined such an extraordinary new chum that I think I may be pardoned for describing him and his advent into the Lost Legion, as it was represented by Lonsdale's Horse. It happened this way. One morning I was returning from drill when I met the worthy Quin who accosted me, saying, "Plaise, sor, there's a man in yer tint who tells me he's come to stop." "Who is he?" said I. "An officer or a civilian?" "Sure, sor, 't 'ud puzzle Ould Nick to tell ye but he's dressed beautiful an' carries a sword that's a trate to look at, while the cheek of him's unbounded; maybe he's the Prince Impariel himself,[25] sor."

I went to my tent where, reclining on my deck chair, was a young man of some two-and-twenty summers, who rose with some difficulty on my approaching him, tendered me his hand and offered me a letter; at the same time expressing a fervid hope that it was near tiffin-time. Previous to opening the letter I took a good look at my visitor, and faith he was an object worthy of scrutiny.[26] Let me commence with his wearing apparel, for indeed he was clad in raiment such as I had never seen before in a camp of Lost Legionaries. To begin with his hat was a

25. Louis Napoleon, Prince Imperial of France (1856–79), only son and heir of the deposed Emperor Napoleon III, served as an observer on Chelmsford's staff, and was killed when his patrol was ambushed by Zulus on 1 June 1879.
26. The bizarre hero of this yarn is surely fictional.

GUARANTEED NOT TO AMBUSCADE LIQUORISH PROPENSITIES.

veritable sombrero, beautifully embellished with a broad gold band and voluminous lines to say nothing about an immense pendent plume of white ostrich feathers that, curling half-way round his hat, fell gracefully over his shoulder. The *chapeau* was splendid but the remainder of his habiliments far surpassed it in grandeur, for his tunic was made of purple velveteen, brass-bound all over, white doeskin riding-breeches and tall jack-boots, such as are used by His Majesty's Horse Guards, to the heels of which were buckled huge Mexican gilt spurs. Troth he actually blazed in the brilliant sunshine and fairly rattled when he moved, for he had fastened on to his short, fat carcase every blessed patent contraption that an oily-tongued, outfitting tradesman could persuade a moneyed new-chum mug to purchase, as being absolutely indispensable to a young gent contemplating going to war, so that had it not been for a huge scimitar like the one Blue Beard flourishes in pantomime, and a brace of revolvers carried most ostentatiously, I might have mistaken him for a peripatetic Christmas tree on the trek. I opened the letter and glanced through it; it was from a pal on the staff and was laconic, simply informing me that the bearer, Mr M'Cuckoo, had been sent out to the General with strong letters of introduction, requesting him to place the sucking hero in a rough irregular corps, so that he might obtain copy, as the said S.H. intended to take up literature as a profession, and it was thought that six months' service at the front, in a corps of Colonial Horse, would be highly beneficial to him, as he intended to write a book on the Colonies also. He had made himself an infernal nuisance at the base, so that the General, knowing Lonsdale's Horse to be composed of the very toughest material out of Hades, had directed the M'Cuckoo to be sent to garner copy in their ranks, and my correspondent led me to believe that, so long as the General never saw him again, no questions would be asked, even should he, the M'Cuckoo, meet with an untimely death, during the process of his garnering. I gazed at the poor young man with a feeling akin to pity for well I knew that like a youthful bear he had all his troubles before him, so I said to him compassionately, "See here, young man, have you not made an error? A trooper's life in an irregular force is by no means an easy one, and you will find very many of your comrades rough and prone to make it hot for men whose manners differ from their own. In fact I think you had better study Colonial human nature from a distance, you will find it more conducive to personal comfort and you can gather copy, whatever that may be, at your leisure." Now my advice was good and was kindly meant, but it is quite astonishing, when you come to think of it, how much good advice we have all tendered gratis during our peregrinations through this world, and devil a bit of it has ever been acted on. It was so in this case, for the new chum waxed indignant and assured me he was quite competent to hold his own, and was capable of roughing it with anyone, as he had camped out for a week, during the previous summer, on the banks of the Thames.

Well it was no business of mine to argue with him, so sending for a Troop Sergeant-Major, I took him to the office tent where he was duly attested and handed over to the Troop Sergeant-Major, who in due course introduced him to perhaps the toughest tentful, and oh, Lord, that's saying something, of men in Lonsdale's Horse. Well the officers' tiffin bugle went and we were all busily employed rustling our curry and rice when in came the new chum. "Major Browne," quoth he, "I am surprised at your sending me to consort with such low, common fellows as there are in that tent. I should much prefer joining your mess and living with the officers." The poor devil had got so far in what might have been an eloquent harangue when he was unceremoniously waltzed out of the mess tent and relegated back to the company of the low, common fellows in his troop's lines. The following morning I was not in the least bit surprised, when weighing off prisoners, at having him brought before me charged with creating a disturbance in the camp. But oh, what a terrible change one short twenty-four hours' residence, in the tents of the ungodly, had effected in the person and habiliments of the whilom gay and festive new chum, for I could see with half an eye that my prognostications *re* the young bear and his troubles had come to pass, and that *ursus juventus*[27] had decidedly come to grief while garnering copy in the fold of the Lambs. Faith he was a deplorable object, for his face looked as if he, or someone else, had been burnishing the inside of a camp kettle with it, and he had a pair of the blackest eyes I have ever seen in my life. Troth and maybe it was only right they should be in mourning, if they could but see the devastation that had befallen their owner's magnificent garments. For alas! the gorgeous sombrero had had its roof kicked out and minus gold band and penache[28] hung loosely in the wretched defaulter's hand instead of being knowingly cocked on the side of his head, and if the state of the *chapeau* was deplorable what word could describe the pitiful condition of yesterday's resplendent purple, brass-bound coat, to say nothing about the immaculate white breeches and lustrous jack-boots, all of which looked as if they had been drawn through a duck puddle and a very dirty puddle at that. Well might the unfortunate seeker after copy have exclaimed, with Moses or the other old fossil, "*Sic transit gloria mundi*,"[29] for by the Lord Harry he had been changed from a splendid outfitter's model, that might well have been exhibited in the window of a West End emporium, into a scarecrow that would have failed to frighten

27. *Ursus juventus* is Latin for young bear.
28. A panache is a plume of feathers.
29. Latin for 'thus the glory of the world passes away'.

the callowest of young rooks. "You are charged," said I, "with fighting and creating a disturbance in the camp. What have you to say?" "Please, sir," he replied, "I created no disturbance and did very little of the fighting. I only refused to peel potatoes, as I consider it is derogatory and menial to do so, and when that man Hicks told me I was slushy's mate and ordered me to skin spuds I refused and called him a low fellow, requesting him at the same time to confine his remarks to his other low companions, whereupon he used disgusting and calumniatory language and went so far as to insult me by throwing a potato at me which hit me in the eye, so I threatened to horsewhip him and he assaulted me most brutally, then the Sergeant-Major came up and I was put in the guard tent and I wish to lodge a complaint against all the men in the tent, their conduct having been most ungentlemanly." I was not surprised at his last remark but turned to his antagonist, also in durance vile under the same charge, and demanded his excuses. He was a diminutive Cockney sailor but, small as he was in stature, his hide covered a sufficiency of brazen blackguardism to have superabundantly rationed a giant, and as at one time he had been, at least as I was creditably informed and could well believe, the terror of Tiger Bay and Ratcliffe Highway,[30] he was without doubt a tough enough nut even for Satan's back teeth to crack. Well, I looked at the *multum in parvo* of villainy[31] and could scarcely forbear laughing at the comical expression the little scoundrel wore on his scarred and weather-beaten but otherwise droll phiz, as he answered me: "Vell, your vorship, the last gent as spoke 'as perwerted the truth for yesterday 'e comes hinto the tent where hi being horderly, was a-peeling taters and says hi to 'im, 'My lord dook, if you'll be so kind as to divest yerself of them gadgits, and yer Sunday-go-to-meeting clobber and 'elp me to skin these 'ere spuds ye'll do more good nor yo've hever done afore;' hand vith that 'e starts in hand says 'e, 'Yer howdacious, low-born skut,[32] hif yer dares to hagain haddress yer disgusting hobservations to me hi'll kick yer blooming hinnerds hout,' whereupon hi sez to him, 'My Lord Marquis, go heasy,' but 'e hups hand 'eaves the blessed taters at me and haggerawates me by plunging 'is 'ead hinto the blooming bucket han' kicks up such 'ell that the Sergeant comes along hand runs us into the ruddy clink. 'E's dangerous 'e his, yer vorship, hand I'm feared of 'im, hi ham," and I believe the little beast winked but whether from cheek or nervousness who could say. However as he had visited the orderly room tent before I gave him seven days C.B.[33] while the M'Cuckoo I admonished, sending for him later on, to my

---

30. 'Tiger Bay' is sailors' slang for rough docklands, and the Ratcliffe Highway murders in 1811 took place near the London Docklands.

31. *Multum in parvo* is Latin for 'a great deal in a small space'.

32. A 'skut' is a worthless, contemptible person.

33. C.B. is Confined to Barracks, an official punishment for a minor military crime.

tent, when I gave him some more good advice and offered to give him his discharge. This however he refused to take, and I admired his pluck, as he asserted he had joined in pursuit of copy, and copy he would have, and if copy meant black eyes, faith he captured copy for he was never without one, more often a brace of darkened optics, during the whole time he was in Lonsdale's Horse.

About this time Lonsdale came up, himself, from Cape Town,[34] bringing with him some sixty men and forty horses, so I fondly hoped I should now be allowed to proceed to the front; but alas! no such luck, as his accounts were in a state of inextricable confusion and his presence was needed at the base so as to try and disentangle them. I was therefore ordered to remain in charge of his Lambs until such time as he could straighten up matters and act as his own shepherd; truly my luck was in decadence. A week or two passed and I received some more cases of equipment, but ye gods! what trash it was; shoddy is not the word to use when describing it, for the tunics fell to pieces as the men tried them on, and as for the riding-breeches, they split across the knees and seat when the men tried to mount. If the clothing was bad, and it was damned bad, the saddlery was worse. You could not have hung a cat with the head-stalls or reins, they were so rotten, and I took one of the saddles and tore it in half, through gullet-plate and cantle, with my hands; snapping the stirrup leathers afterwards in the same manner. Nevertheless I managed to get another troop equipped and dispatched to the front and was then left with some hundred and twenty tatterdemalions, in rags of brand-new uniforms, without a horse for them to ride on, or a rifle for them to use.[35] The men themselves were disgusted, many of them having come out from England, at their own expense, for the purpose of seeing some fighting, and here they were stuck, a few miles out of Durban, without a hope of smelling powder. One day the Acting Adjutant-General[36] came out and inspected our camp together with the rotten equipment. He informed me there was no chance of receiving other stores from imperial sources, nor could he hold out any hopes for a further supply of horses and under these circumstances he asked me what I should suggest doing with the men, whereupon I recommended their immediate disbandment as it was utterly useless keeping them, where they were, doing nothing. I was somewhat prompted by my own desires in giving this advice and maybe,

34. Lonsdale sailed from the Cape on 3 May 1879 (see p. 169, n. 21, above) and arrived at Durban on 9 May.

35. Three troops of LMR eventually joined the Divisional Troops of the 1st Division in its advance up the coast (see p. 171, n. 26, above).

36. This could be one of several officers on the staff of the South Africa Field Force, or one of the staff officers of Lines of Communication and Base, most likely Major Butler (see p. 188, n. 17, above).

I was a little bit selfish in doing so, but the truth is I was heartily sick of Lonsdale's Horse and simply hungered to get back to the front, which I knew I should not be able to do so long as that gang of irresponsibles remained as a menace to the peaceful inhabitants of Durban.

Floored by a Mule

TWO days after the Assistant Adjutant-General's visit I received orders to march the unemployed Lambs back to Durban, where they were to be embarked on board the hired transport *Ontario,* on which they were to be paid off, taken down to Cape Town and disbanded; the A.A.G. not wanting Durban to be overrun by such a mob of undesirables.[1] So far so good, but you can fancy my disgust when I found out I was under orders to shepherd them down to the Cape; for the A.A.G. informed me, that as he was sending an imperial paymaster with his pay-chest, down in the ship, for the purpose of settling up with them, he did not think it safe for either of these to journey, in such company, without my being there to protect them; so that he must request my compliance with the order. Moreover he had another reason for sending me to Cape Town which he explained to me as follows. A vast number of mules had been purchased, in both North and South America, for transport purposes and these playful, domestic animals were being sent over from the land of their birth to Cape Town in sailing-ships, from which, on their arrival at the Cape, they were transferred to steam-ships and sent on to Natal.[2] Well it seems there had been an awful mortality among these quadrupeds *en route* from Cape Town to Durban, some ships losing over twenty per cent. of their cargo; so that the General,[3] knowing I had had considerable experience with the long-eared stock, and, maybe, imagining, that because I could manage human roughs, I should also be able to manage animal ones, desired me to go down the coast in the *Ontario*, which was fitted up for the purpose of carrying live stock, so as to get rid of one batch of kicking bipeds and bring up another of

1. Three of the four troops of LMR joined the 1st Division, while the fourth (possibly A Troop) was disbanded before going to the front, its horses being declared unfit for service. The *Natal Mercury* of 9 June reported that 'Lonsdale's Horse is to be thoroughly re-organised, and all the worthless fellows will be weeded out.'

2. H-B exaggerates the number of mules purchased in America. The greatest number of mules on the army's establishment in Zululand at any one time in 1879 was 4,246 colonial mules and only 387 American ones. A mule-wagon carried 2,000 lb and was drawn by eight mules (War Office, *Field Operations*, pp. 171 –3: Appendix E. Transport in South Africa).

3. Presumably Major Butler, the AAQMG.

kicking quadrupeds; he evidently considering the latter cargo to be the most valuable, as he exhorted me to take great care of the mules, and to see none of them died or had to be thrown overboard, but he expressed no anxiety whatever about the men, and evidently cared not one jot if they were all thrown overboard, so long as he, individually, never saw them again. Lonsdale's Horse was by no means popular, at that epoch, among the imperial authorities but he essayed to hearten me up by informing me the ship would proceed straight to Cape Town and back again, not calling in at any of the intermediary ports, and that on my return he would facilitate my efforts to rejoin Colonel Glyn. He also assured me that my late services were fully appreciated, although they had been rendered far from the fighting line, in fact, being an Irishman,[4] he had a fellow-feeling for a poor countryman in distress; for was not he himself jammed at the base? and he blue mouldy for want of a bating or other warlike divarsion; so with only a grumble, to myself, I took my Lambs to Cape Town and got rid of them. On reporting myself to the O.C., Cape Town, whom I found to be a fussy old woman,[5] he or she informed me that the cargo of mules were ready for embarkation, that they were to be shipped by contract and that I had nothing to do with them, until such time as the vessel would be loaded and ready to go to sea. To these arrangements I demurred, stating that, in my humble opinion, the great mortality among the mules had been caused by faulty loading and I expressed a wish to be present and superintend the embarkation of the long-eared animals myself. Faith if I had asked him for a subscription of a tenner, for the purpose of furnishing little niggers with flannel petticoats and moral pocket-handkerchiefs, he could not have been more perturbed.[6] The silly old image simply bubbled like an infuriated turkey-cock, demanding if I thought he and his officers did not know their work (I would willingly have wagered good money that the only animals of the asinine species they had ever handled was when they shaved themselves) and finished up by ordering me not to go on board the ship until she was ready to start, nor to interfere with the embarkation in any way.

Truly England need not have sent so far afield for mules, she had very many of her own breeding, that no great trouble would have discovered,

4. Irish bearers of the name Butler trace their ancestry to the Anglo-Norman lords who invaded Ireland in the twelfth century.

5. H-B is referring to Colonel Fairfax Charles Hassard, RE (1822 –1900). In 1879 he joined Chelmsford's Headquarters Staff as Officer Commanding Royal Engineers in South Africa and the Field. But in the aftermath of Isandlwana, while in command at Helpmekaar, he suffered a nervous breakdown and proceeded by order to Cape Town where he remained in command until the end of the war.

6. Another swipe by H-B at well-meaning evangelical Christians and their efforts to succour and convert African children.

however orders are orders so I went nowhere near the docks for three days, but on the evening of the third I received a written order, directing me to report myself on board the ship at 2 p.m. on the following day, so as to take over military charge of ship and mules.[7] This I did, accompanied by two naval officers, who were going round to Simon's Bay in the *Ontario,* and by the blessed piper who played before Moses, the state of that ship would have shocked an atheistical anarchist. She lay alongside the western end of the inner dock, and her decks together with the wharf were crowded with a mob of drunken coloured men and women among whom, here and there, appeared the red coat of a soldier. With great difficulty, and then only by the free use of my own and Quin's riding-whips,[8] were our party able to reach the ship's bridge, and there I found the O.C. Cape Town in a state of nervous excitement that was simply pitiable. It seems that I was to take up with me two hundred Cape bastards,[9] who were to look after the mules *en route*, and to act as drivers when we reached Natal, and in their contract of enlistment it was stipulated that they should receive one month's pay in advance, so that they could hand it over to their families previous to the ship's sailing.

Now as these people could give no guarantee that they would keep their part of the contract, provided they had been paid on shore, the O.C. had decided that they should be paid on board, hand over their money to their women folk and then go to sea. This was a lovely theory, one well worthy of a Staff College man,[10] but when it came to be tested, like many other theories emanating from the same source, it was mighty nigh impracticable; for as each Cape boy had brought with him a dozen or more relatives and friends to see him off, the family parties together with the drivers themselves had succeeded in getting beastly drunk on vile Cape smoke,[11] and had gathered round them all the low and criminal, coloured riff-raff of Cape Town. Again no one knew who, among this unruly and drunken mob, were the real drivers and who were not, also there were hundreds of coloured scoundrels present who would gladly

7. The following account of H-B and the injury he sustained on the *Ontario*, although much embroidered in his exuberant style, is based on fact. On 8 June 1879 the *Eastern Province Herald* reported that 'Major Brown [*sic*], Lonsdale's Horse, met with an accident on board the 'Ontario' on Saturday night [7 June]. He embarked in charge of a large number of muleteers and in charge of the mules and horses for Natal. When on duty on the lower deck he was kicked by a mule sustaining an injury to the upper part of his tibus [tibia] – layed [*sic*] up for a month it was expected.'

8. Quin seems at this stage to be have been serving at the LMR's depot as Provost Sergeant.

9. H-B means Khoisan men, or 'Coloureds' in the terminology of the time.

10. In other words, in H-B's estimation an officer with much theoretical, but little practical training or experience.

11. 'Cape Smoke' was a rough, cheap brandy made of either peaches or grapes.

have drawn a month's pay and then given us leg bail and indeed most of the drivers would, did they but get the chance, play us the same trick. True we had on board some thirty soldiers, but they were men belonging to different regiments, and most of them defaulters who had been left behind in Cape Town jail and who were now being sent up to join their respective corps. These men, having obtained Cape smoke from the boys, were now not only very drunk but inclined to be mutinous so that they were quite useless and the O.C., notwithstanding the fact that he was a great authority on pigeon rearing, was at his wits' end to know how he was to pay the drivers and get the ship away. On our mounting the bridge he was walking up and down, metaphorically wringing his hands, blaming everyone with senile wrath and on my saluting said querulously, "Why have you not reported before, sir? You should have been here hours ago; see what a confusion your dereliction of duty has caused." I had no intention of being jumped upon by a man who ought to have been retired from the Service as useless years ago, so I whipped out his own written orders, and as a quartermaster at that moment struck four bells (2 p.m.) he could blame me no further on that tack, so he attempted to shuffle out of his responsibility by ordering me to see the Cape boys paid, and then to take myself and ship to sea, or to the devil, or anywhere else I had a mind to go to, so long as I rid him of my presence. This was not complimentary but I did not care a tinker's curse for his wrath, so I plainly told him, it was no duty of mine to pay the drivers, but if he would send me a party of twenty-five artillerymen, from the castle, to clear the ship and keep order, I would be responsible for the payment of the darkies and go to sea but insisted that I would inspect the mules previous to doing so. He raved at what he called my d——d colonial impertinence but I stood to my guns and refused to go to sea until I had thoroughly inspected the stalling of my cargo, as there was a heavy sou'-easter blowing and I knew that a ship, loaded with live stock, would roll awfully in the heavy sea that must be running outside the bay.

Seeing that I was determined, he at last gave way and said in a grumpy manner, "Very well, your orders are to proceed to sea the moment the drivers are paid; you have nothing to do with the stowage of the mules, that has been done by contract. I shall go to the castle to have my lunch and will send you the party of artillerymen you so needlessly require, and I shall report your conduct to the General." And with this parting shot the old fellow took himself off. By the skipper's advice the ship was hauled into the dock entrance where she lay moored, so that no one could either board her or leave her without using the single gang plank that communicated with the dock wall, then the artillerymen being in sight, the paymaster brought forth his chest and the fun began. The first lot to start the tambourine a-rolling and give us trouble were the

Tommies, some twenty of whom being by now mad drunk were decidedly dangerous, so much so that one of them made a most unprovoked attack on a commander in the R.N. who, dressed in full uniform (he had just come from Government House), was speaking to me. Over into the scuppers rolled the representative of the senior service, where for a minute he lay, brass-bound cocked hat, epaulettes, sword and all, muttering in his amazed astonishment, "Floored, by gad, by a drunken swaddy."[12] The half-mad brute was making another rush at his victim when I landed him a straight right-handed drive under the ear which knocked him down an open hatchway. Then ructions started, his maddened comrades rushed at us four officers but they had no chance. Quin and the ship's officers sprang to our assistance as did the sergeant and the sober men of the party, while the paymaster and his clerks, thinking the stramash[13] to be a prearranged attempt to rush the pay-chest, drew their revolvers and sat down on the top of it. Forcing their way through the mob, up rushed the stalwart gunners, and in less time than it takes a cat to comb its whiskers the mutineers were knocked down, then picked up, and so as to assist them in keeping their equilibrium they were humanly lashed along the weather rail, so that the south-easter could sober them up nicely, which in a few hours it did. Then came the job of paying the Cape boys.[14] Driving all the mob aft, I ordered all the boys who had signed on to file along the port alley way, on to the fore deck, which one hundred and forty of them did, and as each boy was paid, he was allowed a minute or two to hand his cash to his friends and then he was politely requested to step down the fore-hatch, and while doing so he was relieved of any unnecessary cargo he might be carrying in the way of Cape smoke. Some of them resisted and these were promptly lashed along the lee-rail so that the ship should be evenly trimmed; for all things should be properly attended to on board a ship about to sail.

It was by now sunset and after I had had the ship cleared of all the coloured rabble I had a much-needed drink. I had previously dispatched Quin, and a corporal of the 17th Lancers, who chanced to be on board, down below by way of acting as scouts and they, on their return, reported that in the cellar (as Quin termed the lower deck) were nearly one hundred loose mules who, *sans* head-stall or rheim, roamed about playing up hell and kicking one another to death; "and, sor," finished up Quin, "it's more than a man's life is worth to go among thim." So much for contract stowage. I was disgusted but in no ways surprised for I was by

12. 'Swaddy' is slang for a private soldier.

13. 'Stramash' is Scots for an uproar or brawl.

14. By 'Cape boys' (now a derogatory term) H-B likely means Cape Coloureds, or men of mixed ancestry. But he could also mean immigrants of mixed race from the island of St Helena, also known as 'Cape boys'.

this time acclimatized to the incompetence of the majority of the young officers sent out from England for special service, and I cussed the silly old woman who had refused to allow me to superintend the embarkation of the mules.

However it was no use cussing, the mules must be head-stalled,[15] rheimed and put into their stalls, if we wanted to save a single one of them alive. It was blowing half a gale of wind and the job must be done at once, so stripping off my uniform and donning an old pair of overalls down I went accompanied by Quin, the corporal of the 17th Lancers, two members of the crew and some half-dozen of the least drunken drivers. I also took the precaution to request the paymaster and the two naval officers to come with me, so as to be able to substantiate my report, in case I should get into hot water for refusing to put to sea until my cargo was properly stowed, and then down we dived into the bowels of the big Dominion, four-decked, liner.

A Kentucky mule may be safely backed to kick the eye out of a mosquito, just as a pastime, but when he feels thoroughly aggravated and really means conscientiously to do his darndest his saltatorial powers are quite beyond human ken, for although he is only supplied by Nature with a brace of hind legs, yet these are so marvellously gifted that they are able to kick you in fifty different places at one and the same moment, while his muscular development is such, that even one kick, which may be likened to a stroke of lightning, will in all probability cause a family bereavement. Bad scran to them, I hate them, and have just cause so to do, as I will tell you.

The *Ontario* was a four-decked ship and when we reached the orlop deck,[16] and, by the dim light of a few ship's lanterns, gazed down into the murky depths of the lower hold, we saw a sight that might well make the bravest of the brave give pause, for few men have the ambition to be kicked to death by a mob of ungodly and unsympathetic mules and there in that wet, dark, lower deck were nearly one hundred of the beasts, who without a vestige of halter, head-stall or rheim were cruising about, and so as to keep their hands, or perhaps I should say feet, in practice, were trying to kick one another to bits.

Troth, the thuds of the rib roasters, that were being served out, did not sound alluring, while their shrill squeals seemed to ejaculate—" Tommy, Tommy, come and be kicked." There is no earthly use in looking at a distasteful job; buckle to and do it, has always been my motto, so down I went closely followed by Quin and the corporal, as well as by the two sailors, as soon as they had thrown down the Cape darkies, who were

15. To be head-stalled means to be put into a halter.
16. The orlop is the lowest deck in a ship.

more than half inclined to funk it and hang back, but encouraged and assisted by the shell-backs down they came, some of then even faster than they intended. Ye gods! the job was no fancy one, scores of the beasts were down on the wet, slippery deck, though even, as they lay prone there, they still lashed out with an ardour that would have been highly commended had it not been so deucedly unpleasant. Well we tackled to and defending our legs with hand-spikes, managed with much trouble to get them, with the exception of four who were already dead, rheimed and into their stalls. We had then to tackle those still on their feet, many of whom as they rushed about kicking and squealing fell on the deck, or colliding with the bulkheads, stanchions, and one another, knocked chunks off themselves and notwithstanding all our care, occasionally, succeeded in dealing one of us a shrewd kick. Well this phantasmagoria (troth, I'm not sure if that's the right word to use but it wants a long, hard one to depict the devil's dance we had that night with those mules, in the dimly-lighted, olfactory hold) had lasted till past midnight and we had got them all rheimed and safely into their stalls with the exception of four, who lying as they did, in a corner, were hard to come at, especially as they were very busy with their heels. Quin, the corporal and myself were gingerly attempting to noose one of them, when a Cape canary,[17] holding a light, stumbled and fell among the struggling brutes, where, by all the rules of the game, he should at once have had the gruel, medical men call brains, kicked out. Now a drunken Cape boy, more or less, counts nothing, and had I paused to consider that fact, in political economy, I might have sat tight and not made an ass of myself, but you see for a few hours we had been working together and, in accordance with the Lost Legionary law, were at least, for the time being, mates, so like an impulsive fool I immediately jumped into the turmoil.[18] Seizing the half-drunk bounder by the scruff of the neck and the seat of his pants I threw him, quite unhurt, clear out of the danger but in doing so my feet slipped on the wet, slippery deck, and down I fell, flat on my back, among the half-mad, wholly vicious mules, who at once proceeded to do their best to kick me to flinders. Fortunately I kept my head, and by doing so saved it, for I instantaneously jammed it between the thighs of one of the recumbent brutes, at the same time holding out my arms, which Quin and the corporal seizing, drew me out by, on to the clear deck, where I lay and used improper language. Of course I knew, in a moment, I was badly hurt, but as I was not sure where, I dispatched the corporal up on deck to report the occurrence to the senior naval officer, with the

17. H-B is referring pejoratively to the supposedly yellowish skin-colour of the 'Cape boy'.

18. H-B is only too clear where in his estimation a 'Cape boy' stand in the racial hierarchy, but congratulates himself that the comradeship of the Lost Legion nevertheless asserts itself.

request that he would send round to the mail-boats and borrow a medico, as there was not one on board our hooker and in the meantime, as the mules had struggled a bit clear, I set the rest of the party at work to finish the job. This they had just completed when two doctors arrived. These gentlemen had been holding a symposium[19] on board the nearest mail-boat, and although their back teeth were nearly a-wash, as a consequence of pouring down libations in honour of sweethearts and wives, as all good sailors and soldiers should, on a Saturday night, so soon as the week's work is over and done with, not before, mind you, still on hearing a man had been hurt hurried to his assistance. A stretcher was soon rigged, on to which I was carefully lifted, quickly hoisted up to the open air and deposited in the skipper's deck cabin where it was quickly discovered that my right leg was broken in two places, my right knee-cap fractured and three ribs caved in, besides which there was hardly a spot on my *corpus*[20] that did not bear witness to the wonderful dexterity with which an evilly-disposed mule can handle his feet. May the cuss of Cromell rest on the long-eared bastes,[21] and I include in my toast their relations, viz., silly old O.C.'s, fraudulent contractors and drunken Cape canaries, for surely these are anathema. Well the two festive sawbones did their level best for me, but alas, although their spiritual intentions were good, still the spirits they had imbibed prevented anything like successful surgery, for when, next day, we anchored in Simon's Bay, my dear old friend, Fleet Surgeon O'Malley,[22] coming on board to see me, was simply horrified, and declared that all the bandages and splints, with which I had been bound, might just as well have been made fast round the ship's funnel as round my body and limbs in the way they were.

No sooner were the mail-boat doctors ashore, than we put out to sea and my word we caught it, the gale having increased so that the light ship, loaded with live stock, plunged heavily and rolled dangerously. My word, I smelt Hades with the chill off, for when I had been carried into the skipper's deck cabin, to which the kind-hearted sailor had insisted on my being taken (he met a seaman's death, a few years afterwards, going down in his ship the S.S. *Barossa*),[23] I had been placed on a velvet-covered settee that ran athwart ship, so that when she rolled I slid along it from port to starboard or vice versa, sometimes standing nearly upright and

19. A 'symposium' in this context means a drinking party.

20. *Corpus* is Latin for body.

21. 'The curse of Cromwell on ye' remains one of the harshest an Irishman can utter.

22. Deputy Inspector of Hospitals and Fleets, Fleet Surgeon James N. J. O'Malley served on board HMS *Boadicea* when, between March and June 1879, it took part in operations during the Anglo-Zulu War.

23. The only SS *Barossa* to be identified was built in 1938 and burnt out in 1942 in the Japanese bombing of Darwin.

sometimes on my head while it took Quin and the corporal, the latter being a bad sailor, all they could do to hold me on to the settee. However the longest night must have an ending and although I suffered agonies, still I was a tough bird in those days, and had had to bear pain many a time before, so I made the best of a bad job; for what can't be cured should be endured without howling and I had learned that maxim previously in the New Zealand bush.

We dropped anchor in the South African naval port[24] at 9 a.m. and O'Malley lashed up my broken bones and had a proper cot swung for me so that when we went to sea again, which we did the same afternoon, I suffered less pain of body but was awfully cut-up, as I knew full well that there was no chance now of my getting to the front and being in at the death; faith it was cruel hard luck.

We reached Durban in due course of time and, notwithstanding a rough passage, we did not lose a single mule more *en route,* nor did we lose one during the time we were disembarking them, while nearly all, if not all of the other ships, lost a very heavy percentage of their animals; and I assert the loss of these most expensive and much-required transport animals was wholly due to the dishonesty of the contractors and the ignorance together with the culpable negligence of the officers told off to superintend the work.

I have spun a true yarn about my trip in the *Ontario,*[25] and had I gone to sea when fussily ordered to do so with ninety-eight mules in the lower hold, all loose, every one of them would have been shark's meat by morning. I disobeyed my orders and by doing so, not only saved the country some thousands of pounds in cash but also landed the animals alive and fit to do the work, for which they had been purchased in America, and which they could not have done had they been thrown overboard.

True I had got broken up in saving the mules, but then the mules would not have required to be saved, had they been stalled when put on board in the proper manner, so it was not my fault, who had been sent down, much against my own will, to carry out an unpleasant piece of necessary work, and I considered that it was my duty to carry out the task at the risk of my life and limb, just as if I had been ordered to undertake work of a more congenial nature in the field. Some of you, my unsophisticated readers, may imagine I received kudos for the way I carried out my orders, thereby landing a full complement of mules; also a few of you may think I obtained compensation for the severe injuries I had received in the performance of my duty but you would be wrong, for I never received one word of thanks,

---

24. Simon's Town.

25. Unfortunately, H-B protests too much and is not spinning 'a true yarn' about his 'trip in the *Ontario*'. After being badly kicked by the mule, he did not sail on to Durban, but remained in Cape Town. See p. 208, n. 1, below.

nor one penny in the way of gratuity, although it is quite true I never asked for either.

John Bull, Esq., is a paradox, those of us who have served the Empire, in the Lost Legion, know it, alas! too well. A frontier war breaks out and owing to a disaster (probably caused in the first place by the authorities' parsimony and lack of foresight, such as Isandlwana) takes place; in a moment John opens his cash-box and pours out millions of pounds sterling, many of which falls into the clutches of dishonest contractors and others who, never risking their hides in action, batten like foul carrion crows at their country's expense. The climax is over, the danger past, and John Bull,[26] no longer in a stew, buttons up his pocket and behaves in a manner that would disgrace an American-born Jew educated in Aberdeen.[27] He is not man enough, or it is not convenient, or it would not suit the party in power to raise a scandal by bringing the big vultures to book, making them toe the line and disgorge their ill-gotten hoards, so he deliberately breaks the promises his representatives have made and robs the men, where practicable, who have risked life, limb and health in fighting his battles. What I have written above is severe, possibly bad policy, but it is the bald-headed truth and I will give you one personal experience of John Bull's roguery.

In an interview I had with Lord Chelmsford at Rourke's Drift, Colonel Glyn being present, I mentioned the fact that the majority of my officers and non-coms., being poor men, would suffer severely through losing all they possessed at Isandlwana. Whereupon his Lordship assured me, that the officers and white non-commissioned officers of the 3rd Natal Native Contingent would be amply compensated for their losses. Some short time afterwards, by Colonel Glyn's orders, myself together with the remainder of the officers and non-commissioned officers of the 3rd Natal Native Contingent made out our claims for compensation and handed them in; my own being for seventy-five pounds,[28] little enough to ask for considering I had lost two horses, for one of which, being salted,[29] I had paid fifty pounds.[30] A board of which Major Dunbar of the second 24th was,[31] if I remember rightly, president inquired into these claims

---

26. John Bull was a popular national personification of the United Kingdom, especially in political cartoons, little used since the early twentieth century.

27. H-B is deploying the stereotypes of Jews and Scots (especially from Aberdeen) being incredibly tight-fisted.

28. Purchasing power today of about £11,550.

29. A 'salted' horse was one that had recovered from trypanosomiasis or 'sleeping sickness' and was believed to have acquired a measure of immunity.

30. Purchasing power today of about £7,700.

31. Major William M. Dunbar (1833–1900), 2/24th Regiment, served with the 2nd Battalion in Natal and Zululand from July 1878 until 11 May 1879 when, as a brevet lieutenant-

and I know that as far as my own was concerned it was approved and passed. Isandlwana happened in January 1879, my claim was approved in February of the same year, since which date thirty-three years have passed and up to the present moment, although during the years 1880 and 1881 I made numerous applications to the War Office for this sum and other amounts of money due to me, and although they never disputed the debt, I have never received one penny. Five times since that date, throwing up lucrative employment and suffering heavy monetary losses, I have at a moment's notice gone to the front when my services have been asked for by the Empire's representative,[32] and old and crippled as fever and wounds have rendered me, I am still game to risk filling a trench should an invader's bullet find its billet in my worn-out carcase.

Now I maintain that if the labourer is worthy of his hire and compensation, when injured, working for his employer, surely the man who is hurt or loses his health or property while being on active service, is entitled to the same consideration, from the Government he has fought for, and if this be the case, surely while John Bull was casting away millions in extravagance and useless expenditure, he might have paid the few pounds he in honour owed to the poor devils who had faced the music. John Bull however is not constituted on those lines; he had thrown away the millions while in a state of funk, the danger was now over, the men having done their work were no longer necessary, therefore let them slide and if possibly he can rob them of a few shillings, why so much the better, he can flatter his soul by calling his meanness, Retrenchment.

colonel, he took temporary command of the 1st Battalion during the advance of the 2nd Division. Major W. C. Ball, Army Pay Department, was the Staff Paymaster, and might have been the officer H-B was referring to.

32. After the Anglo-Zulu War, H-B served in the Bechuanaland Expedition, 1884–5; the uSuthu Rebellion in Zululand, 1888; the First Matabele (Ndebele) War of 1893; the Second Matabele (Ndebele) War and the Shona Rebellion, 1896–7.

Chapter V

A Life Thrown Away

WELL now I have lodged my protest and had an old war-dog's grumble against the rotten, mean imbecility of John Bull and his red-tape brigade, let me trek on although as I left myself on board the *Ontario* with a skinful of broken bones I was in no condition to be inspanned and had to remain several weeks on board before I could land, when as I was informed there was no accommodation for me in the military hospital I had myself conveyed to Pine Town where I regained convalescence at my own expense.[1] Truly John Bull is a generous master to serve. Whilst sojourning at Pine Town I was waited upon by one of the men who had served with me in the 3rd Natal Native Contingent as a non-com. and also previously in Pulleine's Rangers, the reason for his call being to obtain a certificate for his three years' service. In the course of conversation, he informed me that after my departure from Rourke's Drift he and some of my other men had joined Bettington's Horse and that he, individually, had been one of the party which had accompanied the ill-fated Prince Imperial on his last ride.[2]

1. H-Bs' claim to have spent several weeks convalescing on board the *Ontario* and then four weeks in Pinetown is pure fabrication. In fact, he married in Cape Town on 25 June 1879, eighteen days after being kicked by the mule, and was in that city all that time. He pretends to have returned to Natal to give the impression that he secured a first-hand account of the death of the Prince Imperial of France, the subject of his next tale.

2. Bettington's Horse was No. 3 Troop of the Natal Horse, and was comprised of officers and NCOs of the disbanded 2/1st and 3rd NNC. The party that accompanied the Prince on patrol was made up of Captain Jahleel Brenton Carey, 98th (The Prince of Wales's) Regiment, who was on Special Service with the 2nd Division and was attached to the staff of the Assistant Adjutant and Quartermaster, General Colonel Richard Harrison, RE, a Zulu guide, and Sergeant Robert Willis, Corporal J. Grubb, and Troopers Robert Cochrane, Nicholas Le Tocq, W. Abel and G. Rogers, all of Bettington's Horse.

So, which of these men of Bettington's Horse was H-B's purported informant? Troopers Abel and Rogers were killed alongside the Prince, and that rules them out. The names of Willis, Grubb, Cochrane or Le Tocq do not appear in the admittedly incomplete medal rolls of Pulleine's Rangers or in the muster rolls of the 3rd NNC. In any case, Grubb in his evidence to Captain Carey's court martial declared he had served for sixteen years in the Royal Artillery and fought in two South African campaigns, excluding the Ninth Cape Frontier War.

Now I had met the Prince on his way up country and like everyone else, who had had the same honour and pleasure, had been greatly impressed by the gallant youngster's debonair manners and charming vivacity so like every other officer and man, in the country, deeply deplored his untimely death. Knowing my visitor to be a cool hand under fire, albeit by no means a smart soldier, I asked him to give me his version of the lamentable episode and these are the inferences I drew from his yarn. On the morning of the 1st of June, a small party of Bettington's Horse, together with a few of the Native Contingent, were detailed to accompany Lieutenant Carey, 98th Regiment, who was employed as Deputy Assistant Quartermaster-General, to examine the road along which the column was to advance from Itelezi Camp and of which Lieutenant Carey was to make a sketch. The escort paraded, and just as they were moving off, they were joined by the young Prince, who was attached to the general staff and very keen to see all that he could of the war. The small party rode out along the track for a distance of about five miles until they were some two miles from the Inshallami Mountains[3] and nigh to the Edutu kraal, the ground they had ridden over being open country consisting of low undulating hills interspersed with occasional dongas. It was a country a mounted party, engaged in scouting, should have kept all their wits on deck while crossing, doing their work as quickly as possible and getting away as rapidly as they could; for a scout, with any knowledge of the game, would be well aware that his patrol must have been spotted on the numerous skylines by the enemy, and that if such an enemy were like the Zulus, mobile and enterprising, the betting was ten to one they would try to cut him off.

However the ordinary British officer was as ignorant, in those days, of scouting as a chimpanzee is of skating, so that the observations having been made, the small party actually halted at the edge of a large patch of mealies and incredible as it may seem, off-saddled. This was a direct insult to the goddess of Chance and Nemesis was quickly dispatched to avenge such an outrage on common sense. My informant stated that neither himself nor his companions felt comfortable but of course said nothing although the natives who were with them grew very restless

Of the remaining three, only Le Tocq's experiences accord with the yarn H-B relates below. It is he who was described as 'riding on his stomach' in Cochrane's evidence available to H-B in the redacted 'Proceedings of the Court Martial' printed in Norris-Newman, *In Zululand*, pp. 310–11. Further accounts of Le Tocq's actions, including his own evidence, were equally available to H-B in D.C.F. Moodie's *History of the Battles and Adventures of the British, the Boers, and the Zulus* (1879), of which the Anglo-Zulu War sections are reprinted as *Moodie's Zulu War*, pp. 147–8, 151, 152.

3. Presumably, by 'Inshallami Mountains' H-B means the Mhlungwane Hill, just over two miles from where the Prince's party was ambushed. The alternative, Nhlazatshe Mountain, is nearly thirty miles away.

and somewhat excited. At last the order was given to saddle up, and they had started to do so, when someone shouted out "There are Zulus among the mealies," and two shots rang out; immediately there was a confused bustle, each man striving to complete the necessary girth buckling, etc., and before they had time to mount, a ragged volley, of from ten to twenty musket shots, was fired at them. The narrator went on to say that no further order was given, or at least he heard none, but saw Lieutenant Carey and two of his own comrades riding away at a gallop and at once did his best to mount and get clear. His horse, however, always a restive brute to mount and perhaps scared by the firing, tried to bolt but he managed to throw himself across the saddle, lying on his chest, and his horse following the others, he was carried out of immediate danger in that manner. He stated that, while hanging on in this way, he passed the Prince who seemed to be running by his horse's side, holding on to the holster, and evidently trying to vault into his saddle, which, as it was subsequently ascertained, he failed to do, owing to the holster tearing away in his grasp, as it was discovered to be constructed of brown paper, and so the death of the Prince Imperial may be partly attributed to the roguery of a dishonest tradesman.[4]

At a short distance from where the party had off-saddled, was a shallow donga, and my informant's horse had carried him some little way past this place, before he could struggle into the saddle, and when he had done so he reined in and looking back saw the Prince, on foot, running up the donga, closely pursued by a lot of Zulus; and that was the last glimpse any white man saw of the Prince Imperial alive.

The fugitives continued their headlong flight towards the camp until they met Colonels Wood and Buller; patrols were sent out and the remains of the unfortunate Prince were carried reverently back to the Itelezi Camp, on a stretcher made out of lance shafts, the most becoming bier for a soldier, and then sent via Durban to England.[5] Of course there have been plenty of yarns spun as to the actual killing, but I think that, most probably, the gallant youngster, finding escape impossible, faced his enemies, did his level best, and fell with his wounds in front, a sacrifice to ignorance. In the first place, why did his party off-saddle at all, five miles in advance of the camp, where every lynx-eyed Zulu was sure to be on the look-out for scouts and patrols? Again if it was necessary for them to do so, owing to their horses being knocked up, the only possible

4. This is a myth, but suits H-B's oft-repeated contempt for unscrupulous suppliers. In fact, the stitching on the leather strap of the near-side holster gave way as the Prince clung to it in his efforts to mounts his stampeding horse.

5. For a comprehensive and authoritative account based on all the evidence of the Prince Imperial's death and the conveyance of his body to Britain, see Knight, *With His Face to the Foe*, pp. 199–246, 251–6.

excuse for their off-saddling, and in this case not a legitimate one, as proved by the rapidity with which they bolted, why in the name of all that's holy should they have selected the edge of a mealie field for their halting-place? There was plenty of open ground close by, and anyone with the gumption of a gowk,[6] although he might not have had any previous war experience and have even passed through the Staff College, would have selected a spot to halt on from which he could see an approaching enemy. It must surely have been self-evident to them all that their small party must have been spotted and be under the observation of numerous hostile natives. Moreover, why did they not all, when they had crossed the donga in safety, rein up and try to make a stand? There were five mounted men who had their rifles, and I have not the slightest doubt but that they might have given an exceedingly good account of themselves. Retreat, at the worst, was always open and five mounted men, in fairly open country, can do a lot provided they keep their heads. Again the Zulus are vile shots, so I think the betting would have been in favour of the Prince getting away, had a stand been made and a strong front shown. I therefore think I am quite right when I state that the Prince was a victim to the ignorance of one of the fundamental rules of scouting. Thank God it is very rare indeed in the British service for a stand not to be made when there is any prospect of success, though I fear my remarks on scouting, in case of another war with savages, will still be found to be in evidence.

After four months' sojourn in Pine Town my leg was well enough for me to travel, so, not caring to remain in Natal for the summer, I determined to proceed to Cape Town and decide there on my future movements. The Zulu War was over, Cetewayo was a prisoner, all the irregular forces had been disbanded, Sir Garnet Wolseley, who had assumed the command in place of Lord Chelmsford,[7] knew not Joseph and anyhow I was far too lame to take a hand in the storming of Seccokonie's Mountain;[8] in

---

6. 'Gowk' is an abusive Scottish term for an awkward or foolish person.

7. General Sir Garnet Wolseley (1833–1913) was appointed by the British government on 26 May 1879 to supersede Chelmsford, but Chelmsford, who doggedly continued to act as if he were still in command in South Africa, only resigned on 9 July once he had won the battle of Ulundi. King Cetshwayo was captured on 28 August and was taken off at Port Durnford on 4 September for exile in the Cape. On 1 September Wolseley imposed his settlement of Zululand, abolishing the monarchy and dividing the former kingdom into thirteen little chiefdoms that posed no military threat to British territory. By the end of September all British forces had withdrawn from Zululand. The Natal Mounted Volunteers and other corps called out during the Anglo-Zulu War were all disbanded over several months, it being the turn of LMR during August and September 1879.

8. H-B is referring to Wolseley's storming on 28 November 1879 of Tsate, the stronghold of Sekhukhune woaSekwati, the Maroteng Paramount, during the Second Anglo-Pedi War of 1879.

fact, two medical men whom I consulted, expressed grave doubts as to whether I should ever recover the proper use of my right knee, which had been twice damaged before—once playing football, and once by a revolver bullet; and they assured me that, even should I again be able to use it, I should suffer great inconvenience and much pain from it to the day of my departure to that bourne set apart for sailors, fiddlers and Lost Legionaries. Troth and their surmises were correct, for, although it has helped to carry me many thousands of miles since then and perhaps, thanks to my having been tomahawked in the left knee, I have never noticeably limped, still at the present moment, as I sit here writing, it is giving me unsophisticated gip, and I shall presently lay down my hated pen and solemnly cuss those mules and their progenitors, they, by the inexorable laws of Nature, having no descendants, back to the time of Adam. Blankety, blankety, blank, Amen.

Having made a few remarks anent these mules and rubbed my poor old knee let me resume my pen and continue my yarn. Taking ship from Durban I reached Cape Town where I lived quietly for some months, this being the first repose I had known since childhood.[9] I had married,[10] as most Lost Legionaries do, when laid on the shelf, and my wretched knee prevented me from joining in any sport, except boat-sailing, even misbehaving so badly as to break again, of its own accord, the first time I essayed to play cricket; so that it was long over a year before I could trust it at all, and then I suspicioned it as untrustworthy for years afterwards.

Well the Basuto War broke out, and although I took a hand in it, and it was in Timbuland [Thembuland in the Transkei] that I lost my faithful friend and servant Quin,[11] still I am not going to write about it in this book

9. As noted above, H-B had remained in Cape Town since being kicked by a mule, and had not returned to Natal. He does not mention that in September 1879 he resigned his commission in LMR, and that he wrote on 25 September 1879 to the Cape Colonial Military Secretary requesting a commission in the Cape Mounted Rifles. (The exclusively white Frontier Armed and Mounted Police, formed in 1855, the only full-time military unit in the Cape military establishment, had been augmented in 1878 when all Cape African levies were disbanded, and was renamed the Cape Mounted Rifles.) In his letter of application accurately stating his military service in South Africa – and significantly making no reference to having fought at Gingindlovu – he added the false claim that he had 'served several years in the New Zealand Mounted Constabulary taking part in the campaigns of 1866, 1868, 1869 and 1870 during which' he had been 'many times in action and several times wounded'. In any event, he failed to secure the commission he sought in the Cape Mounted Rifles.

10. H-B married Dolphina Johanna Spolander (1856– 26 May 1904) in Cape Town on 25 June 1879. She was the daughter of Andreas Spolander, who had emigrated from Sweden and was employed as an undertaker with the European Burial Society. She and H-B had six children, four boys and two girls. Two of the boys died in infancy.

11. H-B elects not write about his part in the Gun War and the Transkei Rebellion (1880–1), although he did serve. The context is complex. In 1868 the rulers of the independent

but so as to complete this chapter I shall spin you a yarn of how, owing to that war, an astute though I can't call him a respectable Englishman, got to windward and made a rise out of some unsophisticated Dutchmen.[12] Well it was this way. The war broke out and, being purely a Colonial one, the Cape burghers were called out. This they hated, for although an up-country Boer is a brave man, the Dutch in Cape Town and its surrounding districts are perhaps the rottenest cowards on earth; so consequently many of those, called out for service, offered large sums of money for substitutes

---

kingdom of Lesotho placed themselves under British protection to prevent the Boers of the neighbouring Orange Free State from seizing more of their land. In 1871 the British passed the administration of Basutoland over to the self-governing Cape Colony, whose magistrates challenged chiefly power and attempted to enforce the Cape's hugely resented policy of disarmament, the Gun Act of August 1878. In February 1879 Chief Moorosi of the Phuti revolted, and it required an eight months' siege by Cape forces to reduce his mountain stronghold. Then, in September 1880 the Basotho broke out in a full-scale rebellion, known as the Gun War, in which they took every advantage of their mountainous terrain and now illegal firearms to hold the Cape colonial forces to a stalemate. In February 1881 the belligerents concluded a ceasefire, the first step toward Basutoland becoming a Crown Colony in 1884 with considerable internal autonomy.

Meanwhile, in late October 1880 the amaMpondomise and some of the abaThembu in the Transkei territories administered by the Cape, broke out in their own rebellion for much the same reasons as had the Basotho. Caught unprepared, the Cape authorities had to turn to loyalist Africans and raise fresh settler volunteer units. Converging columns were sent into the rebel areas, and by December 1880, through scorched-earth tactics, had suppressed the rebellion and restored colonial authority.

H-B is coy about his military service in these conflicts, doubtless because he did not take part in active operations, and was not entitled to the campaign medal which he nevertheless later wore. (*See Appendix:* Hamilton-Browne's Medals.) Having failed to secure a commission in the Cape Mounted Rifles, he enrolled as a sapper in the Cape Town Volunteer Engineers (henceforth CTVE) engaged in making roads and other public works. With the outbreak of hostilities in the Transkei, on 15 November 1880 Captain Tennant of the CTVE wrote from the Kei Road Camp in the Eastern Cape to the Officer Commanding, Lines of Communication and Base: 'I have the honour to inform you that finding that a Captain and one Lieutenant are insufficient to carry on the duties necessary in conducting a hundred (100) men, and as our byelaws provides that all officers must be elected by the Corps, I called upon the detachment today to elect an acting Lieutenant in place of Lieut Serrurier who is left behind in Capetown [*sic*] and from what I have ascertained is not likely to join us for some time, if at all. The election was unanimous in favor of Sapper George Hamilton Brown [*sic*], who I strongly recommend for your favorable consideration and trust you will without delay signify your approval of the same' (Cape Archives Repository, DD 1–7: Cape Town Volunteer Engineers, cited in Simpson, 'Imperial and Colonial Officers'). H-B's promotion was approved, and from 26 November 1880 to 4 January 1881 he served as Lieutenant and Quartermaster to the CTVE. However, it seems he remained in a support role in the Cape and because he took no part in the fighting was not awarded the Cape of Good Hope General Service Medal (*see* Appendix: Hamilton-Browne's Medals).

As for Quin dying in Thembuland during the Transkei Rebellion, we only have H-B's word for it because there is no trace of him in the casualty returns.

12. It has not proved possible to trace Trooper William Jones (if he ever existed), the subject of this yarn.

to risk their skins in their places. Well one day a man called at my house and requested me to furnish him with a character, as he had served for a considerable time under me, in Pulleine's Rangers and Lonsdale's Horse, in the latter of which I was in no ways responsible for his enlistment and from which corps he had been discharged with ignominy. Now in both of these regiments there had been very many unadulterated blackguards but if I had been called upon, on oath, to assign the cake to the biggest scoundrel in the combined outfits, I should unhesitatingly have called out Trooper William Jones and he would have stepped out of the ranks with a smile and gleefully owned up to the soft impeachment. Well he asked me for a written character and claimed one as his indubitable right. This I allowed but said, "See here, Jones, you are entitled to a character, if you demand one, but the only one I can give you would cause the gate-keeper of Gehenna to refuse you admittance.[13] Do you still want it?" "I do, sir," he replied, "although there is nothing you can say against me bad enough to describe me. I know I am a hard case," and then he added with a grin, "and quite unrepentant." I therefore took a piece of official paper and wrote a character, such as would have made Satan himself pause before engaging its bearer as a scavenger or cinder-sifter in Hades, signed it and handed over the document for his perusal. He read it, smiled, thanked me and withdrew. Some three weeks afterwards I was on board the English mail-boat, seeing a friend off, when just previous to the boat's departure, who should swagger up to me, dressed in gorgeous, hand-me-down apparel, but W. Jones, Esq. His greetings were polite and effusive, although he had not the temerity to offer me his hand but made many kind inquiries about my health and the progress my leg was making towards convalescence and wound up by saying, "I can't leave South Africa, Major, without again thanking you for your kindness, in furnishing me with that character which has proved itself to be an Aladdin's lamp. May I ask you to step into the saloon and crack a bottle of champagne with me?" I declined the proffered refreshment but as he had aroused my curiosity *re* the benefits he seemed to have acquired through being the possessor of a written character which would have made Old Nick squirm to have in his possession, I asked for an explanation, which without the least demur he at once gave me as follows. "Well you see, Major, I worked the oracle this way. You know, sir, that the cowardly Dutch burghers, round about the Paarl and Stellenbosch, are giving big bounties for substitutes, so that directly I got the written character from you, I went to those parts and soon heard of a rich farmer who wanted a substitute for his son. I went to him, he offered three hundred pounds cash, horse and outfit. I closed. He took me to the veldt-cornet[14] who asked me

13. 'Gehenna' is a synonym for Hell.
14. A *veldkornet* or field cornet was an officer with the equivalent rank of a lieutenant in a commando or volunteer burgher unit.

for my character. I showed him the one you had given me; he accepted me and signed me on. I pouched the cash, took the horse and outfit and that night legged it. I made for another dorp, where I sold the horse and outfit and got another, together with a bonus of three hundred pounds, from a Dutchman, who had just got married. I daresay I could have done better out of him, as he was in a hell of a funk at the thought of getting killed, but you see, Major, you had trained us never to linger when making a raid, so we went to the veldt-cornet, who when he had looked at my character, at once took me on as a substitute, and the same night I cleared out and went to another dorp, where playing the same game won the same stakes. Then I thought I would steer clear of the villages, so visited out-of-the-way farms, at each of which I showed the inhabitants the character, telling them it was an official document, authorizing me to register the names of all young men fit to bear arms. The farmers were only too anxious to make me handsome presents, provided I would omit their sons' names from my list. I took the presents, and here I am, a first-class passenger, bound for Old England, with nearly fifteen hundred thick 'uns in my pouch; true I might have made more, but I am not an avaricious man, and I would far sooner look at that breakwater (the breakwater was being built by convict labour) from over the stern of this ship than work on it."[15] "Yes," said I, "but how was it that these people, reading such a character, as I gave you, should have been so taken in?" "Read it, sir," the scamp replied, "devil a one of them read it, and for a very good reason, as not one of them could read a word of English; it was the lion and unicorn fighting for the crown, on the top of the official paper, that did the trick, and that's what I wanted, when I troubled you for a character. So long, Major, there's the 'all for the shore' bell ringing, good luck and many thanks as it's through you I'm in for a high old time."

As I limped down the gang plank the old text, "Out of evil cometh good," came into my mind and I wondered if it were an appropriate one under these circumstances; anyhow I had never before heard of a rascal making a big profit out of a darned bad character. Still Mr Jones made an egregious error; he should have remained in South Africa and gone up to Kimberley, where the peculiar talents with which he was so gifted would have, in a short time, placed him in the front rank of South African financiers and, like some of them, he might have become the possessor of a house in Park Lane and a place in the upper circles of English society.[16]

15. The Cape Town harbour breakwater was begun in 1860 and extended in 1905.

16. H-B is likely referring to Alfred Beit (1853–1906), the Jewish Anglo-German diamond magnate and philanthropist who in 1894–7 built Aldford House, a grand quasi-Jacobean-style mansion in London's Park Lane. H-B could also be thinking of the millionaire Jewish Anglo-German merchant banker, Sir Ernest Cassell (1852–1921), who was a good friend of King Edward VII and owned Brook House In Park Lane.

Chapter VI

A Kimberley I.D.B. Reminiscence

SHORTLY after the end of the Basuto War I determined to go back to New Zealand but before doing so was persuaded by some friends to run up to Kimberley, so as to have a look at the big hole.[1] This I did, and reached the far-famed diamond fields just as they were in the transition stage, between the old methods of working and the new; for although steam-hauling engines were already employed, yet there were many of the old horse wins as well as the old, horse-driven, washing gears, still working, while the standing wires of the aerial tramways looked like gigantic spider webs, the tubs running up and down them helping out the illusion, by resembling the insects themselves. The epoch at which I reached Kimberley was also one of immense excitement; individual diggers were selling their claims for large sums of money and big blocks of shares, to company promoters. The inhabitants were mad, fortunes were being made every day and even I allowed myself to be drawn into the vortex. In less than a fortnight the slump came and I found myself stone broke, which served me right, for what business has a clean-bred Frontiersman or Lost Legionary to meddle with stocks and shares, unless they should be the stocks of rifles, or the sharing of rations and hardships. However it is not my intention to write about the polygenous blackguards, nor the countless good fellows I rubbed shoulders with in the tin city of the veldt; they will require a book to themselves as I do not care to mix up yarns, of the clean deeds of H.M. Imperial and Irregular troops, with the foul chicanery and rascality of I.D.B.'s, Company Promoters, B.S.A. Co.'s guinea-pigs and fraudulent contractors,[2] in the same work.

1. From mid-July 1871 to 1914 when work on the mine ceased, up to 50,000 miners dug the Big Hole with picks and shovels, yielding 6,000 lb, or 13,600,000 carats, of diamonds. The Big Hole has a surface of 42 acres and is 1,519 ft wide. It was excavated to a depth of 790 ft.

2. On 30 October 1888 the agents of the Cape-based mining magnate Cecil Rhodes (1853–1902), in the hope of finding fresh mineral riches in Mashonaland and Matabeleland north of the Zambezi River, cozened Lobengula Khumalo, the Ndebele king, into giving Rhodes

True many of the former either fill forgotten graves or are to be found in the gutter or the workhouse, while many of the latter may be sought in the seats of the mighty, and the bosom of fashionable society, so I will just spin you one yarn, that occurred in Kimberley during my abode there, and pass on to the Bechuanaland Expedition of 1884 and 1885.[3] Let me call it "The Biters Bit."

THE BITERS BIT
(*A Kimberley I.D.B. Reminiscence*)

As the weary traveller approached the diamond fields, in the early eighties, sick and worn out with the very many miles of monotonous veldt he has had to traverse from the rail-head, then and for some years afterwards located at Beaufort West,[4] the first noticeable objects that struck his bloodshot and dust-filled eyes would be huge mounds of grey earth; and on making inquiry as to what they might be, he would be informed they were the tailing heaps and debris from the four mines, Kimberley, or the new rush as it was called by the old diggers, Du Toits Pan, Bultfontein and old De Beers, and after passing through some of these heaps he would eventually arrive in the tin-built town of Kimberley,[5] where he would find himself a unit of perhaps as cosmopolitan a crowd as ever assembled together on this earth; while as for languages, he might just as well have landed among the builders of the Tower of Babel, on the day they knocked off that big contract, when the necessity for interpreters was first required.

Crawling out of the coach, in which he has spent four or five miserable days and nights, he enters the Central Hotel and asks for a room. He may get one, or he may not, and he may consider himself extremely lucky should he, in the event of getting one, have the sole use of it. Let us suppose he obtains one, when he is shown into an iron box 10 by 8 feet in which he removes, with a scant supply of water, as much of the thick layer of red dust that adheres to him as he may. No sooner has he spruced up, to the best of his ability, than he adjourns to the verandah and orders the most cooling drink he can think of, so as to try and wash down the residue of dust that still sticks in his throat. Maybe he selects a bottle of

---

a free hand in neighbouring Mashonaland. On the strength of the Rudd Concession, as it was known, Rhodes obtained a Royal Charter on 29 October 1889 to form the British South Africa Company (henceforth BSAC) following the amalgamation of his Search Association with his previous competitor, the London-based Exploring Company Ltd. The objective was to pre-empt Portuguese territorial ambitions by conquering the region, and then to colonise and exploit it economically.

3. See pp. 223–34, below.

4. Beaufort West in the central Karoo was founded in 1818. The railroad reached the town in 1880.

5. Kimberley, originally known as New Rush, was officially named on 5 July 1873 after the Earl of Kimberley, the Secretary of State for the Colonies.

Bass,[6] which comforts him greatly so that he does not even sigh when he pays half-a-crown for the same-sized bottle that on the mail-boat cost him threepence;[7] for has not the price of everything desirable risen at every stage of the journey, from Cape Town to the Diamond City. Thank goodness there goes the gong, so he enters the large dining-room and is shown a seat. The dinner is a good one, considering where he is, and looking round the room he is at once struck by the various types of men who surround him and astonished by their conversation. The men are of every white nationality under the sun and are diggers, mine-managers, business men, up-country traders, diamond buyers and adventurers of all sorts, amongst them the Semitic race predominating.

Eating their dinners and drinking drinks, the price of which astonish him, all their conversation is centred more or less on the mines and he hears the price of wood, the jargon of the share and diamond market, the difficulty of procuring labour, mixed up in inextricable confusion, running through which are frequent references made about a set of people called I.D.B.'s, who are invariably spoken of with such prefixes as usually indicate hatred and contempt. Tired out he goes to bed and next morning, after breakfast, he goes out to view the wonderful tin city. It is not my intention, however, to give you a description of Kimberley in the days before bricks were made, and the great De Beers Company ruled supreme,[8] let us therefore suppose our new chum meets a friend who shows him round and explains to him the run of the ropes. Of course the first object of interest to be looked at is the big hole and they turn down old Main Street, after a glance at the huge market square full of high-piled-up produce wagons, to examine one of the marvels of the world. Old Main Street used to consist chiefly of bars, around the doors of one of which is clustered a number of evil-looking, overdressed, underbred men, on whose faces, both Semitic and European, are stamped the lowest traits of bestiality and whose voices indicate them to have sprung from the foulest purlieus not only of London but of all the big cities of the world. Near them are also gathered a crowd of flash, gaudily-dressed niggers evidently acting in conjunction with their white prototypes, whom they ape in manners and dress. These clusters of villainy, for scoundrelism is writ in big letters all over them, naturally draws the attention of the new chum, who demands who and what they are, and is at once informed they are I.D.B. runners and touts, when of course he asks who are the I.D.B.'s

6. Founded in Staffordshire in 1777, by 1877 Bass Brewery was the largest brewery in the world, and Bass Pale Ale was exported throughout the British Empire.

7. Purchasing power today, respectively, of about of about £19 and £2.

8. The De Beers company was founded in 1888 by Cecil Rhodes who was financed by Alfred Beit and the London-based N. M. Rothschild & Sons bank. When H-B was writing, the monopolistic De Beers controlled 80–85 per cent of rough diamond distribution worldwide.

and learns that the mystic letters stand for Illicit Diamond Buyers, when he at once requests information about them and their nefarious traffic.

The intelligence he gains is astounding, for he learns that over one-third of the gems found in the mine never get into the hands of their legitimate owners but that the largest and most valuable of the diamonds are discovered in the first place by the raw, working Kafir, who tempted by his gaudily-dressed tribesman, acting on behalf of one of the white scoundrels, secretes and sells it at a fraction of its value to the said white scoundrel, from whose dirty, bejewelled hands it passes on, at a largely enhanced but still far under the market value, to the princes of the trade, whose lightning changes from Petticoat Lane to Park Lane,[9] and who with a touch of the magic wand have transformed the ancestral fried-fish donkey tray into a thousand-guinea motor-car and a string of race-horses, have filled sober-minded business people with envy and astonishment. He will also learn that an elaborate special Detective Department has to be run, solely to check this awful rascality, that Act after Act has been passed by the Colonial Legislature to try and put a stop to it, that a special court composed of three judges, sits to try its cases, and although the punishment for the infringement of these Acts has been increased, until a sentence of ten years' hard labour on the breakwater, together with a fine of £2000 may be inflicted,[10] that still the illicit trade thrives and increases, while its princes may be looked for among the members of the Kimberley Club,[11] the diamond market, the leading merchants of the town, yea and even among the directors of the principal mining companies themselves. It is impossible in a work such as this to give a full account of the ramifications of the traffic or the laws promulgated to put a stop to it but I will spin you a yarn, how on one occasion some guileless foreigners (if I remember rightly Bulgarians) played a game, not only on the crafty I.D.B.'s but also sold their astute enemies the Diamond Field Detective Department.[12]

I must mark time for a moment, so that I may point out to you that one section of the Diamond Trade Act rendered anyone, not being properly

9. From 1882 Jewish immigrants, fleeing persecution in the Russian Empire, began settling in the vicinity of Petticoat Lane in the East End of London. H-B is insinuating that through the illicit diamond trade these poor, allegedly disreputable Jews were joining the rich capitalists of Park Lane in the West End.

10. The Cape Colony's Trade in Diamonds Consolidation Act of 1882 (in force when H-B was in Kimberley) prescribed a maximum penalty of a £1,000 fine (purchasing power today of over £150,000), or fifteen years' imprisonment, or both for being in unlawful possession of uncut diamonds.

11. The exclusive Kimberley Club was founded in 1881 by Cecil Rhodes with a men-only membership.

12. The following yarn has not been verified, and was doubtless one in common currency at the time.

authorized, liable to the severest punishment, for being in the possession of a rough and uncut diamond, unless such person held a permit granted from the Detective Department, and that every accredited agent of a mining company, licensed diamond merchant, or others whose business authorized him to be in possession of rough, uncut diamonds, had to keep a register, which had to be handed in to the Detective Department once a week, describing every transaction on the part of the dealer, or every day's find on the part of the miner, which return had also to contain a description of every stone above a certain weight; so that the Department knew all about every gem legitimately disposed of on the fields. It also, in various ways, received information about other stones and sometimes made seizures of large parcels of illicit stuff, which the I.D.B.'s were trying to smuggle out of the country, on one occasion seizing illicit diamonds to the value of £60,000.[13] Now for the yarn. It was during the eighties that the heads of the Detective Department were much disturbed and the reason of their perturbation was, that they had information that a number of very large valuable stones were changing hands in the illicit market. Of that there was no doubt, but the Department could get no information as to how they got there, as they certainly had left no trail while passing through the hands of the usual go-betweens, and it was therefore obvious they must have passed direct from the hands of the thief to those of Messrs —— (here halt, no names no pack drill), a fact not to be believed, for such big fish as the princes and dukes of I.D.B.'dom were far too cute to deal direct with Swartboy, Coffee, Tinpot or any of the raw niggers who acted as skirmishers in the dangerous game.[14] Still there was no doubt that many big stones had lately been passed and from the head of the Department down to the meanest trap-boy,[15] everyone was on the *qui vive* with doubled vigilance; until, at last, it was discovered that this small gang of inoffensive foreigners, Bulgarians for choice, were the fountain from which the glassy stones passed into the hands of the I.D.B. aristocracy. But how did these Bulgarians get hold of them? They were unknown to the snarks of the Department,[16] they had no dealings with Kafirs, and when tempted by traps sternly declined to have anything to do with them. How then were they to be handled, so that they and their belongings might be searched, at such a time as it would be likely they should have incriminating evidence on their persons?

13. Purchasing power today of about of about £9,240,000.

14. This is a selection of the derogatory personal names diggers gave to Africans at the diamond diggings.

15. 'Trapboy' is a slang term for a young male involved in the illicit sale of drugs, or in this case, uncut diamonds.

16. A 'snark' is the elusive, fictional character of Lewis Carroll's poem 'The Hunting of the Snark', and is here used allusively to refer to a fruitless search.

The head of the Department was at his wits' end, any day these fellows might leave the Diamond Fields and be out of his reach; while they remained there was still hope that, through them, he might rope in one of the big fish, perhaps even that big Triton Barnabas himself.[17] Something must be done. At last one man suggested that, late one evening, these simple foreigners should be mixed up and included in a pretended row, that police should be handy, to run the rioters in, so that on the victims being searched, at the police-station, something might be found on them that would justify their detention. This low-down trick was played the following night, and the three poor simple souls, strangers in a foreign land, all of a sudden found themselves mixed up with a seemingly drunken mob of brutal Britishers and before they could extricate themselves, a strong posse of police swept the whole crowd, paying particular attention to the inoffensive, much-protesting foreigners, into the police station; in which den of iniquity and injustice the indignant Bulgars found insult heaped on injury, as not only were their sacred persons overhauled but to their astonishment, the men who had been the cause of all the trouble conducted the search, which resulted in the discovery of three most magnificent rough and uncut diamonds. The naughty foreigners were at once locked up and the disguised detectives returned to their office to receive the thanks and congratulations of their chief.

The special court sits, the three judges take their seats, and the benches and standing-room within the court-house are crowded with the I.D.B. fraternity, among whom are many of their princes and dukes, all anxious to see and hear a case which so much concerns their industry, and excites their sympathy. Would that I could paint the scene of the interior of that court: the vile, low-type faces of the I.D.B.'s and the hang-dog-looking blackguards in the dock, but I must get on. Well the charges are read out, the section and Act quoted, and the Public Prosecutor, thinking he has got an easy task, after stating the case for the Crown, sits down with a smug, satisfied look on his fat face. Then up jumps the defending counsel who allows that what his learned friend has asserted is quite true, in so far that the things at present before the court were found on the persons of his clients but at the same time declared their innocence of contravening the Act, as the said Act only related to diamonds, while the articles found on his clients were not diamonds at all but only remarkably good imitations of the precious gems, and as the Act said nothing against imitation diamonds being carried about either cut or uncut, and that, as there was no other law in the land that prohibited a man carrying about

17. Triton is a Greek sea god, usually represented as a merman with the lower body of a fish. Barnabas was one of Jesus's disciples, notable for mentoring others. Hence H-B's double allusion to the IDB ringleader.

on his person imitation diamonds, he demanded the immediate release of the prisoners.

Had a shell popped through one of the open windows and alighted on the table with its time-fuse fizzing, it could not have caused more consternation in that court than this line of defence. Up jumped the Public Prosecutor, who declared that the things in question were diamonds, that they had been valued and examined by the leading experts on the fields; and he stuck to his guns, so did his learned brother, and the arguments waxed furious, until the final test, that of the file,[18] was employed and amid a scene never before witnessed in that court, the stones of contention were declared not to be stones at all, and therefore not diamonds, and the bottom fell out of the case against the simple Bulgars.

If the chagrin was keen on the part of the Department, there were but few signs of triumph on the faces of the I.D.B.'s. The writer of this yarn was seated close to the bench and had a full view of the auditorium, crowded, as previously mentioned, with the fraternity, among whom sat many of the leading spirits of the trade, and possessing a keen sense of humour he relished watching the expressions that came and went on the facile countenances of the princes of the I.D.B.'s, noting fear, consternation and sorrow as the defending counsel made his assertions as to the spurious nature of the goods, and the hope and joy that shone transiently when the Public Prosecutor declared them to be good stones, while at the finals, when without doubt they were proved to be false, the Semitic faces elongated with horror, consternation and despair and the groan that went up was heartrending, as it was made evident that the guileless Bulgars had been off-loading spurious trash among the very smartest of a very sharp fraternity, pocketing good money for worthless goods, so that if the Department had to put up with a great deal of chaff, still the wailing and woe for lost shekels among the aristocracy of the I.D.B.'s was very great. As for the Bulgars, they had to be kept for a long period in durance vile and then smuggled out of the country or they would soon have fallen victims to the fury of the I.D.B.'s, the princes of whom had for once been caught and sold at their own game.

18. A steel file would have cut glass or paste imitation gems, but not real diamonds.

Chapter VII

Yarns of the Bechuanaland Field Force

IT was in 1884 Sir Charles Warren organized the B.F.F. to drive the Boer filibusters out of Vreiburg and Mafeking where they had started two Burlesque Republics and had played Cain with the niggers. However I beg to refer my readers to the Blue Books of that period, in case they should want any information about the cause of the row. I, personally, like all Lost Legionaries, never bother my head about the cause of a row but am always quite contented, so long as I get my share of any of the fun that may accrue from it.[1]

1. In the early 1880s warfare between the Tswana chiefdoms along the western borders of the ZAR drew in Boer freebooters as allies who claimed land as their reward. In July 1882 Gerrit Jacobus van Niekerk founded the little Republic of Stellaland and established its capital at Vryburg. In October 1882 Gey van Pittius founded the neighbouring Republic of Goshen with its capital at Rooigrond, ten miles south-east of Mafeking (later Mafikeng and now Mahikeng), originally Molema's Town founded in 1857 by the Tswana Baralong people. In 1883 Stellaland and Goshen unified as the United State of Stellaland.

These were the early years of the Scramble for Africa, and the fear grew in British imperial circles that the Germans, who in August 1884 had proclaimed a protectorate over Namaqua-Damaraland, would use the two little republics as stepping stones to join hands with the ZAR and cut the Cape off from expansion into the interior. To suppress the two Boer freebooter republics and to assert British sovereignty in the region, in October 1884 Major-General Sir Charles Warren, RE (1840–1927) was sent out as Her Majesty's Special Commissioner in command of the Bechuanaland Field Force to intervene militarily. Known as the Warren Expedition and consisting of 4,000 British and Cape colonial troops (see p. 226, n. 11, below), the force marched north from Cape Town in December 1884 and achieved its aims without bloodshed. The ZAR agreed to negotiate, and in March 1885 Warren established a fixed boundary with the ZAR. The Boers of Stellaland accepted British authority, while those of Goshen moved back to the ZAR.

On 23 March 1885 a British protectorate was proclaimed over the Batswana north of the Molopo River, and in April the Warren Expedition advanced north to extort the agreement of the Tswana rulers. On 30 September 1885 Bechuanaland south of the Molopo River became the Crown Colony of British Bechuanaland (on 16 November 1895 it would be incorporated into the Cape Colony), while the country north of the river was confirmed as the British Protectorate of Bechuanaland. His mission successfully accomplished, Warren was withdrawn.

Well the Expedition, as it was called, had among other units three regiments of Mounted Riflemen: No. 1, the Jam-eaters, raised in England; No. 2 raised in Cape Colony, and No. 3 raised in Kimberley, where I was then located; and although I at first held back, for I was in a very good position at the time, making money and not expecting any fighting, yet on the arrival of a shave (rumour) in Kimberley that the 6th Inniskilling Dragoons had been attacked and cut up at Fourteen Streams,[2] I at once volunteered, threw up everything and joined the 3rd M.R.[3] Up to the time I joined good men had been hard to get and the 3rd M.R. was still short of over 100 men. In raising an Irregular Regiment, everything depends on an officer being known, liked and trusted, both in action and out, before men who have seen service will throw up good billets to join and no old hand cares to serve under officers they do not know.

As I said before the evening I joined, the 3rd M.R. were still nearly a fourth of their number short and the Colonel was at his wits' end to know where and how to get them.[4] I told him I could get them at once and to his astonishment I recruited over one hundred picked men, most of them old hands, in less than forty-eight hours. So much for my reputation gained in the past wars. These men, all of whom had thrown up good billets, proved themselves to be the finest and best-conducted men in the regiment, and the regiment itself, together with the 2nd M.R., were certainly the two finest irregular corps ever embodied in S.A. In fact the whole expeditionary force was splendidly found, equipped and organized, so that had we been properly used, as we should have been had not Mr Gladstone been then in power, all future Transvaal rows would have never

2. Fourteen Streams was where Warren, with an escort of the 6th (Inniskilling) Dragoons, met President Kruger in January 1885 to make an agreement regarding the ZAR's western boundary.

3. On 1 January 1885 H-B was commissioned as Captain and Officer Commanding 'C' Squadron (comprising two troops), 3rd Mounted Rifles and served throughout the course of the Warren Expedition. Each regiment of Mounted Rifles consisted of eight troops of sixty other ranks apiece. The officers dressed in corduroy like the men, wore slouch hats and carried Martini-Henry rifles. The 1st Mounted Rifles (Methuen's Irregular Horse), raised in Britain, was commanded by Colonel Paul Methuen (1845–1932), Scots Guards, who succeeded as the third Baron Methuen in 1891; the 2nd Mounted Rifles (Carrington's Horse), recruited in the Cape, was commanded by Lieutenant-Colonel Frederick Carrington (see p. 41, n. 5, above). He had raised the Frontier Light Horse in the Ninth Cape Frontier War and commanded the Cape Mounted Riflemen in the Gun War, when he was severely wounded; and the 3rd Mounted Rifles (the Kimberley Horse) – H-B's unit – was commanded by Lieutenant-Colonel Hugh Gough (see next note).

4. Lieutenant-Colonel Hugh Sutlej Gough (1848–1920), 10th (Prince of Wales's Own Royal) Hussars, had been ADC to the Commander-in-Chief, India, 1876–81. He had seen action in the Second Afghan War, 1878–9, and in the Anglo-Egyptian War, 1882. He volunteered to serve with Bechuanaland Field Force and raised the 3rd Mounted Rifles.

taken place and S.A. might have been settled at once and for ever.[5] As is well known we had no fighting during Warren's Expedition. The filibusters either remained quietly on their farms or returned to the Transvaal, where their leader, Groote Adrien De la Rey,[6] a vile scoundrel and the cold-blooded murderer of Bethell and Honey, two Englishmen, promptly bolted and took refuge with Oom Paul,[7] who refused to give him up. Neikirke, the mock president of the Vreiburg Burlesque Republic,[8] was arrested and made prisoner and the Field Force was encamped in cantonments along the Transvaal border for six months during which time we had some very good shooting while the Powers that were talked, and then we marched back again and were disbanded. So much for an expedition under a Liberal Government.

It was on this expedition that the small tin discs with a man's number and regiment stamped on it, so as to secure identification in case of death, were first issued in S.A. These were the cause of some rather clever verses written by Sergeant O'Harra of the 6th I.D.,[9] which describe the feelings of the officers and men, composing the expedition, so much better than I can, that I insert them here. They were recited and sung at all our camp-fires during that time and they still are heard at Regimental smokers all over S.A. up to this date.

THE B.F.F. TIN-POT MEDAL

"Oh, father! tell us, father, whose eye is bleared and dim,
Like some ancient tallow candle, an unsnuffed and seedy glym:
Oh, tell us of the medal you wore upon your breast
When you marched up thro' Stellaland, a-chucking of a chest.

5. W. E. Gladstone's second Liberal administration lasted from April 1880 until June 1885. The Transvaal Rebellion (First Anglo-Boer War) broke out in December 1880. Despite a series of defeats, the reinforced British forces were poised to counter-attack, but the Liberal government had no stomach for further military intervention. An armistice was signed on 21 March 1881, and by the Pretoria Convention of 3 August 1881 the Transvaal Territory regained its independence as the ZAR. This temporarily ended the British drive to confederate South Africa, but it was soon resumed and culminated in the terrible Second Anglo-Boer War of 1899–1902. H-B has a point. If the British had suppressed the Transvaal Rebellion, there might well have been no future necessity for Britain to assert its dominion over South Africa at the price of war.

6. Adrianus Johannes Gysbertus de la Rey (1835–99), known as 'Groot Adriaan' (Big Adriaan), was a dominant figure in the western Transvaal. It was to him that the Tswana chiefs ceded the territory that became Stellaland and Goshen (see p. 223, n. 1, above).

7. Paul Kruger (1825 –1904), known as 'Oom Paul' (Uncle Paul), was President of the ZAR from May 1883 to May 1902.

8. Gerrit Jacobus van Niekerk (c. 1849–96), President of Stellaland (see p. 223, n. 1, above).

9. The conveniently Irish Sergeant O'Harra, 6th (Inniskilling) Dragoons, is presumably a pseudonym adopted by H-B, the true author of the following doggerel.

"And tell us of the battles and the victories you won,
And the hardships you encountered there beneath an Afric sun;
Relate to us the legends of the Dutchmen whom you slew,
Though often told they're beautiful and wonderfully true."

"I will, my son," the old man said, in beery voice and low,
"It happened 'twas in '85, that's forty years ago,
That brave Sir Charles Warren, he, with twice two thousand men
Marched bravely up thro' Stellaland, and then marched down again.

"And oh, it was a goodly sight to see each gallant boy
In his putties and cord breeches and his coat of corduroy;[10]
But midst this pomp and splendour, why the thing that looked the best,
Was the medal of the B.F.F. each wore upon his breast.

"Ay! that was a medal surely, lad, no bright and shining star,
No bronze gew-gaw for marching that, and glittering from afar;
But a simple tin-pot medal, with this touching legend stamped,
The number of the tramper, and the corps with which he tramped.

"Nor was it worn outwardly, as if for side or show,
But jealously lay hidden, down all in the depths below;
Amidst those lively animals we picked up on the veldt,
The fleas and ticks and others, that with Norfolk Howard spelt.

"It was a stout and goodly force,[11] composed of the Dragoons,
Of Volunteers three regiments and some Pioneering coons:[12]
Three batteries of Artillery were also with the chief,
Besides the men who fed the troops on wretched Bouilli Beef.[13]

"Then there were the Telegraphists, their poles all in a row,
Which when they had not tumbled down, brought news from down
      below,
Brought us news of other soldiers, and the victories they won,
While we sat still and grumbled, for our sport had not begun.

10. Local civilians were surprised to see British soldiers wearing rough corduroy suits instead of scarlet tunics and with their white helmets stained a dirty brown.

11. The Bechuanaland Field Force of some 4,000 men was made up of the Royal Scots, the 6th (Inniskilling) Dragoons, two batteries of field artillery and one of Gardner machine guns, three regiments of mounted rifles, a detachment of Royal Engineers with balloon and field telegraph sections, a pioneer corps, and a corps of African guides.

12. African Pioneers.

13. Bully beef, the soldiers' tinned ration of corned beef.

"And we also had a corps of Guides, some gents of sable hue,
Though why they called them Guides, I don't think anybody knew;
Unless it was that they were unacquainted with the way,
So 'Domine direge nos,'[14] we howled when led astray.

"One day the Engineers, who were possessed of a balloon,
Sent the old chief Montsioa up (a captive) towards the moon;[15]
And it was a spirit-stirring sound to hear his women swear,
As they saw their lord and master floating gaily through the air.

"For 'tis the usual belief, in Montsioa's town,
That when a chieftain dies he takes a lengthy journey down;
While a missionary murmured, as he gazed up to the sky,
'How strange that soldiers are the first to send my flock on high.'

"But at last there came an order just as if some fairy wand
Had set us all in motion and we marched on Rooi Grond:[16]
And there we saw the Dutchman's flag float bravely o'er the plain,
So we played at body-snatching,[17] and we then sneaked home again.

"Of course there was a grand review, a true red-letter day,
When all the Dutchmen came and grinned and grinning rode away;
So each put back his sabre in obedience to the call,
And bethought him of his medal, which made amends for all.

"So then we marched from Mafeking and Sitlagoli too,
Through Vreiburg, Taungs,[18] in fact we marched the whole of Boerland
    thro',
And treking down West Griqualand,[19] at last we reached the Cape,
Each man convinced that he at least had played the garden Ape.

"So you see we fought no battles on that glorious campaign,
For not a man was wounded, not a warrior was slain:
And the doctors had an easy time, as doctors always will,
Campaigning with a General who's fighting with a quill.

14. *Domine Dirige Nos* (Latin) 'O Lord Direct Us', the motto of the City of London
Corporation.

15. Montishwa a Tshidi was *Kgôsikgolo* (chief) of the Baralong (r. 1849–96). The Warren
Expedition was accompanied by the first three observation balloons ever used by the British
Army in the field.

16. The village of Rooigrond, (Red Ground) capital of Goshen (see p. 223, n. 1, above).

17. A footnote at this point in the original says: 'The gallant poet here refers to the
exhuming the body of Captain Bethell murdered in cold blood by the Boers.'

18. Taungs (now Taung), a small town in British Bechuanaland south of Vryburg, named
after Tau, the Chief of the Bataung people.

19. The British Crown Colony of Griqualand West (including Kimberley) was annexed on
27 October 1871. On 18 October 1880 it was incorporated into the Cape Colony.

"Thus you see, my lad, the medal that I once wore next my skin,
Is no blood-stained medallion, 'tis a simple bit of tin:
But the sight of it reminds me how I wore it on my breast
When I marched up thro' Stellaland, a-chucking of a chest.

"But, youngster, there's a moral, just to end my simple rhyme;
Don't you ever go a-soldiering in all your future time:
But if you should be mad enough, of Africa keep clear,
And whate'er you do, you idiot, 'Don't you never volunteer!'"

SERGEANT O'HARRA,
6th I.D.

And now for some camp-fire yarns. The Colonel who commanded the 3rd M.R. was without exception the very best and smartest cavalry officer I have ever served under,[20] who although very strict on all points of duty, gained at once the respect and esteem of all the Colonial officers and men who served under him, and these would have blindly followed him to Hades had he seen fit to trek there.

This, let me tell you, is by no means usual with irregular forces, as I regret to say that most Imperial officers, utterly ignorant of very many things in the way of veldt life, and Colonial warfare, are often too foolish to take advice from men who have grown up at the game, and are in consequence looked down on and laughed at by their men, who although acknowledging their courage yet do not care to serve under them, at least not before they have learned Colonial ways and the men are able to trust them. Well we were the last regiment to be equipped and left the base camp at Barkley West[21] on a broiling hot day to march to Taungs.[22] I was on that day merely in charge of my troop but the Colonel next morning put me in command of the squadron,[23] removing the Imperial officer who had been squadron-leader to other work.

It was by no means a pleasant march; all the kit was brand new, so were the horses, many of them only half broken in, and they had only been handed over to us the evening before we started. The next night before we reached the outspan, where we were going to bivouac, the heavens opened and down came torrents of rain. For two years there had been a drought, and of course the rain at once turned the sun-baked flats, over which we were travelling, into a sea of mud and water. I was in charge of the advance guard and had reached the outspan when the Colonel splashed up to me.

20. Lieutenant-Colonel Gough, 10th Hussars (*see* p. 224, n. 4, above).

21. Barkly West, on the north bank of the Vaal River, twenty miles north-west of Kimberely, was named after the Governor of the Cape from 1870 to 1877, Sir Henry Barkly.

22. Barkly West to Taung is some eighty-five miles.

23. 'C' Squadron, 3rd Mounted Rifles.

He was in rather a rabid state and made very many pungent remarks, on bullock transport, the weather, the horses, the men and S.A. in general, and was just finishing his oration, when, from the rear, up rode a trooper at a hand gallop. When he reached us, he tried to rein up, but his horse slid in the mud, and his new girth straps having stretched his saddle turned over so he landed just in front of the peppery Colonel with a thud and a splash like a whale breaching. This started the Colonel off again. "My God," said he, "is this the way troopers are taught to approach their commanding officer in S.A.?" Then to the poor wretch who, covered with mud, had managed to recover his feet, "What do you want, who sent you here, what is it, can't you speak?" The unhappy trooper, who had been trying to clear his mouth of a fid of mud, stuttered out, "Captain So-and-so, that day in charge of the rear-guard, told me to tell you one of his horses is dead and what's he to do." Again the Colonel started and made unkind, if truthful, remarks about some officers, then turning to me said, "Ride back, Major Browne,[24] find out what's the matter, put it right and hurry up those infernal wagons."

It was by now pitch dark, the rain coming down in sheets of water that converted the flat into a lake but I managed to splash back past the column, past the long line of wagons, with their labouring spans of oxen, till I stumbled in the dark against a small group of men and horses standing in the road. Now the captain I was looking for was a very tall Irishman and his one sub. was a small Englishman, who had held a commission for some years in a crack Hussar regiment. They were both well-known characters in Kimberley, both thundering good fellows, but both of them were fonder of the whisky, that is white, than of the wine, that is red. I pulled up my horse and said, "Is Captain So-and-so here?" "He is, Major, and so is Lieutenant Dickey," answered a voice I recognized as belonging to the Captain, though it was slightly disguised with spiritual comfort. "Well," said I, "the Colonel has sent me back to inquire into the trouble, what is it?" "Shure Trooper O'Flyn's little hos has dropped dead, sor. What will we do at all at all?" "Well," said I, "if the horse is dead the only thing to do is to hold a board on it. There is no vet with the column, but we are here three officers. I as senior will act as president, you two gentlemen will act as members. We have no pens, ink or paper, and if we had we could not use them on a night like this, so that I will write out the proceedings of the board to-morrow and we can sign it then. Where is Trooper O'Flyn?"[25] "Here, sor." "Well tell us how your horse died." In a voice in which whisky and sorrow blended equally the trooper replied, "The little hos carried me like an angel but all at once he fell wid me and

---

24. H-B's rank was actually captain, not major: another case of his self-promotion.

25. Yet another comic Irish soldier for one of H-B's yarns.

died. God rest his soul." "Well, Lieutenant Dickey, what do you attribute its death to?" The Lieutenant who will be recognized by all Kimberley old hands by his nickname Dickey, answered with drunken gravity and becoming military promptness, "Bots, sor."[26] "Now, Captain So-and-so, what do you consider was the cause of the horse's death?" "Dispensation of Providence, sir," quoth he. "Well," said I, "as none of us can see the horse, much less judge the nature of its death, to-night, we will ride back to-morrow, should the Colonel deem it necessary, when perhaps you gentlemen will alter your opinions and I may have the chance of forming one. In the meantime, O'Flyn, take off the horse's kit and carry it into camp." The trooper, muttering to himself, dragged off the saddle, bridle and head-stall, then vexed at having to carry them through the mud and rain into camp, kicked the dead horse, at the same time apostrophizing it, "Lie there, you onlucky baste, bad scran to yer soule,"[27] and at once the supposed dead animal jumped up and ran away into the outer darkness while the rearguard and myself went into fits of laughter, which were not checked by the yells of Trooper O'Flyn, who sat down in the mud, swore he was bewitched, and refused to be comforted. There was not much damage done as the horse would rejoin the others, so calling the officers aside, I administered a word of warning to them and, also, I must confess, imbibed a strong tot from their bottle, then splashed back to my men, who were making down a very uncomfortable bivouac.

We slopped through the mud to Taungs, remained there four days, and then marched to Vreiburg,[28] where the 3rd M.R. halted, and remained encamped. We had a very good time there, as far as shooting and sport went, but as most of my men had given up good positions and billets in the hopes of fighting we found the time hang heavily on our hands.

Among the duties we had to undertake was the guarding of the ex-president of the aforementioned Burlesque Republic.[29] He was a fat, dirty, greasy Dutchman, and what the deuce the General[30] wanted with him the Lord only knows, but as he was the only prisoner he (the General) had been able to capture he may have prized the evil-smelling brute at a higher figure than any of the rest of us did. This animal was reported to have had a hand in the murder of Honey; whether he had or not I do not know but he was the greatest coward I ever met and quite capable of doing anything underhand. Now a shave went round that the Boers were going to try and release him. I never believed it myself as I failed to understand

26. The bot fly (*Dermatobia hominis*) infests humans and animals with its larvae, causing itchy raised skin lesions.
27. 'Scran' is Irish slang for inferior food, or grub.
28. Vryburg is forty-four miles north of Taung.
29. Gerrit van Niekerk, President of Stellaland.
30. Major-General Warren.

what they could want with the beast, and I am sure he was neither use nor ornament to us, but evidently the General thought otherwise and must have been very nervous about the safety of his only trophy. For one night at 10 o'clock we were ordered to parade two squadrons to escort the bounder down to Taungs for greater safety, and I was sent with one of my troops to remove him from the building used as a gaol, put him in a wagon, and fetch him along to the parade ground, where the main party had fallen in.

I proceeded to the gaol and found the news had been broken to him by Captain Pusey of the Police, who was personally in charge of him. He had been in bed when Pusey came to him and I never saw a man in such an awful state of funk in all my life. He walloped about on the earthen floor of the room, crying like a child. He refused to get dressed, begging on his knees for his life, and refused to believe us when we swore he was not going to be hung right out of hand. At last I told him that if he would not dress himself and get into the wagon I should tell my men to throw him in neck and crop, naked, as he was. Eventually we got him into the wagon and started, reaching Brussels that night, Drei Hartz next night,[31] and Taungs the following afternoon. Here our prisoner was handed over to a guard of the Royal Scots who proceeded to fix bayonets. This was quite too much for him, he threw himself on the ground, seized hold of my spurs and refused to let go of them, insisting that if I went away the Tommies would put their knives into him, so at last he had to be removed by force and taken into the fort, howling with fear. I never saw him again and I never want to. He was tried for the murder of Honey and acquitted, was let go and bolted to the Transvaal, where Oom Paul made a magistrate of him, for such men were the delight of his heart, so that the General lost his only trophy but the 3rd M.R. were relieved from the duty of guarding the cur.

The following day we started our return journey and after a cold march, reached Drei Hartz,[32] where we bivouacked. The horses were picketed, the two wagons drawn up in line, about twenty yards apart, and the men lay down by troops in front of their horses.

There was but little fuel, consequently no camp fires, so after a scrambled dinner of tinned sausages and a pipe, the officers lay down by one wagon, the other being appropriated by the guard. The night was bitterly cold but we had plenty of blankets and so slept well and comfortably. Next morning I woke up before daybreak, my usual custom, and found the whole camp enveloped in a dense fog, so thick that I could not see the horses picketed a few yards in front of me and could only just

31. Brussels and Dry Harts are tiny hamlets between Vryburg and Taung.
32. It is twenty-seven miles from Vryburg to Dry Harts.

distinguish the Colonel lying beside me, he being on the extreme right of the line of officers. Now given a dark morning with a dense fog, it is very easy for a man to mistake one wagon for another, and under the same circumstances two lines of sleeping men rolled up in brown blankets very much resemble one another; anyhow I was lazily contemplating a morning pipe when a figure loomed out of the fog and coming up to us let fly a terrific kick at the Colonel with the words, "Get up, you lazy bounder, and do your sentry-go!" Up started the Colonel with a yell, trying to get rid of the blankets in which he was wrapped, and exclaimed, "I'm not a lazy bounder and I won't do sentry-go." The mysterious form, muttering "Good Gord," promptly disappeared in the fog. The Colonel seized me—I was feigning sleep and smothering my laughter—and said, "Browne, Browne, wake up! A fellow's kicked me and told me to do a sentry-go. Who is it?" "Oh, impossible, sir," I said. "It must have been nightmare." "Nightmares don't kick," he snorted, rubbing himself, "and I can feel it."

I called the Corporal of the Guard, whom I knew to be the real offender, but of course he knew nothing and swore it was impossible. Then the Colonel lay down again, cursing all Colonial and Irregular troops, especially the 3rd M.R. (of whom by the way he was very proud). Scarcely had he fallen asleep again, when for a second time a figure came out of the fog and gave him a rousing kick, saying, "Get up, you lazy bounder, and blow the reveille." Again the Colonel yelled and again the figure uttered a pious ejaculation and disappeared. "Browne, Browne," cried the Colonel, "I'm not a lazy bounder and I won't blow the reveille. Get up and find the swine who kicked me. I'll be blanked if I'll be turned into a football by your infernal men."

I groped my way round the lines but of course could not find the culprit and returned to try and persuade the Colonel that the sausages overnight were to blame for his nightmare. This only annoyed him. He got on my trek, I got the hump, and that day's march was a very miserable one. It was also one of Bechuanaland's worst days. A strong, cold, cutting wind sprang up; certainly it blew away the fog but it raised clouds of dust that simply smothered and choked us. The advance guard, for the day, was under one of my subs., a very smart and efficient officer. Suddenly the Colonel ordered his trumpeter to blow the "Halt." In the raging dust storm my sub. did not hear it, so took no notice, and the Colonel, foaming with rage, ordered the trumpeter to gallop ahead and bring him back. Then the Colonel gathered all the junior officers together, and after telling them collectively and individually all their failings wound up with, "And now, gentlemen, I'll see if you know the bugle calls." He started the trumpeter through his repertoire, asking the officers in tum what each call meant, but the officers were sulky and not being famous for their knowledge of music either could not or would not answer correctly. I was riding by myself away on the flank, dreaming of the long drink I would have when we got into camp and paying no attention to the trumpet-calls, when suddenly the Colonel shouted, "Major Browne, what was that last trumpet-call?" Taken by surprise and following the train of my thoughts, I blurted out, "Grog, sir." I believe it was really "Right wheel!" and the Colonel's language I leave to your imagination. He cursed us all for fully five minutes but shortly afterwards rode over to me, remarked the day and the dust were sinful and tendered me his flask, which was thankfully accepted, and there the matter ended.

Chapter VIII

We All Went A-Hunting that Day

TOWARDS the end of our service, my squadron was sent on post duty between Vreiburg and Taungs. All chance of fighting was over but the country swarmed with game, especially small buck and hares.[1]

We were to leave Vreiburg in the afternoon and on the same morning one of my sergeants, whose father was a well-known M.F.H. in England,[2] suggested to me the advisability of starting a bobbery pack of hounds. I gave my consent and detailed himself and two of his pals to collect all the stray animals of the canine species that overran the camp and the rising town of Vreiburg. This they did with the assistance of two lady dogs and conveyed some twelve couple of curs of various breeds to Brussels (where my headquarters were to be) and shut them up in one of the stone forts the R.E. had built there. I marched my squadron to the same place and encamped outside the fort, but the howling and yelping of the imprisoned animals effectually prevented any of us getting to sleep that night. Next day I gave the order for a voluntary parade without arms and with stripped saddles. Every man turned up; the sergeant and his two pals, who had raised the pack, had also raised some Tommies' old red tunics and appeared as huntsmen and whips. Well the fort gate was opened and out rushed the glad pack. Great Diana,[3] what a pack it was, some twenty-five animals in all, ranging from half-bred deerhounds to terriers. There were bull-dogs, wagon dogs and dogs of every known denomination and many without any denomination at all, but such as they were I meant to hunt with them, so getting the men into extended order I gave the word to advance and we moved off with the huntsman, whips and pack in front of the line.

We had only proceeded a few yards when up got a hare, right under the hounds' noses, some of whom went after her. I gave the word to gallop and

---

1. As the Bechuanaland Field Force now languished, patrolling along the frontier until October 1885, officers indulged their passion for shooting and, as in H-B's yarn, riding to hounds in extemporised fashion where the quarry turned out to be a hare.
2. Master of Foxhounds.
3. The Roman goddess Diana was the patroness of hunting.

in a moment pandemonium started. The hare ran close on two hundred yards then turned and came back on her own spoor.

As I said before she had been followed by some of the dogs, so she had, and they were after her still but the remainder and by far the greater number of curs had at once joined in a free fight. Then the men, most of them wild, reckless young fellows, on the word to gallop, had closed in after the hare, tried to turn with her, met others who were behind them, ran into one another and upset each other all over the shop.

What with the worrying and yelping of the dogs, the galloping and shouting of the men, the ejaculation and cuss words of the huntsman and whips trying to part and straighten out the heap of fighting dogs, one might have thought Old Nick had broken loose, while to render confusion worse confounded some sixty native pioneers who were passing at the time, on the line of march, threw down their arms and joined in the hunt, howling like wild beasts. Faith it was a sight one would only see once in your life, so I slipped off my horse, sat down on an ant-heap and laughed till I could laugh no more. Presently a new element appeared on the scene for the white officer and his non-coms., enraged at the desertion of their niggers, started hunting them, a job in which my mad troopers, not knowing what was up, and some of the dogs, joined, so that what had started as a peaceful hunt might have become a second Chevy Chase and ended the Lord only knows how.[4] Luckily I got hold of my trumpeter and ordered him to blow the regimental call and the rally, which he did, and my men answering, I got them together, when such hounds as could be collected were escorted back to kennel.

Well, well, it's nearly twenty-five years ago, but I still laugh at the recollection of that hunt and my first and last attempt at running a pack of hounds.

What became of the hare I don't know, but I managed to pacify the pioneer officer, who accompanied me back to camp, and after I had lunched him, consented to relieve me of the majority of the pack and take them back to Vreiburg. I retained however two very good half-bred deer-hounds, and a fairly well-bred pointer, and with these had capital sport. There were moreover in the close vicinity to the camp very large herds of springbok and blessbok so that myself and my men had plenty of shooting and fresh meat.

---

4. Inspired by the battle of Otterburn (1388), *The Ballad of Chevy Chase* is an English ballad (the oldest known version dates to the mid-sixteenth century) that tells of a large mounted hunting party led by the English Earl of Northumberland into the Scottish Borders which was attacked with great slaughter by the Scottish Earl of Douglas.

The Jew Smouser and the Irish Priest

ONE wretched cold, wet evening I was sitting alone in my tent feeling very lonely, when I heard the sentry challenge and a mule-cart drew up. "Holloa," said I to myself, "who on earth can this be? I only hope he wants to stay the night. It will be company anyhow and I know the larder is full." Presently I heard a voice, that I recognized in a moment, say, "Is this Major Browne's tent?" and I jumped up and opened the flap, saying, "Come right in, Ikey,[1] out of the cold and wet." In a moment there entered a big German Hebrew who spoke English with a Yankee accent and who was well known, if not respected, all over S.A.

Now in this country no one might call Ikey a desirable acquaintance for he was a Hebrew in whom there was much guile, but up-country on a cold, cheerless night he was a treasure to a lonely man with the hump. For Ikey had travelled much in very queer parts of the world, had done many queer things, alas, many of them not quite honest, but he was the very best raconteur I have ever met in my life with a marvellous fund of dry wit that was simply irresistible.

His life had been one of adventure. In Germany, as a boy, during the early forties, he had been a revolutionist, had been taken prisoner and condemned to death; he had escaped from a fortress, got on board an English ship and been landed, penniless, in America, had drifted out to California, and been one of the men who had hoisted the Black Bear flag.[2] Always a revolutionist he had joined most of the filibustering expeditions of those times. He had been one of the prisoners, to the Mexicans, who had to draw for the black beans, in that ghastly lottery, at La Senora, and was in fact the very individual to make a lonely man pass a very pleasant evening, provided that lonely man did not fancy himself strong at games of chance, especially with cards.

There are thousands of yarns spun about Ikey from the Zambezi to Cape Town but I will only inflict one on you, which although an ancient chestnut in S.A. may be new in England.

1. 'Ikey', from the proper name Isaac, is derogatory slang for a Jew.

2. The California Republic, or Bear Flag Republic, was an unrecognised breakaway state from Mexico in 1846 in what is now Sonoma County, California.

Ikey, years before the date of my meeting him, was a smouser,[3] *i.e.,* a man who travelled about the country trading with the scattered Dutch farmers and especially buying their wool. A smouser's great source of profit is making quick calculations when buying and selling by which the farmer, quite ignorant of arithmetic, parts with his goods at half their value or gives double the price for what he purchases.

Well, Ikey was a smouser, and one day he visited a farmer, bought his wool and then said after it had been weighed and the price fixed per pound, "So many pounds at so much comes to so much," mentioning a sum about half the actual total. But the farmer said, "Nein, it should be so much," stating the real figure, and produced a ready reckoner! Was Ikey cornered? Not a bit. With an air of surprise he said, "Let's look at that book."

The farmer handed Ikey the book and with exultation pointed out the place.

Ikey looked at the calculation, with a sneer, then taking the book he turned to the title-page and then pointing to the date of publication said with a laugh, "Why, mein dear chap, you have got hold of one of last year's books. This year so many pounds at so much makes so much," and he won his case as the farmer looked at the date, shook his head, cursed the man who had sold him the book, declared he had been swindled and gave in. So he had been swindled only not by the man he blamed. Well, this was the old sinner who claimed my hospitality and, I must confess, I welcomed him with more pleasure than I should have bestowed on a much better man.

We had a good dinner, the rum bottle was produced, and over our pipes we sat and yarned until Ikey proposed a game of cards. Now I knew Ikey to be a professional gambler and even if I had fancied myself at cards, I should never have dreamt of pitting my skill against his, but playing for money is one of the few vices that has never appealed to me. Yet Ikey was my guest, I must amuse him, and a few games at euchre, at a tickey (3d.) a game, could hurt no one, so I consented.

Ikey produced a pack of cards and before we began said to me, "Major, shall it be with or without?" meaning should each man cheat or play fair, and of course I answered, "Oh, without Ikey, without."

Well we played two or three desultory sort of games, frequently laying down our cards and yarning, until I at last spotted Ikey pass the Joker.

At once I threw down my hand and said with a tone of sorrow and reproach, "Oh, Ikey, without, Ikey, without."

At once he messed up the cards and ejaculated, with well-feigned surprise and petulance, "Mein Gott, Major, that comes from the cursed

3. For *smous,* *see* p. 23, n. 26, above.

force of habit," and we both burst out in a laugh. Well I marked that night with a white stone,[4] for although Ikey may have robbed me of sixpence, his entertaining yarns and shrewd wit were worth far more. Good luck to the old sinner be he alive or dead.

I don't think there are any more yarns, worth spinning, about Warren's Expedition. It was a splendid Field Force thrown away, and at last the date came for us to march back to Barkley West to be disbanded.[5]

I mentioned in my yarns of the Transkei the celebrated Father Walsh. He was with the B.F.F. as R.C. Military Chaplain and we were great friends.[6] I was to see him for the last time on the march down country, and although I knew it not, was to say good-bye to one of the best and whitest men it has ever been my lot to meet in this world. A soldier, a gentleman and a priest. God rest his soul!

Well as I said before he was serving in the B.F.F. as R.C. Chaplain and was the admiration of all the men for his gallant defence of a fort, which I have previously mentioned.[7] He was in very bad health, though none of us knew how bad, for his big heart kept him going while his cheery voice and hearty laugh were as mellow as of yore, although he knew well that his days were numbered and the tale short.

We were moving down country by squadrons, mine being the last, and one day, on the line of march, I was riding at the head of it. It was a beastly, cold dusty day. We had the wind in our teeth, and the dense clouds of dust and grit driven by the gale choked our eyes, mouths and nostrils, and was so bad that we had considerable trouble to force our horses to face it. The day before, during a halt at a store, two men had got drunk, and as punishment I made them walk behind the wagons and carry their saddles.

Presently Father Walsh overtook the column and rode up to me with, "The top of the mornin', Major, to ye." "God be wid your reverence," said I. "It's a bad day," says he, "but glory be I've a drop of comfort in my off wallet that maybe will remove some of the dust from your throat." With that he pulled out a bottle of whisky. "Drink hearty," said he, "the Queen, God bless her," and I had a good pull. Then coming close to me he whispered, "Major dear, there's those two poor fellows, tramping behind the wagons, through all the dust, wid heads on 'em like concertinas and tongues down to their waistbelts. You know what it is, me son! Now, Major dear, mayn't I just fall back and give 'em a drop of comfort?" "You may not, Father," says I, "for they are under guard." "I can square the guard," he wheedled. "I'll have none of your Jesuitical tricks with my men, Father," says I. "Have

4. An obsolete expression meaning to note something to be remembered with pleasure.

5. The Mounted Rifles were disbanded in October 1885.

6. For Father Walsh, *see* Chapter V, pp. 46–9, above, and its n.3.

7. *Ibid.*

another pull, Major me son, the dust's still in your throat," says he. I did so and then catching his eye I could not help but laugh and said, "Well, Father, it's yourself that has the wisdom of a serpent; be off with you and maybe, so long as I don't know about it, it will be all right." He fell back to the rear. Some time afterwards he ranged up alongside of me looking very disconsolate. "Father," says I, "my eyes are full of dust." "Rub them, me son," says he. "But my throat is full of dust too." "There is water in the Vlei,[8] two miles ahead," he murmured still under a cloud. "But is there no drop of comfort in your off-side wallet, Father dear?" said I. "There is not, me son," said the holy man with emphasis. "Father," says I, "I'm afraid you have not been abstemious this morning." "Sorra a drop of the blessed stuff has passed my lips this day," he groaned. "But that long divil of a Scotch Presbyterian Corporal of yours has got a swallow on him as long as an ostrich, bad luck to the baste."

Then realizing that his effort to square the guard had cost us dearly, I fired my last shot at him. "Oh, Father," said I, "I have always given you the credit of possessing the wisdom of a serpent, but a man must be as innocent as a sucking dove who would trust the only bottle of whisky into the hands of a black Presbyterian Scotchman, on a day like this. Oh, Father, it's ashamed of you I am." A few more words and he said, "Maori my son, ride this way," and he edged me out of earshot of anyone. In a moment the whole personality of the man changed, from the roistering, bantering comrade to the sincere and noble priest. "Maori," he said, "we don't belong to the same Church" (but the words he uttered were far too sacred to be written here). When he had finished, he grasped my hand and wrung it. "Good-bye, Maori," said he again, and after raising his hand in a blessing, he put spurs to his horse, and cantered away. Struck dumb with astonishment, I watched him, admiring his fine seat in the saddle, and thought to myself, "The Queen, God bless her, lost a fine dragoon when you joined the priesthood."

We reached Barkley West, paid off, disbanded the men, and in five days after the Holy Father had passed us *en route* I drove into Kimberley and found all the flags in the town half-masted. "Holloa," said I, to the first acquaintance I met, "what's the matter?" "Why," said he, "Father Walsh died last night."

Yes, it was too true, and the gallant priest knew he was dying when he said good-bye to me, but he would not tell us, for fear of causing sorrow to the wild and reckless boys he loved so well, and whom he had tried to guide by precept and example. Never had there been, never will there be, such a funeral in Kimberley as when the remains of this noble priest and soldier were conveyed to his last camping-ground, followed as they were

8. A *vlei* is a marsh, or wetland.

by every class and every denomination of creed in that cosmopolitan city. Yea, not only followed but deeply regretted by all and everyone in that sinful community. His memory is however still kept green, in the hearts of the old hands who knew him, and many a yarn is still told and many a pannikin still raised, round the camp fires in S.A., to the memory of Father Walsh, priest and soldier.

Chapter IX

So Long!

AFTER the disbandment of the 3rd Mounted Rifles I turned to mine work again but have no space in this book to describe the life led on the Diamond Fields by a Lost Legionary out of harness; suffice it to say I suffered much for my folly in throwing up lucrative employment for the purpose of bearing arms while a Liberal Party was in power. Towards the end of 1886 a great boom in the volunteering movement set in through South Africa when it was determined to start two regiments in Kimberley. One of these, a mounted regiment named the Diamond Field Horse, was the resuscitation of a corps that had won considerable reputation for itself during the Colonial and Griqualand West rebellions of 1877 and 1878, and to this regiment I was appointed adjutant.[1]

The regiment, consisting of four squadrons of cavalry, together with a battery of four seven-pounder field-guns, quickly filled and was a very fine one indeed; as at that time there was in Kimberley a large number of men who had previously served in the late wars or in one of the numerous South African Mounted Police Forces. These men all knew their work, had a liking for it, and joined readily, and it was a real treat for me to have the handling of such a fine body of men. The officers too, albeit some of them had but a vague idea of drill, were rattling good fellows, and as

1. H-B was appointed Lieutenant (permanent), 'A' Troop, Diamond Fields Horse (henceforth DFH), on 13 July 1887. His commission was partly on account of his now habitual false claim that he had fought in the New Zealand Wars, 1867-8-9 and had also been present at Gingindlovu (Cape Archives Repository: DD 7–188). He was promoted Captain and Adjutant on 1 January 1890 and resigned from the corps on 1 July 1891. Despite the captions to two photographs in this memoir in which he is identified as 'Major' H-B, it does not appear he achieved this permanent rank.

The origins of the Diamond Fields Horse (H-B writes Diamond Field Horse, but 'Fields' in the plural was the official style) lies in the diamond-rush days and the British annexation of Griqualand West in 1871. To bring law and order to the new Crown Colony, the administration encouraged the formation of part-time volunteer units. Among them were the Kimberley Light Horse and the Du Toitspan Hussars, both formed in 1876, which amalgamated in 1877 to form the DFH. In 1878 volunteers from the DFH served in the 9th Cape Frontier War. In 1878 the DFH fought in the Northern Border War in Griqualand West and adjacent territories, and volunteers served in the First Anglo-Pedi War of 1878. The DFH also participated in the Gun War of 1880–1.

Capt. Wollaston.   Lieut. Dowling.   Capt. W. Graham.

Major Hamilton-Browne.   Major T. Maxwell.   Capt. Ward.

A GROUP OF OFFICERS OF THE DIAMOND FIELD HORSE.

all of them did their best for the good of the regiment it throve in a most wonderful manner.

The Diamond Field Horse was the first real permanent volunteer corps I had ever served in and I was much struck and greatly surprised by the rapidity with which it gained proficiency, and I am convinced that from a properly-organized volunteer corps (provided the men have sufficient elan and the officers are competent) a vast number of good useful men can be produced from its ranks in a very short time.

At this distance of time I look back with pride and I think myself laudation is in this case pardonable, that although I never had the good fortune to be able to put the last finishing polish on the Diamond Field Horse which can only be accomplished under fire, and though shortly after my leaving the corps in 1891 it dwindled away to nothing,[2] still many of the men who had received their sole military training from me in the ranks of the Diamond Field Horse came to the front, made big names for themselves and rose to high rank in the late Boer War. This being the case I utterly fail to see why civilian troops should not be of immense use for the defence of this country provided they are judiciously trained as irregulars.

The Boer irregulars, bad as a vast number of them were, both in quality and discipline, proved a hard nut for our Imperial forces to crack and in far too many instances forced our scientifically-trained officers to hoist the white flag. Now much has been written and talked about the Dutchman's wonderful shooting powers and men who have only served a dog's watch in South Africa have declared the Boer to be a far better shot than the Englishman. This is all tommy-rot for in the thirty years I passed in South Africa I never discovered this vaunted superiority of the Dutch marksmen either at target, game or nigger shooting over Englishmen who were accustomed to the rifle. The principal reasons the British lost so heavily without administering compensating punishment were chiefly because they were usually the attacking party and did not make the full use of such cover as the nature of the ground afforded; while their opponents, skilfully hidden behind rocks and in shelter trenches, held their assailants at great disadvantage. Moreover, as they occupied positions which they themselves had previously chosen, they had carefully measured and marked the various ranges over which the British troops were forced to pass.

Now, what I want to point out is that Great Britain possesses very many thousands of highly-trained rifle shots who keep themselves in constant practice, and although it would be as useless to try and empty

2. This was not entirely the case. The Victoria Rifles, raised in Kimberley in 1887, and the Kimberley Scots, raised in 1890, amalgamated in 1890 to form the Kimberley Rifles. The DFH and the Kimberley Rifles amalgamated in 1899 to form the Kimberley Regiment.

the sea with a sieve as to pit these men to manœuvre, or fight in line against highly-trained continental troops, still I would defy any column of the latter to advance across country in face of these marksmen for they would be lashed both in front and on flank by an incessant hail of well-directed bullets, each of which would be fired by men knowing their distance from the object and able to plug a bull's-eye three times out of four shots at 600 or 800 yards. Naturally you may say, oh, but the column would be screened by a cloud of cavalry. True, but how many of those cavalry, horse or trooper, would be alive after they had reached within 1500 yards of those picked marksmen. Not many, I gamble, would survive to advance another 500 yards. Oh, but you remark, the column would detach strong parties of skirmishers. Yes, they might, and those skirmishers being forced to advance, even in extended order, across open fields would rapidly be picked off and soon meet the fate of the defunct cavalry screen. Then again should the column deploy into line and start volley-firing they would only present a broader target to their hidden assailants while their bullets might sow the fields without doing further damage. Of course artillery would be employed to search the ground in front of the advancing enemy, but good shots behind good cover or firing from out of ditches have but little to fear from artillery fire, while the gunners, together with the gun horses, would meet the same fate as our men suffered at the Tugela. Naturally I am not such a lunatic as to imagine that an invading army could be defeated, or its advance be permanently stopped, by a few thousand riflemen, but what I do maintain is, that its progress could be seriously hampered, that no reconnoitring party could be sent out, that no mounted officer could live, and that its field hospitals would soon be chock-full, provided it should be assailed by a few thousand such snipers, split up into small parties and judiciously led, as Great Britain could produce. At present very many of the best individual shots are in the territorial regiments, where they are comparatively useless as a few good marksmen cannot, on active service, improve the shooting of a mass of incompetent men, but should these picked shots be drawn from their regiments, be supplemented by the crack shots out of the various rifle clubs, be banded together and be properly trained as irregular troops you could form ten or a dozen regiments that, provided each corps thoroughly knew its individual district, could hamper, check and at the same time administer such unsophisticated Hades to an invading force as would make that force fall an easy prey to the British regulars and also give time to the latter to mobilize in sufficient strength to compel the invaders to fight a decisive battle under the most disadvantageous circumstances.

Now my argument is based on the proviso that these marksmen should be properly trained as irregulars, and this could be very easily done without much expense or trouble to the men themselves, and while I am on the stump let me give vent to my ideas drawn from the experience of many years' irregular warfare, and from having had to handle and lick into shape many hundreds of men taken from every class of society; a vast number of whom were the scum of the universe who knew no more about discipline or drill than an imp fresh from the equatorial regions of Hades knows about snowballing or ice cream. Yet in a very short space of time they were fit and ready to face warlike natives in the field when they rendered a good account of themselves. Now the crack shots of Great Britain have most of them been, more or less, at some period of their lives, under discipline, so that the vast majority of them know quite enough of the simple drill suitable for irregular troops, and as they would not require to be instructed in the rudiments of musketry most of the training that young soldiers and territorials find so irksome could be dispensed with altogether.

To make corps or rather troops (for each county's or combination of county's regiment should be divided into bands of not more than fifty or sixty men, each under its captain or leader) thoroughly proficient they must first of all learn the topography of their own district, the exact distance from ridges, woods or any commanding positions that at some future time they may be called upon to hold against an advancing enemy and the salient landmarks that enemy would have to pass during its advance. They should learn every short cut to and from such defensible positions, every lane, cross road and ditch leading in its direction, that would enable parties of the enemy to approach them by unawares, and also in case they themselves were forced to retreat they might be able to do so as expeditiously and safely as possible. All this might be done during the winter on their half-holidays or Sunday outings, and they might make their trips either on horseback, bike or Shanks' mare, the men doing the latter bearing in mind that heaps of information *re* distances and the length of time it takes for infantry to march from place to place, to say nothing about spotting cover an enemy might make use of, can be better acquired by the humble foot-slogger than by his comrades the pig-skin polisher or the bike rider. Still a combination of parties would be obviously the better way to acquire knowledge, and plans or maps could be made and tested when they subsequently discuss the day's work and observations in their headquarters or club. In this club they could be taught by lectures and discussions the great theory of irregular fighting, which is to inflict as much injury to your assailants as you can and take as little punishment as possible in return.

And now let me tell you how this can be done. In the first place, every man must be taught to fight on his own initiative although acting under and strictly obeying orders. This would not be difficult to inculcate as the men to be trained are all brainy men who can think and reason for themselves else they would never have been able to attain a place among the picked shots of Great Britain, and would therefore be able to comprehend and act upon instructions infinitely better than the raw boys who as a rule fill the ranks of the territorials. Should this system of theoretical instruction be carried out judiciously a very few days in the year would be necessary for regimental mobilization, as the various units could be taught to take cover and act independently by themselves so that the yearly fortnight in camp that causes such inconvenience now could be dispensed with. Of course a very large percentage of these irregulars must be mounted, and for the sake of rapid action should be well horsed, care being taken that the nags should be able to jump and the men able to stick on their backs during a smart gallop across country so as to pound any regular cavalry sent in pursuit of them while falling back from positions no longer tenable. This should be easy as their supplies of rations, stores, etc., being located in rear of them, they could work with stripped saddles while their pursuing enemy would be heavily handicapped, being encumbered and weighted by all the paraphernalia that a cavalry horse is forced to carry. Nor would any O.C. of cavalry be very keen on pursuing small bodies of lightly-equipped mounted men over a country, any ditch, hedgerow or wood of which might ambush a hundred or more Bisley prize-winners.[3] Now very many of these crack shots can already ride, others of them could be taught, while those who have no taste for horseflesh could still render immense service as cyclists, or even as foot-sloggers, as the latter could hold positions from whence, taking care their line of retreat should be always open to them, they could deal out death at long ranges with but little risk to themselves provided they would only learn to take cover. In the preceding paragraph I wrote the words woods, etc., now I wonder if any of the men responsible for our national safety have ever given a thought to the use that could and should be made, in case of an invasion, of the woods, coppices and spinneys so plentiful in England and if so what steps they have taken to train our officers and soldiers in the art of bush fighting. Perhaps they think that the men would instinctively and immediately acquire this most useful though difficult accomplishment, and that therefore there is no necessity for special training. Should this be the case they are blind, besotted idiots, and I recommend them to call to mind the disasters suffered by our troops in the old American wars, the incapacity of the regular troops in New Zealand from 1860 to 1866, and the unburlesquable comedies called combined movements round

3. The Sovereign's Prize is a British full-bore rifle shooting competition established in 1860 and now still held at Bisley Camp.

the Pieri Bush and Thaba Indoda during the South African campaign of 1878.[4] Now I never yet met an Imperial officer or soldier who, at the first go off, had the faintest idea of bush fighting, and I do not blame them for their ignorance, as how could they possibly become trained bush fighters when most probably the majority of them had never in their lives before ever entered a wood thicker bushed than Hyde Park, while the ordinary training of a soldier teaches him to fight collectively rather than individually, the latter being the first and most important lesson for a neophyte in bush warfare to learn. Most of the woods in England, being game preserves, are *tapu*[5] as training grounds to our troops yet in case of an invasion they would be the scenes of the most desperate fighting, and in many bloody encounters the successful defence or combat in a wood might mean victory or defeat to one or the other. This is a well-known fact yet there is not one single body of men, and probably not one single officer, who has been trained to bush fighting in England, while I am creditably informed that a certain number of German Jäger regiments are put through a yearly course of instruction in forest warfare,[6] and if such be the case may the Lord fight actively on our side should ever our untrained Tommies have to try conclusions with accomplished bush fighters in even an English wood. I have stated that the majority of the woods in this country are *tapu (i.e.* forbidden) to troops for training purposes and that even during the autumn manœuvres they are kept sacred from the profane tread of a soldier. I am not going to argue on the rights and wrongs of private property, but surely there are some wood-owners patriotic enough to allow small parties of responsible men, under the guidance of their own gamekeepers, to penetrate into their coverts, learn their geography, the lay of the land, the density of the thickets and how to get about inside it, and when it was found they did no harm to the game, even to allow them to practice skirmishing within their most sacred recesses. Should landowners permit this they would be rendering their country a far greater service than they wot of.

I must apologize to my readers for writing these last few pages, but I have been actuated by the sole wish to render my King, Country and Flag one more trivial service, hoping that an old Frontiersman's ideas, rough and incomplete though they are, may perchance fall into the hands of some man in a position to make use of them. But then when I see the

---

4. Anti-insurgency operations between March and early June 1878 during the later stages of the Ninth Cape Frontier War in the Pirie and Lotutu Bush around Ntaba ka Ndonda were in fact successful in flushing out the Xhosa irregular fighters and ending their resistance.

5. *Tapu* is a Māori religious restriction on something sacred, in other words, forbidden.

6. *Jäger* is a German military term referring to light infantry units suited to patrolling, skirmishing or scouting, often in conjunction with cavalry. The British equivalent would be Rifles regiments.

profound words and writings of a great man like Lord Roberts treated with contempt[7] what hope can there be of anyone paying attention to the scribblings of an unknown old war-dog such as myself, so let me continue my yarn now quickly drawing to a close.

Well, I was appointed Adjutant of the Diamond Field Horse and was serving with them in 1888[8] when Dinizulu's Rebellion broke out,[9] and one fine day I received an urgent telegram from the Imperial authorities requesting me to proceed to Natal without a moment's delay, and in less than two hours I was in the train and on the trek once more for Zululand.

The silly policy of the Liberal Government in allowing Cetewayo to return to Zululand had culminated in perhaps the most awful and bloody civil war the world has ever seen, in which neither man, woman nor child was spared, while Mr Gladstone's well-known cowardice encouraged a gang of Boer filibusters to enter Zululand, where they, defeating Usibeppo, a loyal chief, who had foolishly trusted to the promises made by Britain's representatives, had seized a huge tract of country and in spite of English troops being on the spot held the stolen land, which they called The New Republic. Truly if ever a man disgraced his country and his flag it was Mr W. E. Gladstone. But I am not writing a history of Zululand; it would not be a pleasant task for a man who honours the traditions of his country to do so. Dinizulu after the defeat of Usibeppo took up his abode in a small but very dense bush, one side of which bordered on the New Republic, and the fear of offending a handful of dirty Dutch land-grabbers, located on stolen property, prevented the authorities from allowing the General to intrude on what was really English territory, surrounding the bush and hiving Dinizulu in his fastness.[10] I travelled from Kimberley in company

7. *See* p.175, n.43, above.

8. H-B was not appointed Adjutant of the DFH until 1 January 1890.

9. Dinuzulu's Rebellion, more usually the uSuthu Rebellion, broke out in April 1888 in the British Colony of Zululand, and was not finally suppressed until September 1888. (*See* next note.)

10. H-B's account of events in Zululand up to the period of his participation in the suppression of the uSuthu Rebellion is downright garbled. The situation was as follows.

On 1 September 1879 the British abolished the Zulu monarchy and fragmented the defeated Zulu kingdom into thirteen chiefdoms, but did not annex them. The Liberal government permitted King Cetshwayo on 11 December 1882 to return to the central portion of his former kingdom. Civil war ensued between him and Zulu chiefs who had been collaborating with the British to suppress the aspirations of the royal house, most notably Zibhebhu kaMaphitha, the Mandlakazi chief. Cetshwayo was defeated and died a refugee in British territory on 8 February 1884. His heir, Dinuzulu kaCetshwayo (1868–1913), resumed the civil war against Zibhebhu, and with the aid of Boer filibusters defeated him at the battle of Tshaneni on 5 June 1884. In return for their military support, Dinuzulu ceded the north-western third of Zululand to these Boers, which on 22 October 1886 the British recognised as the New Republic. To contain the New Republic, on 19 May 1887 the British annexed the with Colonel F. Carrington and Captain Thompson,[11] it being intended that the former should raise a brigade of irregulars and that myself, Thompson, together with Major Dear,[12] were to serve on his staff. Previous to our arrival at Etchowe (then headquarters)[13] a party of the Inniskilling Dragoons, supported by two companies of the Staffordshire Regiment, had advanced to the bush, reconnoitring, but being attacked by overwhelming numbers had been forced to fall back.[14] On this reverse

remainder of Zululand as the Colony of Zululand and imposed their administration. Dinuzulu and his supporters, the uSuthu, increasingly resented British rule and the favouritism shown towards their old antagonist, Zibhebhu, whom the Zululand administration regarded as a useful counter-weight against Dinuzulu's royal pretensions.

On 26 April 1888 Dinuzulu broke into open rebellion. The uSuthu besieged several magisterial posts and in a running skirmish on 2 June 1888 at Ceza Mountain, Dinuzulu's stronghold in the thick bush bordering the New Republic, repulsed the British force sent to arrest him (see n. 14, below). Dinuzulu then proceeded on 23 June 1888 at Ndunu Hill to rout Zibhebhu and the Mandlakazi, whom the magistrate at Ivuna had called upon for assistance, and by the end of June the British had lost military control over much of the colony.

It proved necessary to reinforce the Zululand garrison, increasing its strength to 1,000 regular troops under the personal command of Lieutenant-General Henry Augustus Smyth (1825–1906), who had been appointed GOC South Africa on 23 January 1888, and to raise 2,000 African levies and auxiliaries across Zululand. The counter-offensive was launched at the beginning of July with a victory over the uSuthu on Hlophekhulu Mountain on 2 July. Having regained control of central Zululand, during July a British column next reasserted dominance over the coastal region. At the time when H-B arrived in Zululand in late July, preparations were being made for joint pacification operations by two columns. The easterly Coastal Column under Major A. C. McKean was to advance up the coast enforcing submissions. The westerly Flying Column under Lieutenant-Colonel R. G. R. Martin (with which H-B would serve) consisted of the three battalions of Carrington's Levy (see n. 16, overleaf), a company of the Eshowe Levy, and a company of Zibhebhu's Mandlakazi Auxiliaries. It was to march northwards in support of McKean from Nkonjeni, the British forward base in central Zululand where on 1 August Lt.-Gen. Smyth had set up his headquarters. The Coastal Column reached the Ivuna magistracy in northern Zululand on 6 August, and the Flying Column joined it there the next day. On 18 August the joint columns, now under Smyth's direct command, marched back through the coastal regions securing uSuthu submissions, and reached Eshowe on 30 August.

11. To garrison British Bechuanaland and the Bechuanaland Protectorate, in September 1885 a regiment of mounted riflemen, known as the Bechuanaland Border Police, had been raised under the command of Lieutenant-Colonel Carrington. Captain Thompson has not been identified.

12. This is probably Major George Russel Deare, born in Canada in 1852, the officer commanding the volunteer corps at Port Elizabeth known as Prince Alfred's Volunteer Guards, which had served in the Gun War of 1880–1.

13. Fort Curtis, constructed in October 1883 in the little village of Eshowe, was the British base for operations in Zululand. Since 1887 Eshowe had been the seat of the Resident Commissioner of Zululand.

14. H-B is referring to the skirmish at Ceza on 2 June 1888 (see n. 10, above). A squadron of the 6th (Inniskilling) Dragoons, a company of Mounted Infantry of the 1st Battalion, The

the Field Force had been reinforced by a battalion of the Royal Scots
and two machine guns, the whole being massed at Entongeneni and
Inkonjene [Entonjaneni and Nkonjeni], where they awaited the advent of
the staff before crossing the Black Umvolosi [Mfolozi] River and twisting
Dinizulu's tail.[15] Everyone had moved on, with the exception of the
General, when we reached Etchowe and then we learnt that the General
had modified his plans and that Colonel Carrington was to serve on the
H.Q. staff, while Dear, Thompson and myself were to take command of
three battalions of Natal Kafirs.[16] This was not pleasant news for me as I
had experienced the joys of commanding Natal Kafirs in 1879; however
I had never been a grumbler and was not going to start that obnoxious
game now, especially as there was every prospect of some good fighting
in front of us, which was not to be sneezed at even with the drawback
of having to share the diversion with cowardly Natal Kafirs. I therefore
thankfully accepted the good luck the gods had sent me and cussed not
the concurrent misfortunes, for is not this the hard-and-fast custom of
Lost Legionaries when about to engage in the gentle pastime of war? As
we were to take over our Christy Minstrels[17] at Entongeneni [Entonjaneni]
we drew horses from the Remount Department and proceeded there as
rapidly as possible, the niggers being brought in and handed over to us
the day following our arrival by the resident magistrates, who gave us as
many instructions *re* the treatment of the sable beauties as a fussy old lady
gives a new maid as to the handling of her pet lap-dogs. We were allowed
no time to train or organize our savages as next day we started for the
Black Umvolosi [Mfolozi], which in due time we reached and crossed,
and together with a squadron of Inniskilling Dragoons and the Royal
Scots took post, in two parties, on a ridge some ten miles from the Quasa
[Ceza] Bush in which Dinizulu and his hostile Usutas [uSuthu] had their

---

Royal Inniskilling Fusiliers, a company of Mounted Infantry of the 1st Battalion, The North
Staffordshire Regiment (Prince of Wales's), along with a company of Zululand Police and
Mnyamana's Auxiliaries, all under the command of Captain E. G. Pennefather, were engaged.

15. Dinuzulu was still ensconced in his fastness on Ceza Mountain and his submission was
required.

16. Carrington's Levy consisted of three battalions of untrained African levies numbering
1,760 men. They were raised by magistrates in the Colony of Zululand, and not Natal as
H-B states. The men wore usual Zulu dress. To distinguish them from the similarly attired
uSuthu, they tied a red cloth around their heads, just as the NNC had done in the Anglo-Zulu
War. They were armed with their traditional spears and shields, although a few would have
carried obsolete muzzle-loading firearms.

17. 'Christy Minstrels' refers to the actors in any blackface minstrel show, and is used
by H-B as a derogatory epithet for the members of Carrington's Levy. See *also* p. 167, n. 7,
above.

Surg. Maj. Callender.   Paymaster Ettling.   Maj. Hamilton-Browne and family.

D.F.H. CAMP AT SPEITFONTEIN 1890.

stronghold.[18] The General and his staff joined up during the afternoon and camped with the Dragoons some 200 yards from where the Royal Scots, with whom I was, bivouacked.[19] At dark I posted parties of my natives on outlying picket, but these heroes fled back into camp about 9 p.m., declaring the Usutu had come down to attack them. Every preparation was made to resist an attack, and having doubts as to the truth of my natives' report I volunteered to leave the camp on a scouting expedition which I did alone, not wanting to be hampered by a white companion who being a new chum would naturally know nothing about scouting and I placed no confidence whatever in the Natal Kafirs [Carrington's Levy]. Well, out I went alone, charmed at getting a chance of again playing the old game I loved so well and, for a wonder, found that the pickets had told the truth as I quickly discovered the bivouac to be threatened on two sides by several bodies of the Usutu, who however made no attack but simply contented themselves with jeering at us from a safe distance. Next day Captain R. Baden Powell, who was on the staff, was sent to locate a rebel kraal, his escort consisting of mine and Thompson's battalions of natives and a squadron of Dragoons.[20] We reached the place, but found all the fighting men had cleared out, which so emboldened my cowardly beauties that they murdered two wretched old men before I could stop them. As we returned to camp in two parties by different routes my gang flushed a big mob of cattle the herds of which were driving them as fast as they could towards the Quasa [Ceza] Bush, which plainly showed that they belonged to the enemy and were therefore fair loot. This being the case, accompanied by some of my men I went in pursuit and after a smart gallop headed them. The herds, all of whom were armed, bolted and my men coming up we captured the cattle and drove them into camp where I took care the whole outfit, both white and black, were liberally supplied with fresh meat, a godsend to Tommies most of whom had lived on iron rations for months. A few days after the above capture some assvogels (vultures), I mean civil authorities, appeared on the scene, who declared the cattle belonged to friendly natives and that I had followed

18. On 9 August four companies of the Royal Scots under Lieutenant-Colonel Thompson and a squadron of the 6th (Inniskilling) Dragoons established the Nsukazi Fort just north of the Mfabeni hills between Ceza and Ivuna, despite the site being unfavourable because of the thick bush.

19. Smyth's visit of inspection to the Nsukazi Fort was only a fleeting one. On 15 August he left Nkonjeni with his staff to take command of the joint column at Ivuna for the march back to Eshowe.

20. Brevet Major Robert S. S. Baden-Powell (1857–1941), 13th Hussars, was the nephew of Lieutenant-General Smyth. He was serving in Zululand on his uncle's staff as his Acting Assistant Military Secretary. In later years he would achieve fame during the siege of Mafeking in the Second Anglo-Boer War and as the founder of The Boy Scouts Association, but at the time he was recognised as an authority on polo and pig-sticking.

and captured them over the border of the New Republic. Whereupon I was ordered to render my reasons in writing for committing the heinous crime of crossing the boundaries of a neutral state with armed men. The reasons I gave were as follows:—First, that it was a recognised law in case you started a fox in your own country you could follow him into your neighbour's where, provided you did not dig him out of an earth, you had a perfect right to hunt and kill him. Secondly, that I did not know where the frontier line of the tinpot New Republic was, and moreover was quite sure that on this point no one else was better informed than I. These reasons I sent in to H.Q. and as I heard no more about the matter I presume they were considered quite satisfactory. I was, however, ordered to hand over the balance of my capture to the civil magistrates, which I did without regret as all the fattest and best beasts had been reduced to sirloins and beefsteaks and the residue were either cows or poor animals not fit to be butchered.[21]

A few days afterwards we made the advance to attack the bush, Thompson and myself being ordered to make a night's march so as to reach the place at daylight, which we did, but the final movement was delayed until the arrival of the General, who did not put in an appearance till noon and it was past 2 p.m. before he and his staff had finished their lunch when we were ordered to advance. In the meanwhile Dinizulu, deeming discretion to be the better part of valour, deserted the bush, and retired into the New Republic, where he surrendered himself to the Boer filibusters, who unfortunately did not kill him, but handed him over to the British to whom he has been a cursed nuisance ever since.[22] The

21. Richard H. Addison (1857–1921), the Resident Magistrate of Ndwandwe District of Zululand in which the incident took place, was called upon to investigate. His official reports to the Resident Commissioner of Zululand and to Field Cornet P. M. Bester of the ZAR (Laband, 'Dick Addison', pp. 166–7) diverge significantly from H-B's disingenuous account of what turns out to have been a discreditable episode.

Addison wrote that on 11 August at Dlebe Mountain, some seven miles west of the Nsukazi Fort, African scouts from the fort clashed with uSuthu raiding over the Zululand border from the Vryheid District. (The New Republic, without the capacity to maintain itself as an independent state, had in fact ceased to exist on 20 July 1888 when it was incorporated as the Vryheid District in the neighbouring ZAR.) Baden-Powell led out a punitive expedition against what he supposed were the uSuthu raiders. The problem was that Baden-Powell, despite being the recent author of *Reconnaissance and Scouting: A Practical Course of Instruction*, in this instance lacked the requisite skills and possessed no clear idea of where the border lay. Consequently, during the course of the operation his force violated the territory of the ZAR. And to make his error all the more egregious, when Carrington's Levy killed twelve supposed uSuthu and took fifteen prisoner, as well as capturing 146 of their cattle, it turned out that they were not uSuthu at all, but were the adherents of Mnyamana kaNgqengelele, the loyalist Buthelezi chief and ally of the British.

22. During 6–7 August, Dinizulu disbanded the remnants of the uSuthu at Ceza and crossed the border into the ZAR. The British insisted he be handed over to them, and after

following day I discovered a strong party of the enemy down in a deep valley and received orders to attack them, when just as I was gleefully moving off to do so, the General received a dispatch from the Governor of Natal. What its contents were I don't know, but it so disgusted the old gentleman that he immediately gave orders for the Field Force to abandon the district,[23] so instead of having a nice little fight I was directed to march my men back to Etchowe and disband them.[24] Nothing eventful occurred during our retrograde movement, and after remaining a few days in Etchowe, Colonel Carrington and the rest of our party returned to Durban, myself utterly disgusted at having no fun after travelling so far in search of it, but then what can you hope for if you go soldiering when a Pro-Boer, Pro-Nigger, Anti-British Government is in power. Two days after reaching Durban the General with his staff arrived and Colonel Carrington with myself accompanied them to Cape Town, where I, bidding them farewell, returned to Kimberley. There I resumed my duties as Adjutant of the Diamond Field Horse, with whom I served till March 1891,[25] when I was sent up in command of the De Beers Company's Expedition to Mashonaland.[26] However, I must leave the account of my long journey, the privations of the early settlers and the shameful treatment they received from the hands of the British South African Company to another book, when perchance I may be able to open

---

an abortive attempt at flight, on 15 November Dinuzulu gave himself up in Pietermaritzburg. He and the other uSuthu leaders were put on trial in 1889 for high treason, and Dinuzulu was exiled to St Helena. He remained there until 1898 when he was returned to Zululand (incorporated on 30 December 1897 into the Colony of Natal) as a lowly government *induna* (headman). Despite what H-B writes, Dinuzulu gave material and welcome assistance to the British military during the Second Anglo-Boer War. However, he was subsequently tangentially implicated in the Bhambatha Rebellion of 1906. He was arraigned for high treason and sentenced to prison in 1909.

23. It was always Smyth's strategic intention to march the joint columns back to Eshowe from Ivuna (*see* p. 248, n. 10, above). However, as H-B observes, Smyth was repeatedly irritated by messages from Sir Arthur Havelock, the Governor of Natal and Zululand, whose interference in military planning he resented as unwarranted.

24. H-B and Carrington's Levy reached Eshowe on 30 August. By 30 September the British considered the rebellion suppressed and on 2 November the Zululand garrison was reduced to its normal level.

25. H-B officially resigned from the DFH on 1 July 1891.

26. In his daughter Violet's certificate of baptism in Constantia near Cape Town on 25 July 1891, H-B put down his profession as major in the Chartered Company's Pioneer Forces.

On 27 June 1890 the 'Pioneer Column' of 500 BSAC paramilitary Police and almost 200 semi-trained civilian volunteers, led by Frederick Courtney Selous, advanced into Mashonaland. A protectorate was proclaimed by an Order in Council of 9 May 1891. The Pioneer Column was disbanded on 1 October 1890. Its members, who founded Fort Victoria and Salisbury (now Harare), were rewarded with generous land grants and mining rights. Information has not been found concerning the BSAC expedition H-B commanded in Mashonaland in mid-1891. But, in any case, that (as H-B might have said) is another story.

the eyes of the British public to the acts of some of the men whom at present they regard as little Imperialistic tin gods; anyhow this yarn is finished and it is the earnest hope of an old Lost Legionary that those of you who have been good enough to wade through it won't be overbored with its prosiness.

So Long!

THE END

A bemedalled George Hamilton-Browne,
as depicted in the frontispiece of
With the Lost Legion in New Zealand.

Appendix

Hamilton-Browne's Medals[1]

The frontispiece to *With the Lost Legion in New Zealand* shows a photograph of the balefully glowering, shaggily moustached author, 'Colonel' Hamilton-Browne. He is wearing a military-style tunic and is sporting four medals. A similar set of medals was for many years in the collection of the late W. P. Dawson. It is still held in a private collection, and the photographs of it are reproduced here with the owner's authority.

Besides the matter of provenance, these four medals raise several interrelated questions. Firstly, are the medals in the private collection the self-same ones Hamilton-Browne was photographed wearing? They seem indeed to be identical, but without being able to inspect the medals shown in that frontispiece, it is impossible to tell. Secondly, are the medals in the private collection the original medals awarded to Hamilton-Browne, or are they replacements? Thirdly, and most significantly of all, bearing in mind his long career as a con man, what right had Hamilton-Browne to wear them? These last two questions will be addressed when the medals are discussed below.

Moving from the left, the New Zealand War Medal was a campaign medal authorised in 1869 to be awarded to Imperial and Colonial troops who had fought in the New Zealand Wars of 1845–7 and 1860–6. By falsely putting the date of his birth back to 1844 from 1851, Hamilton-Browne could make his conceivable, oft-repeated claim to have served as a very young man during the later stages of the wars, as well as during the subsequent campaigns against Tītokowaru (1868–9) and Te Kooti (1868–72). The problem is that he did not land in New Zealand until January 1872, just as the last shots were being fired in Te Kooti's War. So, although he wore the New Zealand War Medal, Hamilton-Browne had no right to it whatsoever.

Nevertheless, his name is engraved around the rim of the medal in the private collection. Since he had not been awarded the medal, how had this come about? The answer might lie in a letter Captain Gilbert Mair of the New Zealand Mounted Rifles wrote to the *Otago Witness* in May 1916, soon after Hamilton-Browne's death. Mair had been stung by the old, fictitious yarns the newspapers were

---

1. My thanks to Adrian Greaves, Cameron Simpson and Peter Weedon for sharing their vital knowledge of Hamilton-Browne's medals with me.

Left & below left: The group of medals believed to have belonged to, and been worn by, George Hamilton-Browne. From left: New Zealand War Medal, South Africa General Service Medal 1877–9, Cape of Good Hope General Service Medal, British South Africa Company Medal. As the text explains, H-B was not entitled to the first and third of these at all, and the clasp on the second credits him with more service than he actually performed.

———————

repeating about the defunct 'Colonel's' exploits in the New Zealand Wars. His letter set about debunking them, and he went on to explain how Hamilton-Browne had laid his hands on the New Zealand Medal he had been photographed wearing in *With the Lost Legion in New Zealand*. Mair wrote that he had been assured by Lieutenant-Colonel Walter Gudgeon, CMG, a famous veteran of the wars, that the medal had been purchased by Hamilton-Browne at Runanga 'from a comrade, G. Hunter Brown, only the "e" being required to make it correspond with the spelling of his own name'.[2] Lieutenant-Colonel Gudgeon's 'explanation' could well have been no more than a yarn worthy of Hamilton-Browne himself, but it speaks to how widely his specious claim to the medal was known and discussed in New Zealand in military circles.

Second from the left, the South Africa General Service Medal 1877–9, instituted in 1880, was also a campaign medal. It was awarded alone or with one or more of seven claps designating in which campaigns the recipient had served. The Transkei Rifles medal roll indicates that Hamilton-Browne was eligible for the medal with the 1877-8-9 clasp as shown in the photograph, 3,520 of which were awarded. However, there is something odd here, for he served only from February 1878, when he arrived in the Cape, to September 1879, and did not fight during 1877 in the early stages of the Ninth Cape Frontier War. He should therefore have been awarded instead one of the 1,180 1878–9 clasps. But Hamilton-Browne made repeated claims at the time (and in *Lost Legionary in South Africa*) to have served in 1877 and needed to sustain his story. One can only suppose that the award of the 1877–8–9 clasp was made on the deceptive, unquestioned information he proffered, and which was duly captured in the 'Statement of the Services of the Volunteers' register. It should be noted that besides the fabricated claim to have served in the Ninth Cape Frontier War from 1877, in the same register he equally falsely set down that he had fought in New Zealand from 1865 to 1872, and had been present at the battle of Gingindlovu in the Anglo-Zulu War.

The South Africa General Service Medal 1877–8–9 in the private collection has a chiselled engraving along the rim of the silver medal: 'G. Hamilton-Browne, Comdt.' However, the name on a silver medal can be skimmed down by a competent jeweller and replaced by another, and expert evaluation in London has confirmed that this is indeed the case here. In Hamilton-Browne's defence, we know from the medal roll of the Transkei Rifles that he never collected the original medal awarded to him, and it would have been returned to Woolwich to be melted down for re-use. If he wanted to wear the medal to which he was entitled, he

2. *Otago Witness*, 24 May 1916: letter to the editor, Captain Gilbert Mair, 15 May 1916.

The engraving on the South Africa General Service Medal from Hamilton-Browne's group has clearly been applied to a medal originally issued to someone else, and does not use the name or rank by which H-B was known to the authorities at the time.

needed to acquire one and rename it. When he had it re-engraved, he had clearly forgotten (or never knew) that according to the medal roll of the Transkei Rifles, it was 'Lieutenant Brown [*sic*], George Hamilton' who was awarded the medal, and not Commandant Hamilton-Browne with a hyphen and an 'e' to Brown.[3]

The Cape of Good Hope General Service Medal, third from the left, was likewise a campaign medal authorised by the government of the Cape Colony and approved by Queen Victoria in December 1900. It was a retrospective award for members of the Cape Colonial Forces who had taken part in campaigns in Basutoland (the Gun War) in 1880–1, the Transkei (Tembuland and Griqualand East) in 1880–1, and in Bechuanaland in 1896–7. Clasps for the three campaigns were authorised. The medal was awarded to surviving veterans only upon application. The medal in the photographed group has the clasp for Basutoland. Unfortunately, a search through the medal roll of the 5,154 recipients yields no Brown, Browne or Hamilton-Browne. In 1880–1 he served with the Cape Town Volunteer Engineers and on 15 November 1880 he was appointed lieutenant. Elements of this unit fought mainly in the Transkei Rebellion, but it must be supposed that Hamilton-Browne remained at base in the Cape Colony throughout and saw no active service there (he is uncharacteristically reticent about this episode in *Lost Legionary in South Africa*), and was thus not eligible for the campaign medal. Nor, according to the medal roll, did he apply for it.

He wore it nevertheless, and his name is on the rim of the medal in the private collection. The London experts have confirmed the medal's authenticity, but this still leaves an insuperable problem. Of the fifty-one medals awarded to members

---

3. National Archives, Kew: WO 100/49: Medal roll of the Transkei Rifles, where Lieutenant Hamilton-Browne's medal was marked 'returned to Woolwich'.

of the Cape Town Volunteer Engineers, forty-eight carried the Transkei clasp, and three the Transkei and Basutoland clasps. Not one had the sole Basutoland clasp.[4] The conclusion is that Hamilton-Browne acquired this medal with the Basutoland clasp from someone who had served in a unit other than his – and it mattered not a jot that this proved it could not have been awarded to a member of the Cape Town Volunteer Engineers since he had no right to it anyway – and (notwithstanding expert evaluation) had it skimmed and the name of the original recipient replaced by his. No other solution presents itself. As with the New Zealand War Medal, for Hamilton-Browne to wear it was a deliberate deception.

The fourth medal in the row is the British South Africa Company Medal, issued by the BSAC and sanctioned in 1896 by Queen Victoria for the mainly colonial and locally-raised troops who had fought in the First Matabele War of 16 October to 24 December 1893. Recipients received the medal with the name of the campaign, 'Matabeleland 1893', inscribed on the reverse, as in the medal in the photograph. In 1897 the award was extended to those engaged in subsequent campaigns, and two claps were issued, as with this medal. The 'Rhodesia 1896' clasp went to those who had fought in the Second Matabele War from 24 March to 31 December 1896, and the 'Mashonaland 1897' clasp was awarded to those who had seen action in subsequent operations from 24 March 1896 to 31 October 1897. All the medals were engraved with the name of the recipient.

In this instance, Hamilton-Browne had genuinely earned the medal and clasps he wore, having served as a major in the Salisbury Horse during the First Matabele War, and as the major in command of the Umtali Rifles (Volunteer Corps) during the Second Matabele War and in Mashonaland. He is down in the medal roll as 'Major George Hamilton Browne, Salisbury Horse'.[5] Moreover, it has been confirmed by the present owner that his name is engraved on the medal rim and its authenticity has been confirmed.

What this inquiry serves to prove, is that of the four medals Hamilton-Browne habitually wore, he was entitled to only two. But that was typical of the con man he always was.

---

4. Cape of Good Hope General Service Medal roll: AngloBoerWar.com/medals-and-awards/non-boer-war/292-cgh-gsm (accessed 21 January 2025).

5. British South Africa Company Medal roll: AngloBoerWar.com/medals-and-awards/non-boer-war/1721-british-south-africa-company-medal (accessed 22 January 2025).

Sources Cited

Alderson, Edwin Alfred Hervey, *With the Mounted Infantry and the Mashonaland Field Force, 1896* (1896)

Baden-Powell, Robert, *The Matabele Campaign; being a narrative of the campaign in suppressing the native rising in Matabeleland and Mashonaland* (1897)

Brendon, Piers, *The Decline and Fall of the British Empire* (2007)

Castle, Ian, and Ian Knight, *Fearful Hard Times: The Siege and Relief of Eshowe, 1879*, (1994)

Clarke, Sonia, *Zululand at War 1879: The Conduct of the Anglo-Zulu War*, (1984)

Colenso, Frances E., assisted by Lt.-Col. Edward Durnford, *History of the Zulu War and its Origins* (1880)

Cooper, Barbara, 'George Hamilton-Browne; An Investigation into his Career in New Zealand', *Bay of Plenty Journal of History*, Vol. 33, No. 2, 1985

Dawnay, Guy C., *Campaigns: Zulu 1879, Egypt 1882, Suakim 1885* (c. 1886; reprinted 1989)

Durnford, Lt.-Col. Edward C. L. (ed.), *A Soldier's Life and Works in South Africa, 1872–1879: A Memory of the Late Colonel A. W. Durnford, Royal Engineers* (1882)

Gilling, Bryan D., 'George Hamilton-Browne', *Dictionary of New Zealand Biography* (1993)

Greaves, Adrian, and Ian Knight, *Who's Who in the Zulu War. Vol. 1: The British; Vol. 2: Colonials and Zulus* (2006, 2007)

Hallam Parr, Capt. Henry, *A Sketch of the Kafir and Zulu Wars: Guadana to Isandhlwana* (1880)

Herron, Kristine, *Georg Hamilton Brown: A Misjudged Man* (2019)

Hodes, R., and R. H. Reznek, 'The intertwining of antisemitism and racism in modern South Africa, c. 1880–1939', *Jewish Historical Studies*, vol. 55, 2024

Hummel, Chris (ed.), *The Frontier War Journal of Major John Crealock 1878: A Narrative of the Ninth Frontier War by the Assistant Military Secretary to Lieutenant-General Thesiger* (1989)

Knight, Ian, *With His Face to the Foe: The Life and Death of Louis Napoleon, the Prince Imperial* (2001)

——, *Zulu Rising: The Epic Story of Isandlwana and Rorke's Drift* (2010)

Laband, John, 'Dick Addison: The rôle of a British official during the disturbances in the Ndwandwe District of Zululand, 1887–1889', MA dissertation, University of Natal (1980)

——, *The Shadow of Isandlwana: The Life and Times of General Lord Chelmsford and his Disaster in Zululand* (2023)

Laband, John (ed.), *Lord Chelmsford's Zululand Campaign 1878–1879* (1994)

——, *Charlie Harford's Anglo-Zulu War: The Memoir of a British Lieutenant, 1878–1879* (2024)

MacDonald, Robert H., *The language of empire: myths and metaphors of popular imperialism, 1880–1918* (1994)
Molyneux, Maj. W. C. F., *Campaigning in South Africa and Egypt* (1896)
Moodie, Duncan C. F. (ed.), *John Dunn, Cetywayo, and the Three Generals* (1886)
——, *Moodie's Zulu War*, (1988, reprinted selection from D. C. F. Moodie, *History of the Battles and Adventures of the British, the Boers, and the Zulus* [1879])
Morris, Donald, *The Washing of the Spears* (1965)

Norbury, Fleet Surgeon Henry F., *The Naval Brigade in South Africa during the Years 1877–78–79* (1880)
Norris-Newman, Charles L., *In Zululand with the British throughout the War of 1879* (1880; reprinted 1990)

Peers, Chris, *Rorke's Drift and Isandlwana 22nd January 1879: Minute by Minute* (2021)

Simpson, Cameron, 'Imperial and Colonial Officers of the Anglo-Zulu War of 1879' (*forthcoming*)
Sisman, Adam, *An Honourable Englishman: The Life of Hugh Trevor-Roper* (2011)
Smith, Keith, T*he Wedding Feast War: The Final Tragedy of the Xhosa People* (2012)
Stevenson, Lee, Ian Knight and Adam Baynham-Jones, *Rorke's Drift: By Those Who Were There* (2023)

Tylden, G., 'Commandant George Hamilton-Browne of the Colonial Forces', *Journal of the Society of Army Historical Research*, Vol. 37, No. 152 (1959)

War Office, Intelligence Division, *Narrative of the Field Operations Connected with the Zulu War of 1879*, (1881; reprinted 1989)
Wood, Field Marshal Sir Evelyn, *From Midshipman to Field Marshal* (1906)

Newspapers and Periodicals

Dublin Times, Dundee Courier, Evening Post, The Gleaner, Gloucester Graphic, Grahamstown Journal, Illustrated London News, Natal Mercury, New Zealand Mail, Otago Witness, Sheffield Evening Telegraph and Star, The Sketch, Sporting Times, Times of Natal

Professor John Laband

John Laband collapsed and died unexpectedly on 5 August 2025, at his home in Greyton, in South Africa's Western Cape, shortly after completing work on this book. He was seventy-eight.

John was an outstanding historian in the field of colonial conflicts in southern Africa, and in particular the Anglo-Zulu War. He was educated at St John's College in Johannesburg, and underwent service in the SADF, guarding forlorn outposts in South West Africa (Namibia) in the apartheid years, before completing his education at the (then) University of Natal in Pietermaritzburg, and at Cambridge University in the UK. He secured a post as a lecturer at UNP specialising initially in British colonial history in India; in 1979, however, the centenary of the Anglo-Zulu War made him realise that much of the study given to that conflict remained rooted in either British Imperial or local settler perspectives, and that the Zulu perspective had been largely ignored. Working with fellow lecturer Paul Thompson John produced *A Field Guide to the War in Zululand* (1979), the first serious attempt to map the conflict's historic sites. Writing during the painful years of the apartheid endgame – a time when any study of African culture and history was regarded with official suspicion, and when the sort of field research in designated 'black homelands' necessary for such a work was discouraged – John and Paul produced a number of well-researched academic books and monographs of the war which began to reshape understanding of the conflict. John's interest in the Zulu side of the story resulted in his PhD (*Kingdom in Crisis; The Zulu Response to the British Invasion of 1879*, 1992, which was later expanded into his book *Rope of Sand; The Rise and Fall of the Zulu Nation*). The fall of apartheid and the introduction of free multiracial elections in South Africa in 1994 required considerable reshaping of the historiographical landscape, and John was central to the emergence of a new integrated approach which incorporated Zulu perspectives. He continued to lecture in Pietermaritzburg, rising to professorship and Head of the Department of History; on leaving he was made a Fellow of the University. In 2002 his expertise was recognised internationally when he was offered an appointment at the Wilfrid Laurier University in Ontario, Canada. When he returned to South Africa in 2015 Wilfrid Laurier awarded him the accolade of Emeritus Professor of History.

John and his wife Fen settled in Greyton, and, having retired from teaching, John threw his considerable energy into fresh writing. His output included a look at the impact of Portuguese settlement in southern Africa, *Bringers of War*, (2013), and a concise and insightful study of the complex and divisive history of the struggle for land, *The Land Wars; The Dispossession of the Khoisan and AmaXhosa in the Cape Colony* (2020). Mostly, however, he continued to write about the 'wars of Confederation' in the 1870s – the wars that resulted from Sir Bartle Frere's attempts to bring the Boer republics and independent African kingdoms under a British umbrella.

As usual, his interest remained in 'the other side of the story' – his *Zulu Warriors* (2014) was in fact a look at the military systems of not just the Zulus but the various African groups who opposed British expansion in the region, whilst his *The Transvaal Rebellion* (2005) and *The Battle of Majuba Hill* (2017) were concerned with the Anglo-Transvaal War of 1881. Mostly, however, he continued to be inspired by Zulu history, editing new editions of existing works and memoirs – like this one – and producing new studies like his history of the Zulu monarchy, *The Eight Zulu Kings* (2018), and *The Assassination of King Shaka* (2020). In 2020 he ventured into the world of alternative history with *The Fall of Rorke's Drift* which wondered how a Zulu victory in that most famous of British Imperial battles might have affected the wider outcome of the war. In 2022 he published *The Zulu Kingdom and the Boer Invasion of 1837–40* which offered his typically well-researched and unbiased analysis of one of the most contentious episodes in Zulu history.

His last full-length work was a detailed biography of Lord Chelmsford, the ill-fated British commander in Zululand, *The Shadow of Isandlwana* (2023). This book was short-listed for the Society of Army Historical Research's Templer Award in 2024, and John was invited to London to receive the Society's Fellowship in 2025.

John Laband was undoubtedly the leading South African academic historian of the nineteenth-century Zulu kingdom, but his influence went far beyond academia. His focus on thorough research, his refusal to be swayed by decades of enshrined bias and mythology, impacted on others working in the same field in the UK and across the world, effectively reshaping interpretations of the 1879 campaign to the extent that investigations restricted to the old colonial sources are no longer viable. His passing has left a gulf in Anglo-Zulu War studies which is unlikely to be filled.

Ian Knight
Chichester,
November 2025